TWO GENERATIONS

IN PERSPECTIVE

TWO GENERATIONS IN PERSPECTIVE

Notable Events and Trends 1896–1956

———————————————

Edited by Harry Schneiderman

———————————————

With a Foreword by Louis Finkelstein

MONDE PUBLISHERS, INC.

New York

Designed by Meyer Miller

DEDICATED ON THE OCCASION
OF HIS SIXTIETH BIRTHDAY TO

ISRAEL GOLDSTEIN

*Rabbi, Jewish Community Servant, Zionist Leader,
Advocate of Equal Rights for all Men, Good Government,
and Morality in International Relations*

ON BEHALF OF THE COMMITTEE OF SPONSORS:

Itzhak Ben-Zvi, *Honorary Chairman*
Louis Finkelstein, *Chairman*
Charles H. Silver, *Associate Chairman*

PREFACE

As its title indicates, this book is a survey, from many points of view, of the most meaningful developments in Jewish life, in the United States and abroad, during the past six decades, the most eventful, the most tragic, and yet, in some ways the most hopeful in Jewish history.

The book opens with a comprehensive historical survey of Jewish life, especially in America and in Palestine, and later in Israel, during the past sixty years. This survey is followed by several other chapters of a background character, such as those dealing with Zionism in the United States and in other countries, and a chapter tracing the development of community organizations in the United States.

Part Two of the book is devoted also to the background of the period, but in the special field of religion in the United States. This is followed by two groups of chapters giving authoritative, factual information regarding specific organizations and movements. The first group is concerned with Jewish communal activities at home and abroad; the second, with public causes in the general community. It is hoped that in this manner, the book may serve to present a vivid composite picture of the most significant events and trends in Jewish life during the past half century, the most momentous in modern Jewish history.

As it will be seen, this book is dedicated to Dr. Israel Goldstein. It was prepared and is published in his honor. The sixtieth anniversary, in 1956, of his birth was widely celebrated in both the United States and Israel. The many organizations and institutions which he has served or is serving as a leader, regarded the occasion as a welcome opportunity to express their gratitude for his active participation and their admiration of the skill, ability and devotion which marked his leadership.

Because of these tributes, a number of Dr. Goldstein's close friends and admirers came to feel that a complete record of the more important of his many activities on behalf of the general, as well as the Jewish community, would be not only an enduring tribute but also an inspiration to others, as well as a useful and illuminating survey, and evaluation of significant developments during the period spanned by Dr. Goldstein's career.

Following the historical and descriptive chapters of the book are several personal tributes to Dr. Goldstein, including one from Dr. Itzhak Ben-Zvi, the President of the State of Israel; these are followed by a comprehensive biography, based in part on Dr. Goldstein's reminiscences of his childhood and youth. The volume concludes with a selection of excerpts from Dr. Goldstein's addresses and writings. From these excerpts the reader will acquire a knowledge of Dr. Goldstein's views on many important subjects, which may stimulate thought and encourage continued support of high endeavor toward the advancement of the welfare of humanity.

Preparation of this volume was made possible by the willing and eager cooperation of the contributors, many of whom were glad to give up valuable time to what all regarded as a labor of love. The Editor is eager to express his grateful appreciation of their cordial cooperation. He wishes also to express his heartfelt thanks to Dr. Louis Finkelstein, chairman of the Committee of Sponsors, for advice and for the enlightening foreword contributed by him. The Editor expresses his grateful appreciation also to the Hon. Charles H. Silver, associate chairman of the Sponsors' Committee, for his aid. Thanks are due also to Mr. Itzhak J. Carmin who, in behalf of the publishers, gave valuable cooperation and encouragement. The Editor joins him in expressing thanks, for their assistance, to the Hon. S. Cecil Hyman, Consul General of Israel, for his valuable cooperation, to Mr. Meyer Miller, who designed the book, and to Mr. William Uhl, the printers' representative who guided it with patience and skill through all the steps of production.

Because he knows and admires Dr. Goldstein, it was a genuine pleasure for the Editor to have been associated with the production of this volume. From its interesting contents he has come to know Dr. Goldstein better and to admire him more. He is happy to have this means of felicitating Dr. Goldstein on the completion of a half century of dedication to the service of the Jewish people and of humanity in general, and to express the fervent hope that he be spared for many more years to continue his beneficent labors.

The Editor

FOREWORD

Israel Goldstein is one of the most dedicated servants of the Jewish and general community in our time. The chapters of this book reflect a remarkable diversity and an equally remarkable consistency of service to noble causes. The State of Israel, the Synagogue, sufferers from persecution, American minorities, the disadvantaged everywhere, have been, and remain to this day, primary subjects for his concern. Leaders in a vast array of enterprises to help mankind have participated in the preparation of this book; yet they are but a fraction of those who admire the genius for organization, the insight, and the zeal of the energetic and gifted man whose sixtieth birthday is being celebrated through this volume.

The Jewish Theological Seminary of America, from which he was graduated as Rabbi in 1918, thrills with happiness as her son receives the accolades of so many distinguished servants of the community.

An older contemporary may indulge in reminiscences about Dr. Goldstein's youth, the days when, a leader in the Morais-Blumenthal Society (the student organization of the Seminary in those days, named for the celebrated founder of the institution, and the first chairman of its Board), he first showed the high promise fulfilled in the tireless labor of four decades. He was Solomon Schechter's favorite preacher among the students; and indeed his was the last student sermon that great teacher was destined to hear. He was a favorite pupil of Israel Friedlaender, who saw in him a potential scholor in the field of Biblical literature. He won the respect of Alexander Marx, who wanted him to become an historian of American Judaism. He had the respect and admiration of Morris D. Levine, a remarkably dedicated saint of that day.

Sol M. Stroock, later chairman of the Seminary Board of Directors, was so fascinated with the ability and promise of the young rabbi, that Israel Goldstein was called to the pulpit of Congregation B'nai Jeshurun, which he has served to this day.

Yet this dazzling and singular ability to arouse affection, respect, and admiration did not (as often happens) cost Israel Goldstein the friendship of his colleagues. They recognized his rare gifts and his even rarer assiduity and powers of organization and concentration, and assumed from the beginning that his destiny was to achieve unusual distinction, helping to create as well as helping to write modern Jewish history. One of the reasons that he aroused so little jealousy in his brother students was doubtless that he felt none. He pursued his path, zealously and devotedly, and helped others so willingly that they could not begrudge him his superior gifts. He carried on his work, accepted the laurels which came to him, and continued his service, unaware apparently of the nature of his own excellence—a modesty which continues to this day, and which will survive even this book.

As Israel Goldstein enters on his seventh decade, he cannot be unconscious of the great change which has come over America and a large section of the free world, in part through his own efforts and those of his colleagues in Judaism and other faiths. There is a hunger abroad for the word of God, such as none of us anticipated in our youth. The readers of this volume will include many wracked with the thought of the morrow, whose nature depends so greatly on whether we can rise to the challenge. Science and technology have done their work in creating a world where whole nations can have the kind of plenty known only in the courts of kings in earlier generations. But this power itself suggests the perils which surround royalty in a time of revolution.

Men are properly asking themselves whether, like the last Tsars of Russia, we are to watch the rising torrents, sure to sweep us away, without any endeavor to escape. Escape cannot lie in doing what has already been done; for that has led to the present threat of disaster.

Religious leadership in 1957 therefore faces an immense challenge—nothing less than thinking through its own commitments, its premises, and its obligations. In the early years of this century, Judaism, especially, was considered even by many devotees, something to be preserved as a museum piece. Nostalgic memories attached to it, and kept people coming to the synagogue, abstaining from forbidden foods, fasting on the Day of Atonement, and in a degree observing the Sabbath. But the young people of today have little inclination for such nostalgia, knowing that they are in danger of their lives. They are concerned for their future; and have little time for preservation of memories of an ineffective past.

There is an awful question which every religious servant has to pose to himself, and which tests his own devotion to his calling. It can be formulated in a hypothetical dilemma which suggests the nature of the alternatives before man. We will all agree with Rabbi Israel Salanter who, in an epidemic, tried to convert some synagogues in Kovno into hospitals, because of the urgent need to house the sick. We might even go further. The commandment to heal the sick and save life is so urgent that if a community were confronted with the choice of maintaining, for a time, its synagogues and religious schools or its hospitals, we should all have to agree that the sick come first.

But suppose the alternative were to maintain either hospitals or religious worship and education over a whole generation. What would our attitude be? Would we regard the preservation and development of man's religious insights as of paramount importance, to be preserved at all costs? Would we affirm that "study of the Torah outweights them all," or would we assume that physical well-being is really more important that the spiritual life? In our time, it is probable that most would yield the houses of worship rather than the hospitals; not out of greater love for man, but out of lack of respect for worship.

But if physical endurance is man's real goal, if longevity is an end in itself, and the spiritual quality of life a secondary "value" to be preserved if possible but abandoned under stress, what fate

awaits western man, when this doctrine spreads to the disadvantaged of the world?

On the other hand, if western man, already possessed of material goods and power, could also achieve the dedication to the
transcendent goals of civilization held out to him by the Prophets,
what a new and blissful prospect would suddenly be open to him!

He might still have to share his knowledge and experience with
the rest of the world. This might cost him much self-indulgence.
He might have to invest a great deal in the prosperity of others
whose lives are now devoted to serving him. But he and his
descendents will escape the fate which sooner or later overtakes
all blind despots—the fate of the Tsars.

In brief, the alternatives facing man in our time are a real
return to real religion—accepting all its implications, moral, theological, and ritual—or ultimate disaster. Mighty America in the
West, and tiny Israel in the East, can lead a world into creative
paths, and save themselves and mankind untold agony, if the
individuals constituting these nations (and others) can but cure
themselves of the notions that pleasure, self-indulgence, and
power are real goods.

The translation of such generalities into practical programs for
education and life is the huge task of contemporary moralists.
There is reason to believe that much can be accomplished, because
the alternatives to spiritual life are so clearly spelled out by the
events and the threats of our day.

But such practical programs require men of practical experience. They also require men with deep love for their fellows, and
with understanding of the teachings of the truly great men of the
past.

Is it, perhaps, to bring about the formulation and the implementation of such a program that Israel Goldstein has been
unconsciously preparing all his life? Has his turn from pure
scholarship and the theoretical issues of religion into the practical
problems of Zionism, philanthropy, religious life, and education
been more than an immense contribution to the solution of immediate problems of human need? Is it possible that what he has
done for men and women, in many parts of the world, was not
only a great end in itself, but also a means to a further goal, still

to be achieved by him? In short, has his life until the present been a preparation for the career which actually is to be his? Will his destiny be that of the great teachers, who spent a third of their lives studying, a third of their lives in practical works, and the final part of their lives in offering instruction to mankind?

The need for the leadership which a man of Dr. Goldstein's stature alone can offer, is so great that I venture to pray that he will be given the strength, the energy, and the time, in which to offer the community as a whole the guidance it needs at his hands. The combination of ingenuity, ability, wisdom, and practicality, which are found in him, can, in my opinion, form the basis for leadership, the results of which can scarely now be estimated. Whether he chooses to give this leadership through the written or spoken word, through further institution building, through influence on young men now entering on the world, can naturally be decided only by him. But I have profound faith and hope that a destiny awaits him even transcending what he has achieved in a career already marked with rare distinction.

Louis Finkelstein

CONTENTS

CONTRIBUTORS

EVERETT R. CLINCHY, Ph.D., New York City, President of the National Conference of Christians and Jews since its inception in 1928.

BEN DAVIDSON, New York City, Executive Director, Liberal Party of New York State.

MOSHE DAVIS, Ph.D., New York City, Provost, Jewish Theological Seminary of America; Assistant Professor of American Jewish History and co-director of the American Jewish History Center of the Seminary.

LEVI ESHKOL, Jerusalem, Minister of Finance of the State of Israel, member of the Executive of the Jewish Agency for Palestine in charge of Colonization.

BENJAMIN B. FERENCZ, LL.B., New York City, attorney; formerly Director General of the Jewish Restitution Successor Organization; Director of operations of the United Restitution Organization, Ltd.; Director for Germany of the Conference on Jewish Material Claims Against Germany, and former Executive Counsel of the Office of Chief of Council for War Crimes, Nuremberg.

LOUIS FINKELSTEIN, Ph.D., S.T.D., New York City, Chancellor, Jewish Theological Seminary of America.

FREDERICK W. GEHLE, New York City, Vice-President, Chase Manhattan Bank; formerly national vice chairman of the commerce and industry division and chairman of the labor division of the British War Relief Society in the United States.

NAHUM GOLDMANN, J.D., Ph.D., New York City, President, World Zionist Organization and Jewish Agency for Palestine; President, World Jewish Congress.

ROBERT GORDIS, Ph.D., D.D., New York City, Rabbi of Temple

Beth El, Rockaway Park, New York; Associate Professor of Bible at the Jewish Theological Seminary; Adjunct Professor of Religion at Columbia University and Visiting Professor of Old Testament at Union Theological Seminary.

ABRAHAM GRANOTT, LL.D., Jerusalem, Chairman of the board of directors of the World Keren Kayemeth L'Israel (Jewish National Fund); member of the executive council of the Hebrew University, and of the Weizmann Institute.

SOLOMON GRAYZEL, Ph.D., Philadelphia, Editor of the Jewish Publication Society of America and corresponding secretary of the American Jewish Historical Society; author of "A History of the Jews," 1947, and other works.

JACOB KAPLAN, Paris, Grand Rabbi of France.

MORDECAI M. KAPLAN, D.H.L., New York City, founder and rabbi emeritus of the Society for Advancement of Judaism; Professor of the philosophies of religion at the Jewish Theological Seminary of America and the founder of the Reconstructionist Movement.

MOSHE KOL, Jerusalem, Chairman of the Youth Aliyah department of the Jewish Agency; member of the World Zionist Executive.

LOUIS E. LEVINTHAL, LL.B., Philadelphia, Judge of the Court of Common Pleas; president of the Zionist Organization of America from 1941 to 1943; member of the Congress Court of the World Zionist Organization since 1946; member of the Actions Committee of the World Zionist Organization.

SAMUEL MARGOSHES, D.H.L., New York City, journalist and editor; formerly vice-president of the American Jewish Congress and of the Zionist Organization of America.

ISAIAH M. MINKOFF, New York City, Executive Director of the National Community Relations Advisory Council.

MAURICE L. PERLZWEIG, New York City, head of the International Affairs Department and the permanent representative of the World Jewish Congress at the United Nations.

JUSTINE WISE POLIER, LL.B., New York City, Justice of the Domestic Relations Court of the City of New York; Chairman of the Executive Committee of the American Jewish Congress and a member of the Executive of the World Jewish Congress.

LOUIS RICHMAN (deceased), New York City, attorney; founder and volunteer Director, Jewish Conciliation Board of America.

ALEX ROSE, New York City, President, United Hatters, Cap and Millinery Intern. Union; vice-chairman, Liberal Party of N.Y. State.

PHILIP RUBIN, New York City, author and journalist.

CHARLES H. SILVER, New York City, industrialist; President of the Board of Education of New York City; President of Congregation B'nai Jeshurun and Beth Israel Hospital.

JULIUS SILVER, LL.B., New York City, attorney and industrialist; member of the Library Committee of the Jewish Theological Seminary and one of the initiators of Brandeis University.

CHANNING H. TOBIAS, D.D., L.L.D., New York City, Chairman of the Board of Directors of the National Association for the Advancement of Colored People.

PIERRE VAN PAASSEN, S.T.D., D.D., New York City, author and Unitarian minister; his books include two on Zionism and Palestine.

COMMITTEE OF SPONSORS

Honorary Chairman: Itzhak Ben-Zvi, President of Israel
Chairman: Louis Finkelstein, Chancellor, Jewish Theological Seminary
Associate Chairman: Charles H. Silver, President, Board of Education of the City of New York; President, Congregation B'nai Jeshurun

Gershon Agron, Mayor of Jerusalem

Maurice Ashkanasy, Former President, Executive Council, Australian Jewry

Peretz Bernstein, President, General Zionist Party of Israel

Samuel Blumberg, Chairman, Board of Trustees, Congregation B'nai Jeshurun

Samuel Bronfman, President, Canadian Jewish Congress

Pinkhos M. Churgin, President, Bar-Ilan University, Israel

George S. Counts, President, Liberal Party, State of N.Y.

Abba S. Eban, Ambassador of Israel to the U.S. and to the United Nations

Fritz Feigl, President, Confed. of Jewish Federations, Brazil

Abraham J. Feldman, President, Synagogue Council of America

Edmond Fleg, Author

Buell G. Gallagher, President, City College of New York

Edward E. Gelber, Former Pres., Zionist Org. of Canada

Nelson Glueck, President,
Hebrew Union College—Jewish
Institute of Religion

Moises Goldman, President,
Jewish Community of Buenos
Aires

Albert M. Greenfield, Banker
and realtor

Rose L. Halprin, Acting
Chairman, Jewish Agency for
Palestine, American Section

Adolph Held, President, Jewish
Labor Committee

Barnett Janner, President, Board
of Deputies of British Jews
and Zionist Federation of
Great Britain

Horace M. Kallen, Professor
Emeritus, The New School for
Social Research

Aba Khoushy, Mayor of Haifa

Mordecai Kirshblum, Former
President, Mizrachi Org. of
America; Member, Jewish
Agency Executive

Herbert H. Lehman, Former
Governor of New York and
member U.S. Senate

Harris J. Levine, President,
Jewish National Fund of
America

Louis Lipsky, Former President,
Zionist Organization of America

James G. McDonald, Former
Ambassador of the United
States to Israel

Theodore R. McKeldin, Governor
of Maryland and President,
America-Israel Society

Israel A. Maisels, President,
South African Jewish Board
of Deputies

Benjamin Mazar, President,
The Hebrew University of
Jerusalem

Robert R. Nathan, Economist

Abraham A. Neuman, President,
The Dropsie College for
Hebrew and Cognate Learning

Jacob Panken, Former Justice
of the Board of Domestic
Relations

Justine Wise Polier, Chairman,
Executive Committee of the
American Jewish Congress

Eva Violet Reading,
(Marchioness), President,
British Section of World
Jewish Congress

Pinhas Rosen, Minister of
Justice of Israel

Cecil Roth, Historian

Louis Segal, Member, Jewish
Agency Executive

Moshe Sharett, Former Minister
for Foreign Affairs of Israel

Israel M. Sieff, Chairman,
European Branch of World
Jewish Congress

Simon E. Sobeloff, Judge, United
States Circuit Court

Joseph Sprinzak, Speaker of
Knesset, Israel

Adlai E. Stevenson, Former
Governor of Illinois

Dewey D. Stone, Chairman,
United Israel Appeal

Alan M. Stroock, Chairman of
the Board, Jewish Theological
Seminary of America

Arieh Tartakower, Chairman,
Israel Section, World Jewish
Congress

Bernard H. Trager, Chairman,
National Community Relations
Advisory Council

Kurt Wilhelm, Chief Rabbi of
Sweden

Isaac Wolfson, Industrialist

Part One

———————————————

BACKGROUNDS

1896–1956

A CHRONICLE OF

OUR GENERATION

---

by Solomon Grayzel

> *One generation passeth away,*
> *and another generation cometh;*
> *And the earth abideth forever.*
> *(Eccl. 1.4)*

A GENERATION cannot sit in judgment on itself. Its successors may reverse or even laugh at its values and standards, as we smile at the values and standards of some generations that have preceded us. What is even more important, no generation can tell how well it is preparing, or how badly it is neglecting, such powers as its successors will need to meet the challenges that they may have to face. Not knowing what these challenges will be, especially in an age of rapid change, how can a preceding generation prepare for them? Yet it is on the basis of such a sense of adequacy or inadequacy on its own part that the future will judge us. If it is hazardous to write the history of an age long past, it is presumptuous to try to point out the rights and wrongs, the good and evil, the encouraging and the distressing in the period through which one has lived and is living, and to measure his generation's success in making it possible for some future generation to live Jewishly on the highest possible level.

But it is tempting. The past sixty years have not been merely turbulent; they have also been exceedingly interesting. We have witnessed vast changes in economics, society and politics, great advances in science and technology, revolutions in the minds of men. The world has been in ferment. Inevitably, therefore, the ferment has been transmitted to the Jewish people as well. The Jews have always lived in the very center of world events, so that their experiences in any period have reflected the state of the human spirit. But is that all? Have our contemporary experiences been no more than reflections of a dynamic era? Has there been —to use a phrase made popular by a modern historian—no creative response to the challenges we have encountered? Have not the Jews drawn upon their accumulated spiritual resources and given a characteristic, distinctive turn to events? An appraisal of the events of the crowded decades just past seems to permit an affirmative answer. Our age has done what it could in the face of innumerable problems, tragedies and opportunities. We have, within the limitations of human foresight, and sometimes through sheer luck, helped safeguard the future of the Jew and his heritage.

In discussing Jewish experience during the generations or two just past, our center of attention will be the American Jewish community. This is natural because the United States is the home of the writer and of most of the prospective readers. Besides, United States Jewry now represents the largest and the foremost diaspora community. The successes and failures of this community must in the end count for more than similar successes and failures in smaller communities. Other communities, especially that of Israel, offer opportunities for contrast and comparison and serve to illustrate the varieties of Jewish attitude toward problems and events.

I. THE NEW DIASPORA

a. *As the New Century Opened*

Henrietta Szold, commenting on the closing year of the nineteenth century, remarked (*American Jewish Year Book*, II, pp. 14, 38) that the Jews were parting with that year, and that century, with no regrets. The strides made by anti-Semitism in its second half belied the hopes and ideals which that century had produced

in its first half. In the next *Year Book* (III, p.15), the first year of
the twentieth century was described as having been marked by
two outstanding events: the work of the ICA (the Jewish Colonization Association) and the appearance of the first volume of *The
Jewish Encyclopedia.* The first was acclaimed as "bearing within
itself the possibility of far-reaching influence upon the future of
the Jewish People as long as the world may endure." The second
was hailed as a work of great scholarship signifying the awakening cultural interests of the American Jew. Events were to prove
that writer over-optimistic on every count. The twentieth century
was to outdo the nineteenth in anti-Semitism. Agricultural colonization was, indeed, to have far-reaching influence; but in Palestine
rather than in the lands of the Diaspora. *The Jewish Encyclopedia*
proved to be an important work; but infinitely much more labor
would have to be undertaken to arouse any considerable interest
among the Jews in their cultural heritage. There is no occasion for
surprise at the optimism which pervades these analyses of the
Jewish situation at the turn of the century; the whole western
world was then aglow with firm faith in uninterrupted progress of
which optimism was a natural concomitant. No one but a few
prophets of doom foresaw the wars and revolutions, the fall of
empires and the rise of savagery which were to afflict the world
within a few short decades. The forces which were to transform
the world were then already in motion, but few recognized them
and fewer still did anything to forestall them. No one can be
blamed for not being a prophet. It is nevertheless remarkable
that perspicacious people like the editors of the *Year Book* failed
to note the relative importance and the likely consequences of the
movements which were to cause a transformation in Jewish life.
They did note the vast migration from eastern Europe; but even
so they did not appreciate what it would mean to the religion and
culture of the American Jewish community, let alone foresee the
changes about to take place in other parts of the world.

b. *The Exodus from Eastern Europe*

The seeds of the revolutionary changes which Jewish life was
to experience in the next half century had already been sown. The
great exodus from eastern Europe had already begun, and out of

it was to stem most of what was destined to happen, in terms of both destructiveness and creativity, in the next two generations. Its beginnings must therefore be described.

Russia and Rumania were the chief culprits. The latter had repeatedly promised to grant its Jews equality of treatment, but was using every subterfuge to avoid doing so. The western nations looked on with some disdain, but did nothing to enforce the promises made them at the Congress of Berlin in 1878. Only the United States openly showed its displeasure, though the practical effects of this attitude were nil. At the same time, the Russian government, for its part, openly proclaimed its intention of eliminating its Jewish population. It embarked upon systematic persecution with whatever efficiency the Czarist government was able to exercise. The pogroms (riots) actually encouraged by the authorities in various parts of the country in 1881 and 1882, and the May Laws of the latter year, which drove the Jews from many towns and villages, left some dead, many homeless and all of the Jews terrified. Thousands fled across the borders into Germany and Austria. They had only the vaguest idea of where they were going and they certainly did not have the means of getting there. For the first time, the Jews of western Europe and America were faced with a vast refugee problem.

It was a problem they would have to face almost continuously and in aggravated form from then on. The revolutionary rumblings in Russia, and the dissatisfaction with their lot of the middle and lower classes in Rumania, continued to make diversionary tactics by these governments necessary as a substitute for an honest facing of their internal problems. Anti-Jewish policies had served other governments elsewhere in the past. Charging a helpless minority with responsibility for all the evils from which the nation was suffering had worked before and would work again. The rulers of Russia and Rumania considered this technique a cheap and clever way of retaining power.

It is easy to forget that the Russian and Rumanian Jews could have solved their problem by becoming Christians; they preferred to face exile. The first question they had to answer was, therefore, "Whither?" A country of expanding industrial capacity offered the best opportunity. Germany, France, England and some of the smaller states of western Europe were, it is true, close at hand, but they were comparatively less well known to the Jews of eastern Europe as lands of opportunity. The United States, on the other hand, while farther away, had already become famous both for its hospitality to immigrants and for the presumed ease with which one could attain a degree of economic independence. There were other places of settlement open to those seeking new homes: South Africa and, to a lesser extent, Australia were opening up to European immigration. In all of these, most of the Jews expected to engage in industry and commerce.

Another theory, however, had become current among the Jews of that age, both in western and in eastern Europe, namely, that there was something wrong about the lack of a farming population among the Jewish people. For centuries the Jews had been excluded from agriculture; now the severance of the Jews from the soil was being turned into an accusation against them. They themselves accepted their economic situation as anomalous and sought ways of correcting it. One group, which called itself *Am Olam* (Eternal People), favored establishing Jewish agricultural settlements anywhere in the world. Another group was equally interested in farming, but their agricultural efforts aimed to achieve also the emotional, national goal of reviving the soil of their fathers in the Holy Land. A movement towards the attainment of this goal had been in existence ever since the early 1860s. It bore the name of BILU and for a time had stirred considerable enthusiasm. Its net results had been small, for the revival of Palestine, then a rocky wasteland inhabited by a small and impoverished Arab population, was too difficult a task for the scanty resources, apart from idealism, which the devoted young Biluists brought with them.

Each of the possible new homelands reacted to the flood of immigration which touched its borders, so that by the year 1900 each had a policy of its own. In the early 1880s, the western Jews tried to stem the tide of Russian emigrants and then to regulate it by giving guidance and assistance. The German Jews, being geographically the closest, established a Central Committee for Russian Jewish Refugees to raise money for the support of the needy among them and speed them on their way. Before long the German committee enlisted the cooperation of the Alliance Israélite Universelle, of the London Mansion House Committee and of others. The European Jewish committees quickly agreed among themselves that the vast majority of the emigrants from Russia must find their way to the United States. A considerable number of American Jews, however, received this decision with no enthusiasm whatever. But the more liberal-minded American Jews prevailed, and the delegate of the Hebrew Immigrant Aid Society sought to make sure only that those encouraged to go on to the United States were physically fit to become self-supporting. For some years these committees functioned separately in their respective countries and jointly at the border stations outside of Russia. Had the flow of emigration lasted a year, or two, or three, or shown some signs of letting up eventually, these committees would no doubt have carried on according to their plans. Unfortunately, the flow increased rather than diminished. The dam which they had tried to set up proved completely useless in view of the situation in Russia. It became clear that all that the Jewish organizations could do was to offer elementary guidance and protection en route; their finances were unequal to anything else. This was the situation in 1900. By then any attempt to direct emigrants to, or away from, any country had been given up. It had become clear, moreover, that the greatest number by far were looking to settlement in the United States. While the number of Jews immigrating thither from eastern Europe had hardly exceeded 50,000 throughout the nineteenth century down to 1880, it rose to about 135,000 in the ninth decade of that century and to 280,000 in its final decade.

Before describing the fate of the immigrants in the United States and how their presence affected the Jewish population already there, two events bearing on the problem of the Jews' search for a home must be dealt with. One of them was hailed as a definite solution, but proved quite inadequate; the other was widely condemned as illusory, but proved to be of tremendous importance. The first was the attempt by German-born Baron Maurice de Hirsch, industrialist and railroad builder, to ease and guide the settlement of the immigrants in their new homes. In

1890, he established in the United States a fund under which immigrants would receive vocational training and be provided with tools. A year later, impressed by the argument that farming was the most desirable occupation for the immigrants, he set up another fund, this time in the huge sum of $40,000,000, for the settlement on farms in North and South America of such Jews as were willing to forego city life. A new organization, primarily under the direction of European Jews, was established under the name of the Jewish Colonization Association, better known by its abbreviated title ICA. Baron de Hirsch was undoubtedly a great and imaginative benefactor. Thousands of Russian and Rumanian Jews heeded his call and settled in the western hemisphere in scores of farming communities from Manitoba in Canada to the southern part of the Argentine Republic, as well as in South Africa and Australia. Some of these farmers succeeded and some did not; some, like those in southern New Jersey in the United States, remained on the land for a generation and some for two. But the Baron's dream of solving the problem of the aimless Jewish emigrants from eastern Europe was hardly realized to anything like the extent he had hoped for. His great wealth did not suffice to achieve his difficult goal, which was nothing less than the reversal of economic habits enforced through more than a millennium. Emotional conviction, not merely logic, was needed to bring about so great a change. This was not yet evident in the year 1900, so that it is not surprising that the American Jews considered the founding of the Jewish Agricultural Society that year as a very hopeful sign.

c. *The Zionist Hope*

Three years before the end of the nineteenth century, on August 29, 1897, a different project was initiated to find a home for the homeless Jews. That day, in Basle, Switzerland, Theodor Herzl opened the First World Zionist Congress. Herzl, the assimilated European Jew, had been touched by the tragedy of the flight from Russia. Like many others among his western contemporaries, he had attributed the uprooting of the Jews from their east European homes to the lack of civilization in those lands. Suddenly, in the course of the Dreyfus Affair, it dawned on him that, where the Jews were involved, western civilization also was not immune to prejudice and cruelty. There was only one thing for the Jews to do, namely, to establish themselves as a nation in a homeland of their own. Herzl did not know at first that his idea had a long history, that many Jews and some Christians had advocated it before him. It came to him with the force of a revelation and he could not rest until he had written it down in the form of a pamphlet, "The Jewish State." He tried to interest his friends, and then a number of wealthy and influential Jews, among them Baron Maurice de Hirsch and Baron Edmond de Rothschild. None of these took him seriously. But when, despairing of these presumably practical men, he turned to the masses, he found enthusiastic support, especially among the Jews of eastern Europe, but also among some of all types everywhere else. For the first time in more than seventeen centuries, since the days of Bar Kokhba, a congress of Jews met to plan national policy for the entire Jewish people. They set forth their aim as "Zionism"; and they formulated their policy in what came to be known as The Basle Program, that is, to work for the establishment of a publicly recognized home for the Jewish people.

The idea made astonishing progress, not so much in realization as in the enthusiastic support which it evoked. It also brought bitter opposition and even condemnation. Both the support and the opposition are interesting, because both reveal the mind of the Jews at the close of the nineteenth century. The fact that the aim was achieved only through a chain of circumstances impossible to foresee fifty years ago would seem to indicate that those people were not far wrong who called Herzl a dreamer and his plans chimerical. That is how Zionism must have appeared to the objective onlooker. But ever so many Jews could not be objective in the matter of national revival. The adoption of Zionism as a goal by so many Jews can be explained, not only by the negative reason, namely, the depth of their hurt over what was happening in Europe—the persecutions in the east and the anti-Semitism in the west—but even more by the creative ferment of the age-old, unforgotten and unforgettable hope of a return to national life. The fervor and the clamor of the opposition equally show that the opponents of Zionism appreciated the depth of feeling upon which the new movement rested. Such opponents argued vehemently that Jewish nationalism was a thing of the past and that its revival would interfere with the universalist mission of the Jews. This was the view of Isaac M. Wise, the leader of Reform Judaism in the United States, who denounced Zionism with all his customary vigor. Moreover, Wise and others asserted, Zionism laid the Jews open to the charge of disloyalty to the country in which they had their home. It was a fatuous argument, and did not justify the heat with which it was advanced, since it was obvious already then that anti-Semites did not need this additional "reason" and that others would not use it.

Most Jews, however, though sympathetic to the aims of Zionism and engaged by the leadership of Theodor Herzl, reacted as most people react to a cause that requires the expenditure of effort and energy—they were content to discuss this evocation of the old hopes without doing much to realize them. There was, indeed, little enough that anyone could do. Local clubs were established in every major city in Europe and America; and federations of such clubs were organized on a nation-wide scale in every country.

Zionism carried on vigorous propaganda: debating, theorizing, educating and collecting small sums in dues and donations. Its chief function was to keep the hope of restoration alive in the older people, and to stir the sense of pride in the Jewish past and dreams of its future in the young. But there was little that was tangible about Zionism at that time. The only place where the appearance of Zionism on the world Jewish scene made a practical difference was in Palestine itself. There, the few colonies that had been established by the idealistic pioneers of the previous thirty years had begun to show signs of despair over the meager results of their labors and the inadequate support they had been receiving from the Lovers of Zion. Baron Edmond de Rothschild had helped and, in the 1890s, so had the newly-founded ICA. The colonists had proved that Jews could overcome major obstacles and become farmers on highly unpromising soil, provided they had an ideal beyond self to stimulate their interest and keep it alive. Their experience had also proved that a country, which had been neglected for centuries, could not be revived without great and constant idealistic support. Now Zionism appeared and, quite apart from the few thousand more who responded to its call and came out to join in the revival of the land, the new movement offered the necessary encouragement and promise of support. Among the more hopeful signs which Miss Szold recorded for the year 1900 was that Zionism was being taken more seriously and that settlement in Palestine was becoming well established and promising.

d. *The Economic Problems of the Immigrants*

The migration to Palestine had no perceptible effects on the flow of emigrants from eastern Europe to other parts of the world, especially to the United States. In fact, at the turn of the century, this migration was still on the increase, so that the problems of the immigrants and those which they raised for the older strata of the Jewish poulation continued to agitate mind and spirit and to lay the foundation for changes destined to take place within the next half century. For it must never be forgotten that the immigrants into most countries came into an existing and ongoing Jewish life. They did not start Jewish life anew. Even in such sparsely settled countries as South Africa and Australia, a Jewish community had already been functioning for decades and the newcomers had to fit themselves into established patterns of life. A completely free hand to make a new start was possible only in some Latin American countries where the older Jewish population was not only small and of the Sephardi tradition, but where the newcomers settled in groups by themselves, either in farming communities sponsored by ICA or, if in the cities, in groups that had little to do with the other Jews already there. Such countries as England and the United States, on the other hand, had Jewish communities with a history and more or less established traditions by which the newcomers were strongly affected. The extent to which they, in their turn, could exert influence towards modifying the existing traditions depended on both the spirit of the country in general as well as on the strength of the Jewish communal organization and the vigor of its traditional life. The differences to be noted between Britain and the United States, at the end of two generations of joint labor by the older stratum and the newer one of their respective Jewish populations, must be accounted as the results of the different conditions which the newcomers found in the two countries.

The problems raised or intensified by the new immigration fall naturally into three categories: economic, social and religio-cultural. In actual life, none of these problems is easily separable from the others. The nature and severity of his economic struggle made it difficult for the immigrant to tell which aspect of his new life he found more distressing: the rapid tempo of work in his new home as contrasted with the leisurely manner of working in the old; the all-pervading, unashamed acquisitiveness, with the rewards of success entailing a complete reversal of social status; or the apparent necessity of giving up his old cultural and religious values and customs in order to attain a degree of comfort and security. From the viewpoint of the community's Jewishness, the difficulties encountered in making a satisfactory adjustment of the immigrants' religious and cultural attitudes were ultimately to prove the most important. But the economic problems were the most immediately pressing and had to be solved first.

When the new immigration started, practically all the countries to which it flowed were in the midst of rapid industrial expansion. The factories in the crowded cities offered the greatest opportunities to the large numbers of rather unskilled workers who needed immediate means of earning a livelihood. As the nineteenth century drew to its close, the possibilities for peddling and eventually opening local stores decreased. A sociologist points to a notable difference between the opportunities open to the east European immigrants and those which had been open to the immigration which had preceded them: the latter had been able to rise to a higher economic and social status within half a generation; the east European immigrant took a full generation to achieve the same goal.

The factories drew them in. Some of them had had a certain amount of experience in the slowly developing industries of eastern Europe; most had had none. For many of them were young people who had had nothing at all to look forward to in Russia and Rumania. A considerable number would have joined the large—altogether too large—class of petty traders in the small Russian towns; it was practically all that the east European economy had permitted them to do. There were also those, a comparatively large number, who were far advanced in their studies at the *yeshivot* and might have become religious functionaries of one sort or another, a class of whom east European Jewry needed a good many while the United States needed very few. In the United States, all alike became factory workers, manufacturing a large variety of articles, chiefly garments.

A modern historian of labor has listed the reasons why so many immigrants of those years went into the needle trades. Many had been tailors in the Old Country, and those who had not plied the needle there could easily learn to do so here, since the new machinery made it a skill easily acquired. The hours of work were long—a twelve-hour day was not at all unusual in the factories at the end of the nineteenth century—but the work itself did not call for the type of muscular exertion of which these men and women were incapable. Most of the factory owners were Jews and, even if of a different tradition and upbringing, a person hailing from eastern Europe and therefore uneasy in the company of non-Jews could feel more at home with them. It was even possible to find in the needle industry shops which kept closed on the Sabbath. Finally, with the industry as then organized, it was possible to graduate, within a fairly short time, into a semblance of independence despite one's very limited capital.

Two-thirds of the Jewish immigrants from eastern Europe, between 1880 and 1914, entered the needle trades; but whatever the industry which they joined, not many of them expected to remain merely workers in a shop. Some labored feverishly to amass the modest sum necessary in those days to set themselves up as subcontractors in a crowded back room, with a few more recent immigrants as workers. This practice aggravated the unspeakable sweat-shop conditions in the big industrial cities; yet it had its brighter side, too, for it was the first step up the ladder of success. Others dreamed of escaping the atmosphere of the clothing or cigar factory by going into "business," if only as pushcart peddlers on the overcrowded streets or as storekeepers in some hole in a wall from which they could dispense soft drinks or sell needles and thread. Still others, more intellectually inclined, or lacking the inner drive and sometimes the toughness essential for success in the existing competitive situation, succeeded after incredible efforts involving much hardship and self-sacrifice, in obtaining an education and eventually entering a profession. Such hopes were certainly not realized in every case. The vast majority eventually became resigned to the wearing labor as their inescapable lot. Their hopes of success were transferred to their children, and their personal disappointments were expressed in dreams of social change.

The physical relocation of so large a segment of the world's Jewish population represented a normalization, even as it created an anomaly. The normalization was in the area of economic life, the Jews now becoming artisans in large and growing numbers. At the same time, these new artisans, still imbued with social and intellectual values which most other workers did not possess, were somewhat out of place in the ranks of labor. This fact was of importance not only for the emergent labor movement, but also for the social and religious developments within the Jewish community.

Before the 1900s, it seemed difficult to organize the Jewish workers into labor unions. Little could be done with them until they learned that their chances for improvement lay, not outside the shop, but within it. Moreover, the Jewish worker's religious training and his experiences as a Jew in the Old Country had taught him to view his situation in terms of broad universal issues. Unionism merely for the improvement of his personal lot failed to fire his imagination. He had to be aroused by calls to his sense of justice and appeals on the basis of human dignity. He still remembered what he had learned in the *heder* of the prophetic message against the oppression of the poor. Craft unionism, as advocated by the American Federation of Labor under the leadership of Samuel Gompers, a fellow-Jewish immigrant, seemed to the average Jewish worker to lack intellectual and spiritual foundations. It stood for a gradual improvement in the physical situation of the worker, while leaving basic conditions unchallenged. Many Jews sought a better mixture of the practical and the idealistic.

Jewish labor could be moved by ideas. Every so often an intellectual would be called in to encourage an embattled group—thus Abraham Cahan had been called in during a tailors' strike in 1884 —but there was no continuous contact between such leaders and the workers. At length, a small group of Jewish intellectuals decided to take matters in hand. Several of them had some knowledge of, or experience in, labor and socialist movements in Europe; others were workers like the people whom they wished to organize, but were at the same time pursuing professional courses in an American college. They founded the United Hebrew Trades (1888) which, within two years, enrolled twenty-two unions with a membership of about 6,000 workers, all of them located in New York City. Jewish labor, as has been repeatedly pointed out, was thus organized from the top down.

It was one thing to organize the Jewish workers into unions, it was quite another to give them ideological guidance. The last fifteen years of the nineteenth century resounded with quarrels within the ranks of Jewish labor. For the question which came to the fore repeatedly, then and in later years as well, was whether labor is to be a tool of socialist theory or socialism the goal of a political party furthering the interests of labor. The plays and counter-plays of radical theoreticians worked havoc with unionism among the Jews. What Daniel DeLeon and his Socialist Labor Party did to the Jewish unions of the last decade of the century was to be repeated under more ominous circumstances some thirty years later. On both occasions, moderate leadership and principled journalism turned the tide.

e. *The Culture of the Transplanted*

Economic and political interests were of course important elements in the life of the east European Jewish immigrant, but they alone cannot explain his attitudes nor those of the next generation. He brought with him ideas which had been spreading in his old environment, and modified them and developed them further in accordance with the demands of the new. This is why the history of the Jews in the United States, and in other countries as well, during the past two generations, cannot be fully understood without recognizing the transformation which Jewish life had begun to undergo in eastern Europe at the very time that the great migration began.

By the middle of the nineteenth century, the literary-cultural movement which went by the name of *Haskalah* (Enlightenment) had become strongly entrenched in the larger Jewish communities of the Russian Pale of Settlement. In fact, in its eagerness for western culture which amounted almost to a denial of their Jewish loyalties, the upper middle class was already going beyond *Haskalah*. The lower middle class and the workers, especially those who lived in the smaller towns and villages, continued to be guided by ancient tradition; Jewish values certainly did not lose their force among them. Nonetheless, as a peripheral result of *Haskalah*, the organized Jewish communities and the old ways and habits were suffering a perceptible loss of authority.

There were several ways in which this new spirit manifested itself at the very time that the emigration from that part of the world was reaching its height. The new literature, which had been produced during the generation or two before, was not so much secular as non-religious and non-legalistic. It was not written for the talmudical scholar but for the man of average intelligence and Jewish education—a fact which, in itself, represented a radical change in the east European literary tradition. It also differed from the new Jewish literature in Germany which, generally speaking, represented historical research with apologetic overtones. The east European Jewish community began to produce native, thoroughly and unself-consciously Jewish *belles lettres*. The new trend penetrated Jewish life in eastern Europe through the medium of the Hebrew language, for one of the aims of *Haskalah* was to encourage the common use of the classical Hebrew tongue. The second half of the nineteenth century, however, saw the development also of a literature in Yiddish, the language of the masses. It entered the field as an assistant to Hebrew, as its handmaiden; but, by the end of the century, Yiddish became Hebrew's outspoken competitor. Mendele Mokher Sefarim (1836-1917), followed by Sholem Aleichem (1859-1916) and I. L. Peretz (1852-1915), led a host of gifted story-tellers, poets and dramatists in creating a literature of great power and attractiveness. It was not only written for the common man and in his language, but also was concerned chiefly with his bitter struggles and disappointments. Whether in Yiddish or in Hebrew, the new literature openly and bitingly criticized the exclusive concern with religion which had been till then the sole mark of culture among the Jews, the communal leadership which had become arrogant, the current religiosity which had grown barren, and the narrowness of the bounds within which the prevalent Jewish educational system had been keeping the minds of the Jews at a time when the world's broad culture was being made available to them.

It took time for the new currents of thought to penetrate the vast majority of the population in the east European environment. Having been brought up close to, or within, the institutions criticized, the majority of the actual readers knew that the accusations were exaggerated intentionally to stimulate reform rather than to destroy. Others, the pious traditionalists, looked upon all this literature as impious nonsense. Now, persons of these two types were likely to be older, more set in their ways and less willing to uproot themselves, except under most unusual conditions. Consequently, the earlier the date of emigration from eastern Europe, the fewer the people of this conservative nature to be found among the migrants.

There were other segments of the Jewish population whose natural rebelliousness against restraint was fed by the critical literary and cultural currents of that age, or who had in any case already lost patience with the traditional Jewish modes of thought and life. This group consisted of the intellectuals who hungered for western culture but to whom, with rare exceptions, the gates of Russian universities were closed. Many went to western universities, many others were self-taught. But wherever they got their education, it was of the type in which the rationalism of the day prevailed. These intellectuals provided the leadership for the variety of ideological groups into which the sons and daughters of the Jewish middle and working classes flocked. They joined the secret revolutionary societies which aimed to westernize and democratize the Russian state. They organized the Bund (1897), which represented, among the Jewish workers, the revolutionary strivings of Russian socialism while recognizing the folk character of the Jewish population and appealing to them through the Yiddish language. Others among the intellectuals, imbued with deeper Jewish loyalties, were captivated by the theory of the Jewish historian Simon Dubnow (1860-1942), who contended that Diaspora Jewry needed no political center to lead a national life, but could continue to live, as it had lived for almost two thousand years, united by its culture in a unique spiritual nationalism. Finally, Russian Jewish intellectuals were also among the first to respond with enthusiasm to Herzl's call on behalf of political nationalism. All these groups, it must be emphasized, represented departures, in greater or lesser degrees, from the purely religious character of Jewish life and all that it meant in terms of customs, learning and spiritual values.

Russian Jewish youth did not consist entirely of intellectuals. The working people and the small town and village Jews sent their sons to *heder* where they became acquainted with the elements of Judaism. Eventually these, too, heard the clamor of the battle for the Jewish mind which was being waged in eastern Europe before the turn of the nineteenth century and continued into the next. A neighbor's intellectual son or daughter, temporarily returned from studying in the big city, the local subscriber to a newspaper, visitors and even peddlers could have planted the seed of doubt or offered a glimpse into a new, different and, therefore, more alluring world. The old ways, being deeply rooted, prevailed as long as the younger people remained in the old environment, so that few changes were perceptible there for another decade or two. But this was the very element of the Jewish population to whom emigration made the strongest appeal. Having emigrated, they were subjected not only to the upsetting effect of so complete a change in environment and the intoxicating sense of freedom from parental and religious control, but also to the revolutionizing influence of newspapers, books, ideas and currents of thought which fitted in with their new-found freedom and their natural desire for rapid adjustment. The young Jew, equipped only with his *heder* education, now heard of the conflict between Science and Religion which was then at its height. Spinoza and Spencer, Darwin and Marx replaced the Bible heroes and the midrashic stories the immigrant had absorbed in the Old Home. He learned that the validity of the manner of life which his home town's rabbi represented had long been disputed. The religion upon which he had been brought up appeared to have no relevance to the economic and social problems which beset him. On the other hand, what he saw and what he was told of Reform Judaism, the new western, religious attitude, appeared strange, alien and even more irrelevant. The older among the immigrants, more fixed in their habits of mind and spirit, hungry for the accustomed forms and ways, made every effort to transplant to the new land the synagogue and other communal institutions which existed in the old. But the younger people followed their intellectual leaders into the new paths which were supposed to lead to happier promised lands.

f. *The Problem of Religion in an Age of Rationalism*

The cleavage between old and new religious attitudes was more evident in the United States than in other countries. To some extent this was due to the unusual sharpness of the economic struggle in which the newer immigration was involved. It was due also and above all to the fact that traditionalism in general was weaker in America than in other predominantly Anglo-Saxon countries. In Britain, the immigrants also went through a period of social and religious conflict; but the spiritual dislocation was not as sharp, primarily because of the better communal and religious organization, which the immigrants found already in existence, and the greater regard for tradition which characterized the old population and with which the newcomers quickly fell in line.

In the United States, by the end of the nineteenth century, the immigrants of the so-called second migration, that of the period down to 1880, had become adjusted to life in America. Economically, linguistically and politically, they considered themselves fully acclimatized citizens, and were so considered by their Christian neighbors. In large part, the Jews of 1880 were second and even third generation Americans, so that many were far removed from the intellectual outlook and emotional attachments of east European Jewry. But they had not succeeded fully in solving their religious and cultural problems. By the end of the century, the religious life of the older strata of the Jewish population already showed the three groupings which have maintained their identity to this day. Many vain attempts to establish a nation-wide union of congregations had been made by the lovable and far-sighted Isaac Leeser (1806-1868) and by the energetic Isaac M. Wise (1819-1900). The latter succeeded in establishing such a union of congregations (1873) in the Middle West and a college for the training of rabbis, the Hebrew Union College, in Cincinnati (1875). For a decade, it still seemed possible that these organizations could serve as a nucleus for union. In 1885, however, Wise and his colleagues, some of them more radical than he, joined in the formulation of the Pittsburgh Platform which voiced principles more extreme than any Reformist trends then existing in Europe. In immediate reaction, Sabato Morais (1823-1897), Leeser's successor as minister of the Mikveh Israel Congregation in Philadelphia, and a number of other rabbis and lay leaders of more traditional views, began working for similar institutions to counteract Reform. The Jewish Theological Seminary of America opened its doors in 1886. It was hoped that around it would group themselves all the tradition-loving elements of the Jewish community in the United States. But it became clear, within a very few years, that a considerable part of the Jewish population was not content with the program of the Seminary and hardly satisfied with the moderate views of those who sponsored it. The growing immigration from eastern Europe after 1880 had resulted in the establishment of numerous synagogues and the arrival of many rabbis who wanted neither affiliation nor even cooperation with the existing institutions. At the turn of the century, while the Reform and the traditionalist pulpits resounded with sectarian disputation, the more recent immigrants turned away disdainfully from both.

A large number of these immigrants remained untouched by any of the religious viewpoints. The Americanized Jewish population was no more immune, than the immigrant group, to the allurements of current non-religious and anti-religious ideas. The former did not, on the whole, find Karl Marx as attractive as the younger immigrants found him; but the other ingredients of nineteenth century intellectualism affected them quite as much. Rationalism, humanism and even atheism found many devotees. The Ethical Culture movement (1876), founded by Felix Adler (1851-1933), a former student for the Reform rabbinate, attracted many Jews. Religion had ceased to be the center of Jewish life in the sense in which it had been its focus for millennia.

The growing religious indifference was blamed then, as it has been ever since, on the inadequacy of existing means for transmitting Jewish knowledge. From the very beginning, the Jewish population made valiant efforts to overcome the difficulties in the way of giving their children a Jewish education. Towards the middle of the nineteenth century, it had looked as though the solution might be the all-day Jewish school with a curriculum of both secular and religious subjects. The development of the public school system, however, put an end to this experiment. Some traditionalist synagogues, in various parts of the country, established afternoon religious schools; others met for a few hours on Saturday and Sunday; but the basic institution to emerge from that period was the Sabbath or Sunday School. Through the Union of American Hebrew Congregations, the Reform group tried to coordinate such educational efforts by founding the Sabbath School Union in 1886. As Reform Judaism was to learn in the decades to come, it was naive to imagine that a few hours a week would suffice to transmit any appreciable part of the vast Jewish cultural heritage.

The east European immigrants, accustomed to a much more profound and extensive Jewish education, were compelled to seek a solution of their own. By the end of the nineteenth century, they were employing three methods of achieving their goal. One was the Old World institution, the *heder*. It became, when transported to the United States, an afternoon school conducted usually in a dingy room by a person frequently ill-equipped for his task and almost always unable to cope with his charges. A

second method was that of the "private rebbe," an itinerant ped-
dler of instruction, who went from home to home and gave the
boy of the house a few minutes of Hebrew reading practice per
day. It rarely went beyond mechanical reading, presumably
preparatory to the boy's participation in the synagogue service; it
could hardly have been called Jewish education.

The third and most promising means of transmitting Jewish
Education in the last part of the century was the *Talmud Torah.*
Like the *heder,* it was an institution transported from eastern
Europe. After undergoing some changes, it became a semi-pub-
lic afternoon school, organized and supervised by responsible
Jews of a neighborhood, using a course of study with gradations
and goals appropriate for its time and people, and employing
as good a staff of teachers as was then available. The Machzikei
Talmud Torah in New York and a similar school in Chicago were
established in 1883 and served as models for other cities. In 1886,
the Etz Chaim school was established in New York with a more
ambitious course of study, including Talmud, thereby laying the
foundations for a rabbinical *yeshivah.*

With elementary education making comparatively little progress, it was clear that adult education must be called upon to
help redeem the situation. In the spring of 1888, representative
leaders of Jewish religion and culture met in Philadelphia to
establish the Jewish Publication Society for the production of
Jewish reading material in the English language. This idea, too,
had been thought of long before by the spiritually alert Issac
Leeser. But his effort (1845-1851) as well as another in the
1870s had failed. Better organization, wider sponsorship, the
availability of more popular books and authors, and a larger public from which to draw members contributed to the greater success of the third effort. Under the active guidance of Mayer Sulzberger, and with Henrietta Szold as its editor-secretary, the Society introduced Israel Zangwill to the English-reading world
and, also before the end of the century, published a translation
of Graetz's "History of the Jews" in a somewhat abbreviated form.
Meant to serve the needs of the second and third generations
of the already established population, the Jewish Publication

Society became an increasingly potent force in the supplementary Jewish education of all strata of the American Jewish community.

g. *Americanization and Philanthropy*

Another long-existing institution also underwent a conscious transformation. Social and literary clubs for Jewish young people had been in existence since the 1840s. In the 1850s, such clubs re-organized themselves into Young Men's Hebrew Associations. The literary aspects of the clubs had been rather superficial before, and their Hebrew aspect meant just as little now. But, the YMHAs, and the YWHAs, were useful in that they served as meeting places for Jewish youth, where debates, dances, musicals, theatricals, and amateur athletics were conducted. They offered lectures and courses on Jewish subjects, established libraries, and took note of holidays and special Jewish events. Frequently, they housed Sabbath and weekday schools for the poorer Jewish children. The coming of the new immigrants, moreover, provided the score or more of such institutions throughout the country with opportunities to join in the Americanization program which the older stratum of the Jewish population began to consider all-important.

All segments of the Jewish population were interested in the work of Americanization. The newly-arrived, being for the most part young, ambitious and intellectually hungry, knew that the sooner they acquired the language and manners of America the sooner they would feel and, they hoped, be made to feel at home. They enrolled in classes in English and quickly Americanized their names and their clothes and aped what they could see of the manners of America. It takes almost no imagination to realize that progress in these respects did not at once ease the sense of strangeness and uprootedness which the immigrants felt. The adult immigrant needed time to forget the environment and give up the habits of mind and body in which he had been reared, and inwardly to accept the new way of life. Moreover, one does not learn to feel at home; he must be made to feel at home. The American Jewish population of longer standing, for its part, did all it could for the immigrant except take him to its bosom. Humanly speaking, one could hardly have expected the older Americans to treat as equals people of strange language and customs, poverty-stricken and, in many cases, somewhat foreign in manners. Amid the growing trend to define aristocracy in terms of wealth and length of American residence—operative within the Jewish group as well as in American society—the Jewish immigrant appeared to be lowering the standing of the older Jewish residents on both scores. Not that Jews of any type or kind would, under any circumstances, have been accepted in the Gentile society of that day, but the presence of the immigrants served as an excuse for the practice of general exclusion. The Jewish Americans of long residence more than suspected that their non-Jewish neighbors lumped all Jews together. Some impatience and bitterness were, therefore, inevitable on both sides.

Classes in English and in citizenship, public lectures in Yiddish and in English, reading rooms and recreation facilities for young and old—these and dozens of other means were used in the drive to Americanize the immigrants in as short a time as possible. In New York, the Educational Alliance was a magnificent institution built for such purposes in the heart of the immigrant district in the East Side. Similar buildings were erected in other large cities. Incomparable work of social service was done by such institutions as the Henry Street Settlement in New York, directed by Lillian D. Wald, and Hull House in Chicago, directed by Jane Addams. These settlement houses and many like them in the midst of the city slums performed many services admirably and pioneered in social work which proved of great advantage to the entire community. The National Council of Jewish Women, organized in 1893, also plunged into the work in behalf of the immigrants. Its members were active in the settlements; its chapters took under their care children who showed signs of becoming delinquent; they charged themselves with the protection of girl immigrants.

There was, of course, no limit to activities of a charitable nature. Long before the beginnings of the east European immigration, the Jews of the United States had established a network of charitable institutions. Indeed, as religion became progressively less important as a bond of union among all Jews, charity emerged, to some extent, as a substitute for it. The vast new and constantly growing population multiplied old problems and created many new ones. Hospital and orphange facilities had to be expanded, direct support had to be provided to prevent homes from breaking up, stranded people had to be helped. The challenge to the established Jewish community was such as to confront it with the alternatives of allowing its charity system to break under the strain, or to develop philanthropy to such an extent as to lead the entire field. The Jews of the United States met all philanthropic emergencies.

Charity functioned exceedingly well. Cooperation, planning, the scientific approach, the substitution of professional for volunteer help, the supervision of workers—these and other evidences of efficiency became characteristic of its various areas of activity. Even the need to avoid wastefulness in the collection of funds was not lost sight of. Beginning with Boston in 1895 and Cincinnati in 1896, federations of Jewish charity organizations developed in most of the larger cities in the country. By 1900, a national conference of Jewish charities met annually. One important reason for this progress was the presence in the Jewish community of excellent leadership in the field: Morris Loeb and Lee K. Frankel, for example, among the social experts, and Jacob H. Schiff, Adolph Lewisohn and Daniel Guggenheim among the philanthropists. The fact to remember, however, is that the entire Jewish community was behind them. There was a challenge and it was met in the traditional Jewish fashion, though by methods as different and complex as was the problem which faced the Jews of that day.

The situation was, of course, not a happy one for the beneficiaries of this charitable activity. They were not so much ungrateful as resentful. All too frequently it was the givers who were really at fault. Their condescension, even while doing good, was obvious whether on the part of the kind ladies who did volunteer work in the settlements or on the part of the men who would rather work *for* the immigrants than with them. No charitable institution of those days invited representation on their boards from among the people who were most concerned. Everything about the immigrants was disparaged, sometimes including their religion. They were asked to break completely with their past, a request which could not work with the older people but succeeded with their children, thus multiplying rather than decreasing the problems of the home. To the natural economic and cultural cleavages there was thus added a social cleavage which went even deeper. The breach between the "uptowners" and the "downtowners"—as they were known in New York—or by whatever similar names they were known elsewhere in the country, was not to be healed until the total situation had become transformed during the lifetime of the second American generation of the twentieth century.

The immediate result of the mutual irritation was to drive the immigrants back upon their own resources. It encouraged the immigrants' natural tendency to re-establish in their new home the various institutions to which they had been accustomed in the old. But transferring the east European small town completely proved impossible. All the immigrant was left with to bridge the miles and the centuries, the manners and the hopes, were the synagogue and that artificial re-creation of old world society which came to be known as the *landsmanshaft*. At the meetings of the latter, as in the traditions of the former, he could relive temporarily the good old days when life was simpler and less upsetting. Besides, such organizations served as resources for mutual help. Rather than turn in time of need to the established "charities," with their searching and degrading investigations, the immigrants preferred to turn to assistance funds of their own. Before long, they began establishing new institutions. The Russian Jews of New York, for example, as early as 1892, founded the Hebrew Free Loan Society with a capital of $95; it is still in existence, though many of its imitators in other large cities no longer are, and proudly boasts of having lost in bad loans throughout its career no more than one half of one percent of its total funds, which by now run into half a million dollars. So, too, before the century came to an end, hospitals, old age homes and orphanages were founded by east European Jews in various parts of the country. The avowed reasons for such duplication of existing institutions were that the old ones did not make the east European Jew feel at home, that they provided no Jewish atmosphere, that they did not observe the dietary laws. Henrietta Szold, in her review of the last year of the century mentioned above, refers to the charge that this was unnecessary duplication by saying that it may have been ill-advised but that it was certainly not discreditable.

The course of events in other parts of the world was in many respects no different than in the United States. Everywhere, except in eastern Europe, at the end of the nineteenth century, the old established Jewish populations, despite some evidences of latent anti-Semitism among their neighbors, enjoyed a rather increased sense of at-homeness, while the newcomers among them were struggling hard to overcome their economic and spiritual dislocations. Israel Zangwill's charming sketches of Jewish life in London's crowded Whitechapel could as easily have reflected New York's East Side. The continental cities of western Europe did not have these problems to the same extent. The German police knew how, quite unofficially, to discourage immigrants from settling in that country. France and the other west European states offered comparatively few economic opportunities. Of non-European countries, South Africa began to attract considerable numbers—for some reason, mostly Lithuanian Jews—because it offered the greatest promise of opportunity and freedom. The same reasons made Canada also a goal of immigration. Thus, the foundation was laid for the English-speaking countries eventually becoming the foremost centers of Jewish population.

Available estimates indicate the Jewish population of the world in the year 1900 to have stood at the following approximate figures:

United States	1,058,000
Canada	16,000
Latin America	9,700
Russia	5,700,000
Austria-Hungary	1,870,000
Rumania	1,300,000
Germany	568,000
Turkey	350,000

United Kingdom	148,000
Netherlands	97,000
France	72,000
Italy	50,000
Bulgaria	22,600
Rest of Europe	33,650
Northern Africa	320,000
South Africa	10,000
Asia (except Turkey)	60,000

The total slightly exceeded 11,500,000.

This was the body, scattered and weak, of the Jewish people which was destined to meet the numerous revolutionary changes of the next half century. If the threats of disintegration and tragedy were already visible, the forces to counterbalance them were also asserting themselves. Looking back upon the final years of the old century, one cannot help noting that old hopes were being revived, new organizations were brought into being, efforts at adjustment were never slackened, ingrained values were gaining strength. These were some of the characteristics with which the Jews entered into the new and more dangerous age.

II. EXPERIMENTS IN ADJUSTMENT

a. *For a Measure of Security*

The new century was merely a date on the calendar; it did not mark any sudden transformation in the ways of the world or any alleviation of the problems that faced mankind. As far as the Jews were concerned, the changes that were taking place were at the time imperceptible. Equally imperceptible and just as unabating were the efforts, physical and spiritual, which ongoing events aroused among the Jews of all types and classes.

Emigration from eastern Europe continued; indeed, it increased. The average annual immigration of Jews into the United States, between 1900 and 1913, exceeded 100,000, close to ten percent of the total. Jewish migration to other parts of the world was relatively as large. Everywhere this sharpened the problems of relations with the non-Jewish population and within the Jewish community. In the United States, on a number of occasions, Congress passed restrictive immigration measures in the form of literacy tests (1896, 1909, 1915), which were vetoed by the presidents. In Great Britain, the labor unions were persuaded that immigrants competed unfairly with native labor and lowered the standard of living. A parliamentary commission held hearings, recommended restrictions, and the government did nothing further about it. Immediate danger of a closing of the gates was thus averted, but the Jews of older residence were impressed with the need to do something to avert its recurrence.

If the irritations incident to the arrival of large numbers could not be averted, they could, it was believed in some quarters, be mitigated by directing immigrants away from the overcrowded cities. The ICA, of course, continued to function in both North and South America. The Jewish Agricultural Society, in the first ten years of its activity, cooperated with ICA, to settle over three thousand Jewish families on farms in New England, New York, New Jersey and states farther west. It not only continued to guide these families and give them instruction, but it tried also to give agricultural training to such others as showed some interest in going into farming. The way of the novice farmers was hard. Frequently, they were compelled to supplement their income by taking in summer boarders or by working part time in factories. Frequently, when they came to terms with their new life, it did not appear likely that they would be able to make farmers out of their sons and daughters. With the trend in the general population away from the farm, it seemed rather unreasonable to look for its reversal among Jews.

Even temporary success in this respect was, however, a gain, since it removed that many families from the slums of the cities. Other experiments toward the same end were therefore tried. In 1901, the Industrial Removal Office was established. Its aim was to persuade immigrants to move farther inland in the United States, where opportunities for adjustment might be better. The IRO succeeded, in the course of a very few years, in transferring some 40,000 to the smaller towns in the interior. As quickly as these left the eastern seaboard, others took their place. It seemed necessary also to prevent the very debarkation of immigrants in the crowded centers. The wise, kindly, philanthropic Jacob H. Schiff espoused the idea which came to be known as the Galveston Plan because that southern port played the chief role in it. Immigrants were to be persuaded at ports of embarkation in Europe to avoid the eastern seaboard of the United States and to enter the country through the south. It was hoped thereby to shunt considerable numbers into the more sparsely settled portions of the country. The plan began to operate in 1907 and there were indications that it might achieve the objectives sought, when World War I interrupted its development.

Having hurdled the difficulty of transferring themselves from their stepmotherslands to their new homes, the immigrants had to turn to the pressing problem of earning their livelihood. This, too, did not come easy. But the conflict and uproar was accompanied by quiet adjustment and comparatively rapid acclimatization. Again the progress of events in the United States must serve as the example because it illustrates the process on the largest canvas.

The center of the struggle was the Jewish labor union. As the century opened, the focus of union labor activity was away from ideological disputes and towards the use of unionization for material improvement. Both the United Garment Workers (UGW, organized in 1891) and the International Ladies Garment Workers Union (ILGWU, organized in 1900) finally came into their own during the first decade of the new century, as did the unions of the furriers, capmakers and others. In one city after another, strikes were productive of greatly improved conditions, and their victories heartened the workers and prepared them for the greater struggles to come. Moreover, union efforts now had the sympathy of the liberal elements of the population. It had finally dawned upon people that the factory workers could really not be blamed, as they had been for decades, for the slum conditions in which they lived, as long as the length of their working day sapped their energies and the low pay made decent living conditions a luxury.

With the economic revival, after the comparatively slight depression of 1907, the various needle industries began to prepare for showdown strikes. The most spectacular was the strike of the 20,000 girls who worked in shirtwaist factories in New York. It began in November 1909, and had the full sympathy of the New York public. The strike lasted for three months, but it ended in an almost complete victory for the girls. A few months later, in July 1910, the workers in the cloak-and-suit industry went out on strike. In this case, too, the employers were forced to yield a substantial victory to the strikers. Especially interesting in this case was the use of public opinion to work a change in the relations between workers and employers. The vast majority of the workers and employers being Jews, both sides were appealed to on the basis of safeguarding the reputation of the Jewish population. Jacob H. Schiff and Louis Marshall, who commanded the respect of all concerned, urged a cessation of the violence which characterized strikes in those days and the arrival at a settlement without waiting for the total surrender of one side or the other. Louis D. Brandeis, then a noted Boston lawyer, worked out a plan for a permanent board of grievance which was to refer all future disputes to impartial arbitrators. In modified form, this plan was to remain part of union-employer relations in the needle industries from then on.

Despite some setbacks, internal wrangling and constant recriminations between employers and employees, the Jewish labor unions came through the period of World War I strengthened and more popular. The sweatshop was a thing of the past, destroyed less by government action than by labor victories; working conditions were incomparably superior to those of the previous decades; wage rates bore a closer relation, than formerly, to the cost of living. No one could say any longer that Jews were incapable of unionization. It was, in fact, clear that the Jewish unions were among the strongest and most intelligently led in the United States.

Yet it was already clear, by the time of World War I, that the needle industries and other trades, in which Jews had preponderated to the extent of almost ninety percent of the workers, would not long retain this ratio. The large immigration of the century's first decade and a half tended to cover up the fact that the second generation of American Jews was turning to other areas of economic activity. On the whole, it was a period of expansion for small business. Seen in retrospect, it does not appear to have taken long for factory workers and peddlers to turn into grocers, butchers, tinsmiths, cigar-store owners, opticians, and dozens of other kinds of vendors. Some seized the opportunity, because they had the imagination, to enter and develop new fields. Thus, the nascent motion picture industry, still manifesting itself during the century's first decade in little more than penny arcades, was taken hold of by a number of immigrants and turned into a new, vastly popular form of entertainment. Whether this insight was a re-assertion of innate individualism, or of trading habits become fixed through generations, or of a desire for more rapid economic advancement, or of dissatisfaction with a life of manual labor—whatever motivation, good or not so good, is ascribed to it, the fact is that in a society which glorified the middle class, the Jewish immigrant population had begun its ascent into that class. If so much is to be explained on the basis of folk habit, one must attribute to Jewish character also the interest which the second generation displayed in so-called white-collar occupations. Immigrant parents made every effort and sacrifice to send their children to high school and, if possible, through college. The highest goal—even higher than to be a businessman—was law or medicine for a son, and teaching or, at least, secretarial work for a daughter. As Jews, having overcome great obstacles, sought to enter new and more respected economic areas, whether business or professional, they encountered new—in Jewish experience old—obstacles placed in their way by non-Jews already in the field.

b. *The Tide of Anti-Semitism*

There was a moment during the nineteenth century when the Jews of Europe were justified in looking forward hopefully to the disappearance of anti-Jewishness. The moment proved all too brief. When, during the Age of Rationalism, it became no longer fashionable to hate Jews for religious reasons, the racial reason, that is, anti-Semitism, was substituted. It proved even more serviceable than old-fashioned Jew-hatred as an excuse for condemning and hating Jews, since it is possible for a person to change his religion but quite impossible, according to the scientific theories of that day, to change one's racial character. The German-speaking countries, where Jews were making spectacular economic and, therefore, social progress, became the homeland of the anti-Semites. In France, towards the end of the nineteenth century, anti-Semitism played a crucial role in the political upheaval known as the Dreyfus Affair. The forces of liberalism triumphed after six years of bitter conflict which showed at every turn how deeply ingrained in the minds of the people was the dislike of Jews. Britain, with the broad sense of fairness and tolerance which had become characteristic of that country, had abolished, some forty years before the end of the century, the last disabilities that had been imposed on the Jews. Nevertheless, the anti-immigration movement at the beginning of the new century had about it a slight odor of anti-Semitism. The Scandinavian countries, and Italy as well, were almost completely free from this spiritual blight. Russia and Rumania, of course, were an entirely different case.

A considerable anti-Semitic literature, mostly in German, circulated in Europe around the turn of the century. The anti-Semites even banded themselves together in an international league which met periodically for consultation and propaganda. An occasional "ritual-murder" scare, in various parts of the Austro-Hungarian empire, served to show that religious prejudices were still prevalent among the backward populations. The failure to permit Jews to become officers in the German army or to promote them to professorships in the German universities was also a holdover from former days and could not be credited directly to the influence of the new anti-Semitism. Nevertheless, though it seemed to show no practical results, anti-Semitism was planting, in the hearts of men, seeds that in time would bear their poisonous fruit.

Jews reacted with indignation and fear. They issued leaflets and books as counter-propaganda, dignified and intelligent enough, but perhaps for that very reason unpersuasive. Appeals to reason against an irrational emotion were bound to fail. Virtually every country in Europe had a defense organization to combat anti-Jewish propaganda and to guard against infringements of the rights of Jews. But the chief immediate results of this revival of anti-Jewishness was its effect on the Jews themselves. They became over-sensitive and over-careful. A large measure of the opposition to Herzlian Zionism among the Jews of western Europe is traceable to the fear that sympathy with the rebuilding of the ancient land would be misinterpreted as lack of loyalty to their native country.

Anti-Jewishness in the United States began differently and has given promise of ending differently, but some of the intermediate steps and some of the reactions on the part of Jews were not unlike those of Europe. European religious prejudices were imported with every group of settlers even in Colonial days; under prevailing conditions, however, these prejudices could not thrive or have any lasting influence. When the national government came into being, it refused to recognize divisions according to religion; the Bill of Rights guaranteed the separation of Church and State. That there were occasional lapses into prejudice on the part of individuals must be taken for granted; but the attitude toward Jews on the part of the population as a whole must be set down as proof that, where opportunities for economic betterment are plentiful and agitators scarce, the average sensible human being will not hold against his neighbor the fact that the latter differs from him in custom and religion. In the course of the nineteenth century, there were several occasions when the United States entered official protest, on humanitarian grounds, against mistreatment of Jews in foreign lands. It did so more vigorously where Jewish citizens of the United States were affected, not on the ground that the people maltreated were Jews, but on the ground that they were citizens, among whom the government of the United States made no distinctions because of religion. As late as 1887, President Grover Cleveland appointed a Jew, Oscar S. Straus, as minister to Turkey, in large measure in order to show the prejudice-ridden Europeans that the United States did not practice discrimination. It can be said that the United States had grown to maturity as a nation without showing any substantial evidence of Old World anti-Jewishness. Among the general population, however, the prejudice showed signs of spreading as the new century opened.

Many factors contributed to this change of atmosphere. One

historian attributes it to the growing economic distress of the farmers, especially in the Middle West, and to the rise of an American aristocracy. Agitators tried to persuade the former to accept the idea, borrowed from the anti-Semitism of Europe, that alleged Jewish control of finance lay at the bottom of all troubles; the charge was that the Jews controlled Wall Street. The self-appointed aristocrats, largely representative of the real financial power in the country, desired no intrusion into their ranks and looked on with dismay at the climb of some Jews up the economic ladder. Such attitudes at the top seeped down quickly. The immigrants were blamed for the rising tide of anti-Jewish feeling: their numbers, their manners and the slums they were accused of creating. It was a persuasive explanation, and many among the older strata of Jews were also prepared to accept it. The hollowness of the argument was immediately apparent through the fact that the completely assimilated German Jews were at that time also not spared the pains of prejudice. Moreover, as the children of the Jewish immigrants, though all but indistinguishable from the rest of the American population, began looking for occupations in fields in which Jews were formerly not conspicuous, the number of Jews exposed to hostility and discrimination increased. Restrictions began to appear on every side: against Jews desiring to move into better neighborhoods, against those seeking admission to better or socially more recognized schools, against their entrance into the legal, medical or engineering profession. Certain economic areas, like banking or the heavy industries, were completely closed to Jews. Restrictive advertisements, whether by resorts or employers, became common.

The American Jews had no organization to combat this intangible yet real menace. They became as ill-at-ease and, therefore, as apologetic as the west European Jews. The natural outlet for their discomfort was the same type of protest and explanation. Rabbis from their pulpits refuted every possible charge; but their audiences were Jews. The papers read and published by the American Jewish Historical Society (founded in 1892) concentrated on the part played by Jews in the birth and growth of the nation; but they again reached a small number and these almost exclusively Jews.

An event occurred in 1903 which indicated that anti-Jewishness was not yet so deep-seated as many Jews feared. The pogrom in Kishinev was another symptom of the czarist government's desire to draw the attention of the people away from the reforms which the country desperately needed. Organized by the government itself, the riots resulted in about forty lives lost, some six hundred people injured and much property destroyed. The civilized world was horrified. Protest meetings were addressed not only by Jews but also by distinguished representatives of the Christian population both in Britain and in America; conscience appeared to be still alive. Another indication of the fact that anti-Jewish feeling was not yet deep among the Christian population of the United States, was the warm participation of leading non-Jews in the celebration, in 1905, of the 250th anniversary of the arrival of the first Jews in North America—the same event of which the 300th anniversary was recently celebrated.

Realizing that, on the whole, the American people were not hostile to Jews and that the United States Government represented public opinion in its firm and unequivocal condemnation of persecution in foreign lands, some of the foremost American Jews were encouraged to implement suggestions that had been made in the Jewish press for the organization of a general committee to serve the same purposes as were served by similar bodies in western European countries. Such an organization had existed in the United States from 1859 to 1878. It was called the Board of Delegates of American Israelites and comprised representatives from a number of Reform congregations; it was merged with the Union of American Hebrew Congregations with the understanding that this work would be continued by a special committee of the latter organization. The fact was that, at the time of the Kishinev massacre, no organization existed in the United States that could appeal to the entire Jewish community for relief funds, or that could approach the Government, in the name of all the Jews of the United States, to lodge a protest against the outrage with the Russian Government.

As a consequence of this situation, an *ad hoc* committee had to be set up to raise funds for the relief of the surviving victims of the Kishinev massacre and others that followed. Happily, the leaders of this committee, which included such widely known and highly respected persons as Oscar S. Straus, Jacob H. Schiff, Cyrus L. Sulzberger, Louis Marshall, Adolph Lewisohn, and others of similar stature, enjoyed the confidence of American Jews generally, who responded generously to the appeal for contributions. The funds raised were transmitted to representative Jewish bodies in Russia, which also were raising money there, for application to the needs of the situation.

The fact that an *ad hoc* committee had to be formed to meet this crisis was another factor in convincing Jews, who were regarded and were turned to, when emergencies arose, as leaders of the community, that a permanent representative body was urgently needed. How such a body should be organized was the subject of prolonged and earnest debate at two conferences, held in New York City, of individuals selected because they were known to be recognized as leaders in their communities. There was much difference of opinion as to the basis of organization, but there was no difference of opinion on the need of such a general committee; the only point on which there was majority agreement was that such a committee should be established, and Mayer Sulzberger, who was in the chair, was instructed to appoint a committee of fifteen which would co-opt forty-five additional members to constitute the general committee; later the number was increased from sixty to seventy-five. On November 11, 1906, these men met and established the American Jewish Committee.

One of the first steps taken by the new organization was to deal with what actually constituted a civil disability for American Jews. This was the fact that the Russian Government refused admission to that country of Jews from the United States, regardless of the place of their birth. This policy was a flagrant violation of the Treaty of Commerce and Navigation, concluded between the United States and Russia, in 1832, and the United States Government had protested against the policy repeatedly for almost half a century. The American Jewish Committee began by approaching President Theodore Roosevelt and his successor William H. Taft, both of whom regretfully replied that the United States Government could not see its way clear to taking any action other than continuing its diplomatic protests. Following this unsatisfactory response, the American Jewish Committee decided to demand and to agitate for the abrogation of the treaty of 1832 on the ground that, so long as it continued in force, the civil and political equality of American Jews as citizens of the United States was actually abridged under the laws of the land, of which treaties are a part. Resolutions requesting the President to take the steps prescribed in the treaty to bring about its abrogation were introduced in both the Senate and the House of Representatives. Representatives of the American Jewish Committee, accompanied by leaders of several other Jewish organizations, appeared before the appropriate committees of the Congress and argued in favor of the resolutions. The case was strengthened by the fact that the American Jewish Committee learned that the embargo against the admission of American citizens did not affect only Jews but also Catholic priests and Protestant missionaries. Backed up by an aroused public opinion, which was the more ready to support the breaking of this bond with Russia because of the pogroms, the House of Representatives passed the abrogation resolution by a vote of three hundred to one; before the Senate was ready to consider this measure, President Taft notified that body that he, through diplomatic channels, had given the Russian Government the year's notice of this abrogation required by the treaty. The Senate thereupon adopted a resolution approving the President's action.

It was a victory which pleased Jews and re-affirmed the American guarantee of political equality. As was expected, it had no effect whatever on Russia. Two years later, Russia offered the world the spectacle of a thoroughly medieval "ritual-murder" trial. In 1911, a Jew by the name of Mendel Beilis had been arrested on the trumped-up charge of having killed a Christian child for non-existent purposes of the Jewish religion. The real culprit, the mother of the dead child, was easily identifiable; but, despite the protests of liberal Russians and of groups of leaders in many western countries who ridiculed the "ritual-murder" fable, the Russian Government openly went to great lengths to have the Jew, and through him all Jews, convicted. The dastardly plot failed, not because of the protests and other expressions of disgust of the civilized part of the world, but because there simply was no evidence.

c. *Zionism Under Herzl*

It is not surprising that large numbers of the Jewish population of the Russian Empire were eager to escape from such an atmosphere and such pressures. What calls for explanation is why the vast majority chose to stay or hoped to go elsewhere than to the countries in which they or their children could expect material improvement. The explanation lies in their spiritually satisfying life. The inner life of the Jews of eastern Europe was now, in the decade preceding World War I, more active than ever. It was also more varied. One cannot divide a population into clear-cut segments but, with a great deal of overlapping, the following groupings could be discerned among the Russian Jews of that day. The largest group maintained, deepened and purified, the characteristic east European Jewish religious life, both hasidic and non-hasidic. Such people were suspicious of the newly-formed Diasporas, already notorious, as far as they were concerned, for their religious laxness, if not outright Godlessness. Such Jews migrated only when their personal situation became quite intolerable or when family ties drew them to the distant land. At the other extreme, was a group whose hopes were centered in Russia's coming revolution. For there was a growing number of western-educated and increasingly assimilated Jews who felt that Russia could not long postpone democratization. Rather close to the latter were the workers and intellectuals who formed the backbone of the socialist, revolutionary, Yiddishist town dwellers of the Pale. Between the two extremes were those whose views, whether inclining more to the religious or more to the socialistic, were mingled with a sense of Jewish nationalism; whose cultural interests, though broad, were drawn to Hebrew as their language; whose humanist sentiments, though inclusive, could be traced back to the Bible and other Jewish sources of idealism, and were connected closely with the highly productive Hebrew and Yiddish literature of the day. The usual centers of migration did not attract them, being considered by them culturally barren. This group constituted the body and the hope of the Zionist movement.

There was a sense of urgency about Dr. Herzl's activity in behalf of the cause which he represented, almost as though he knew how short his life would be. His visits to the Sultan and the Kaiser, to Russian diplomats and British statesmen, to wealthy Jews and influential Christians; his correspondence, the institutions he saw established to further the movement's aims, his arguments and negotiations before, at, and after the Zionist congresses—all testify to the intensity of his desire to achieve the Zionist aim in the shortest possible time. His almost feverish activity indicated his obsession by the idea; but it indicated also his conviction that Russian Jewry, perhaps European Jewry and, possibly, even world Jewry, had to be saved at once or the Jewish people would perish. It was a conviction touched with prophecy. Quite as prophetic was his description, in his "Altneuland," of the progressive, efficient, modern Jewish state which would be in existence fifty years later. The two prophecies were joined in his mind, as they were destined to be joined in fact.

Herzl wanted to save the Russian Jews who, all objective observers agreed, had to abandon the empire of the czar. With anti-Semitism almost everywhere in evidence, the best solution of the so-called Jewish question clearly was a homeland of their own for the Jewish people. But despite half a dozen years of active contact with some of the best among the Jewish people, Herzl, with his assimilationist background and inadequate Jewish upbringing, still did not realize the depth of Jewish attachment to Palestine. When the British government suggested Uganda in Africa as a place where a semi-independent Jewish community could be established, Herzl decided to place before the World Zionist Congress about to meet, in 1903, the proposal that the British offer of Uganda be accepted as a *Nacht-Asyl,* a temporary asylum. He was shocked by the effect which the suggestion produced on the delegates representing the very Russian Jews whom he was so anxious to save. They viewed it as an abandonment of their dearest hopes, a betrayal. They would not hear of Uganda nor of any other temporary asylum, but only of Palestine. The compromise arrived at, namely, to send an investigating commission, was merely a cover-up for a retreat from the entire scheme. It was to be Palestine, the ancient homeland, or nothing. A number of Zionists, on the other hand, considered this stand quite unrealistic. Israel Zangwill, for example, noting the rising tide of objections to Jewish immigration into his native England and into America, and fearful of the effects of assimilation on the future of the Jewish people, felt that a quicker solution had to be found than the one which Zionism offered under its self-limitation to Palestine. The Jews, he argued, could not wait until the Sultan was persuaded to grant the charter to Palestine upon which Zionist hopes were based. Zangwill, therefore, seceded from the Zionist organization and founded the Jewish Territorial Organization (ITO) which looked for a Jewish home, or Jewish homes, wherever it or they could be found. He had to admit eventually that his apparently easier task proved at least as difficult; he was still searching for other homes when Zionism began taking giant steps forward.

Another aspect of the east European view of Zionism was a source of surprise to Herzl. He was impatient of the method of slow colonization which the Hovevei Ziyon had been pursuing for the quarter century before. Given to thinking in political terms, he considered colonization the wrong way to begin. The proper first step was to obtain a charter from the Sultan guaranteeing Jewish autonomy within the Turkish Empire. Admittedly, he was not getting far in that direction. That was why he tried to use the influence of the Kaiser and to bring whatever other pressure he could on the wary Abdul Hamid. Once the charter was obtained, he believed, the Jewish masses would flow into the land and rebuild it and their Judaism with it. He was astonished to find a substantial number of Zionists, mostly east Europeans, taking quite the opposite view. They considered the people's culture more basic than any political arrangements. Ahad Haam (Asher Ginzberg, 1856-1927), the foremost interpreter of the Jewish spirit of that day, as well as all the other participants in the stirring revival of Hebrew culture, were more concerned with the people than with the land or with national autonomy. Chaim Weizmann, then a young scientist, was among the leaders of the opposition to Herzl.

Opposition, dissappointment, ceaseless labor destroyed Herzl. He died at the age of forty-four. Everyone, the east European Jews most of all, recognized that the cause had lost its great leader. Everyone feared that Zionism would collapse. But it went on, though without the drive of Herzl's personality and his resourcefulness. David Wolffsohn, Herzl's successor in the presidency of the World Zionist Organization, was a mild-mannered businessman who had all he could do to keep things going. Yet the organization and the institutions which Herzl had founded continued to function. The work for a charter and other political plans were now relegated to second place. The opposition had triumphed in a way it certainly had not wished, but the fact was that it had the field practically to itself. Palestine was to be built through agricultural settlements and cultural renaissance.

Two ideals motivated the young people whose arrival in Palestine between 1904 and the outbreak of World War I is designated the Second *Aliyah* ("ascent"): the ideal of reviving the Jewish nation on its ancestral soil and the ideal of socialism, which they understood to mean a non-exploiting society. They objected to the employment of Arabs because, for one thing, this would limit the opportunities for Jewish immigration and, perhaps more important, it would turn the Jews into supervisors of a peasant Arab population. Their views found expression in the personality and writings of the remarkable A. D. Gordon (1856-1922). Arrived in Palestine in 1904, at the age of forty-eight, he insisted on becoming a common laborer. He evolved the principle of "the Conquest of Labor," indeed, the holiness of labor. Fortunately, too, the World Zionist Organization established a labor office in Palestine in charge of the wise and gifted Dr. Arthur Ruppin (1876-1942). Moreover, the Organization soon succeeded in persuading the new Turkish Government (1908) to permit the acquisition of land by Jews. The newly established *Keren Kayyemet* (Jewish National Fund) became the purchasing and holding agency of the national soil, to which it retained title but which it let the colonists work. Thus a number of colonies were founded in every part of the country. They took various forms: collectivist, both economically and socially, cooperative, or individual in ownership. Not all the problems were solved, but the entire Zionist enterprise began to take shape and give promise.

There were other significant developments, during this brief decade and a half, testifying to the creative vitality of the *Yishuv* (the Jewish settled community in Palestine). The organization of the *shomerim*, a band of Jewish armed guards, to protect the colonies from nocturnal incursions of Arabs bent on theft, lent an air of frontier romance to the history of the period. The foundation of Tel Aviv, a new suburb on the sandy outskirts of Jaffa, which began to mushroom into a city, was another foreshadowing of the future. As important as any manifestation of vitality was the emergence of Hebrew as an every-day spoken language. Poets and publicists and novelists had been urging such a development for a century, not without some bitterness against Yiddish which they identified with exile and spiritual subservience. What could not be achieved by arguments and pleas in the larger centers of eastern Europe, the tiny but ardent settlement in Palestine willed into existence.

The process had begun in the days of the First *Aliyah*. It seemed natural for those who came to revive the ancient land to desire to revive its ancient language. They adopted the Sephardi pronunciation, modifying it slightly, ostensibly because they persuaded themselves that the language had thus been spoken in ancient times. In all likelihood, there was here, too, the subconscious motivation of wanting to break with the exile, the ghetto and all that it had brought into Jewish life. The Second *Aliyah* fortified the earlier decision of bringing the Hebrew language to life. In the schools that were established the children were taught in Hebrew only. Unfortunately the classical Hebrew, which was available, did not suffice for the modernity which was equally a part of the new *Yishuv's* heritage. Now, however, the influence of Eliezer ben Yehudah began to be felt. A man of indomitable spirit, he made the speaking of Hebrew a principle of life with which he brooked no compromise. If the Hebrew vocabulary was inadequate, he single-handedly undertook to enlarge it. In his many-volumed dictionary, he drew upon Arabic and he Hebraized western terms. Later Hebraists changed many of his locutions, but he had laid the foundations of the revived language.

The intense loyalty which the *Yishuv* had begun to feel to the Hebrew language came to the surface when they thought it was being threatened or even slighted. The *Hilfsverein der deutschen Juden* opened a technical school in Haifa. Arguing that Hebrew was not yet ripe for effective use in scientific studies, the directors announced that the school would use German in the technical courses. At once, pupils and teachers went on strike. It is by no means certain to this day that the German directors wanted to side-track Hebrew, but they had obviously touched a very sensitive nerve in the spirit of the community. The long and heated argument had the effect of making the World Zionist Organization take on educational functions along with its other activities. Above all, the struggle made it perfectly clear that Hebrew was to be the language of the future among the Jews of Palestine.

The *Yishuv* was thus taking firm root. Years of development still lay ahead, hard struggles in every sphere; but there was every reason to expect that, in the course of some generations, a healthy community would grow up and prosper. Suddenly, a world-shaking tragedy loomed out of the west and threatened to destroy all that had been achieved. Yet, out of that tragedy, came the un-expected—that charter recognizing Jewish rights in Palestine for which Herzl had worked and because of which he had been derided and opposed. This, however, is a story so closely connected with the western Diaspora that attention must once more be centered there.

d. *Varieties of Judaism and Experiments in Unity*

It had been Ahad Haam's contention, from the very beginning, that what the Jews were experiencing was a crisis of Judaism rather than a crisis of the Jewish people. Total and ignominious assimilation, he maintained, was a greater and more imminent danger than anti-Semitism in the west and persecution in the east. Both Herzlian Zionists and the defense organizations which had grown up in the various countries of western Europe put the solution of social and political problems first. The advocates of strengthening the Jewishness of Jewish life in the western communities were indeed numerous and sometimes vociferous, but hopelessly divided as to aims and means.

Religion, more than any other aspect of Jewish life, revealed the wide divisions which existed among Jews. In Germany, advocates of greater Reform organized a union in 1908, and extreme Orthodoxy countered by establishing a world union of its own under the name of Agudath Yisroel (1912). In France, the consistorial system (1905) aimed to unify French Jewry on a religious communal basis; but that did not prevent the east European immigrants from establishing synagogues quite independent of the Consistory. At the same time, a Reform movement appeared and also established a synagogue in Paris. In England, where Judaism had a long tradition of unity because of the official and unofficial functioning of the United Synagogue and its Chief Rabbinate, there came into being an Orthodox *Kehilla* on the Frankfort-German model, a federation of synagogues of the east European type, as well as a liberal synagogue taking its cue from American Reform Judaism.

Nowhere was religious division more apparent and more articulate than in the United States. The emergence of three distinct religious viewpoints by the beginning of the twentieth century has already been mentioned. Of the three, the Reform group alone was well organized. The Union of American Hebrew Congregations was a flourishing body; Isaac M. Wise had given it extraordinary leadership. On his death (1900), the presidency of the Hebrew Union College went to Kaufmann Kohler, a great scholar and theologian. Reform might eventually have become the dominant religious view of American Judaism, had it not been characterized during that crucial decade by religious radicalism, social exclusiveness and anti-Zionism. Orthodox Jewry had, indeed, made a feeble effort at strength through union when, in 1888, it had invited Rabbi Jacob Joseph of Vilna to become the chief rabbi of the Russian Jewish congregations in New York. The plan failed completely. The chief rabbi's authority was flouted by his colleagues and not supported by laymen. At his death (1902), the situation reverted to chaos. The Union of Orthodox Jewish Congregations, which had been organized in 1898, proved far too weak. No area of Jewish life, from *kashrut* to education, was given the necessary supervision. The congregations were not only independent of one another but also antagonistic to each other. The Yeshivah (the Rabbi Isaac Elhanan Theological Seminary, organized in 1896) enjoyed but minor status when European-trained rabbis were readily available. Not till 1915, with the appointment to its presidency of Bernard Revel (1885-1940), did the institution begin to exert influence on American Orthodoxy.

The Jewish Theological Seminary had been marking time since the death of Sabbato Morais (1897). The institution's appeal to Americanized traditionalist Jews, by and for whom it had been founded, had never been either vigorous or effective. Its sole contribution had been the preparation of a number of scholarly rabbis who could preach in English to congregations which still maintained the orthodox ritual. The entire situation changed with the coming to the Seminary's presidency of Solomon Schechter. He was a scholar and a sage, a brilliant writer and an ardent fighter in behalf of a living, functioning, traditional Judaism. Behind him stood some of the finest spirits in American Israel: Jacob H. Schiff and Louis Marshall, though themselves identified with a Reform congregation; Cyrus Adler and Solomon Solis-Cohen, who had been brought up in the Sephardi congregation of Leeser and Morais; and many other important individuals, though comparatively few congregations. Dr. Schechter set forth his goal for American Judaism as organized traditionalism grounded in learning. He began to build on the model of the Breslau seminary which had been founded by Zechariah Frankel in the 1840s. He invited first-rate young scholars like Louis Ginzberg, Alexander Marx, Israel Friedlaender and Mordecai M. Kaplan, to serve on the Seminary's faculty. He laid the foundation of what was to become, under the guidance of Professor Marx, one of the foremost Jewish libraries in the world. Under him, the Jewish Theological Seminary began to graduate rabbis who could challenge the leadership of the Reformers. In 1913, Schechter founded the United Synagogue of America, dedicated to what he preferred to call Historical Judaism, but which has come to be known as Conservative Judaism.

All of these religious movements and institutions combined, it must be remembered, did not command the adherence of all the

Jews in the United States, any more than similar movements and institutions claimed the loyalty of all the countries of Europe. A substantial minority of the newly-arrived immigrants as well as of the older residents were indifferent to affiliation with organized religion of any kind. This reflected the trend in the general population, though among Protestants more than among Catholics. That the lack of affiliation was more apparent in the Jewish group may be accounted for by a number of considerations: the impression that adjustment demands the obliteration of all differences, the special susceptibility of Jews to rationalist influences, the inability of immigrant parents to transmit their heritage in the terms of their new environment, and, finally, the patent fact that Jews can express their Jewishness in ways other than public or even private worship. Each of the numerous organizations which claimed the loyalty of Jews—B'nai B'rith lodges, *landsmanshaften*, the Workmen's Circle, Zionist clubs, or any number of others of a philanthropic nature—could claim to be an expression of the Jewish spirit.

This fragmentation of Jewish life may have made it colorful and interesting, but it also made it chaotic. The disorganization had long troubled some of those who stood at the forefront of Jewish life, but it took an ugly incident to stir them to action. In 1908, the Police Commissioner of New York City published an article in which he voiced current anti-immigrant prejudices by saying that half the city's criminals were Jews. In the face of a storm of protest, the Commissioner retracted the ill-advised and easily-disproved accusation. But the incident showed how important it was for the Jews to draw together in defense of their common interests. Judah L. Magnes, already a powerful influence in American Jewish life and, though at the time a rabbi of the Reform Temple Emanu-El, loved by the Jews of the East Side of New York, decided that it was time to act. Characteristically, he was concerned, not so much with defending the good name of the Jews, as with bringing to the fore their latent spiritual qualities. The Jews of New York must organize on a democratic basis to deal with the variety of problems which confronted them. Thus, in February 1909, the New York *Kehilla* came into existence.

The name of the city-wide organization was reminiscent of the

Kahal, the official Jewish community which had functioned for many centuries in every town in Europe. The new body itself was in effect quite different from the old *Kahal.* It consisted of representatives of every variety of Jewish organization, based on its membership—synagogue, lodge, philanthropy and all the rest. The "down-towners" were there and the "up-towners" too, for Magnes sought to tie the American Jewish Committee, be it ever so loosely, with the Jewish efforts for internal unity. The aims were as broad as Magnes' hopes were high: "Nothing Jewish should be foreign to the Jewish community of New York." It was going to institute supervision of *kashrut,* to improve Jewish education, to gather statistics in various areas of Jewish life, to strengthen and democratize philanthropy and to participate in any number of other activities. There was great enthusiasm, which carried over to other cities. A similar *Kehilla* was actually formed in Philadelphia and there was talk about it in other cities as well.

Yet the glowing hopes came to little. After the first year or two, enthusiasm waned. Magnes' popularity kept it going for almost a decade, but by 1918 it petered out completely. The reasons for its demise were inherent in the Jewish population and in Magnes. Jews among themselves had not yet overcome suspicions and prejudice based on their places of origin. Too many toes were being stepped on in the plans for various kinds of supervision. There was still too much antagonism between the socially and economically distinct portions of the city's Jewish inhabitants. The intellectual differences could not be bridged. Above all, World War I broke out and interest was diverted to the tragic plight of the Jews in Europe. Magnes himself, courageous and outspokenly idealistic, moved against the current of American sentiment both with regard to the War and the revolutionary events in Russia, and so fell under a cloud. Losing him, the *Kehilla* lost its vital spirit and ceased to function.

Nevertheless, all was not lost. The *Kehilla* of New York left a legacy in the form of several institutions which continued to exert a constructive influence on Jewish life. Among these was a school for Jewish social workers which functioned for a number of years. There was, above all, the Bureau of Jewish Education which soon began a fruitful career under the direction of Samson Benderly (1876-1944). He brought system into the organization, and method into the conduct of the Jewish school. He surrounded himself with promising young college men whom he inspired to make Jewish education their life work. By persuading several important schools to pay their teachers a living wage, he raised the prestige of the Jewish teaching profession. By encouraging the preparation of new textbooks and urging the adoption of Hebrew as the language of instruction, he brought new spirit into the child's introduction to Jewish life. His cause was aided by the arrival in the United States of a number of excellent teachers as well as by the inspiration deriving from Zionist thought. Through the Bureau, Benderly, aided by a substantial fund given by Jacob H. Schiff, knew how to translate all this into program and curriculum. Before long, many of the larger Jewish communities made serious efforts to coordinate their schools through similar bureaus of Jewish education.

The *Kehilla*, despite its failure, proved that forces making for broad unity were stirring within the Jewish population. Actual cooperation during days of peace and for the difficult purpose of inner reconstruction required more self-effacement than was as yet possible; too many memories and too many prejudices still divided group from group. But already a generation was growing up in whose spirit a common upbringing was to outweigh the divisive influences of the past. Moreover, even before that generation came into its own, a challenge was hurled at the Jewries of the west, especially that of America, which compelled them to assume responsibilities from which they would ordinarily have shrunk as beyond their powers.

III. WAR AND ITS CONSEQUENCES

a. *Between Two Fires*

It has been pointed out often that in time of war Jews suffer in double measure: as part of the embattled nations and as Jews. Every army in World War I had its Jewish soldiers, usually in a ratio higher than the proportion of Jews in the nation's population. By accusing the Jews of being shirkers, anti-Semites succeeded in proving the high scale of Jewish participation. For several governmments, among them both the German and the Russian, undertook to investigate the matter and came up with astonishingly high figures. Tens of thousands of Jewish soldiers met their death on the battlefields and an unusually large number of Jews in every army was cited for bravery.

Anti-Semites usually lie low during the period of actual fighting. In the lands of the czar, however, official anti-Jewishness was quite as rampant as in time of peace. Since most of the fighting was done in the western provinces of the empire, which coincided for the most part with the Pale of Jewish Settlement, the Jewish civil population was in almost greater danger than the fighting forces. Many were ruthlessly uprooted on suspicion that they would side with the enemy. The fact that the commanders of German occupation forces, in one or another province, dealt kindly with the Jews, in order to win their support, was sufficient for the Russians to accuse the Jews of collaborating with the enemy. When a city was won back by the Russians, the Jews paid heavily for the comparative quiet which they had enjoyed under German occupation. Throughout the duration of the war the Jews of eastern Europe suffered every misery.

Its end was even worse. The havoc of war was followed by the horrors of revolution. The democratic Kerensky government, which replaced the czar and which Jews the world over hailed with delight, was soon overthrown by the Bolsheviks. A double war began. On the one hand, there were the forces of reaction which, moving across the Ukraine, organized anti-Jewish pogroms in every town they captured or were about to evacuate. On the other hand, there was the ruthless communist policy of exterminating the middle class in which the Jews were largely represented. Religion, Jewish studies, Zionism, the Hebrew language—all were pronounced counter-revolutionary and punished with Siberian exile, if not death. To be sure, the communists took an official stand against pogroms, but this stand was largely theoretical in view of the chaotic conditions. On balance, the cure for czarism was as bad as the disease.

The cries of distress, which reached the Jews of the more fortunately situated west, from the beginning of the war and long beyond its end, touched the heartstrings of all who heard them, especially the Jews of America. Two national relief committees were organized almost at once to meet the situation. Before long, they joined in a single body under the chairmanship of Felix M. Warburg (1871-1937). The American Joint Distribution Committee for the Relief of Jewish War Sufferers, soon to be known in Europe as "The Joint" and in America as the JDC, began to distribute the funds raised by the relief committees, in what would before then have been considered incredible amounts. The efficiency of the distribution equalled that of the collection. There were even martyrs connected with the transmission of the funds to the Jews of the eastern provinces: Professor Israel Friedlaender and Rabbi Bernard Cantor, while on their mission of peace in eastern Ukraine, were shot down by a band of Ukrainian marauders (1920). Without the funds gathered with such devotion and distributed at such risk, it is certain that scores of thousands would have succumbed. But, as far as the Jews of the United States were concerned, the war emergency had a result of an entirely different kind, which astonished them more than anyone else. It showed them ready to meet a challenge, willing to shoulder responsibility and capable of a degree of cooperation which gave promise of a brighter communal future.

b. *Promise and Retraction*

In addition to the war problems of eastern Europe, danger threatened the Jewish community of Palestine. Some 85,000 Jews were living there when the war broke out, half of them of the First and Second *Aliyot*. Many of the younger Jews were forced into the Turkish army; others fled. Suspecting its sympathies with the Allies of the West, the Turkish commander decreed the destruction of the entire Jewish settlement. Henry Morgenthau, the United States ambassador to Turkey, transmitted a warning of the danger, and the Jews of the United States through President Woodrow Wilson, as well as the Jews of Germany through their government, did what they could to stay the execution of the threat. American Jews came to the rescue. Jacob H. Schiff and the American Jewish Committee joined the Zionist Organization of America in sending the sum of $50,000 to Mr. Morgenthau. It is interesting to recall that payment was made to him in gold from funds in Constantinople belonging to the Standard Oil Company of the United States. Other forces were also at work, so that, at the very moment when the situation appeared exceedingly dark, it took a remarkable turn and began to bring the highest Zionist hopes nearer to realization.

The work of the World Zionist Organization was practically disrupted during the war years. Its leaders were scattered. Its work of building the Palestinian Jewish community had to yield to the labor of preventing the destruction of what had already been built. Chaim Weizmann was in England where, since 1903, he had been teaching chemistry at the University of Manchester and where, during the war years, he performed outstanding service for his adopted country. Shmarya Levin, a former member of the Russian Duma (Parliament) and an extraordinarily effective Yiddish orator, had gone to the United States at the outbreak of war in Europe and kept Zionist interest alive among American Jews. At the same time, a new leader of American Zionism emerged in the statesmanlike Louis D. Brandeis (1856-1941), soon to be appointed by President Wilson to the United States Supreme Court (1916).

Early in the war, both the Allies and the Central Powers began to cast about for ways of gaining the sympathy of the world's population. Each side saw advantages in enlisting the support of Jews everywhere. Each side planned to promise that, as soon as practicable, after the war, Palestine would be turned into a Jewish commonwealth. Germany could not as easily dispose of its Turkish partner's territory as could Britain and France of land belonging to their enemy. A great deal of secret negotiating was done with the Arabs, among the Allies themselves—soon to include the United States—as well as with leading Zionist and non-Zionist Jews. When it seemed likely that Britain's General Sir Edmund Allenby would soon drive the Turks out of Palestine, the fateful announcement was made. On November 2, 1917 in a letter to Lord Rothschild, Arthur James Balfour, British Foreign Secretary, let it be known, on behalf of the British government, that they "view with favor the establishment in Palestine of a national home for the Jewish people . . . it being clearly understood that nothing shall be done which may prejudice the civil and religious rights of existing non-Jewish communities in Palestine, or the rights and political status enjoyed by Jews in any other country." When, a few weeks later, on December 9, which corresponded to the first day of Hanukkah, Jerusalem actually fell to the British, it seemed to everyone that a new era of Jewish history had opened. On December 10, General Allenby made his entry into the city, where the Jews hailed him as their deliverer.

A great deal had to be done before the Balfour Declaration could assume reality. First, the war had to be won by the Allied and Associated Powers. As an earnest of Jewish participation in the war, a battalion of some 5,000 Jews, volunteers from Palestine and the United States, had been organized under Vladimir Jabotinsky, and it arrived in Palestine in February 1918. Some months later, Galilee was occupied by the British, making it possible to extend the work of relief and reconstruction to the entire country. But, before a civil government could be organized, through which the promise of a "Jewish home" could be fulfilled, the transfer of Palestine to Britain, which had made the promise, had to be ratified by the Allied governments. A conference of these Powers met at San Remo in April 1920 and gave the mandate over Palestine to Great Britain, charging it with the implementation of the Balfour Declaration. This action, in turn, was approved by the Council of the League of Nations in July 1922. It looked as though Herzl's dream of a charter, publicly recognized by the civilized world, had actually and miraculously come to pass.

But difficulties could and did arise. They began early. For Zionist leaders, taking the Balfour Declaration very much in earnest, arrived in Palestine prepared to govern; and they immediately clashed with the British military government and some civil servants who quite cynically looked upon the Declaration as merely a promise made under the pressures of war. The Arab upper class soon woke up to the fact that they still had a chance to gain control of the situation. They protested, and they organized riots. Their views prevailed so far that, in 1922, even before the League of Nations had confirmed the mandate to Britain, Winston Churchill for the British Government, in a letter to Chaim Weizmann, issued the first official interpretation of the Balfour Declaration which watered it down considerably. It was explained to mean that the Jews could establish a community in Palestine—they were there "of right and not of sufferance"—but they could not consider it theirs in the sense of developing it as their own country.

This was a blow to Jewish expectations, the first of many that were to follow; but at the time, its full significance was lost upon the Jews preoccupied in building up the *Yishuv.* They were pleased with the appointment of Sir Herbert Samuel as the first High Commissioner of Palestine (1920-1925). They were pleased with the steady flow of idealistic, devoted, hard-working young people from eastern Europe who came as pioneers (*halutzim*) to build the Jewish Home. New colonies, new institutions, new forces were created through the work of this, the Third *Aliyah.* Jews all over the world participated joyfully, as an indication of Jewish hope and character, in the establishment in this poor and struggling country of the Hebrew University on Mt. Scopus in Jerusalem. It was opened with dignified ceremonies in April 1925. Its first president was Dr. Judah L. Magnes.

c. *Minority Rights*

Another situation which Jews met with vigor and imagination, thus turning tragedy into promise, was connected with their hope for reviving Jewish life in the war-stricken communities. For almost half a century the fate of the east European Jews had been uppermost in the minds of their western brothers. Whether as residents in, or emigrants from, those lands of oppression, they had been a constant problem. Now the war had given this problem a new and more terrible twist. The immediate needs had been provided by generosity; but what of the future? Could the Jews be left to the mercies of the new and enlarged states being organized under ultra-nationalistic governments which might be worse than those of Russia and Rumania of the past? The Jews of the Allied lands began to wonder whether some permanent solution could not be found to guarantee the safety and future of the Jews in central and eastern Europe. They hoped to persuade the planners of peace not to overlook the fate of the Jews in the very countries where they were most numerous and most in need of such protection.

As the time approached for the Paris Peace Conference, representative Jews came from the east European countries affected, excepting Russia itself which kept aloof from the entire affair. The Jews of England and France also sent representatives, picked without much difficulty from the outstanding personalities of those communities. In the United States, however, there arose considerable discussion and conflict regarding the choice of delegates to this unofficial Jewish conference. The conflict must be touched upon, not only because it led to the establishment of an important organization in American Jewry, but also because it was, in a sense, a declaration of maturity on the part of a substantial portion of the Jewish population in the United States.

The American Jewish Committee which, since its establishment in 1906, had been dealing with the protection of the civil and religious rights of Jews in the United States and abroad, decided to send delegates to Paris. But there were objections to this assumption of authority on the ground that, although the membership of the Committee consisted of the most prominent men of every city, they were not elected by any local group. The charge, therefore, was that the Committee was undemocratically organized and could not be said properly to represent the Jews of the United States. Moreover, at the beginning of the century, when the Committee had come into being, Jewish leadership was in the hands primarily of German Jews; by 1918, however, the east European Jews, or their sons, had grown in wealth, status and self-consciousness. Many of them had long been chafing under the assumption of leadership by the Jews of presumed German extraction. Finally, although there were Zionists in its membership, the American Jewish Committee's attitude toward Zionism was regarded as at best only lukewarm. Zionist leaders considered the situation ripe for organizing a representative body on democratic lines and formed a committee for the organization of an American Jewish Congress to consist of representatives elected by popular vote in each community. Opposition to the creation of such a representative body was expressed in some quarters, especially by the American Jewish Committee and other organizations, and a heated controversy ensued in the Jewish press. Another source of conflict was the announcement by the proponents of the Congress of their desire to demand of the eventual Peace Conference, not only equal political, civil and religious rights for Jews, but also national rights.

After months of discussion and of negotiation between the leaders of both sides, a compromise was reached. The pro-Congress leaders agreed that the Congress when established should continue only until the task of its delegation to the Peace Conference would be completed; the anti-Congress leaders agreed to the inclusion of a demand for what they insisted be called "group rights": wherever such "rights" were given to other groups of a population, they should be given to Jews as well. It was also agreed that, in addition to delegates to the Congress elected by popular vote, national organizations would also be given representation.

The delegations of the various Jewish communities assembled in Paris represented the majority of the Jews of the world. They soon decided to join forces and thereby strengthen their influence, especially if they could decide on common objectives. They, therefore, organized themselves as the Committee of Jewish Delegations at the Peace Conference. The westerners recognized before long that such principles as equality before the law and the rights of citizenship, which were part and parcel of the western form of democracy, did not completely correspond to the needs of the Jews of eastern Europe. The latter felt that there were aspects of Jewish life which they were as eager to preserve as they were to gain their rights as citizens and which, they were sure, the majority of their non-Jewish neighbors would try to sabotage.

It thus came about that a new principle was accepted into international law. Minority Rights were written into the peace treaties of the Allied and Associated Powers with the new and enlarged states created by them: Poland, Latvia, Lithuania, Czechoslovakia, Jugoslavia, Bulgaria and Rumania, many of which states had regained their independence, some after centuries of foreign rule. Such rights applied not only to Jews, but to all "racial, linguistic and religious minorities" that wanted to take advantage of them (only in the case of Poland and Rumania, were Jews mentioned specifically). It meant that members of a minority were within their rights, if so desired, to use their own language, conduct their own schools, live under their own religious laws and organize their own communities. They could do all this without being looked upon as alien to the state of which they were a part and whose citizenship they were entitled to possess. In educational matters, a minority had a right to a proportional stipend from the state treasury. Thus no majority could destroy a minority's culture under the specious argument of wanting a unified state. The system worked well in some countries for a number of years, and would have continued to do so had the League of Nations had the power to preserve it against just that type of blind nationalism and racialism which the Jews foresaw and against which the minority rights were to serve as a protection.

The first twenty years of the twentieth century appear in retrospect to have been a highly productive period in the life of the Jewish people. The challenges had been many and some of them had gone to the very roots of Jewish life; but the responses to them had been fruitful or, at least, promising. Little has been said so far about the area of culture and religion, for here developments during this period proved to have been inconclusive; moreover, the story of Judaism must be told in unbroken sequence and must therefore be deferred. In other areas of life, however, Jews faced up to every problem. Their attempts to solve them may not have brought lasting results, but even so they showed the strength and resilience of the Jewish spirit. The desire to speed the absorption of the immigrants had resulted in the establishment of social and charitable institutions which eventually benefited the total community. The American Jewish Committee's stand in defending the rights of American Jewish citizens against the prejudices of Russian czarism, was to be a victory not for the Jews, but for American dignity. Jewish labor unions had helped develop some novel methods of cooperation with management. The threat to the physical and cultural survival of the Jews in eastern Europe, apart from evoking an unprecedented philanthropic response, had set in motion a new experiment in the international protection of minorities. The opportunity to build a national home had resulted in an enthusiastic flow of pioneers and in a first act toward the fulfillment of the Zionist aim. If some of these responses to the problems which had faced Jews proved ephemeral, it was because western civilization failed to be equally creative in meeting the forces which challenged it.

IV. TWO DECADES OF RETROGRESSION

a. *Racialism in America*

One wonders about the inability of western civilization to meet its challenges during the period between the two World Wars. It had apparently learned nothing from its experiences during the four years of slaughter: "the war to end war" turned out to have been a war which had engendered hate. The world continued to progress phenomenally in science and the arts and in industry, yet it seemed incapable of taming its fears and curbing its lust for battle. So the western world moved from crisis to crisis until it drifted into a second world war more terrible than the first. The maladies of our civilization became evident during the few decades that preceded World War II: a type of nationalism which, in addition to its old faults, now became twisted into racialism, and a set of religious and psychological values which, while urging personal salvation and security, permitted conscience to atrophy. As usual, the failures of civilization in general became most obvious in the world's relation to its Jews.

Signs of the racialist direction in which nationalism was tending had been evident since the latter part of the nineteenth century. Both the apologies for colonialism on the bombastic grounds of "the white man's burden" and the pseudo-scientific underpinnings of anti-Semitism, with the equally hypocritical concern about the purity of a noble race, stemmed from the same source. Such ideas began to be expressed among the self-appointed upper class of American society and to seep down into the lower economic strata. Their diffusion in the United States was slow, for one thing, because about a third of the population was still conscious of its immigrant origins and, for another, because the industrial leaders were still convinced that they needed further recruits for their labor force. The pompous proponents of Anglo-

Saxon superiority at first remained merely prophets of doom. Soon after World War I, however, the change in economic conditions deprived the labor argument of its potency. Besides, the newer generation found a way of shedding its sense of immigrant inferiority by broadening the definition of the desirable racial strain. Instead of being limited to the Anglo-Saxon, it was extended to the "Nordic." This term included a much larger group—indeed, all white Protestants—and excluded the so-called Latins, Slavs and, of course, Jews. A few decades later, when the Irish had become a political and economic force to be reckoned with, the religious qualification could be softened and Catholics, too, could be drawn into the magic circle. The "scientific" nature of this racial theory had been made plain in the work of Madison Grant, its chief American apostle. This aristocrat and arch-anti-Semite was the one who made the fateful transition from the glorification of the Anglo-Saxon race to the enthronement of the Nordic. Such thinking became characteristic of many outstanding leaders of American thought and contaminated American society.

Whether originally an importation from Europe, or a result of resentment on the part of the older American families at being economically eclipsed and socially elbowed aside by more recent strata, racialism, or nativism, was given a tremendous impetus by post-war conditions. The fever-pitch of wartime idealism suffered a let-down as a result of the peace; the anti-German and then the anti-Bolshevist hysteria had to be replaced by another emotional outlet; the transition from a war to a peace economy involved a depression and was accompanied by considerable labor troubles which were blamed on foreigners. All this showed itself in the phenomenal development, during the 1920s, of the ridiculous and rowdy Ku Klux Klan and in the surprisingly widespread and ugly anti-foreignism.

What Henry Adams, Madison Grant and Lothrop Stoddard accomplished for the intellectuals, Henry Ford did for the masses. A simple-minded man, he, like tens of millions of others, sought a simple explanation for all the ills of the world. Nothing seemed simpler than a plot by a people whose survival and presumed prosperity had always appeared inexplicable except on the assumption of sinister plotting. Ford fell victim to the persuasiveness of a czarist ex-Russian propagandist who elaborated on a plot of the Jews, first to ruin, then to seize control of the world. "The Protocols of the Elders of Zion" were the supposed minutes of secret meetings of Jewish leaders, towards the end of the nineteenth century (timed to coincide with the first World Zionist Congress). Though an obvious hoax, based, as was later disclosed, upon an old satire directed against Napoleon III, the Protocols were given wide currency by Ford's *Dearborn Independent* and accepted as true by every frightened nativist in the country. An atmosphere was created which helped deepen prejudice even among those who recognized the story's stupidity.

Under such influences, the United States, during the 1920s, became for many Jews and members of other minorities a land of restrictions rather than opportunities. With the descendants of many former immigrant groups charged with mongrelizing the "pure Nordic blood," with citizens of foreign origin under suspicion of fomenting labor and social unrest, with prospective immigrants from eastern and southern Europe held up as inferior, One-Hundred-Percent Americanism came to mean first of all the restriction of immigration. The literacy test, finally passed over President Wilson's veto in 1917, proved completely ineffective in meeting the situation when large-scale immigration resumed in 1920. Over 50,000 monthly crowded Ellis Island, among them a large number of Jews and a great many Italians and Slavs. This influx frightened the nativists out of their wits. The law of 1921 limited immigration to five percent of the number of foreign-born in the United States according to the census of 1910, and it was provided that the total number of immigrants, during any one year, should not exceed a quarter of a million. Still the restrictionists were not satisfied. In 1924, a new law was passed in which the basic census was that of 1890 and each nationality was limited to two percent of the number it had had in the population at that time. Although families of citizens were exempted from this calculation, the immigration was in fact limited to a tiny number, except for the so-called Nordic countries most of which could never fill the quotas allotted them. The United States thus legally adopted a racialist policy; Italians, Slavs, Greeks and indirectly, also, Jews were, in effect, declared inferior and unwanted. Prejudice, under the guise of science, had won a resounding victory which could not be undone even when, a few years later, prosperity having returned and the hysteria having abated, the saner and more truly American elements once more prevailed.

The spirit of restriction extended to other areas of life as well. It not only kept more Jews from coming into the country, but also limited the activities and opportunities of those already in the United States. Divisive practices were shameless. Hotels, resorts, dwellings, as well as jobs were closed to Jews and some other minorities. At the same time, Christian restrictionism and exclusiveness were justified by the assertion that Jews were clannish. Most shocking was the complete surrender to the prevalent prejudices by leaders of American culture. Quota systems had long existed in the more important professional schools; now similar quotas were adopted by undergraduate colleges, even such as functioned in large centers of population. Culture, like banking or automobile manufacturing, was going nativist. Much of the literature of the day reflected this spirit of the age.

b. *The Flowering of the Defense Organizations*

The Jews of the United States were thus faced with a new situation—not new in Jewish history, for it recalled not too vaguely conditions and attitudes which had led, in centuries gone by, to exclusion from Christian and Moslem society—but new in the United States. Previous instances of discrimination had been few and scattered; now, with the number of Jews in the country greatly increased, such instances became widespread and assumed the aspects of social policy. The situation was all the more painful because the American Jew had fallen in love with America and took pride in its freedoms and its spirit of equality. He drew solace from the knowledge that many true liberals were raising their voices to criticize the prevalent hatreds and he put his hopes in the fundamentals of Americanism. Yet, he felt that some action on his part was called for. To be sure, nothing could be done for the time being about the restrictions on immigration. The harshness of the law, as distinct from the spirit behind it, had been somewhat mitigated by the exemption from its operation of close relatives of American citizens. Besides, Latin America, South Africa and parts of western Europe were available as places of refuge for the hard-pressed of eastern Europe. But something had to be done about the invasions of their personal rights and the wild accusations which were being levelled against the Jewish people.

Although the Jews of the country had not achieved unity, they did occasionally succeed in speaking with one voice. Thus, in December 1920, twenty of the most important national Jewish organizations responded to a call by the American Jewish Committee and issued a repudiation of the charges identifying Jews with Bolshevism and with the Protocols. Again, in 1924, when about 15,000 would-be Jewish immigrants, on their way to the United States under the law of 1921, were stranded at ports of embarkation because they were not able to comply with the requirements of the new law of 1924, there was wholehearted cooperation in dealing with this problem. The Committee and the American Jewish Congress jointly convoked a national conference, which created the Emergency Committee for Jewish Refugees which, in the course of a few years, helped these refugees to return to their former countries or to find homes elsewhere. On the whole, however, Jewish defense efforts varied in accordance with the nature of the groups and classes into which American Jewry was divided or the leadership which they followed. The American Jewish Committee, though less exclusive than formerly, was still representative of the wealthier and older stratum, and pursued the quiet, dignified methods which it had adopted from its inception. In letters to individuals and in public statements, Louis Marshall, the Committee's president, denounced and refuted anti-Jewish assertions and publications. He scored his greatest success when, in 1927, he obtained from Henry Ford a complete retraction of, and apology for, the libels and insinuations which his publication had been spreading for almost a decade. Another defense organization, the Anti-Defamation League, was an arm of the B'nai B'rith, which had just entered upon a period of rapid expansion as a result, in part, of having opened its membership to growing numbers of second-generation east European Jews. The ADL, organized in 1914, was therefore in a sense representative of the middle class Jew, eager for a more direct and vocal defense of his rights and his good name. It undertook to answer all attacks, to explain all presumed shortcomings, to refute every accusation. This task proved to be a somewhat disappointing one. Very few of the masses of non-Jews, who were easily led to suspect the Jews when some fiery demagogue described them as satanic conspirators, ever got to read or came to hear the defense. In fact, such demagogues used the ADL's efforts to unmask their dishonesty as evidence of persecution at the hands of the Jews. On the other hand, vocal defense also had considerable advantages. The non-Jews, whether infected with anti-Semitism or not, got to know that the Jews were reacting vigorously to the accusations fired in their direction. Fighting back brought a measure of respect.

The American Jewish Congress, originally formed only for the purpose of representing American Jewry at the Versailles Peace Conference in 1919, was followed by a permanent organization established in 1922. It made an effort to be representative of the entire American Jewish community, by inviting to membership both national organizations and especially established local groups. Its program was broad, including civic and national, defensive and educational activities. It recognized that a minority's firmest allies are the liberal forces of the nation, that all minorities, whether racial or religious, face common problems and must come to one another's defense, and that the American tradition of democracy was the best guarantee of personal and religious security. On the assumption that no apologies were needed for a minority's right to exist, the Congress from the first tried to put the anti-Semites and the reactionaries on the defensive. This broad, liberal, fighting program fitted the character of Dr. Stephen S. Wise perfectly, and it became characteristic of the Congress of which he was the head from its establishment until his death. In fact, the Congress did not limit its activities to defense. It participated actively in Zionist work and early adopted a program of adult Jewish education. Democracy and good sense demanded that, if an organization expected the intelligent participation of its members, it must make them aware of the background and the nature of its activities.

Here then were three different responses to the problem of anti-

Semitism in a democracy. The differences noted have been, of course, variations of emphasis rather than limitations of policy. There was considerable overlapping of activity among all of them. It may well be that they arrested the spread of the moral ailment of anti-Semitism during the later 1920s. The next decade, however, brought new and even greater danger. Until the 1920s, anti-Semitic activities in the United States and elsewhere in the west were uncoordinated. Now, a determined enemy of the Jews, one well supplied with vast resources, took control; the situation became ominous on a world-wide scale.

c. *The Communist and Fascist Attacks*

The 1920s witnessed the beginnings in Europe of the trend towards the tragedy which was to overwhelm the world and destroy more than a third of the Jewish people. The framers of the Treaty of Versailles had thought to safeguard the peace by imposing a democratic system of government upon the states defeated in the war and upon those which emerged from the break-up of the Russian and Austrian empires. They had hoped to assure the reign of justice among peoples by creating a League of Nations and by including in the League's charter those clauses for the protection of minorities which the representatives of the Jews had urged upon them. Unfortunately, democracy was alien to most of the nations in central and eastern Europe, while international justice proved to be an ideal for which the nations of the world were not yet prepared.

The mild, socialistically-inclined republic established in Germany was spiritually not strong enough to combat the resentment against defeat which gnawed at the hearts of the population. The assassination of Walter Rathenau (1922), a very able leader of the new government who had been working toward a lasting peace with France, was the first open expression of bitterness which took an anti-Jewish turn. No matter how stupid it sounds, it is a fact that the reactionaries and ultra-nationalists of Germany accepted the theory that the defeat was due to Germany's betrayal by its Jews. The majority of the population at first ridiculed the small National Socialist group led by the ex-corporal Hitler; but nothing was done to counteract his insidious anti-government propaganda which used anti-Semitism as its means for attracting party members. It appeared silly for a government to imagine that its survival depended on the defense of the Jews; yet that proved to be the case. As for the German Jews themselves, staunch German patriots, thoroughly assimilated into German culture, they could not imagine that their Christian compatriots would let them down by succumbing to Hitler's rabid doctrines. They did what they could to present facts in self-defense. The rest of the National Socialist program seemed to them understandable enough, for many German Jews shared the widespread resentment against the Treaty of Versailles. Like most Germans, they did not think that Hitler would ever attain power: a civilized people like the Germans, they thought, could never succumb to the rowdy tactics of the Nazis. And they were certain that if, by some remote chance, he did win an election, he would never carry his anti-Jewish threats into execution.

The problems connected with the Jews of eastern Europe seemed much more serious in the 1920s. There was, first of all, the question of Jews in Russia. The Bolshevist government had established itself firmly and embarked ruthlessly upon communizing the country. This meant a complete transformation of Jewish life. From being largely middlemen, Jews had to turn to artisanship. The younger people could perhaps adjust themselves, but the middle-aged and the older people could find no place in farming or industry. They were reduced to performing the most menial tasks or, failing that, to starvation. For a few brief years in the middle 1920s, Lenin felt compelled to slow the pace of Russian communization, and his New Economic Policy temporarily eased the situation of the mercantile class of which Jews formed a large part. During the respite some adjustments could be made; but there is every reason to believe that the ultimate solution of the problem of the Jewish middle-aged came through death rather than adjustment. An even more serious problem confronted Judaism as a religion. Officially anti-Semitism was banned, though, as subsequent events proved, the facts were otherwise than the law. But anti-Judaism was given free rein, with the communists of Jewish origin carrying this program through with incredible ferocity. Most synagogues, like many churches, were closed or confiscated. Jewish religious education was forbidden by law. The teaching of Hebrew and adherence to Zionism were declared counter-revolutionary. Observance of Jewish law and tradition put a person under suspicion and was likely to deprive him of his means of livelihood. Thus not only was the survival of the three million Russian Jews jeopardized, but the survival of Judaism, itself, was also imperiled.

On the other hand, Jews were recognized as a nationality. Yiddish was declared one of the official languages in addition to Russian. The Jews of the larger cities could, if they so desired, send their children to schools in which Yiddish was the language of instruction. Literary and scholarly activity in Yiddish was permitted and actually developed, and a Yiddish counterpart of the official newspaper *Pravda* bore the name *Emmes*, in the Yiddish, not the Hebrew, spelling of the word. Moreover, whether to gain the sympathy of western Jews, or to cast doubts upon reports of the cruel lot of the Russian Jews resulting from the process of communization, or to lessen the appeal which the promise of Palestine was having for some of the Russian Jews, the Soviet government promised to establish in southern Russia a Jewish agricultural settlement which might some day become an autonomous district within the state. The settled population of that territory evidently offered strenuous objection to the plan, hostility to Jews apparently not being quite dead. When this promise could not be kept, the prospect was transferred to the dreary wastelands of Siberia. The outlook for distant Biro-Bidjan was portrayed in glowing colors as a future Jewish state. Twenty years later, the district still had no more than a few thousand Jewish inhabitants.

The most hopeful part of the world's Jewish population in the 1920s, and the most spiritually promising, was still concentrated in the new and revived states east of Germany: Poland, Latvia, Lithuania and Czechoslovakia. New prospects for physical and spiritual development opened up for them under the Minority Treaties. The only one of these countries that had protested strenuously and indignantly against being compelled to put its minorities under international protection had been Poland, the very one that had both the largest number of Jews and the worst record of persecution in the immediate, as well as the more distant, past. The only one of these countries where the Jews were not especially concerned whether or not they enjoyed such rights was Czechoslovakia, whose record in this respect had been good and whose leaders, Thomas G. Masaryk and Eduard Benes, could be trusted to safeguard democracy. To a greater or lesser extent, therefore, the Jews of these and of the other states, which had promised to abide by the minorities system, organized themselves into communities with power to regulate their internal Jewish life without governmental interference. They could, if they desired, establish a school system and receive support for it from state taxes. At the same time, they enjoyed every right of citizenship in their respective countries. Feeling relatively secure, the Jews, with help from the American JDC, began to rebuild Jewish life. There was, of course, no unanimity among the Jews in any of these countries; the arguments among the Hebraists, secularists and religionists of every shade were sometimes acrimonious, and each group insisted on a school system of its own. Nonetheless, it seemed obvious that Jewish life had a future there.

Unfortunately, the minorities system soon began to be sabotaged by the governments concerned. Born out of racial consciousness, each of the Slavic states pursued a racialist policy. To advance the interests of the dominant race, the governments discriminated in its favor in the vast network of civil service and in the industrial and commercial activities directly or indirectly under their control. They established cooperatives which competed with Jewish merchants but employed no Jews. Before the end of the 1920s, the amount of state subsidy to which the Jews were entitled began to shrink and Jewish representatives in government departments were being eliminated. The Poles, of course, set the pace for this policy, and Latvia and Lithuania followed close behind. The Jews were intimidated into not calling their fatherlands to account before the League of Nations, while of itself the League, that is, the combination of great Powers, was morally too weak to act. By the 1930s, the Slav nations received support and encouragement in their anti-Jewish policies from the more terrible example of Nazi Germany. Thus, another achievement of the peace following World War I presaged, by its failure, the greater tragedy into which mankind was to be plunged.

d. *An Empire and its Conscience*

The 1920s proved disappointing also in the progress towards the realization of the glowing promise of a Jewish Palestine. Again the constructive work founded on faith, hope and idealism was done by the Jews, while the non-Jews—Christians and Moslems alike—either attempted to block every Jewish step forward or refrained from giving their promised help.

The decade opened with the Third *Aliyah* in full swing. From 1919 to 1923, some 35,000 *halutzim* (pioneers) immigrated. They built roads and drained swamps; they established colonies and brought new land under cultivation. They made the Valley of Jezreel blossom as in days of old and they made cooperative labor a reality. Never before had the world seen such a peasant class, so avid for culture, so deeply interested in ideas, so consciously a part of the world's hopes. Their successors, from 1924 to 1930, who constituted the so-called Fourth *Aliyah,* were of a somewhat different type. Also east European Jews, mostly Polish, their immigration into Palestine was motivated by despair over conditions in Poland, by the closing of the gates in America, and, above all, by the promise of a national Jewish community in Palestine. They were rather older than those who had constituted the Third *Aliyah* and, therefore, comparatively few of them became farmers; the majority gravitated towards the cities. They raised the population of Tel Aviv from about 14,000, in the early 1920s, to close to 40,000 at the end of the decade, and they developed other towns as well. Their interests tended towards commerce and industry which they developed despite the temporary economic setback which the country suffered in 1926 and 1927. Thus Palestine acquired, in the decade following the granting of the Mandate to Britain, an active and productive population which had risen from 56,000 at the end of World War I, to 84,000 by 1922, and to 175,000 by the end of that decade.

Britain had been appointed by the League of Nations as a partner of the Jews in the creation of a Jewish Homeland in

Palestine. While it performed well the administrative tasks of government, it failed completely to implement the primary aspect of the partnership. Instead, it saw its duty to the Empire first, that is, in terms of keeping a careful watch lest Jewish interests advance too far and too quickly as against the presumed interests of the Arabs. No doubt the British were impressed by awakening Arab nationalism and, desiring to strengthen their position in the Middle East, sought to show themselves as the Arabs' friends. In general, this was the era of appeasement; the world was destined to take a long time to discover that appeasement only whets the appetite of the appeased. Bit by bit, the interpretation of the Balfour Declaration was whittled down. The painful steps in this process cannot be detailed here. It took the form of administrative orders and investigating commissions and White Papers; of granting public lands to the Arabs while the Jews had to purchase land at fantastic prices; of curtailment of Jewish immigration on specious principles; of loudly voiced sympathy for the poor *fellahin* (peasants)—who in reality "had never had it so good"—and irritation with the Jews. Here, in brief, was a series of government actions which not only negated the promise of the Homeland, but also made it impossible for Jew and Arab to get together, and even encouraged the latter to riot and bloodshed.

The Mandate provided that a "Jewish Agency," representative of all the Jews of the world who were interested in the project, should help bring the Homeland into being. There was need for the active cooperation of a great many prominent, well-to-do and influential Jews, some of whom were, in fact, outspoken non-Zionists. The task of building the Homeland needed not only their means, but needed also the prestige they enjoyed among the peoples of the world. It needed, above all, a united Jewish front in the face of the growing coolness of the British Colonial Office to the Jewish aspect of the Mandate. But it took some years of planning and negotiation for the various groups of non-Zionists to agree among themselves, and for all of them together to come to terms with the Zionists. This result was finally achieved in the summer of 1929 after patient planning by Dr. Chaim Weizmann, president of the World Zionist Organization. At Zurich, Switzerland, a group consisting of some of the most distinguished Jews of the world, non-Zionists as well as leading Zionists, adopted a set of regulations for the Jewish Agency called for in the Mandate. In helping to achieve this goal, the great American Jew, Louis Marshall, who died a few days later, rendered the last of his many great services to his people. But even while Jews were congratulating themselves on this achievement, news arrived of another and more serious anti-Jewish outbreak in Palestine. More than a hundred Jews were killed, almost two hundred were wounded, and several isolated colonies were destroyed. The two events occurring simultaneously, symbolized the decade's ceaseless organizing and constructive efforts on the part of the Jews in the face of the lack of government cooperation, intrigue, violence and destruction. In the next decade, the forces of destruction were to gain complete and unchallenged dominance.

e. *The Rise and Spread of Fascism*

The fourth decade of the twentieth century actually opened in the latter half of 1929 with the misfortune of an economic depression which grew in severity during the next few years. Widespread unemployment turned dissatisfaction into bitter discontent, and discontent simmered into rebelliousness. Two revolutionary authoritarian movements profited from the situation: Russian communism and that travesty on the social state which had been named Fascism by Mussolini, the Italian mountebank dictator. Adolph Hitler's National Socialist Democratic Labor Party improved on this, combining his vague socialism with virulent racialism, aggressive nationalism and murderous anti-Semitism. As the decade progressed, militarism, fascism, Nazism and communism gained control of a large part of the world, while the rest groped helplessly, in the midst of economic and social upheavals, to avoid the infection of these flagrant denials of civilization while trying to maintain peace. As a result of its weakness and vaccilation, the democratic west saw China and Ethiopia conquered by force of arms; Finland and Czechoslovakia reduced to servitude; Russia, Germany and Spain subjected to bloody purges; and their own freedom and human dignity openly disparaged and undermined from within. The League of Nations, weak to start with, proved utterly helpless, and almost every other hopeful result of

World War I was practically nullified. Under these circumstances, it was inevitable that the Jews should become the greatest sufferers in Europe.

Events in eastern Europe, in Palestine and in some western countries had been disturbing enough; but all such evil trends and conditions were dwarfed for the rest of the decade by the horrors which centered in Germany. It seemed incredible that Germany would succumb to this barbarism, that its scientists would yield their almost tedious adherence to facts, its clergy their conscience, and its cultured element their common sense. Yet that is what happened in 1933, and the first plank of the Nazi program that Hitler implemented when he rose to power was that threatening the civil, political and economic status of the Jews.

After the first outburst of physical attack on the Jews was over, Nazism having been given a chance to express its gutter nature, Hitler let loose a number of anti-Jewish decrees aiming to remove Jewish influence from German society. Jews were summarily dismissed from civil and academic posts. They could not act as lawyers for non-Jewish clients. Unofficially, but quite effectively, a boycott was enforced against businesses owned or run by Jews. Booted and armed young Nazis, frequently sons or in the pay of competitors, turned customers away from stores. Objectors and those on a previously prepared list of Jewish leaders and other opponents of Nazism were arrested, beaten and sent off to that typically Nazi institution, the concentration camp. In view of what was to happen later, all this chicanery and brutality seems fairly mild. Hitler and his aides evidently still feared the reaction of the rest of the world. But the only ones to react were the Jews, and not even all of them. The American Jewish Congress, under the leadership of Stephen S. Wise, organized vast protest meetings and urged all decent people to avoid buying German goods. Other Jews, however, advised caution, lest the Nazis react even more violently. Such advice was based on the expectation that the civilized world would bring pressure to bear on the new German government. But the so-called civilized world did nothing of the kind. Perhaps if it had reacted, the entire chain of gruesome events of the next decade might have been avoided.

Within the next few years, every conceivable pressure and

humiliation was visited upon the Jewish population of Germany. Before long, every means of livelihood was closed to the Jews. In 1934, in the infamous Nuremberg laws, they were officially deprived of German citizenship and the term "Jew" was defined by decree to mean anyone, regardless of his religion, who had one Jewish grandparent. Thus, the needed target for hatred was broadened. It was further enlarged with the annexation of Austria in March 1938. On November 10, 1938, a day of open rioting was declared in revenge for the killing by a Jew of a minor German diplomatic official in Switzerland. That day, almost all the synagogues in Germany went up in flames.

Six hundred thousand men, women and children, and as many more when those of Austria and Czechoslovakia were added, faced annihilation. Practically all of them were above the average in culture and among the foremost in commerce, science and the arts. Who came to their aid? Unquestionably there were German Christians whose hearts bled for them and some who suffered exile or imprisonment because of their outspoken sympathy for the persecuted Jews. But these were a tiny number and made no impression whatever on the general population. Some churchmen spoke up. Pope Pius XI issued an encyclical on March 14, 1937, in which he opposed racism and condemned the attacks on the Jewish Bible. "Spiritually," the Pope said, "we are all Semites." Even before this, Cardinal Faulhaber of Munich and several other prelates had objected to the inclusion of converts to Christianity among those considered Jews. In 1938, the Archbishop of Canterbury and other members of the Church of England spoke up more directly against the persecution of the Jews; and a number of Protestant clergy in Europe outside of Germany did the like, though within Germany the Protestant clergy remained, on the whole, silent. Such limited, indirect and rather polite criticism of savagery rampant did not offer much evidence of a sensitive religious spirit in wide circles of western civilization.

With their advent to power, the Nazis embarked upon a worldwide anti-Semitic propaganda campaign. Every person of German ancestry everywhere in the world was a potential apologist for Nazism; every anti-Semite was a Nazi collaborator. An especially virulent campaign was conducted in the United States and was almost successful in persuading the population that to attempt interference with Nazi plans was to fall victim to a non-existent Jewish plot. So laden with racialism and anti-Semitism, or so callous to them, had the world's atmosphere become that little refuge could be found for the fugitives from Hitler's fury. Throughout that decade, the Jewish leaders of western countries went hat-in-hand to statesmen and parliamentary committees pleading for the admittance of even small numbers. It was not enough to point out that a refusal meant condemning thousands to death; one had to assure these representatives of civilized Christian nations that the prospective immigrants would not become public charges, or that they were young people of ability and skill, or that they were children who had to be saved from the tiger's paws. Within the United States, as in some other countries, the Jews added to their already burdensome philanthropies the National Refugee Service through which they kept the promise exacted from them that the new immigrants would not become a burden on the general community. In the end, Great Britain, between 1933 and 1939, admitted about 75,000; down to its entrance into the war, the United States admitted some 175,000. The international Evian Conference of 1938, called for the purpose of finding more places of refuge, ended in failure.

Soon after the Nazis captured Germany, the Jews of that country embarked on two constructive activities. They tried to send the very young Jewish children out of the country, and they established training centers for young people so that, equipped with some manual skill, they would be prepared to go to Palestine. Families and individuals, frequently Christians, in various countries like Britain, the Netherlands and Denmark, adopted some of the children. Henrietta Szold, then a permanent resident of Palestine, organized a Youth *Aliyah* for the transportation and upbringing of children there. The young people, along with those older ones who could do so, made their way to Palestine through ordinary channels, though a good many had to circumvent British limiting regulations and enter the country illegally. Altogether the Fifth *Aliyah*, which consisted mostly of German refugees, had brought about 100,000 more Jews into Palestine before the outbreak of World War II.

The Palestinian Arabs, however, decided to join in the widespread anti-Jewish barbarities by means of another uprising. Although the Jews responded with a policy of non-resistance (*havlagah*), five hundred Jews were killed between 1936-1939 and thousands wounded. If, on the one hand, non-resistance had no effect whatever in stopping the Arabs' war against the Jews, the danger from the Arabs did not, on the other hand, stop the Jews from continuing the development of the country with the aid of the energetic and capable newcomers. Britain, of course, sent another investigating commission whose report led to a further effort to appease the Arabs. The White Paper of 1939 limited the number of Jewish immigrants to 15,000 a year for the next five years. The policy was intended to make certain that the Jews would remain permanently a minority of the country's population.

The effect that such palpable hostility in almost every part of the world had on the Jews of the democratic countries was to intensify their defense efforts. A new defensive organization had come into existence in 1933 in the form of a Jewish Labor Committee. Because of its contacts with general labor organizations, this body was able to exert influence on the latter to resist Nazi anti-Jewish propaganda in their ranks. The American Jewish Committee, in touch with Jewish leaders everywhere, including Germany, was able to compile and analyze the propaganda of the Nazi agents in the United States, unmask them and reveal their lies. In 1932 and again in 1934, the American Jewish Congress called meetings of representatives of various European communities for the purpose of taking joint action to combat mounting anti-Jewish feeling. In 1936, the World Jewish Congress came into being for the defense of Jewish rights, Stephen S. Wise and Nahum Goldman being the leaders. The Congress promoted the anti-Nazi boycott, organized public protest meetings and vigorously attacked every denial of human rights. The Anti-Defamation League of the B'nai B'rith concentrated on watching the activities of native fascists and rabble-rousers. Before long, all the defense organizations joined in a General Jewish Council.

The type of danger they had to guard against was exemplified by the activities of the Reverend Dr. Charles E. Coughlin, a Roman-Catholic priest in Detroit. In October 1938, he began a series of weekly anti-Jewish broadcasts over a national radio hook-up. In addition to his spoken diatribes, he published direct and slyly indirect attacks on the Jews. A so-called Christian Front, formed in New York City under his sponsorship, carried on a violent anti-Jewish campaign through street meetings, the boycotting of Jewish merchants and other means. The Jewish defense organizations attempted to answer him in public statements and privately appealed to Coughlin's ecclesiastical superiors. He was eventually silenced, but with shocking reluctance and after surprising delay. Another source for anti-Jewish attacks was isolationism in the United States. Isolationist groups charged that, because of their hatred of Nazism, American Jews were stirring up public opinion in favor of intervention in what was a purely European war. These raucous voices were silenced only by the Japanese attack on Pearl Harbor, on December 7, 1941.

V.   THE ORDEAL OF CIVILIZATION

a. *The Triumph of Savagery*

Since the Hitler war was prepared for, and entered upon, to establish German supremacy over the rest of mankind, it was natural that the Jews should be the first sufferers and that the murderous spirit of Nazism should be directed most ruthlessly against them. This is not the place to speak of the travail of all civilization, of the machine-gunning of fugitives, of the bombing of cities, of the oppression of populations. Eventually the Nazis lost the war against their enemies east and west, but, as has been repeatedly pointed out, they won the physical war against the Jews. Six million people were murdered in cold blood, only because their nature, tradition and hopes were the antithesis of Nazism. Thousands of communities were wiped off the face of the earth, among them some which antedated the presumed natives of the lands in which they had lived and all of which had made significant contributions to local and European civilization.To say that the six years of World War II constituted the most disastrous period in Jewish history in almost two millennia is to presume too much on the power of words to transmit a sense of tragedy. Only a Jeremiah could describe it—the beastliness and the heroism. What made the situation the more horrible was that the conscience of the rest of the world was so little stirred both at that time and later.

There were, to be sure, almost entire nations, like the Danes and the Dutch, and many individuals among the British, Scandanavians and French who defied the Nazis and did their utmost to save their Jewish neighbors. Most of them acted out of sheer humanity; some, especially French Catholics, in their zeal to "save" the children they had hidden, had them baptized; in some of these cases, the protectors of the children refused, after the war, to restore them to their Jewish families. With these exceptions, people who, at great personal risk, came to the aid of the hunted, kept alive faith in the essential goodness of human nature. But there were others, far more numerous, in the invaded countries to the east who helped the Nazis in their destruction of the Jewish population. Poles, Rumanians, Hungarians and Ukrainians by the thousands, fawning upon their conquerors, outdid them in beastliness. In France, there were few such traitors to humanity, but the Vichy Government was under the thumb of the Nazis and paid them the tribute of imitation by disfranchising the Jews and interning them along with Christian liberals and patriots in concentration camps.

Unarmed and completely in their enemy's hands, the peaceful Jewish populations of the countries overrun by the Nazis were stunned by their fate. It was, indeed, hard to believe that human beings could be so coldly brutal, so completely merciless as the invaders. A small number of young Jews, here and there, succeeded in eluding the Germans and organizing themselves into bands of guerilla fighters. They had to contend not only against the German enemy, but often against another, the Christian partisans who were almost as bad. The vast majority of the Jews in eastern Europe, now herded into ghettos, at first refused to believe that their extermination had been decreed. The Nazis kept the torture chambers and the crematories secret. But eventually the secret leaked out. Then some sort of resistance, hopeless though it was bound to be, was organized. The smuggling into the ghettos of small arms took a long time, for this had to be done piece by piece and, even so, arms were hard to come by because the non-Jewish underground forces gave the Jews but grudging cooperation. In time, several ghettos revolted, the biggest and most spectacular revolt being that of Warsaw, which began on April 19, 1943, and continued for some days, until almost every Jewish fighter lay dead in the ruins.

Several countries in southeastern Europe, however, though under the heel of the Nazis during the first years of the war, did not remain completely under their control. An arrangement with the governments of Rumania and Hungary, each with about three-quarters of a million Jews in 1941, was possible, and permission might have been obtained for the emigration of a considerable number of Jews. But where were they to go? No country engaged in the war against Germany was willing to permit them to enter—and to this extent these countries and their leaders must share in the guilt of the eventual murder of hundreds of thousands. There was room for them in Palestine. But Britain, ever hopeful of Arab cooperation which it never got, refused to rescind or relax the immigration restrictions of the shameful White Paper of 1939. A few of those who escaped from the European furnaces succeeded in making their surreptitious way across the Palestine border, to the intense indignation of the British officials in Palestine.

The Arabs everywhere in the Middle East were, in fact, openly in sympathy with the Nazi cause. The propaganda of the ex-Mufti, who had eluded the British and made common cause with the Nazis, bore fruit. An Iraqi rebellion had to be put down by military force. The Egyptians hailed with joy every advance made in North Africa by the German General Rommel. The Jews of Palestine, on the other hand, offered, early in the war, to organize a considerable force and join the British armies. The British Government managed to put all sorts of obstacles in the way of any such plan, even to the absurdity of limiting the number of Jews in a Palestinian force to the very small number of Palestinian Arabs who volunteered. The British apparently preferred defeat to giving the Jews any ground for claims to post-war treatment worthy of allies. Not until 1944, were the Jews of Palestine permitted to organize a separate battalion. Despite all obstacles, considerable numbers of Palestine Jews participated, as groups within the British armies, in battles on almost every front. Behind the lines, in Palestine, Jews performed invaluable auxiliary service. An occasional word of commendation was given them by several regional British commanders; but officially the British Government acted as though none of this had happened. The Jews were, as the saying went in those years, Britain's "anonymous allies."

When the fighting ended with the occupation of Germany, allied soldiers freed the tortured and emaciated inmates of the concentration camps whom the Nazis had not destroyed in their final burst of fury. The furnaces and crematoria in which so many human beings had perished were now uncovered. The feeling of revulsion which seized the soldiers, carried over to the civilian populations of the western nations. Now the world learned the truth about Nazism which it had refused to believe when the Jews told it. In the course of the next few years, some—by no means many—of the perpetrators of the most outrageous cruelties were condemned to death or imprisonment, and for a while ex-Nazis were in disgrace. That was the extent to which the world's conscience stirred over the fate of six million innocent victims.

b. *The Remnants of a People*

Every aspect of Jewish life during the post-war decade (1945-1955) has been affected by the consciousness of two events: the disappearance of Jewish communities in the European Diaspora and the rise of the Jewish state in Palestine. The second was, to a very large extent, the creative response to the first, while both together have evoked forces in the remaining Diaspora communities which have not ceased to modify their life.

At the century's opening, the Jewishly most promising communities were those of eastern and central Europe. Numerically, they accounted for more than half of the world's Jewish population. The ratio was decreased somewhat by the growth of the new Diaspora; but, as late as the outbreak of World War II, the older communities remained preponderant. The contrast between the last available statistics (1939 or 1940) before the war, and the best available figures after its end is instructive. Both sets of figures are offered in round numbers for those countries which came under Nazi rule.

	1939 or 1940	*1945 or 1946*	*Losses*
Germany	150,000	20,000	− 130,000
Austria	190,000	4,000	− 186,000
Italy	45,000	35,000	− 10,000
Poland	3,250,000	45,000	− 3,205,000
Rumania	750,000	425,000	− 325,000
Hungary	725,000	143,000	− 582,000
Czechoslovakia	360,000	100,000	− 260,000
Bulgaria	48,000	28,000	− 20,000
Yugoslavia	75,000	15,000	− 60,000
Greece	75,000	10,000	− 65,000
France	250,000	130,000	− 120,000
The Netherlands	140,000	35,000	− 105,000
Belgium	75,000	20,000	− 55,000
Luxemburg	5,000	1,200	− 3,800
Denmark	2,500	1,500	− 1,000
Norway	1,300	700	− 600

In some instances, the reduction noted was due to emigration. In Germany itself, for example, about 360,000 of the half million Jews there in 1932 are said to have left by 1939. Most of those who remained anywhere in Europe were, of course, exterminated without being recorded in the figures noted above. Many thousands of Polish Jews fled into Russia before the Nazi invasion of the latter, though apparently not so many as was once supposed. In any case, there are no reliable figures for the situation in Russia in general. The Nazi invasion of Russia in 1941-2 overran the very districts inhabited by many Jews, who were treated by the Nazis and their collaborators with the same barbarity as that meted out to Jews everywhere else. Certainly the Jewish losses in the Ukraine exceeded a million. It seems clear, therefore, that the six million figure as the number of Jews done to death during the war years is an underestimate. The number of Jews in the world was reduced by at least a third. The reduction in the spiritual potential is, of course, incalculable.

It is well to recall, moreover, that the termination of hostilities did not bring to an end the tragedy for the exiled and the hunted. Those freed from concentration camps and those in a distant Russian exile had the choice of returning to their former homes. Some did so, often only to discover that those who had benefited from Nazi rule by appropriating the property of Jews were deeply disappointed to see the former owners come to life and claim their own. There was stubborn resistance to returning the property in question. Where there was decency in the governments of the western lands, such disputes were eventually adjusted. Things were different in the eastern countries because too many had profited from the ruin of their Jewish neighbors. The few Jews who straggled back to Poland found no trace of family, friends or populous Jewish community. What they did find was consuming hatred on the part of men and women who were enjoying the fruits of murder, in which they may or may not have participated, but which they certainly had done nothing to avert. The Polish clergy, charging that the returned Jews were communists—there were a few communists in the post-war Polish government—sided with their flocks. There were numerous beatings and murders of returned Jews. The most spectacular of such assaults was the pogrom, deliberately planned and carried out, at Kielce on July 4, 1946. In every possible sense of hearth and fatherland, the Jews were now homeless. There was a renewed flight, this time westward into the displaced persons' camps under American and British control.

The displaced persons' camps remained in the news for several years after the war. They were maintained at great expense to the government and to the Jews of the United States. It seemed impossible to dispose of the few score thousands who were practically all that remained of formerly great Jewish communities. The restrictive immigration laws of the United States remained in force and the west European countries also shut their gates in the face of the DPs. The rate at which homes were found for them was so slow that it looked as though the camps would become permanent monuments to Nazism and to human heart-lessness in general. There was, of course, an obvious solution, namely, to transport the DPs to Palestine. That, in fact, was where the majority of them preferred to go, and there were hundreds, perhaps thousands, who were aided by Palestinian Jews to smuggle themselves into the country. But no large scale immigration was permitted; the British barred the way.

c. A Nation is Reborn

The key to the events of the next few years is the fact that Palestinian Jews—both those who had labored for more than a generation to make the stony land a home for their people, and those who had but recently passed through the European in-ferno—were not disposed to be pawns in Britain's, or anyone else's, imperial politics. The days of *havlagah*, as uselessly prac-ticed in the 1930s, were also at an end; non-resistance to attacks had failed to impress either the Arabs or the British. When the fighting against the Germans was over, the Jews of Palestine strengthened the *Haganah*, their military defense organization which the Arab marauders feared and which the British army tried to suppress. Jews everywhere felt completely justified in demanding that the inhabitants of the DP camps be transferred to Palestine, while units of the British navy used force to prevent the debarkation of those who succeeded in approaching the Palestinian shore.

World opinion, especially in the United States, compelled Britain to do something in self-justification. Towards the end of 1945, the British government consented to have the situation looked into by a joint commission of Britons and Americans. After taking evidence in the DP camps and in Palestine, the commission unanimously recommended the immediate admittance into Pales-tine of 100,000 DPs. But the boorish Ernest Bevin, then foreign minister of Britain, growled his refusal. Naturally, the Jews of Palestine intensified their efforts to thwart the British forces. What the British called rebellion, the Jews called defense of their rights as human beings to receive into their homes their unfortunate brethren whom western civilization was treating as pariahs. To make matters worse, a group of extremists came into being who acted on the principle that the best defense is offense. Rejecting the mild, purely defensive policy of the *Haganah* as one that left the initiative in the hands of the British, this group, which called itself *Irgun Tzvai Leumi* (National Military Organization), under the leadership of Menahem Beigin, did not hesitate to use terrorism when they felt that the occasion required it. The exasperated British put themselves further in the wrong by attacking the ship *Exodus 1947* and imprisoning and later forcibly transporting its 4,500 DP passengers back to a camp in Germany.

The *Exodus* incident occurred at the very time when an international commission, appointed by the United Nations General Assembly, was making still another effort to solve the problem of Palestine and the Jews. Britain herself had placed the matter in the hands of the United Nations and had announced, at the same time, that it would relinquish the Mandate and evacuate the country by August 1, 1948. The General Assembly then appointed representatives of the following states to seek a solution: Australia, Canada, Czechoslovakia, Guatemala, India, Iran, the Netherlands, Peru, Sweden, Uruguay and Yugoslavia. These nations did not find it possible to separate the problem of the DPs from the problem of Palestine. Their decision that Palestine be divided between the Jews and the Arabs was probably less an admission of Jewish achievements in Palestine than of what Christian civilization had done and was doing to the Jews: there literally was no other solution. The United Nations Commission recommended further that Jerusalem be turned into an international city because of its sacredness to Christianity, Islam and Judaism. On November 29, 1947, the General Assembly adopted this proposal.

The reaction of the three participants in the on-going conflict was instructive. Britain sulked. The Arabs screamed. The Jews rejoiced. The promise of an independent Jewish state had been made by a large majority of the nations of the world, and that state would serve as a home for their fellow-Jews wherever they were distressed and persecuted.

Britain did more than prepare to give up the mandate; it relinquished Palestine with unseemly haste. With all their proud tradition of fair play, too many Britons in the Palestine army and government openly and secretly favored the Arab attackers and interfered with the Jewish defenders. Even arms and supplies seemed to be deliberately abandoned where the Arabs would find them. But if this policy was meant to discourage, frighten and disorganize the Jews, it failed of its purpose; the results were quite the opposite. A government had in effect been functioning within the *Yishuv*. As the British let go, the National Commission took hold, and the entire Jewish population cooperated. Every border of the Holy Land was now alive with Arab armies ready to march in as soon as the British left, and gleefully promising to drive the Jews into the sea.

There was something tragic about this British retreat. One cannot help contrasting it with the glorious promise of those other days in 1917 when, having issued the Balfour Declaration, Britain stood forth as the friend of the Jewish people, as the successor to Cyrus of old in sponsoring the restoration of the Jewish Commonwealth. Barely thirty years later, the failure of that promise was being signalized by a decision of the international community which amounted to a rebuke; by the relinquishment of the charge once proudly assumed; by the abandonment of the country to the ravages of internal and external war. To be sure, Britain was leaving a lasting impression on the country: in the roads it had built, in the foundations of civil law it had laid, in the numerous administrative institutions it had developed as a result of its long imperial experience. And yet, all these and many other assets it had created during its rule would have vanished had the impending conflict been won by the side which Britain was encouraging by its untimely departure from the scene. The results of the thirty years of British labor in cooperation with the Jews—the only ones who ever did cooperate—would have, in all probability, been wiped off the face of the earth, and the country reduced to that same picturesque wilderness which it had been before Jewish vitality and creativeness had touched it with life, had the Jews not surprised the world by their successful defense.

On May 14, 1948, in the all-Jewish city of Tel Aviv, a small group of men and women who had been the leaders of the *Yishuv* met at the municipal museum and heard David Ben-Gurion solemnly proclaim the existence of the State of Israel. He recalled the age-old connection between that land and the Jewish people; he reminded the world of the hopes and efforts which had built the community; and he based the Jewish claim to the land on the vote of the United Nations the preceding November. Thus, the Jewish commonwealth was re-born, the third in a period of some three thousand and five hundred years.

At that very moment, however, the new state was being invaded by several armies vowing its extinction. The Egyptians came from the south and the Syrians from the north, the well-trained and excellently equipped Jordanian Arab Legion under British officers struck across the eastern boundary, while Arabs within the state came forward with armies of their own. None among the Arab peoples, and few elsewhere had believed that the fighting which would follow could end in anything but the defeat of Israel. With a population of only 600,000, a tiny fraction of that of its enemy countries, its territory minute and wide open on three sides, its impromptu army ill-equipped, its military leadership of unproved ability, Jewish Palestine appeared to be facing obliteration. Yet, in a matter of weeks, the Israelis were driving their enemies before them and, had not the United Nations intervened and imposed a truce, would have invaded both Syria and Egypt.

The usual explanations for this unexpected outcome have been, on the one hand, the over-confidence of the Arabs and their extremely poor leadership and, on the other, the high morale of the Jews and the superb generalship of their youthful commanders. But this cannot be its whole explanation: the morale itself has to be explained as well as the sudden emergence of courageous and intelligent leaders. The explanation for these phenomena must be sought, not only in the nature of the Zionist ideal and in the recent tragedies that had overwhelmed the people, but also in the moral and intellectual history of the Jews for centuries past. Now, in freedom of body and spirit, the full vitality of the Jewish people could at last assert itself.

Unfortunately, this vitality had to manifest itself first in war, as though to bring to pass, in a different sense from that intended, an ancient prediction included in the prayers for the Ninth of Ab: "For Thou, O Lord, hast consumed it [Jerusalem] by fire, and by fire art Thou destined to rebuild it." Let it be remembered that neither the Zionist ideal nor its program had envisaged conquest. Herzl had worked for an international charter. The settlers in Palestine had acquired almost every inch of the soil they worked by purchase. Many of the Jews of Palestine had felt that they were not yet ready for independent statehood. But they were given no choice. War was forced upon them. Thousands of young men and women, who might have helped build the nation, lost their lives in its preservation.

Arab leaders had been urging the Palestine Arab population to abandon their homes, promising them that they would soon return in triumph and take possession of the property of the Jews who would certainly be annihilated. The Arabs either heeded this advice or were compelled to heed it. In many instances, Jews pleaded with their Arab neighbors to stay; but there was no stopping the mad flight. Tens of thousands left their homes and crowded to the borders of Syria, Egypt, Jordan and Lebanon in the hope of a quick return.

The United Nations was, in the meantime, trying to effect an armistice between Israel and the Arab nations. It became easier to achieve this as the months rolled by and the Arabs lost their enthusiasm for fighting the Israelis. The United Nations had appointed Count Folke Bernadotte of Sweden, chairman of the International Red Cross, a well-meaning diplomat, as chief mediator between the two sides. It became known that Count Bernadotte, perhaps under British influence, was about to use his prestige and his powers to impose on Israel terms which would have drastically restricted the territory under its control. Some Israeli terrorists thereupon assassinated him. It was shocking evidence of the war's effect on morals and no one was more disturbed by this act than the Jews of Israel and of the Diaspora. The United Nations efforts did not slacken, however; Dr. Ralph Bunche of the United States became the mediator and the truce was arranged. The temporary boundaries of Israel were drawn largely in terms of the lines held at the cessation of the fighting. It came about that the lines of demarcation were not easy to follow, that Egyptian and Jordanian territory cut deep into that held by Israel and, most striking of all, that the city of Jerusalem was split into two: the old city, having been overrun by the Arab Legion, was left in Jordanian hands; the new city in the hands of Israel. The most deplorable result of the truce was that the area of Mount Scopus, with its Hadassah hospital and the valuable buildings and library of the Hebrew University, likewise fell to Jordan.

For the time being, the important consideration was that Israel existed. The first country to recognize this fact was the United States, President Harry S. Truman having announced his government's recognition of Israel within hours after its proclamation of independence. Other governments followed rapidly. Within a year, fifty-four states had done so, forty-five of these being members of the United Nations. On May 11, 1949, Israel itself was admitted to the international body. This event did not mean, of course, that even its territorial status was settled. The fighting had seriously upset the boundaries which the United Nations had fixed in its resolution of November 1947. There was, moreover, the difficult question of Jerusalem's status. Originally, it was planned to make of it a separate entity, ruled by an international authority, because of the location within its area of the places sacred to Christians, Moslems and Jews. Actually, such an arrangement would have proved impractical. Jordan objected to it far more than did Israel, which pointed out that, of the thirty or so sacred sites in Jerusalem, only two were within the new city and, therefore, under Jewish control. Many Christians agreed that a Jewish state which did not include Jerusalem would be highly incongruous. Nevertheless, the United Nations refused to modify its original vote on the subject, perhaps because of the opposition of those nations which were influenced by the views of the Catholic Church. In 1953, the Israel government moved all its offices to Jerusalem which was declared, thenceforth, the capital of the state. Several governments, however, have not yet recognized the validity of the move.

d. *The Problems of the New State*

Since the immediate motivation for the establishment of the state was the need of the homeless Jews, it was inevitable that its doors should be thrown wide open to all who wished to come.

The first arrivals were those Jews whom Britain had intercepted during the closing days of the Mandate and had kept in its own DP camps on the island of Cyprus. Simultaneously, the camps in Europe began to be emptied of those who had looked longingly towards the Promised Land. Moreover, in the bitterness of defeat, the Arab nations, those directly concerned as well as others, aggravated the problems of Israel by making life intolerable for the Jews in their lands, so that large numbers, leaving their property behind, escaped to Israel. Scores of thousands came from North Africa and western Asia. The most colorful group of these new immigrants were the naive, pious, hardworking Yemenite Jews. Under the protection of Great Britain, they made their way overland to Aden and thence were transported by air to Israel. For westerners this relocation was called "Operation Magic Carpet"; for the Yemenites themselves it was the fulfillment of the divine promise made through Isaiah that they would "mount up with wings as eagles." (Is. 40.31).

The arrival of so many immigrants all at once naturally intensified and complicated Israel's economic and social problems. The country was not producing enough for its vastly increased population, while the boycott by its neighbors permitted no expansion of foreign trade. Consequently, the support of the new population called for measures as heroic as those that had brought the state into being. The older residents had to ration their food in order to feed the newcomers. A vast retraining program had to be undertaken to fit the able-bodied among the immigrants into their new life. Large numbers had to be housed temporarily in transition camps (*ma'abarot*).

As for the Arab refugees from Israel, none of the Arab countries, despite their great size and sparse populations, was willing to do for its fellow-Arabs what the Israelis were doing for their fellow-Jews. Nothing of the enormous profits from the rich oil lands was given for refugee support. The Arab nations did not, in fact, want the problem solved at all. They insisted that Israel permit the former inhabitants to return. They knew very well that this step, if taken, would make the functioning of the new state impossible both economically and politically and would endanger its very security. There were already about 150,000 Arabs in Israel, who had ignored the advice of the Arab leaders that they leave, and had remained to become part of the new state. In time, Israel admitted many thousands more, so that families might be reunited. Compensation was offered for the property of the others. The refugees had, however, become a weapon in the war of the Moslem nations against Israel. The former continued to insist that they would not discuss peace until the refugees were readmitted to Israel. Israel's answer has been that the problem of the refugees was an item for the agenda in the discussions of peace, not a pre-condition for it. In the meantime, some 750,000 human beings—the number of refugees has grown naturally and by the attraction to them of elements from the other Arab nations seeking free support—have been maintained by the United Nations.

The Jewish population of Israel has risen from about 600,000, immediately after World War II, to more than a million and a half in 1956. Put differently, this means that, exclusive of the children born during the past decade, over fifty percent of the people have lived in the country less than a decade. What is more, they differ from one another as Europeans differ from Asians and Africans, as the German Jew differs from the Yemenite, and all shades in between—linguistically, economically, religiously, in color of skin, in habits of life, in outlook and in hopes. That these different people have undertaken to fuse into one nation is evidence of the power of an idea, whether religious or historical; at the same time, this common undertaking to build a nation forces them to face a number of tremendous problems. The problem of language has been solved: Hebrew remains the uncontested language of the country. It has, indeed, experienced a renaissance, growing in vocabulary and increasing in suppleness to meet every modern need. Compulsory, universal schooling must in time succeed in giving the population a basic cultural unity. So, too, universal military training for men and women must prove, not only a means of defense, but also a force in overcoming, to some extent, the differences arising from environmental backgrounds. Under the influence of that part of Israel's population which hails from Europe, the entire people is culturally very much alive. Its newspapers, books, museums, symphony orchestras and other appeals to mind and heart must eventually develop unity without external compulsion. But the problems that go deeper into the human spirit are not so easily solved.

One of the most serious is, naturally, that of religion. The Moslems and the members of Christian denominations in Israel are, of course, unaffected by religious controversy among the Jews. Within the Jewish community, however, differences of religion range from atheism to the extremest type of Orthodoxy. Continuing the policies of the British, the Israel government has operated with an organized religious community. There is a chief rabbinate; marriage and divorce are impossible without religious formality; the army and other government institutions observe Jewish traditions in *kashrut* and the like. But the extremist religious forces cannot be satisfied with these concessions since they hold that Judaism must pervade all of life. On this theory, the government would have to enforce *kashrut* and Sabbath observance on everyone. On the other hand, a large segment of the population is equally convinced of the need to separate religion from the state. They would even discontinue those connections with Judaism which have obtained until now, letting religion remain, as in western states, a matter for the individual's conscience to decide. The battle has been postponed, but the differences are still unresolved. Sooner or later, Israel will have to decide, in democratic fashion, what its future religious policy will be, and that decision must, in the very nature of things, affect the Judaism of the Diaspora.

It may have been fear of just such a disruptive argument, while the state was still weak, that caused the adjournment of debate on a constitution. For a commission to draw one up was appointed soon after the state was established. Eventually, articles were formulated and brought up for discussion, but it was felt that the time for adopting a constitution had not yet come. More experience of actual government, more crystallization of ideals were needed before definite regulations could be adopted. For the Jews of Israel are fully aware that a basic law formulated by them must express the Jewish spirit at its best and Jewish experience at its noblest. The law, which prevails, pending the adoption of a constitution is, therefore, a mixture of Jewish civil and ethical law and British common law. A judiciary functions with a supreme court at its head. A president is elected by the Knesset, the one-chamber legislature. His position is more like that of the president of France than that of the president of the United States. The actual government is vested in a cabinet and its prime minister responsible to the Knesset, very much like the arrangement in Great Britain and other European countries. Elections are held every four years, or more often if the cabinet finds that it no longer has the support of a majority of the Knesset but feels that it does have the support of the majority of the population. Since 1948, three elections have been held. In all three, Mapai, the moderate socialist party received the largest number of votes; in the first two, the socialists farther to the left, who bear the name Mapam, came next, and the religious forces third. In the last election, Herut, the economically more conservative and politically more activist party, showed marked gains. There were something like a dozen other parties. The government consequently has had to consist of a coalition of parties, quite as is the case in France. The cabinet, like the Knesset, represents a balance of power which reflects the balance of opinion in the population. Thus, in every way possible, Israel attempts to practice the maximum of political democracy; the ultimate result should express the creative will of the people.

The first president of Israel was the veteran leader of Zionism, Dr. Chaim Weizmann. Upon his death, in 1952, the choice of the Knesset fell on the unpretentious, popular, scholarly Yitzhak Ben-Zvi, who had come to Palestine in 1907, with the Second *Aliyah*. The able and dynamic leader, David Ben-Gurion, who had settled in Palestine in 1906, and who had stood at the head of the *Yishuv's* government during the latter days of the British Mandate, was again entrusted with the prime ministry. For a while, in 1954-5, he relinquished his post to his colleague Moshe Sharett, the first foreign secretary of Israel, and retired to a small settlement in the Negev. But when the situation became critical for Israel, Ben-Gurion resumed his former office (November 1955), while the foreign ministry was taken over by Golda Meir (Meyerson), who had been a member of the Israel government from the first.

The ability of Israel to solve its internal problems has not extended into the difficult situation which it confronts in the unabated hostility of its neighbors. As so frequently in the past of the Jewish people, Israel finds itself in the midst of a world crisis. The awakening nationalism of peoples hitherto considered colonies of western nations has brought political revolution to the Middle East. Moreover, it suits the politics of Russia to utilize the state of affairs in the Middle East to reduce the influence of the United States and other nations of the west. Both of these world problems, Arab nationalism and the east-west conflict, have militated against the establishment of peace between Israel and its neighbors. Defeated in war, the Arab nations have been carrying on a guerilla fight. Hardly a day passes without some hit-and-run attack on the Jewish colonies along the borders or on Israel army patrols. The United Nations Armistice Commission, stationed in Israel and in the Arab lands to adjudge such cases and condemn the guilty, has defined its task as preventing retaliatory action as well as attack. The Arab nations, which have loudly proclaimed their intention to avenge their defeat in a second round, succeeded in 1955 in obtaining large consignments of arms from communist countries. With the exception of France, the western nations, have, on the other hand, been unwilling to sell or grant arms to Israel. Under such conditions, it is obvious, the prospects for peace have dimmed considerably.

In the last days of October 1956, Israel, aware of the vast preparations made by the Egyptian dictator Gamal Abdel Nasser to invade and destroy it, and unable to tolerate any longer the unceasing incursions of Egyptian murder bands, sent its army into the Gaza strip and the Sinai Peninsula to destroy the bases from which the attacks were being launched. These objectives were won within a week. But the United Nations again interpreted this act of self-defense as aggression. Israel thereupon agreed to withdraw its forces from Sinai. It made the withdrawal contingent, however, on the United Nations preventing Egypt from re-occupying the Gaza Strip and the entrance to the Gulf of Aqaba. But no sooner had Israel withdrawn than the United Nations as well as the United States went back on the spirit, if not the letter, of the understanding. In the spring of 1957, the situation in that part of the world remained explosive.

VI. THE DIASPORA AFTER WORLD WAR II

a. *Anti-Semitism and Unity*

Not the least important result of the establishment of Israel as an independent state was its effect on the Diaspora. With a mixture of pride and hope, Jews greeted this evidence of the unexhausted vitality of their brethren. Participants in Jewish life were elated. Even those who had become quite alien to any manifestation of Judaism, who had apparently long since succumbed to the cultural pull of the environment, now again expressed interest in Jewish fate. In the United States, however, a small group of those who had always been anti-Zionist, voiced loud objection. They called themselves the American Council for Judaism; in point of fact, their energies have been directed against Zionism and against support for the Jewish state. With this small exception, the Jews of the Diaspora found new unity in their enthusiasm for the state which, in addition to its appeal to heart and mind, offered some compensation for the pain and despair experienced while Nazism was in the ascendant in Europe, and anti-Semitism in the United States.

Israel apart, the Diaspora communities, especially that of the United States, after World War II, once more faced the problems of adjustment and survival. A new generation had by this time taken control, the second or third of even the east European migration. Intellectually and economically this generation did not feel the cleavage with Jews of different origins as keenly as had their parents. Moreover, comparatively few immigrants had entered the United States since the restrictive immigration laws had come into force. Those from central Europe fitted themselves easily into the pattern of American Jewish life. Many of those who brought traditions from more eastern districts of Europe contributed some interesting and important variations to the pattern. But they had practically no influence as yet on the perennial Jewish Diaspora problem of how to articulate the fears and hopes of the Jewish population.

Community organization had taken considerable steps forward during the war. This was so of necessity, since work of rescue and relief was an obligation which American Jews never dodged. The magnificent aid extended to Israel during its life-struggle strengthened the local community organizations. But they remained largely fund-raising rather than functional bodies. Voices were raised occasionally in behalf of some form of representative local community agency. None of the larger communities, however, has responded to any such call, and the characteristic basis of American community life has remained philanthropy combined with defense. There are, indeed, important leaders of Jewish thought who argue that, in the free environment of western democracy, no other basis is possible or even desirable. To attack such nation-wide problems as affect all the local federations, the Council of Jewish Federations and Welfare Funds had been organized in 1932. Its functions being primarily those of research and consultation, the Council is obviously not the body to represent the Jewish population of the United States.

One of the paradoxical notions, widely entertained by Jews the world over, is that anti-Semitism somehow has helped Jewish survival. The fact of survival during the many centuries of oppression lends countenance to the assumption that the enemies of the Jews have kept them alive. It is true that, as the tide of anti-Jewishness rose, in England or America or anywhere else, Jews flocked to the support of defense organizations. It was an understandable reaction on the part of decent men. But this natural defensive attitude has given the false impression of staunch loyalty. It was rarely anything of the sort. It added much to the suspicions with which Jews regarded their neighbors, but it implied no commitment to Judaism or to the Jewish people. It intensified the Jewish sense of insecurity, of not belonging to the majority, but it also made for impatience with all those elements of Jewish life which differentiate Judaism from the surrounding civilization. It thus made for a psychology of escape, of intermarriage and of denial of self. An attitude prevailed which tested every word and deed, every book and undertaking, not by its effectiveness in strengthening Judaism and the Jewish community, but by the impression it was likely to make on the

Christian neighbors. The only other result from this aspect of Jewish experience, during the fourth and fifth decades of the century, was a stronger conviction among those already firm in their Jewishness that little mercy and less love were to be found among many of those who use these terms continuously; and it also made some alienated Jews look back to their origins.

The greater organizational unity which might have been expected from this concentration on defense did not result from it. During World War II, a proposal came forward that the Jews of the United States organize a body which would be representative of them all and thus concentrate their influence on improving the situation of Jews the world over, when the time came for negotiating the peace. The characteristic argument advanced during the discussion of this proposal was fear lest any such attempt at unity be misunderstood by the rest of the country's population. Finally, the idea was accepted and the American Jewish Conference was organized. It held a preliminary meeting in Pittsburgh in January 1943, and its first regular session in New York, August 29 to September 2 of the same year. Although a number of factors inherent in the situation prevented the Conference from leading anything but a shadowy existence, it served a useful purpose in providing a broad Zionist and non-Zionist front in behalf of the idea of a Jewish Comonwealth in Palestine. It also dealt with several other matters of concern to the American Jewish Community. In January 1949, the Conference decided to discontinue its labors.

If the disbanding of the Conference was justified on the ground that its work overlapped the program of other existing organizations, the same argument could be applied to the on-going and expanding activities of the various defense agencies. The American Jewish Committee, the American Jewish Congress, the Anti-Defamation League of the B'nai B'rith, the Jewish Labor Committee, and the local and regional Jewish Community Relations Councils which had come into existence during the 1930s and had since organized a National Community Relations Advisory Council—all of them and others were engaged in more or less the same type of work. Yielding to common sense, and under some pressure from the communal fund-raising organizations, these agencies agreed in 1950 to invite Professor Robert M. MacIver, a noted sociologist, to evaluate their total effort and to submit his recommendations. In his report in 1951, while recognizing the worthwhileness of Jewish defense work both for the Jewish group and for American democracy in general, Dr. MacIver thought it could be made more effective and efficient if various aspects of the work were done by organizations specializing in them and if authority to assign tasks were placed in the National Community Relations Advisory Council. These recommendations did not fall pleasantly on the ears of some of the organizations involved, especially the more influential and well established among them which felt that their very reason for existence was being questioned. Following heated discussion and much negotiation, the American Jewish Committee and the Anti-Defamation League declined to join in the implementation of Dr. McIver's recommendations. The organizations stood by the view that various elements of the Jewish population had a democratic right to combat anti-Semitism in their own way and that unity was therefore neither necessary nor desirable.

Actually, however, the interest of the Jews has veered away from anti-Semitism to a considerable degree since World War II. In the United States, the upward swing of economic life, the proved connection between anti-Jewishness and Nazi as well as communist anti-democracy, and the obviously irrational and self-seeking character of the known anti-Jewish agitators have led most non-Jews to turn a deaf ear to the wild charges which the professional hate-spreaders continue to mouth. There has been, moreover, a marked improvement in the presentation of Jews and Judaism in popular fiction and in the periodical press. That racialist prejudices were still to be reckoned with became clear in 1952, when Congress passed, over President Truman's veto, the MacCarran-Walter Act which retained and, in some instances, intensified existing restrictions on the immigration of presumed non-Nordics. A considerable proportion of the non-Jewish population has clearly not given up its suspicious attitude towards the Jewish minority. Their attention is the prize for which a bid has been made in the past few years by the old-fashioned anti-Semite now joined and supported by Arab and pro-Arab propagandists trying to frighten American Jews away from aiding Israel and to promote a public opinion adverse to the new state. There are, besides, some fields of social, professional and economic activity in which discrimination against the admission of Jews is still practiced. But on the whole, the situation has undergone noticeable improvement and, given peace and prosperity, must continue to improve. With the Jews no longer under direct attack, defense organizations have learned to join their efforts to the general striving for economic stability, social progress and equality of rights for all minorities. The fight against anti-Semitism has ceased to be as spectacular and as urgent as it used to be, and the attention of the Jewish people could be turned to the more deep-seated problems and creative tasks.

b. *New Trends in Religion*

The period of adjustment and conflict left its mark on the Judaism of western Europe and America. It emerged at the end of the half century different both from the Judaism which the immigrants had found on their arrival and from that which they had brought with them. A survey made in 1953, of an eastern American city with a Jewish population of several thousand, may be considered representative of the Jews in the United States in general, especially of those living away from the large centers of Jewish population. Only 30% of that city's Jews expressed strong objection to intermarriage, which had, indeed, risen in that community to 7% of all marriages. Most Jews, however, were more or less conscious of their Judaism, its culture and its values. Far from being discouraging, this record must be considered very good in view of the attractiveness of the majority culture and the numerous problems and difficulties which the Jewish group has had to face under circumstances which made centralized control and direction impossible. That the internal ties would be weakened could have been and was foreseen; but that so many of the third, fourth, and sometimes even later generations, should still have strong attachments to the religion and way of life of a small minority is evidence of Judaism's vigor. Those who remember the dire predictions of a generation ago must feel encouraged by the current quest on the part of the younger generation, especially in the larger cities, for closer contacts with Jewish tradition.

A number of factors may be called upon to explain this unexpected situation. The past quarter of the century has witnessed a reaction against the rather cold rationalism which dominated the thought of the century's earlier years. Whatever the cause for this change in the world in general, the new intellectual climate has also affected the Jews; the trend towards religion—even to mysticism—has not left them untouched. Closely allied with this general trend has been the improvement in the economic status of the Jewish population. Whereas the thinking of the parents had been largely socialist when the factory or shop was central in their lives, the children, now possessed of greater financial resources, even though equally plagued by a sense of insecurity, have taken on the thought-patterns of the middle class. An American Jew, as the above-mentioned survey indicates, thinks of himself as primarily a member of a religious group. Moving into a new neighborhood, he seeks social identification with fellow-Jews. He may neglect his religious observances, but his membership in a synagogue may be taken for granted, especially after his children attain school age. The synagogue as an institution has grown in prominence during the post-war period.

But these environmental and sociological influences on the development of Judaism, being more or less external, could become significant only because Jewish spirit and intellect are alive and functioning. Signs of such life are not far to seek. To begin with, religious discussion and interpretation have never ceased. Jewish thought, at the end of the nineteenth and the beginning of the twentieth centuries, may have lacked the uniformity which it had displayed in former days, but it continued to function on several levels. Hermann Cohen (1842-1918) in Germany, and Kaufmann Kohler (1843-1926) and Solomon Schechter (1847-1915) who, though German-trained, worked in the United States, and a number of other scholars presented the philosophical and theological aspects of Judaism. Such studies were, however, less prominent than the historical. As a pre-eminently history-conscious people, the Jews were more given to the study of the interplay between religion and the conditions of life than to theology, which is by its very nature static. Between the death of Heinrich Graetz (1891), who had seen Jewish history in terms of religious loyalty and rationalistic thought, and that of Simon Dubnow (1942), who described it in terms of culture and community, an incredible amount of research was done into every aspect of the Jewish past. The scientific study of Jewish history (*die Wissenschaft des Judentums*) was carried on with fervor at the seminaries in Europe and by means of numerous monographs and a number of highly scholarly periodicals. In the early part of the twentieth century, similar activity began in the United States. The founding of Dropsie College for Hebrew and Cognate Learning, in Philadelphia in 1907, showed that far-sighted American Jews recognized the importance of such studies. After World War I, a considerable number of the younger European Jewish scholars transferred their activity to America. They prepared the way for the transfer, in the 1930s, of their contemporaries who had stayed behind. Now Palestine and America took over the tasks of Jewish scholarship.

The most effective method by which such scholarly activity was transmuted into guidance for the average person has been the preaching and instruction of the rabbi. The rabbinate as an institution, underwent considerable change as a result of its contacts with western culture. The most obvious of these changes was the growing emphasis on preaching. The rabbi's position is no longer described as "the rabbinical chair," but as "the pulpit." On the other hand, the rabbi never quite abandoned his traditional Jewish duty of teaching, an activity in which he has become increasingly involved. Whether through preaching or teaching, the synagogue is the forum where the rabbi presents his views, in the light of Jewish thought and experience, on the problems of Jewish life and, frequently, also their philosophical backgrounds. The rationalistic emphasis characteristic of the early years of this period, which was followed by the historical, has of late shown signs of giving way to the theological.

The changes in the religious emphases have led to several changes in program. The Reform rabbis, meeting at Columbus, Ohio, in 1937, effected basic modifications in the radical Pittsburgh Platform of 1885. Among these was a positive attitude towards Zionism and a return—hesitant, to be sure—to broad traditionalism. A rather small minority of these rabbis and their lay followers refused to go along with these changes in the philosophy of Reform, but this minority never went quite so far as to secede from the Union of American Hebrew Congregations. At about the same time, Reconstructionism emerged out of the Conservative movement. Eager to give Jewish life philosophical direction in contemporary terms, Professor Mordecai M. Kaplan defined Judaism as a "religious civilization" which adhered to the Jewish historical view of life, expressed itself in accord with Jewish tradition—though not unmodified—and sought to revive cohesive Jewish community living. Others within Conservative Judaism, however, were less eager to find a common philosophical platform than to continue adhering to their basic tenet of continuous adaptation without breaking away from the sources of Jewish tradition. Nor has Orthodox Judaism, though presumably at one on the principle of unchanging tradition, been completely united in the face of the cultural differences among its adherents.

All the trends within western Judaism were alike affected by the revival of mystical religion in the western world in the '40s and the '50s. Among Jews, this took the form of a renaissance of the ideological and theological aspect of Hasidism: recalling that movement's penetrating insight into Judaism and life in general, its religious fervor and its super-worldliness as distinguished from other-worldliness. The name with which this revival is chiefly connected is Martin Buber, who had begun his activity in Germany after World War I and, in the '30s, had gone to Palestine. The wide popularity of the neo-Hasidic attitude among rabbis, teachers and intellectuals, may be further proof of the hunger for a deeper religious spirit; but there is no proof yet that its influence will be lasting.

Hasidism and Orthodoxy of a different, more personal, type entered into the Judaism of the west with the migration from eastern Europe of rabbis, *yeshiva* students and adherents of a number of hasidic leaders. These types of Judaism had continued to flourish in that part of the world down to the time of its disintegration under the blows of communism and the horrors of Nazism. The influence of Rabbi Israel Meir Kagan (the *Hafetz*

Hayyin, 1838-1933), on the one hand, and of the Lubavitcher dynasty of hasidim, on the other—to cite but one example of each type—had been tremendous and widespread. The horrors which the Jews were made to suffer during the fourth and fifth decades of the century intensified their religious loyalties. When these groups of undeviatingly Orthodox Jews arrived in the United States—or in Israel—they served as a nucleus around which clustered many Jews of an earlier immigration. They established schools, *yeshivot* and synagogues of their own. On the whole, this attempt to transplant the east European habits of life into American soil is reminiscent of similar efforts made by immigrants at the beginning of the period under review. Like the earlier attempts, the current one has served to strengthen the totality of Jewish religious life.

c. *Education for Young and Old*

The planned efforts to increase the content and improve the methods of Jewish education, which had begun in the second decade of the twentieth century, gained momentum in the succeeding years. Schools for the training of American-born teachers were opened in a number of cities. Gratz College, established in 1897 in Philadelphia, was the first of its kind; the Teachers Institute of the Jewish Theological Seminary (1909), in New York, was the second. Thereafter, similar schools were established in Chicago, Baltimore, Boston, and in other large cities, as well as several others in New York City. The graduates of these schools joined the devoted and highly cultured teachers who had come from Europe after World War I, so that the newer type of Jewish teacher has deservedly gained in professional status. A new spirit now prevails in the Jewish religious school, where Hebrew began to be taught as a living language and Jewish ceremonials as living, vibrant traditions. Moreover, although the Kehilla movement did not survive, community interest in education, which the Kehilla had awakened, did continue. Jewish community organizations, now to be found in almost every city and town, though primarily philanthropic and defensive in their motivation, have assumed greater educational responsibility. Many of the larger cities have established central bureaus of Jewish education, with trained pedagogues at their head and on their staffs. The American Association for Jewish Education, organized in 1939, consists of laymen who seek to stimulate and guide Jewish education throughout the United States.

In the more recent decades, the trend has been away from the communal school and towards the synagogue school. In his effort to bring more order into American Jewish life at the beginning of the century, Dr. Solomon Schechter, had laid it down as a rule that a synagogue must conduct an elementary Jewish school as part of its congregational function. The graduates of the Jewish Theological Seminary took this advice to heart and established synagogue schools for the children of the members. A little later, the rabbis trained at the Rabbi Isaac Elhanan Theological Seminary (Yeshiva) adopted the same policy. As synagogue affiliation increased, the number of children attending community schools began to fall off. This trend may have been, as some claim, due to the fact that more parents, under the influence of the rabbi, were persuaded to provide their children with a better grounding in their heritage. But because many such parents were evidently not persuaded to subordinate their children's other physical and cultural interests, the number of sessions in the afternoon Jewish schools had to be reduced, so that their general pattern calls for a maximum of some seven hours per week as against the minimum of ten to fifteen hours that was formerly the rule. To make up for this loss of time and other difficulties, reliance has been placed on improvement of the curriculum.

Far more hopeful developments, however, have taken place in several other areas of Jewish educational effort. There has been a substantial growth in post-elementary Jewish education for children of high school age, and successful experiments have been conducted with a few summer camps where Hebrew speech and religious instruction are part of the program. Moreover, an institution quite unlooked for a generation ago has come into being: the all-day Jewish school with a more or less integrated program of Jewish and general subjects. The new hasidic communities have been most active in this type of school and their success has encouraged others to try the like. Already by 1950, there were more than a hundred and fifty such schools, under various auspices, throughout the United States.

The idea of integrating the two cultural areas in which the American Jew must live, spread into adult education. Discussions on the desirability of a Jewishly-sponsored university had begun in the 1920s and gained momentum during the years when colleges and professional, especially medical, schools discriminated against Jewish applicants for admission. The plan was finally implemented when, as a result of the initiative of Dr. Israel Goldstein, Brandeis University opened its doors, in the fall of 1948, under the presidency of Abram L. Sacher, as a non-sectarian collegiate institution, with a well-staffed department of Jewish studies as part of the usual college course. Even earlier—as early as 1928—the Rabbi Isaac [Yitzhak] Elhanan Theological Seminary opened an undergraduate collegiate department. Before long, it accepted non-theological students as well, and eventually added graduate courses. It thereupon changed its name to Yeshiva University. Even a medical school is now part of Yeshiva University.

Other cultural institutions have made similar efforts to strengthen their foundations and broaden their influence. The Jewish Theological Seminary has opened a branch in Los Angeles, the University of Judaism, which has the right to grant graduate degrees in the field of Jewish studies. The Hebrew Union College of Cincinnati and the Jewish Institute of Religion in New York (founded by Stephen S. Wise in 1926) have joined forces, although both institutions continue to function separately.

One of the astonishing manifestations of current Jewish life has been the vitality of the Yiddish language and culture. Yiddish speech, to be sure, no longer dominates the Jewish neighborhoods. The number of Yiddish newspaper readers has dwindled, as was to have been expected. Yet the use of the language has remained considerable and the variety, volume and quality of its literature exceptionally high. An example of an influential cultural institution among the Jews of both North and South America is the Yivo Institute for Jewish Research. Organized in Vilna, the old Lithuanian Jerusalem, in 1925, to promote historical and sociological research, it was forced in 1939 to transfer all its activities to the western hemisphere, with headquarters in New York. Its monthly in Yiddish, its annual volume of studies in Yiddish and English, its monographs, and its valuable library testify to great earnestness and high achievement.

The transformation in the elementary educational picture in the past forty years has been paralleled, though not equalled, by changes in the field of adult education. Every organized Jewish group has adopted an educational program. Synagogues, Centers, B'nai B'rith lodges, Zionist and other groups maintain programs of lectures and study circles, and the National Jewish Welfare Board, the National Association of Jewish Community Centers, maintains a lecture bureau and other services for the enrichment of Jewish programs. Even if the motivation for these activities is frequently social, their popularity bespeaks a revival of a traditional Jewish approach to life. Such study, it must be admitted, is largely on a popular, elementary level. But, at least, the problem presented by intellectual poverty is recognized and the will to solve it is there.

Whether in English, Hebrew or Yiddish, on the adult or the juvenile level, in fiction or works of scholarship, recent literary activity among Jews has been significant. The Jewish Publication Society is no longer the only publisher of books of history and fiction on Jewish subjects; commercial publishers and even university presses have discovered that an interested Jewish reading public exists. The day is past when Jewish scholarship has to subsist on borrowings from Europe. There is, to be sure, much that can be criticized; weaknesses and inadequacies are apparent in every area of Jewish culture and religion; there is still a wide chasm between reality and what might have been expected in spiritual and intellectual productivity from a Jewish community so fortunately placed. It is, nevertheless, undeniable that American Jewish life has, in remarkable measure, withstood the test of time and the challenge of the environment.

THE BALANCE SHEET OF A GENERATION

In 1954-5, the Jewish community of the United States celebrated the tercentenary of its origin. In 1955-6, the Jewish community of Great Britain observed a similar anniversary. Comparisons and contrasts between the small and uncertain beginnings and the size and strength of these two western communities were inevitable. Both communities, however, as well as the Jews of the rest of the world, have undergone, in the past sixty or seventy years, more radical transformations than in the entire preceding millennium. Few periods in the long history of the Jews have been as revolutionary, as tragic and as inspiring. The problems and the difficulties have been of such magnitude as to justify the view that the mere survival of an identifiable Jewish group might well have been miraculous. Yet the Jewish people has not only survived, but has also displayed such constructive spiritual powers as to enable it to add an interesting and, in some particulars, a thrilling chapter to Jewish history.

This most recent period of Jewish history can be summarized on two different levels, so that two different conclusions can be drawn from it. It can be argued that the Jews have been nothing more than victims of historical forces: their migrations, the result of politics and prejudice; their adjustments to new environments, but individual successes; their community organizations, mere manifestations of minority reactions to pressure by the majority; and even the establishment of Israel, an accidental outcome of international rivalries. A case can be, and has been, made for such a view. It is the view of those who see the Jewish people with the jaundiced eye of the anti-Semite or of the alienated Jew, or of those who smugly explain Jewish survival either by the Ahasuerus legend or the more intellectualized terminology of "fossil civilization." According to such views, there is neither sense nor purpose in remaining a Jew; to do so is a manifestation of stubbornness or, worse still, of racial narcissism.

The trouble with such explanations is that, by ignorance or design, they do not explain. Mere stubbornness or self-adulation could not have persisted in the face of terror and martyrdom; above all, these barren attitudes could not have led to spiritual productivity. No people—not even a powerful nation—can be said to be living or dead because it dominates or fails to dominate historical forces. That happens too rarely, if at all, to be considered a realistic test. A better test of a people's vitality is its ability to stand up to such forces and to try to be true to its values no matter how much or how suddenly conditions vary. By this test, the Jewish people has been very much alive during the sixty years just passed. All one need do is consider some of the events mentioned above. Those who emigrated from eastern Europe, for example, did so in large part for economic reasons; but they could have remained at home and improved their social and economic status by losing themselves in the majority. Their religion and culture must have, to put it mildly, meant something to them if it played so important a part in so momentous a decision. And those very much larger numbers who did not emigrate, if one is to judge them by the personalities they produced and the broad human ideas that came from among them, were certainly not a dull and inert mass of humanity. Nor could it have been sheer accident that so many of the adjustments which so many immigrants made in their new homes were so frequently related to, and in harmony with, the intellectual and spiritual values of traditional Jewish life. The sense of mutual brotherly responsibility which created effective philanthropic institutions, both local and worldwide; the unquenchable hope for restoration to free life in the Holy Land which developed a community prepared to assert its claims to self-expression; the literary achievements in every language and the creation of literatures in two languages which were themselves the creations of the Jewish spirit; the social and educational institutions to fill every cultural, religious and philosophical need; even the fervid religious disputations and disagreements within the Jewish community—all of these and more are irrefutable proofs that Judaism is a functioning religion and culture with a great deal to offer to its adherents and to mankind as a whole.

These, it should be noted, were achievements of the Jewish people in an age and under conditions of personal and cultural freedom, especially in the west, but in eastern Europe as well. The Jewish spirit had functioned in previous eras and under less auspicious circumstances, too, but at a much slower tempo and with less variety of expression. The greater needs and challenges of the present day are producing more diversified and more numerous responses. Moreover, because of its functioning in close contact with different peoples and cultures, the Jewish responses can frequently benefit the wider community. In this sense one can talk of Jewish contributions to civilization: in the labor movement, in philanthropy, in social work, in such political inventions as the Minority Treaties, and even in religion when Judaism has been articulate in the presentation of its own point of view. This enumeration naturally takes no account of the individual Jew's activity in the life of the nation of which he is a citizen. The fact that Jews have been and are more prominent in some areas of life than in others may derive from Jewish fate and tradition, but it would take considerable psychological and statistical investigation to prove this. One can only hope that the Jew's Jewishness will continue to mold him into a socially valuable personality as it has, without doubt, made him a member in a socially valuable group.

Such a future is, however, by no means certain. The very survival of the Jewish Diaspora is open to doubt. The number of those losing contact with Jewish values and severing their connections with the Jewish community has been on the increase all through the past generation. This and the falling birthrate among the Jews of the Diaspora will at best probably keep the world's Jewish population merely stationary. What is more, there is every indication that the Jews of the Soviet Union, estimated at about two and a half millions, must also be written off. This loss means that within this one generation the Jewish population of the world has been reduced by half. Pessimists, sociologists and Jewish nationalists—a strange combination—argue that environmental pressures are bound to eliminate the Diaspora entirely. Pressures of various kinds give no promise of abating in the most populous Diaspora community, that of the United States. There is no reason to assume that these and other forces will cease in the foreseeable future to weaken those Jews who are ill-equipped to withstand them.

Herein, therefore, lies the foremost task for the future of Diaspora Judaism. It may yet turn out that of all the costly activities and great institutions created by this generation to meet the problems of our day, the next generation will be most grateful for the all-day school and the Hebrew summer camps for children and for the study circles and institutes and Jewish college courses for adults. For, in the final analysis, the sources of Jewish vitality have been the literature, the ceremonial and the religious teachings which moulded the Jewish personality. The generation just past was able to answer the challenges hurled at it because it was not too far removed from this cultural-religious complex which goes by the name of Judaism. Even a casual view of the Jewish scene reveals that the farther removed any group of Jews has been from this source of Jewish life the weaker have been its Jewish responses. Our generation, therefore, will inevitably be judged by its success or failure in transmitting these ideas and attitudes as functioning realities. Judaism warns against relying on miracles; one may pray and hope for them, but not sit back and depend on their coming to pass. It will be a miracle if a Jewish people survives two or three more generations unless the Jews of the present day take steps to stem the increasing alienation from the sources of Jewish life. Only if the current revival of interest in religion takes on the form of meaningful and plentiful Jewish education will one be able to look hopefully to the future.

But intellect, leadership and organizational forms will have to undergo radical change if any such intensified training in Jewishness is to become the rule. Jewish life will have to assume more meaning than merely another expression of man's need to worship. Leadership, both lay and professional, will have to be judged by more than energy, organizing ability and a social outlook. It will have to understand and react to the problem of transmitting Jewish knowledge and values. The entire community will have to re-organize in terms of a changed focus, away from the centrality of defense and philanthropy. There is practically no evidence at the moment that any such revolutionary changes in leadership and purpose, on any considerable scale, are in the offing in any Diaspora community. There are only scattered individuals and a few comparatively small groups, with little influence on the so-called top leadership, who are deeply enough concerned about maximum Jewish living. From this viewpoint, too, therefore, the outlook is for a Jewish community considerably reduced in size.

Perhaps what is needed is leadership with ability, devotion and prestige, to give voice and direction to the inner strivings of Jewish life. Such leadership has at various times of need arisen in the past. In the meantime, one may look to influences likely to come from Israel. The Diaspora cannot consider the new State as merely a political entity which has already realized the hope of restoration. Unless Torah comes out of Zion, it will not have fulfilled Jewish aspirations. It need not become a theocratic state, and it probably will not; but it must exert cultural and religious influences on Diaspora life as the Jewish community of Palestine did in the distant past. Under these conditions, the Diaspora's cultural contacts with Israel are of the utmost importance. Quite apart from supporting Israel materially, as the Diaspora will have to continue doing for a long time, it will also have to foster Israel's cultural and religious institutions with increasing vigor.

Life in an environment which permits of cultural give and take is bound to be hazardous for a minority. Losses are to be expected. But the past sixty years, like other periods in Jewish history before, have proved the possibility of attaining integrated personality in which Judaism and western culture fuse harmoniously. The process will continue in the coming generations. If prejudices of various intensities do not intervene, the process will be a happier one than it has been in the generation here described. If the Jews are more careful to balance their general culture with a more ample supply of Jewish knowledge, experience and spirituality, the results will be of even greater value to civilization. In any event, the continuance of Judaism and the Jewish people cannot be questioned.

The events discussed in this essay form a proper background for the volume dedicated to Dr. Israel Goldstein on the occasion of his sixtieth birthday. Indeed, many of these events and historical processes are an integral part of his biography. To interpret Judaism, to realize the Zionist hope, to defend the Jewish people, to organize for better community living—to spread knowledge and to inspire hope—he participated in all these aspects of his generation's struggles, as an eloquent, far-sighted and constructive leader. May his influence long continue to be felt!

DEVELOPMENT OF JEWISH
COMMUNAL ORGANIZATION
IN AMERICA
1900-1956

by Isaiah M. Minkoff

ALTHOUGH organized Jewish life may be said to have existed on this continent since the arrival of the first band of Jews in New Amsterdam in 1654, yet it is within the sixty years, more or less, covered by the present review that Jewish communal organization as we know it today took form.

The phenomenal creativeness in organization displayed by American Jewry is closely and vitally related to the scope and vigor of the American society. The forms that Jewish organizations have taken in the United States are, in many respects, indigenously American, being fully as much products of the characteristic American spirit of practicality as of the venerable Jewish capacity for innovation of modes of organization.

To attempt, in the brief scope of a single chapter, anything beyond the merest tracing of major strands in the rich fabric of that Jewish organizational life would be futile. Nor is even that the aim of this chapter. Rather it is to seek in history those influences and tendencies that have shaped the form and directed the course of Jewish organizational development in this country.

Until the last two decades of the nineteenth century, the Jews of the United States constituted a relatively homogeneous population; especially was that homogeneity striking in the light of subsequent dramatic changes. The differences that, in the eighteenth and early nineteenth century, divided the descendents of the comparatively small number of early Spanish and Portuguese Jewish settlers from the later German Jewish immigrants had relatively limited consequences in a period when organized Jewish communal life in this country was very sketchy. Jewish immigration up to about 1880 was moderate in volume; and the immigrants were almost all from western and central Europe. While many of them faced great economic hardships, they accommodated readily to the cultural patterns of the American society. Among themselves, they were drawn together by common cultural and social interests. As they followed the expanding frontiers of the growing nation, or settled in its more established centers of population, they formed congregations and, around these, grew up, as for countless generations before, various charitable and mutual aid activities. The sense of mutual dependence, hammered into the group memory of Jews by a bitter history of discriminations, expulsions and migrations throughout the Middle Ages and into modern times—a history which again and again had made whole communities of Jews dependent for very survival upon the freely-given succor of their more fortunately situated fellow-Jews—led them also to create larger organizations drawing Jews together into fraternal relationships and united endeavors.

The homogeneity of the American Jewish population was replaced by a bewildering heterogeneity as the result of the altered pattern of Jewish immigration after about 1880. That immigration was almost wholly from eastern and southeastern Europe.

The differences between the new immigrants and the already established Jewish groups were many. The cultural settings in Europe from which they had come were worlds apart. Like other immigrant groups, the eastern European Jews tended toward group cohesiveness. There was among them, moreover, a unique striving to preserve their cultural customs and patterns. Yiddish culture, Yiddish literature, the Yiddish theater throve in the new Jewish setting. To many of the older elements, all this seemed merely obdurate resistance to Americanization. Economic disparities were great. The German Jews by then were mainly middle class—merchants, manufacturers, professionals—whereas the east European Jews included a preponderance of artisans and unskilled workers. In the larger American cities, the factories in which the immigrants found employment often were owned by German Jews; employer-employee hostilities sometimes aggravated ill feeling. The political and ideological radicalism of some of the leaders and intellectuals among the east European Jews aroused alarm and anger in the generally conservative German Jewish circles. Economic, cultural and social distance between the established Jews and the newcomers was increased by theological difference. The eastern Jews were Orthodox, whereas the settled German Jewish group had largely embraced Reform Judaism.

But the divisions within the Jewish group were not only dichotomous. The east European Jews were themselves a markedly heterogeneous mixture of nationalities—Russian, Polish, Lithuanian, Galician, Roumanian and others—and the members of each sub-group tended to gravitate toward each other for mutual aid, social intercourse, diversion. *Landsmanschaften*—fraternal organizations of immigrants from particular lands, provinces, cities, towns—were formed literally by the thousands. Ages-old prejudices and animosities were perpetuated.

Yet, even as these separatist influences were constantly being augmented by the influx of newcomers, other factors were at work tending to reduce the divisive forces. Gradually, language barriers were overcome. East European Jews rose from the sweatshops and the push-carts to become merchants and manufacturers, factors and brokers. Their children went to school, college, university. They entered the professions. Families moved out of the ghettos. Economic and social distances narrowed.

At the same time, too, there was, as always, a constant at work, making for unity of effort. This derives in part from the sense of common identification among Jews, based in turn upon common traditions, common historical memory and common religion. Over the years, these influences were augmented by demographic changes within the Jewish population, by external crises that raised problems of common concern, and by developing American patterns of group identification and group relationships.

Internally, the Jewish population underwent great changes: the virtual cessation of immigration after the first great war, the rise of a substantial Jewish middle class, the acculturation of "big-city Jews" to the life of suburbia, the progressive fading of "social distance" between the so-called German and eastern Jews, the growing integration into American life of Orthodoxy and the simultaneous movement of Reform toward restoration of traditional forms. Externally, Jewish persecutions and hardships and needs in various parts of the world called for concerted response by American Jewry: the series of anti-Jewish pogroms in Russia, beginning with the Kishinev outrages in 1903, the displacement of Jews by the first World War, the needs of Palestine, the Nazi campaign of extermination, the creation of Israel, and the perils confronting the young State. All these factors, in their various ways, impelled American Jews toward unity of identification, of purpose, and of effort.

The tendencies toward diversification and the tendencies toward unity in American Jewish life have been in a continual mutually antagonistic flux. Sustaining and giving sanction to both has been the voluntaryism that characterizes the American society. From the outset, the United States presented Jews with conditions unique in the prolonged and frequently tragic history of Jewish migrations. Except in England (a very minor source of Jewish immigration to America), where the Cromwellian revolution had resulted in the readmission of Jews and their entrance into the body politic as individuals, and to a somewhat lesser degree in France, Jews throughout Europe were by statute or edict members of discrete sub-national communities, possessing defined political and regulatory authority and collective responsibility, frequently subject to taxation as a community and empowered to levy taxes upon their own members—in short, corporate entities.

As late as 1919, after the establishment of the Weimar Republic, the Jewish community in Germany levied taxes under governmental authority for the support of Jewish needs. In Poland, as late as 1927, an individual could sever himself from the Jewish collective only by religious conversion or by declaring himself to be without religious conviction.

The United States, by contrast, was a new nation, its national character not yet completely formed. Citizenship was equal for all. Its democratic Constitution, a revolutionary document, not only accorded freedom equally to all religions but forbade the government from concerning itself in the religious beliefs or practices of its citizens. Here was an unprecedented focusing upon the individual as the exerciser of free choices. Even the authority of the government was qualified with safeguards against arbitrary or unreasonable demands upon the citizen. The citizen was free to support, oppose, or remain indifferent to, every cause, movement, creed, faith or organization whatsoever. And this freedom was not merely a negative absence of both compulsion and restraint; it was voluntaryism raised to the status of a principle.

This principle has not only sustained a great diversification of Jewish organizational structures but, by doing so, it has also given wide play to the improvisation, inventiveness, and variety that have contributed so much to the dynamism of American Jewish life. At the same time that this principle has sanctioned and, by sanctioning, encouraged that diversification, it also has sanctioned all sorts of efforts toward unification. Voluntaryism, as a principle, is fully as much reflected in unity as it is in diversification, since within voluntaryism, unity is not imposed but is the product of free choice, and possesses the strength and vigor infused in it by the spirit of common purpose. In the context of a pluralistic culture, with its emphasis on group identification, the principle of voluntaryism has served to encourage inclusive associations of Jews, and thus has given impetus to the creation of united Jewish enterprises in common causes.

I. LOCAL COMMUNITY ORGANIZATION

Origins and Development

By the last decade of the nineteenth century, the heterogeneity of Jewish life in America already had produced a great diversification of organizations, institutions, agencies and associations on every facet of Jewish living—religious, philanthropic, social, cultural, economic, political. Not only did diversified organizational relationships and structures proliferate in these circumstances; but the resourcefulness of all the varied groups comprising the Jewish population also was challenged and stimulated to find effective ways of sustaining their separate integrities in the new environment and of building bases for their fruitful survival and growth. Thus, within the welter of overlapping, duplicative, conflicting activities there went on a dynamic process richly productive of ideas that were to find expression in enduring forms of organization in a later period of leveling and amalgamation.

Federations

The idea of federation was one of these ideas. In its origins, it was an idea for increasing the efficiency of fund-gathering and fiscal administration of relief agencies conducted under the auspices of a particular, rather homogeneous segment of the community. Years later, the idea burgeoned into the concept of a central community organization, but when it was first broached it contemplated the federation of only a relatively few well-established agencies. And, like so many other ideas that have proved fruitful of durable forms of organization, it was in its origins very largely nothing more than a pragmatic response to a felt need among a small number of influential Jewish leaders.

By about 1890, the tremendous influx of Jewish immigrants had created a volume of need for relief and assistance such as had never been contemplated by the nineteenth century American Jewish communities. The charitable services that the German-Jewish communities of that era had built up were engulfed in the flood. True, the newcomers, as soon as they were able, formed their own charitable and benevolent societies. But the burden fell most heavily upon those best able to bear it, the older, wealthier organizations and agencies.

The capacity of all the agencies was overtaxed. The *mish-mash* of separate and competing appeals for funds presented a picture of inefficiency that seemed to the businessmen, who were the leaders in Jewish affairs, to make neither sense nor logic.

These leaders represented the, by then, old established German-Jewish elements. They were men of affairs, successful in commercial enterprises and imbued with business precepts of efficiency and economy in operation. The relief of suffering and want was a practical problem in the realm of humanitarian effort. They put their heads together and devised an efficient business-like approach to its solution.

The leaders of the early federations were not at all preoccupied with theoretical questions of "community." And, as has been said, the early federations made no pretense of inclusiveness. They were limited virtually to those agencies within the communities that were under the leadership of the German-Jewish group, leaving outside disparate agencies that had sprung up under the aegis of the still "unadjusted" newcomers.

Boston pioneered with its Federation of Jewish Charaties in 1895, bringing five leading Jewish organizations together for common fund-raising. Cincinnati followed the next year, joining eight organizations in the United Jewish Charities, which from the outset instituted combined fund-solicitations and allocations. Chicago's Jewish Federation came into being in 1900. (The Boston Federation, however, did not take on the essential characteristic of federation—solicitation of single combined giving for support of all federated agencies—until 1904; prior to that, contributors were asked to give to the separate agencies.) By 1904, there were federations also in Philadelphia, Cleveland, St. Louis, Kansas City, Milwaukee and Detroit. By 1914, the number had grown to twenty-five; by 1917 to forty-seven.

Welfare Funds

Exigencies created by World War I led to the extension of the idea of central fund-raising for purposes not up to then included, by and large, in federation—that is, for national and overseas philanthropies. A number of developments contributed to this enlargement of scope. The formation of the American Jewish Joint Distribution Committee in 1914 suggested the feasibility of a similar merging of appeals at the community level. The constantly increasing separate solicitations by overseas and Palestine agencies caused the idea of one combined appeal to impress many community leaders as the only avenue of escape from utter chaos. While some federations merely expanded their own fund-raising to cover national and overseas needs, others which, in the war and immediate post-war years, joined overall community chest structures could not make such provisions. In cities where this was the case, or where, for other reasons, it seemed desirable to separate the drives for local and for national and overseas funds, the Jewish communities had to create separate agencies. These were commonly called welfare funds. The first ones were founded almost simultaneously in 1925 and 1926 in Columbus, Detroit, Indianapolis, San Francisco and Oakland. By 1936, there were at least forty of them.

Community Relations Councils

Rising anti-Semitism was the chief precipitating agent for the creation, beginning in the 1930s, of another form of Jewish communal structure, the community relations council. Anti-Jewish agitation threatened all Jews and all Jewish institutions. The common threat manifestly called for common defense. In any particular Jewish community, this meant primarily a common, united effort to prevent, counter, overcome or contain anti-Semitism in that community. The entire community was concerned about this effort, for the status and welfare of the entire community were threatened.

To involve the entire community in the effort to deal with this common problem, it was necessary to create a policy-making and local action body fully representative of all segments of the Jewish community. Such was the community relations council. This tended toward inclusion, in addition to the organizations and individuals participating in the local federations and welfare fund structures, of many others not involved in those structures: religious institutions and organizations, civic bodies, fraternal organizations, local chapters or branches of national organizations, lodges, clubs, etc. This inclusive representation was not uniform. Like other Jewish communal organizations, the community relations councils vary widely among themselves.

It soon became evident that Jewish rights could not be regarded as secure in a society that denied equal rights to any group, whether because of religion or race or other irrelevancy. A positive program of advocacy of equal opportunity for all, of support for the traditional American principles of religious freedom and constitutional equality, was developed, including actions looking toward the legal rectification of the disabilities imposed upon minorities and the translation into actual practice of the principles of the democratic faith.

These were issues of national import, and the Jewish communities made common cause with national Jewish community relations agencies in dealing with them. Between the national agencies and the local Jewish community organizations, special problems of relationship developed. The local bodies found themselves differing in some cases with the national agencies. They sometimes questioned the adequacy of judgments formulated, as it seemed to them, in distant offices, without regard to circumstances in the communities or to community opinions and desires. They questioned the undertaking of activities in the communities by national agencies without consultation with the local council. The communities began to voice demand for participation in the planning of national programs which, in the very nature of community relations, had an inevitable impact upon the local community; for it is here that community relations ultimately exist. In 1944, fourteen local councils became partners with the national agencies in a joint coordinating agency, the National Community Relations Advisory Council. They were in the following cities: Baltimore, Boston, Brooklyn, Cleveland, Cincinnati, Detroit, Indianapolis, Los Angeles, Milwaukee, Minneapolis, Philadelphia, Pittsburgh, St. Louis and San Francisco.

Community Councils

Among these were community councils as well as community relations councils. The functional scope of the community councils was broader than that of the community relations councils. In addition to community relations, the community councils concerned themselves with matters of internal Jewish discipline, Jewish cultural interests, arbitration of disputes within the framework of the Jewish community, and the like. Among the fourteen "charter" community members of the NCRAC were several community councils, including notably the Cleveland Jewish Community Council and the Detroit Jewish Community Council. In conception, the Jewish community council is an embracing representative communal body, made up of delegates from all the organizations and institutions in the community, and dealing with all matters of community concern.

This conception found incorporation in the unmistakable and, on the whole, steady tendency throughout recent years toward the development of central Jewish communal organizations.

Trend Toward Central Communal Organization

The homogeneous federation structures of the early years of the century, embracing only selected relief and welfare agencies and governed by boards made up of their representatives, soon began to enlarge their base of participation and to expand their functional scope. They progressively assumed financial responsibility for support of more and more agencies and services and undertook planning functions for the community as a whole, relative to community needs for those agencies and services. National and overseas appeals became recipients of federation-welfare fund financial support, as did a variety of communal enterprises other than welfare, such as community relations, Jewish education, and cultural activities. There was a decline in the tendency to regard services offered by Jewish agencies as charitable contributions by the wealthy for the relief of the poor; increasingly these services came to be looked upon by all as a collective enterprise of the community, carried on in the interest of the community as a whole. All this progress was accompanied by professionalization, of both the administration of federation-welfare fund-council management and the operation of the agencies and services supported by the central fund-raising agency. By accretions of participating beneficiaries, expansion of scope, enlargement of function, and integration of previously separate appeals and programs, there gradually developed many central Jewish communal organizations.

With time and usage, the terms federation, welfare fund, and community council have come to be interchangeable. All denote communal organizations of various types. Some "federations" are also welfare funds and some are community councils as well. Some "welfare funds" are also federations and may or may not embrace community council functions. Some councils are also federations and welfare funds.

National-Local Relationships

The leadership of these communal enterprises, with their broad responsibilities for serving community needs, in time sought to examine with the same analytical attention they gave to local beneficiaries, the programs and the financial requirements of the national and overseas agencies to which they were allocating funds. A number of federations in 1927 organized the National Appeals Information Service, to finance studies of national and overseas fund-raising organizations. Five years later, in 1932, fifteen federations constituted a more formal association with a broader mandate for joint planning and central servicing, the Council of Jewish Federations and Welfare Funds. In 1957, the CJFWF embraced some 250 communal organizations in the United States and Canada.

Under the auspices of the CJFWF, efforts continued for the establishment of relationships between the federations and the national and overseas agencies whereby the local communal agencies might play a role in the analysis of national agency budgets, evaluation of national agency performance, and projection of national agency programs. In 1940, a proposal was advanced for the creation of a National Advisory Budgeting Service, to review the budgets of the national and overseas agencies applying for support to the welfare funds, and to formulate national recommendations concerning agency needs and local responsibilities. After a period of intense debate and discussion, this proposal was finally defeated at the general assembly of the CJFWF in 1946. In 1948, a number of the larger cities in the CJFWF established the Large City Budgeting Conference, to cooperate with national and overseas agencies in the mutual analysis of their budgets, with a view to reaching consensus of opinion on their appeals. Some national agencies were cooperating with the Large City Budgeting Conference in this process in the middle 1950s; others were not.

Relationships of the local communal organizations to national and overseas agencies with regard to finances are in a continuing state of evolution. What is the proper role of the central communal agency? As a representative instrumentality of the whole community, to what extent does it have a responsibility to review the work and the budget of each agency that calls upon the community for support and to seek to assure that each such agency reflects in its operations the desires and needs that are expressed by the communal will? To what extent, on the other hand, is it a fiscal agent? At the extreme, some national agency leaders hold that the communal organization is solely a fiscal agent, raising money that the national or overseas agency might raise through its own efforts.

The New York "Kehillah"

Historically, the various communal structures created by Jewish communities have proved viable to the extent that they have met the pragmatic criteria of community need. Structures created before communities were ready for them soon revealed their ultimately fatal defects. Perhaps the most instructive illustration is to be found in the history of the New York City "Kehillah."

At least from the beginning of the massive east European immigration in the 1880s, the final destination of a very substantial proportion—probably, until well after the turn of the century, a majority—of the Jews coming to the United States was New York. It has been estimated that one-half million Jews—more Jews than there were in Warsaw in 1939—lived in the metropolis in 1900. By the outbreak of the first World War, the number approached the one million mark.

In this teeming environment, every ideological movement, every form of association, every sort of tie, every kind of difference in Jewish life found some manifestation or outlet. The yeasty ferment out of which contemporary Jewish organizational life has developed was nowhere more volatile. Nowhere was there more Jewish wealth or more Jewish poverty; nowhere a greater diversity of origins, purposes and goals; nowhere a greater distance between the "uptowners" and the "downtowners"; nowhere a greater proliferation of organizations, agencies and institutions.

It was not until as late as 1917, that New York City organized a federation. Yet, in 1908, in cooperation with the American Jewish Committee, a "Kehillah" was formed in New York. Known under the name of "The Jewish Community of New York

City," it was designed to be the central representative Jewish
body in the metropolis and its purpose was to further the cause
of Judaism in New York City and to represent the Jews of the
city in respect of all local matters of Jewish interest. Its membership included every incorporated synagogue of some size, every
local federation of Jewish societies, every independent Jewish
society, societies of rabbis, cantors, social workers, etc. Later, it
was to embrace, also, hospitals, social settlements, loan societies,
labor unions, burial societies, social clubs, and a variety of other
organizations.

The constitution of the Jewish Community of New York City
provided for an Executive Committee of 25 members who would
constitute, at the same time, District 12 of the American Jewish
Committee. Under the constitution, the "Kehillah" had exclusive
jurisdiction over all questions of a local character or specifically
affecting the New York community itself; the American Jewish
Committee had exclusive jurisdiction over all questions affecting
Jews generally, not of a purely local character.

While the "Kehillah" created several viable institutions, some of
which continue, under the auspices of successor organizations, to
the present day, its life was brief. There was strife within the
"Kehillah" both over policy and over method of representation.
Yet, perhaps the most important reason for its demise, according
to the leaders of the movement at that time, was the fact that the
"Kehillah" came on the scene too early, that the community was
not sufficiently homogeneous within itself, and that although in
its brief life it demonstrated the effectiveness of joint action, it
also demonstrated that the community was not ready for it.

But, although the "Kehillah" proved abortive, the conception of
voluntary central Jewish communal organization lived and grew
under the stimulus of developments outlined earlier in this
chapter.

II. NATIONAL ORGANIZATIONS

At the Turn of the Century

While Jewish communities were gradually evolving their communal structures, the unique American environment was making

itself felt on national Jewish organizational life as well. By 1900, there already were a considerable number and variety of national Jewish organizations.

The Independent Order of B'nai B'rith, formed in 1843 in New York by a dozen German Jews, by 1900 had 30,000 members in 315 lodges throughout the country and had established district lodges in New York, Cincinnati, Philadelphia, San Francisco, Richmond, Chicago and New Orleans. The Independent Order Free Sons of Israel, founded 1849, had upward of 11,000 members in 103 lodges. Order B'rith Abraham, founded 1859, had nearly 19,000 members in 253 lodges. The Independent Order of Sons of Benjamin had some 14,000 members in 192 lodges. There were perhaps fifteen or twenty other smaller fraternal organizations.

By 1900, the Council of Jewish Women (now National Council of Jewish Women) already had some 5,000 members in 59 sections throughout the United States.

In 1900, there were two organizations of Jewish veterans: the Hebrew Union Veterans Organization, comprising Civil War veterans; and the Hebrew Veterans of War with Spain. These were the forerunners of the post-World War I organization of the Hebrew Veterans of Wars of the Republic, which later became today's Jewish War Veterans of the United States of America.

By 1900, there were several national agencies for the reception and adjustment of Jewish immigrants. Among these were the Baron de Hirsch Fund, founded in 1890 for the purpose of helping immigrants find places in American agriculture and industry. In 1900, the Jewish Agricultural Society was created, with funds from the Baron de Hirsch Fund and the Jewish Colonization Society.

On the religious scene, by 1900, national Jewish organization was well under way. The Union of American Hebrew Congregations, founded in 1873, counted 91 affiliated congregations. The Jewish Chautauqua Society, founded 1893, had 2,000 members. The Hebrew Union College by then was already 25 years old. Some notion of the rate at which new congregations had been established is conveyed by the *American Jewish Year Book* enumeration in its first volume (1900), which reported almost 800 congregations, many in the early stages of formation. The overwhelming majority of them undoubtedly were Orthodox; the newly organized (1898) Union of Orthodox Congregations, at its first biennial convention in 1900, had 96 congregations in the United States and Canada. Conservative Judaism had created the Jewish Theological Seminary in 1886, but it was not until 1913 that the Conservative movement created its own national congregational body, the United Synagogue of America.

By 1900, the foundations of the American Zionist movement had been laid. In the east, the Federation of American Zionists held its first convention in New York in 1898. By 1900, over 50 Zionist societies had been organized. In the west, the Knights of Zion was chartered in 1897. Making its headquarters in Chicago, this was the first interstate Zionist body in America. In 1909, it changed its name to Federated Zionist Societies of the Middle West.

The Zionist movement found virtually no support, at that time, among the influential German-Jewish elements that comprised the B'nai B'rith, and the Reform rabbinate and Reform lay leadership, with rare exceptions, were actively hostile to it. Except for some relatively small Zionist-oriented elements such as Poale Zion (which in 1904 still had only two chapters), Jewish labor likewise was anti-Zionist.

By 1900, there was already a thriving Jewish labor movement. A number of viable unions existed, mostly in various garment trades. Among the most important of them were the United Garment Workers (the Amalgamated Clothing Workers was organized in 1912), the International Ladies Garment Workers Union, the United Cloth Hat and Capmakers Union. The United Hebrew Trades, founded in 1888, exerted substantial influence in building unions of Jewish workers. There was already an influential Yiddish press. The Forward Association, which published the *Jewish Daily Forward,* became the ideological seedbed of Jewish socialism. Jewish labor groups had formed their own fraternal organization, the Workmen's Circle, in 1892; in 1901 it was reorganized as a national order.

Even before 1900, several abortive attempts already had been made to create some sort of representative body of American

Jews as a whole. The Board of Delegates of American Israelites, created at a conference of fourteen communities in 1859, called to consider action in regard to the infamous Mortara forcible conversion case (1857), functioned for two decades. In 1878, it merged with the then young Union of American Hebrew Congregations which, through a Board of Delegates on Civil and Religious Rights, continued the work of the older organization. In 1891, a fresh attempt was made to create a central national body in the form of the Jewish Alliance of America. Dissension between the older and newer groups brought about its early demise.

Overseas Relief Growth Since 1900

Catastrophe befalling Jews abroad has been a recurrent stimulant of Jewish organizational activity in the United States. From the Mortara incident to the present crisis of Israel and the Egyptian expulsion of Jews, each time that Jewish lives and fortunes were jeopardized somewhere in the world, American Jews rose in protest and exerted themselves to provide assistance to the persecuted and distressed. Each time, too, the resultant concerting of concern and effort led to a fresh formation of more inclusive association of American Jews in almost every area of Jewish communal life. None of these produced what their authors contemplated, yet each contributed toward the present picture of Jewish organizational forms and relationships.

The dreadful pogroms in Russia touched off by the Kishinev massacre in 1903 evoked an immediate, spontaneous horrified reaction in American Jewry and a great compassionate outpouring of aid for the suffering victims. In the absence of any central body through which either political representations or philanthropic effort could be organized, a National Committee for the Relief of Sufferers from Russian Massacres was created by a group of Jewish communal leaders.

World War I and its aftermath profoundly affected Jewish organizational activity. By producing problems that were the common concern of Jews as Jews, irrespective of many of the differences that divided them, the war and post-war developments supplied a variety of impulses toward unity.

The relief of distress and suffering among Jews in war-ravished Europe quickly came to be viewed as a common cause of American Jewry and this consensus resulted in one of the earliest consolidations on a national basis of philanthropic efforts for overseas needs. Characteristically, American Jews had responded swiftly to the needs of Jews made dire and urgent by the war; but they had done so as segmented groups. Shortly after the outbreak of war, a conference of Orthodox rabbis and lay leaders in New York City set up the Central Jewish Relief Committee. Somewhat later, another conference, this one of national organizations, called by the American Jewish Committee, formed the American Jewish Relief Committee. Subsequently, under Jewish labor leadership, the People's Relief Committee was formed. The shortcomings of duplicative distributions of funds becoming soon evident, the Central Jewish Relief Committee and the American Jewish Relief Committee, in October, 1914, created the American Jewish Joint Distribution Committee; later, the People's Relief Committee also became a JDC constituent. For some time, the JDC had responsibility only for distribution of funds raised by the three relief committees; only later, did it take over the fundraising function as well.

The Zionist Movement

The impact of World War I and its aftermath upon Zionism was dramatic. The Zionist movement had manifested a constant striving toward unification. In 1909, Zionist youth clubs had merged into Young Judaea; and in 1912, Zionist women's groups had combined in Hadassah. But no single inclusive Zionist organization had emerged in America. Because World War I isolated the world Zionist leadership, which had its headquarters in Germany, American Zionism had to devise an independent executive instrumentality. The immediate impulse was toward consolidation of all Zionist resources and energies. In 1914, a conference of Zionist groups—B'nai Zion, Young Judaea, Hadassah, Keren Kayemet, Mizrachi, Poale Zion, and the Federation of American Zionists (which by then had absorbed the Federated Zionist Societies of the Midwest) created a Provisional Committee for General Zionist Affairs as overall executive, which was acknowledged in 1915 as an official body by the World Zionist leadership in both Berlin and London.

When the United States entered the war in 1917, another national convention of American Zionists, for the purpose of creating a permanent organization, ended in schism, both Poale Zion and Mizrachi withdrawing because of dissatisfaction with the representation that was to be accorded them in the proposed Zionist Organization of America. The ZOA was accordingly launched the following year as an association of all the General Zionist groups, excepting Hadassah, which remained independent.

Almost immediately after the issuance of the Balfour Declaration, a schism developed over ideology, fund-raising methods and various programmatic issues; this resulted in the withdrawal of a faction that insisted upon independence from the World Zionist Organization and that espoused recourse for funds to private initiative and philanthropy rather than mass or public solicitations. The ratification of the British Mandate for Palestine by the United States in 1921 came at a propitious time to bolster the ZOA and help it over the crisis caused by this withdrawal.

The American Jewish Committee

Meanwhile, there was a continuing search for a basis upon which a central representative organization of American Jews could be built. In May, 1906, a small group of Jewish leaders, including some who had been instrumental in creating the National Committee for the Relief of Sufferers from Russian Massacres a few years earlier, met with a small number of other Jewish communal leaders who had come on their invitation, to discuss the possibilities of creating such a representative body. A subsequent conference was held several months later. Agreement on the desirability of a representative organization was general. Discussion revolved chiefly around the question of how the individuals that should comprise the body were to be chosen, whether by some form of popular election, by delegation from organizations, or otherwise. In the end, the following plan won majority assent in the conference: the presiding officer was to appoint a committee of fifteen, which was empowered to coopt additional members of their choice. Thus, in November 1906, was the American Jewish

Committee formed. Virtually all of its originally named and coopted members were drawn from the established German-Jewish elements, as was the membership still at the time, for the most part, of the B'nai B'rith. It was the expectation of the founders that, in emergencies, this small body would be able to mobilize American Jews to take appropriate action.

The American Jewish Congress

When, however, the outbreak of World War 1 presaged an emergency of unprecedented magnitude, the Committee's announced intention to act on behalf of Jews at an eventual peace conference met with strong opposition from important segments of American Jewry, which pointed out that the Committee was a self-appointed, self-perpetuating body that had no mandate from American Jewry. The resulting controversy led to the formation of a broad inclusive instrumentality which, although *ad hoc* in its original form, provided the basis for a permanent American Jewish organization.

The suggestion for a "Congress of American Jewry" had been broached by the leadership of the New York Kehillah in 1915, when events in Europe already were placing American Jewry in a new position of world responsibility. The suggestion found a widespread favorable response, but this was later hedged about with reservations, especially those of the American Jewish Committee and the Jewish labor movement. Some were reluctant to become parts of any organization that would be dominated by Zionists. The Jewish labor groups, moreover, felt themselves ideologically out of sympathy with the "bourgeois" leadership of the major elements involved in the planning for the proposed congress. Their opposition, at the time, was expressed through an *ad hoc* organization, the National Workmen's Committee on Jewish Rights in the Countries at War and in Roumania, which comprised the United Hebrew Trades, the Workmen's Circle, the Jewish Socialist Federation, Social Territorialists, Labor Zionists, Bundists, and Farband-Labor Zionist Order.

The American Jewish Committee, and a number of other national organizations associated with it in this position, insisted that a congress should have a strictly limited scope and not be a general quasi-legislative body or representative assembly; and that it should be temporary, disbanding when the specific purposes for which it was created had been achieved.

The American Jewish Congress was organized, finally, along such lines. As constituted, it was inclusive of a number of national Jewish organizations; it was limited in scope to dealing with problems relating to the war and the terms of the peace as they affected Jews throughout the world; and it was to disband when this mission was accomplishd. After the issuance of the Balfour Declaration, the tasks of obtaining approval of the Declaration and of the designation of Great Britain as Mandatory for Palestine were added to the program of the Congress.

Accordingly, in 1920, after unanimously accepting a report from its delegation to Paris, the Congress voted its own dissolution. But those who, from the outset, had sought the creation of a permanent, representative American Jewish Congress remained in the assembly hall and laid the foundation for today's American Jewish Congress. This came formally into being in 1922. It included then only Zionist groups, others being embraced after a reorganization in 1928.

National Jewish Welfare Board

War-time needs also produced a wholly new American Jewish instrumentality which became the nucleus of a national merger of many Jewish recreational and social agencies. The Jewish Welfare Board was created to serve Jewish members of the United States armed services. Following the war, it extended its services to veterans and to other Jewish young people.

Meanwhile, YMHA's, YWHA's, Centers, settlements, and similar institutions had grown apace. The National Council of Young Men's Hebrew and Kindred Associations, founded in New York in 1913, included 70 member organizations. It later (1921) merged with the Jewish Welfare Board, which thus became the national association of Jewish centers in the United States.

Toward Deeper Sense of Common Cause

The war was a turning point in the history of American Jewish life. It cut off the flow of immigration from Europe, which had included an average of nearly 100,000 Jews annually during the seven pre-war years. And after the war, before the flow could be resumed, a new immigration statute erected a dam against it through which very few could enter. With the major source of new and different elements thus virtually cut off, American Jewry developed more rapidly toward homogeneity.

Gradually, social distances narrowed. Many of the eastern European immigrants rose to positions of wealth and prestige in business and the professions. They began to compete for leadership in communal and other affairs with those who traced their origins to the earlier German-Jewish immigrations. The children of many eastern Jews were already men and women of affairs; they were just as "American" as others who traced their ancestry to earlier arrivals in this land. Within the frame of reference of American concepts of equalitarianism, attempts to maintain distinctions of social status, based on birth or origin, became in any case untenable.

There was a new conception gaining currency, too, of the nature and composition of the American society as a whole. The "melting pot" in which newcomers were to lose their identities and merge into a sort of alloy that could be cast into a standard "American" mold no longer seemed a workable concept. What actually appeared to be happening was the simultaneous persistence of many cultural patterns, modified by the conditions of American life, combining and interacting to make not a uniform but a *plural* American culture. In the course of time, this observation of cultural pluralism became transmuted into a principle. Even by the 1920s, this was evident in the changing emphasis in the programs of social settlement houses and other similar agencies offering educational, cultural and recreational services. These were turning from "Americanization" of immigrants to a much more open acceptance and appreciation of the varied cultures represented in the groups from which their clientele was drawn. In Jewish centers and Y's a corresponding tendency could be observed.

But the concept of pluralism had a much deeper and more extensive influence upon Jewish organizational life. This principle of friendly co-existence and mutual acceptance of difference—even its nurturing—within embracing bonds of common interest and concern, which was proving its viability in the general American society, plainly was not less relevant to the structuring of Jewish organizational relationships in the light of common Jewish causes. Applied to Jewish life, the principle of pluralism meant cooperation on an equal-status basis of Jews and Jewish groups of every social, economic, cultural and ideological stripe for common purposes of major import overbalancing the divisive effects of differences. There have been many such common causes. Since World War I, they have for the most part centered upon philanthropy, both for domestic needs and for the needs of Jews abroad; growing support for the building of a Jewish homeland; and defense against anti-Semitism, and the fostering of conditions conducive to Jewish security and dynamic Jewish living.

The "leveling" tendencies within American Jewish life, the concept of pluralism, and the inexorable pressure of common problems combined to produce a strong force for unity. Under the pragmatic pressure of exigent circumstances, organizations and agencies that had been sharply divided—as it must have seemed to their founders in earlier periods, irreconcilably divided by unbridgeable gulfs of ideological or other difference—found themselves uniting in pursuit of common causes.

United Philanthropy

In the field of philanthropy, the most dramatic of such unions was that represented by the United Jewish Appeal. This was organized in 1939 to consolidate the fund appeals of the American Jewish Joint Distribution Committee, the United Palestine Appeal and the National Refugee Service. The first of these has already been discussed. The United Palestine Appeal had been organized in 1927 to represent Keren Hayesod and Keren Kayemeth. The National Refugee Service, organized by a number of national bodies concerned with immigration, to assist in the settlement of Jewish refugees from Hitlerism, combined later with the Department for the Foreign Born of the National Council of Jewish Women to form United Service for New Americans; and in 1954, this agency was united with the long-established Hebrew Sheltering and Immigrant Aid Society (HIAS) to form United-HIAS Service.

Closing Zionist Ranks

In the Zionist movement, the forces working for unity likewise proved increasingly strong, aided by the progressive diminution of ideological or "political" controversy over the creation of a Jewish homeland. Such controversy tended to lose cogency in the face of continuing persecutions of Jews in European countries. Non-Zionists joined actively after the middle 1920's in aiding Palestine's settlement. Britain's vacillation in its administration of the Mandate aroused universal concern and consternation among American Jews and drew them into closer concordance. The British White Paper of 1939, restricting Jewish immigration to Palestine and Jewish land-purchase there, drove American Zionists to larger exertions in behalf of establishment of a Jewish homeland. An Emergency Committee for Zionist Affairs was formed in that year and in 1942, at an Extraordinary Zionist Conference held in New York, the historic Biltmore Platform was formulated. The Emergency Committee became the American Zionist Council. It waged an unrelenting fight against the White Paper and appealed for unrestricted Jewish immigration to Palestine and the prompt establishment of a Jewish state. Hitlerism, the decimation of European Jewry, and the tragedy of the surviving remnant wiped out almost every practical division among America's Jews over the question of material support for Palestine. By the mid-forties, only the numerically insignificant adherents of the American Council for Judaism could be counted in opposition.

Cooperation in Defense

American Jews found common cause, too, in the fight against anti-Semitism. This took on an increased urgency in the post-World War I period, when native anti-Semitism became virulent. The Ku Klux Klan was revived and showed alarming growth. Simultaneously, Henry Ford launched his notorious campaign against the Jews, based on the discredited *Protocols of the Elders of Zion.* Several anonymous books were published, in which it was charged that Jews were the cause of world unrest, including the Bolshevik revolution in Russia. Prejudice was translated into open discrimination. American Jews were severely jarred.

Many Jewish organizations had long regarded the combating of anti-Semitism as among their functions. The Board of Delegates of American Israelites had been formed in part for this purpose and, around 1900, various Orthodox and other denominational bodies with similar aims were created. Organization of the American Jewish Committee in 1906 and the American Jewish Congress in 1916 have previously been dealt with. In 1913, the B'nai B'rith established the Anti-Defamation League to deal exclusively with this problem. From the twenties on, the ADL, the American Jewish Committee, the American Jewish Congress, and the Jewish War Veterans of the U. S. worked in their several ways to thwart and counter the tide of prejudice.

It was in the thirties, however, after the rise of Hitler and the extension of the Nazi anti-Semitic propaganda campaign to this country, that anti-Semitism grew to such proportions as to raise fears that a really dangerous coalition of pro-fascist groups might achieve political power.

The defense organizations were stimulated to increased efforts. They launched strenuous campaigns of defense, initiating processes that were to grow, with time and events, into a major Jewish contribution toward the drive for practical realization of America's constitutional principles of equality of opportunity without regard to religion or race or national origin.

In 1933, the Jewish Labor Committee united many Jewish labor elements in a new national organization, one of whose primary aims was the combating of anti-Jewish discrimination. The Jewish Labor Committee united for common purpose many diverse groups in the Jewish labor movement: the Workmen's Circle, the Jewish Daily Forward Association, the Jewish Socialist Farband, the Achdut Avodah (Left Poale Zion), the United Hebrew Trades, the International Ladies Garment Workers Union, the Amalgamated Clothing Workers of America, the United Hatters, Cap and Millinery Workers International Union, as well as unions of painters, furriers and workers in provision and food industries. The varied ideological and political views represented among the leaders and constituencies of these organizations have not been permitted to interfere with unity of effort for the common purposes that over-arch the differences.

Under pressure from the leadership of major Jewish communities, various tentative efforts were made toward coordination of the work of the national Jewish community relations agencies, as they later came to be called. A Consultative Council in the middle thirties was short-lived. The American Jewish Congress and the Jewish Labor Committee, however, cooperated effectively for several years in a Joint Boycott Council, directed to the boycotting of German goods. In 1938, four national defense agencies —American Jewish Committee, American Jewish Congress, Jewish Labor Committee and Anti-Defamation League of B'nai B'rith—in response to continuing community pressure, joined in the General Jewish Council. When the American Jewish Committee and the Anti-Defamation League combined their fundraising activities in the Joint Defense Appeal in 1941, the American Jewish Congress promptly withdrew.

National Community Relations Advisory Council

As the result of growing community pressures, culminating in action by the general assembly of the Council of Jewish Federations and Welfare Funds in 1944, an inclusive advisory council of both national and local agencies was created—the National Community Relations Advisory Council. This was a viable successor instrumentality to the General Jewish Council. By then, a number of Jewish communities had created their own local councils for coping with anti-Semitism and related problems. These councils demanded the right to participate with the national agencies in a process of joint policy-formulation and program-planning for the work in which they were all engaged.

Fourteen local councils met the criteria for membership established by the NCRAC and they, together with the American Jewish Committee, the B'nai B'rith, the American Jewish Congress and the Jewish Labor Committee, constituted its initial constituency. By 1950, the Jewish War Veterans and the Union of American Hebrew Congregations had been added to the membership and the total of local agency constituents had grown to twenty-eight.

"Cooperation in the common cause" became the motto of the NCRAC. It made progress toward cooperation among the participating organizations, but institutional rivalries and frictions among the national organizations continued, and there were unresolved conflicts between national and local agencies also. To the end of developing a relationship that would eliminate more of these features, the Large City Budgeting Conference, an association of the largest communities belonging to the Council of Jewish Federations and Welfare Funds, financed a study, undertaken by Dr. Robert M. MacIver, professor emeritus at Columbia University, with the co-operation of the NCRAC member agencies. Dr. MacIver's report, submitted in 1951, was subjected to intensive analysis and discussion. In 1952, a set of recommendations deriving from this process was drawn up and submitted to a plenary session of the constituent agencies of the NCRAC. At that session, a modified plan for cooperative relationships was adopted by overwhelming majority vote. The American Jewish Committee and the B'nai B'rith, whose representatives had opposed the recommendations, withdrew from the NCRAC. Since then, the membership of the NCRAC has been enlarged by the inclusion of the national congregational bodies of Orthodox and Conservative Judaism—the Union of Orthodox Jewish Congregations of America and the United Synagogue of America—and of additional community councils to a total of 36 in 1956.

American Jewish Conference

As in 1917, so in 1943, as the end of World War II appeared in sight, a movement developed for an inclusive and representative body to speak for American Jews on questions affecting the postwar status of Jews throughout the world and the upbuilding of Palestine. On the initiative of the B'nai B'rith and with the backing of 32 national Jewish organizations, the American Jewish Conference was formed in August 1943. Delegates participating in its first convention included 379 chosen at local and regional electoral conferences and 123 from 64 national bodies. The Conference brought forth, with unanimous approval, a number of demands regarding war criminals, immigration to Palestine and other matters. Over vigorous but numerically minor opposition, it also adopted a resolution urging establishment of a Jewish Commonwealth. The American Jewish Committee voted against this resolution and shortly afterward withdrew from the Conference. Subsequently, the Jewish Labor Committee withdrew in protest against inclusion in the Conference of the Jewish Peoples Fraternal Order and the American Jewish Labor Conference. In 1946, it was suggested that the Conference become a permanent body. There was substantial opposition to this proposal. In 1949, the Conference was finally disbanded.

Conference of Presidents of Major National Jewish Organizations

The most recent organizational move toward cooperation in common causes came in response to the growing threats to Israel's security and indeed to her very existence as a result of Soviet-abetted Arab belligerence. In 1954, an informal Conference of Presidents of Major Jewish Organizations was convened. It has continued as an informal interconsultative body. The formation and the continuance of this Conference reflects the virtual unity of American Jewish support for Israel, which already has been remarked upon. During the latter 1940s, American Jewry made unprecedented exertions in behalf of the Jewish settlement in Palestine. Material assistance reached a peak in 1948; representations to governmental and international bodies, and other forms of moral support were similarly without precedent in scope or in the extent of their backing by American Jewish organizations. The creation of Israel, her recognition by the United States and other powers, her heroic and successful defense against Arab attack, her absorption of hundreds of thousands of Jews driven by oppression and persecution from many parts of the world resulted in a further solidification of support.

Under the auspices of the Conference of Presidents, national conferences were held in 1954, 1955 and 1956 in Washington and New York, and a number of regional emergency conferences in January 1957. Various representations to the United States Government were made in the names of the Presidents during that critical period. In February 1957, the Conference of Presidents comprised the heads of the following seventeen national Jewish organizations: American Zionist Committee for Public Affairs; American Trade Union Council for Labor Israel; National Council of Jewish Women; Jewish War Veterans of the United States; Union of American Hebrew Congregations; Union of Orthodox Jewish Congregations of America; Hadassah, the Women's Zionist Organization of America; American Jewish Congress; Jewish Agency for Palestine; Jewish Labor Committee; B'nai B'rith; Mizrachi Organization of America; American Zionist Council; Zionist Organization of America; United Synagogue of America; Central Committee Labor Zionist Organization of America and the National Community Relations Advisory Council.

CONCLUSION

There never has been a blueprint for organized Jewish life in America, either national or local. On the contrary, the forces that have fashioned Jewish organizational life and determined its course have been many and varied—demographic changes within the Jewish group, economic growth, social shifts, the leveling of differences; external problems and crisis, from the Mortara affair, through the Nazi decimation of European Jewry, to the realization of the State of Israel; growth of desire for "belonging," for group identification; development of the concept of cultural pluralism, of diverse groups working together for common ends, notwithstanding differences; the recurring need for pragmatic solutions of emerging problems affecting the whole of American Jewry; the voluntaryism that both sanctioned diversification and gave impetus to free association and unification in common causes.

Those forces have exerted both centripedal and centrifugal influences—making for diversification when the Jewish population was most heterogeneous, for unification in the common cause as the Jewish community grew more homogeneous. Today, there seems small doubt that the forces making for common cause are in the ascendent, both at the community level and on the national scene. It is more evident in the communities, where the growth of central communal organizations reflects an ever-increasing maturity. With this maturity has come a fuller realization by the communities of their aspirations, and of their desire to play their proper role in the formation of policies and the resolution of issues that confront the Jews of America as a national group. In national Jewish organizational life, with its institutional rivalries and its powerful organizations conducting large and valuable programs, there has been a greater persistency of separatism. But the signposts cannot be ignored or misread. They point unmistakably to the same goal of greater unity in the common cause.

AMOR FATI

ISRAEL'S YOUTH AND ITS FUTURE
RELATION WITH WORLD JEWRY

by Nahum Goldmann

THERE IS ONE aspect of the psychological and intellectual be-havior of the people of Israel which seems to me of crucial im-portance in the evolution of the character of Israel and its future relation with world Jewry. I can deal with it only very briefly in this short essay. I refer to a deep-seated tendency among many Israelis, especially the Sabras, those born and bred in Israel, and specifically Sabra youth, to adopt a posture of indifference and, sometimes, to stimulate ignorance regarding the terrible tragedy of the Nazi period which deprived us of one-third of our people.

This, of course, is not the posture of Israel's acknowledged leaders and spokesmen, nearly all of whom grew up in Europe, were nurtured on its Jewish culture, and lost friends and relatives in the Nazi holocaust. The Nazi period will forever remain a dominating element in the compound of their thought and emotion. But Israel's youth, including the children of its acknowl-edged leaders, shows a very pronounced reluctance to face up to the gruesome facts of our recent past and seems determined to cast them out of its memory.

A characteristic illustration is the attitude of Israel's young toward the Yad Vashem Institution, financed in part by the Gov-ernment of Israel and the Jewish Agency for Palestine, and in part by the Conference for Jewish Material Claims Against Germany. The purpose of this Institution is to collect, preserve from oblivion, survey and analyze all documentation pertaining to the Nazi period, and to transmit this evidence of the greatest tragedy of Jewish history to future generations. The scholars of the Hebrew University in Jerusalem, who direct this undertaking, have complained to me time and again that notwithstanding generous scholarships and grants, Israeli young scholars and post-graduate students just do not respond to invitations to undertake this research. These are young men and women who wish to devote their lives to the study of Jewish history. Yet, they seem completely uninterested in undertaking a study of this most recent period, which is an open, still lacerating scar on the memories of our generation. Only a very strong, albeit subsconscious, desire to escape the horrible truth of this tragedy can explain this surprising and unnatural phenomenon.

This attitude seems to me more than incidental. It has deep intellectual and emotional roots. Theoretically and benevolently, one might argue that a people creating a new State and launching a completely new historical career, radically different from its patterns of life in the past 2,000 years, may be anti-historical, as young people generally are, setting its face to the future, turning its back on the past. This, however, is not true of Israel's youth. On the contrary, one of its most spectacular characteristics is its deep and passionate interest in ancient Jewish history. The most popular pasttime of young Israelis, besides dancing and singing, is archeology. It has become the hobby of thousands of young people. Past generations of Jews were more preoccupied with the Talmud and talmudic literature than with the Bible. To Israel's children, even those wholly devoid of religious sentiment, the Bible has become a subject of profoundest interest and greatest fascination, the expression of a deep urge to sink their roots deep in the soil of the country, to fuse with the contours of its landscape, not only by living in the land and working on its soil, but also by establishing direct contact, as it were, with the most ancient past and the mythos of their ancestors who had inhabited that land. This deep desire to establish their legacy by retracing the past of their people is one of the most stimulating and creative phenomena, an effort to establish an aristocratic basis for their return, and to assert themselves as the successors and heirs to the kings and the prophets. But while seeking passionately and doggedly a direct association with that portion of Jewish history that was performed on Israel's soil, they are patiently leaping across a time-distance of 2,000 years to the periods of the kings, the prophets and the Maccabees, as if the many generations of the Diaspora had been a dismissable interlude, to be forgotten, if it cannot be erased. It is as if they were seeking by this leap from the present to the ancient past to disassociate themselves from the long night of Diaspora humiliation.

Let us again cite the Nazi period as a concrete example. In the passionate discussions, several years ago, about the reparations agreement with Germany, we who favored negotiations with Germany, were moved by a moral obligation to facilitate the re-habilitation of Nazisms' victims. Sabra opponents of the negotiations, however, were moved primarily by their hatred of the Nazis, the root and cause of the tragedy, and not by concern for the fate of its survivors.

This is an understandable tendency. The State of Israel means for them the end of persecution, suffering and degradation. Having become, after 2,000 years, a majority in a country of their own, they have set out with a furious tempo to acquire all the attributes of a "normal" people living in its own country. Israel's political and other policies are often revealing of the passionate desire of the Israelis to demonstrate that they are masters of their own destiny and that no external factor can interfere with their purpose. In fact, Israel is a revolution, not an evolution; it is a leap, not a gradual advance. The Israelis do not wish to be reminded that they had ever been a minority, that they, the masters of today, had been slaves for 2,000 years. And because their enslavement was never more complete, their humiliation never more base than during the Nazi period, it is precisely this period that they seek to banish from their consciousness. Recently, a young Israel scholar with whom I pleaded that he undertake research into the Nazi period, concluded our discussion by saying that he was prepared to undertake a study of 19th century anti-Semitism up to the Nazi period, but not a study of that period itself.

An understanding of the motivations by no means reconciles us to the grave psychological and spiritual implications of this

attitude. If we could be sure that this is a temporary phenomenon, characteristic of this generation alone, we would adjudge it
a healthy effort to obtain psychological compensation for centuries of inferior status. I am afraid, however, that this is not the
case. Nascent intellectual and emotional attitudes of young States
and peoples have a tendency to solidify and to leave a lasting
and indelible impress. What is most important in the life of a
people and a country is its beginnings, its initial course. The
famous saying by Goethe *"Das Gesetz nach dem Du angetreten"*
(the law which you began) is even more applicable to peoples
than to individuals. There is the inherent peril that this escapism,
this subconscious casting aside of 2,000 years of history, this naive
and dangerous delusion that the new Israel can begin where the
old Israel terminated, might become a permanent element of the
psychological and intellectual behavior of the Israel of the
future. Such development would spell intellectual and moral
disaster. Peoples, like individuals, pay a horrible price for attempts at *"Verdraengung,"* at forgetting the traumatic facts of
the past. One of the bases of modern psychology is the contention
that facts concealed in the subconscious must be brought to light
lest they suppurate into frustrations and neuroses, destructive of
the spirit and the soul. The same principle applies even more, to
groups and to peoples. To be creative, a people must base itself
on the full record of its achievements, on its total past. Otherwise
it loses its dignity and historical *raison d'etre,* and by placing
itself out of its historic focus, it distorts its image in world history.
This is true of every people; the greater a people's history, the
truer this is. It is, therefore, doubly true of the Jewish people. Our
Diaspora history alone, a tenure of two thousand years, is longer
than the history of most modern peoples, and its erasure from
memory would distort all Jewish history and reduce it to
absurdity.

Our history started with the Egyptian Diaspora. Some of our
greatest achievements were attained in the Babylonian Diaspora,
which was followed, after an interval, by the third Diaspora that
has lasted for two millennia. The question is not whether the
Diaspora was good or bad. Because historical developments are
not a matter of choice, they are not subject to such judgments.

An Israeli nation, that would strike the Diaspora from its memory and from its day to day life, would exclude itself, to put it extremely, from the history of our people. Such an outcome would, in turn, result in the violation of historical fact, and would ultimately sever Israel from the rest of Jewry, reduce it to a small state in the Near East, encircled by an ocean of Arabs, and transform it, eventually, into a satellite of the Arab world. The element that makes Israel a unique and a great nation is its intimate kinship with the entire Jewish people. It is a little state in geographic terms, but it is great and can become still greater by preserving its links with globally-dispersed Jewry, and contributing, through this channel, to trends and developments throughout the world. Its geographical limits may be what they are, but its spiritual limits can be the globe itself. An Israeli people severed from two thousand years of creative achievement in the Diaspora would deprive itself of the benefits of these values and would create something quite apart from our tradition, something that might not fit at all into the pattern of Jewish civilization.

There are no leaps in history. A people's present is a result of its entire past. A people is creative only if it continues its past by synthesizing the thousand trends and tendencies of all periods of its history into the pattern of its future. To leap from the present directly to the Maccabees and Prophets is a foredoomed undertaking. That is where the danger lies in the escape from Diaspora history.

This dangerous tendency is only in its incipient stage. Israel's life has not yet crystallized, it is still a search, an experiment, without irrevocable commitments. That is why it is so essential to take cognizance of these dangerous tendencies before they assert themselves fully. The Israelis' pride in their liberation from the Diaspora is healthy and justified. It is the realization of the essence of Zionism. Yet, moral noblesse commands Israel not to forget the agony of the past, and the instinct of spiritual self-preservation commands it to comport itself not only as the spiritual progeny of the Prophets and the political heir of the Maccabees and the great kings of Judaea, but, also as the successor to the martyrs and heroes of the *Galut*, of the Mishnah and the Talmud, of Maimonides and Yehuda Halevy, Spinoza and Einstein, Bialik and Mendele Mocher Sefarim. Only by absorbing the totality of our history, both its achievements and its humiliations, its glories and frustrations, will Israel be able to lay the foundations for a new future in accord with the greatness and uniqueness of our people's history.

Israel has to learn what Nietsche once called *"Amor fati"* (love of one's destiny). One of the fundamental prerogatives of individuals and peoples is the right and capacity to chart their own course. One of the cardinal principles of Jewish tradition, primarily its religious aspects, is that man must accept with gladness whatever destiny has been determined for him, yet exercise his choice as a co-architect of its design. Israel must not repudiate this principle. We have survived as a people because we have accepted alike, the tragedies and the triumphs of our history, and have worked with the materials of our destiny to create our unique character. Israel must advance into its future with an *amor fati* attitude regarding its past. Only then will it be able to shape a historic frame of reference that will be accepted and shared by future generations of the entire Jewish people.

ZIONISM'S IMPACT

ON JEWISH LIFE

---

by Samuel Margoshes

THE IMPACT OF Zionism on Jewish life of the past half century is, to me, not a historical process viewed dispassionately and from a distance. I have lived through it and in it. I have witnessed most of it. In some of it, I have personally participated. And I have publicly commented on part of it as a working newspaperman, as editor and as columnist.

Zionism has wrought a profound and thoroughgoing revolution in Jewish life. When we compare the Jewish world of today with that of fifty-sixty years ago we are confronted with vast changes in every area and on every level. Of course, these changes have been due to many factors, including events of world historic importance. During this momentous period no less than four million Jews migrated from east Europe to the American continents. The transfer of the Jewish center from the Old World to the New World was tragically completed by the Nazi mass murder of six million European Jews. In the meantime, in Palestine, the work of building up the Jewish Homeland was proceeding at an ever-accelerating pace.

The spiritual core of this revolution, the source that gave it its meaning and its dynamism, was the worldwide Zionist Movement. Zionism has always had a double energy and a double purpose, directed equally toward Israel and toward the Diaspora. By the very act of focusing Jewish effort and Jewish aspiration on Palestine, it gave the Diaspora communities a sense of their unity and a sense of their power that they had not had for centuries.

I

The extent of the impact of Zionism on Jewish thinking can be gauged by the depth of penetration of three ideas that form the nucleus of Zionist ideology.

The first of these is the unity of the Jewish people. This idea now seems so axiomatic that it is hard to remember that it had to be fought for and worked for, and that it is an idea that still has powerful opponents in the Jewish as well as in the non-Jewish world.

When Herzl launched the struggle with his cry, *"Wir sind ein Volk—EIN Volk,"* he was defamed and attacked by the powerful assimilationist forces that then led Jewry. Many outstanding scholars and community leaders joined with the *Protestrabbiner* in denying their Jewish nationality and insisting that they were Germans, Frenchmen or Englishmen of Mosaic persuasion. This isolationist and apologetic point of view is still vigorously defended by the American Council for Judaism and has many gentile adherents, including such strange bedfellows as former Assistant Secretary of State Henry Byroade and the authors of the most recent edition of the Soviet Encyclopedia.

But the isolationists have been isolated, and today they are fighting a rearguard battle—and losing. The Zionist idea of the unity of the Jewish people has conquered the Jewish world. There is hardly a segment of Jewish society that has not adopted it or that does not act on it, even if, as is the case with the American Jewish Committee, it does not always find it feasible publicly to profess the doctrine.

The second basic idea of Zionism is the responsibility of each local Jewry for all Jewries. This idea, a natural consequence of Jewish unity, is, of course, as old as the dispersion. In imperial Rome and in medieval Europe, all Jewish communities contributed to the ransoming of captives. The modern form of Jewish brotherly aid, transcending national frontiers, was embodied in the Alliance Israélite Universelle, founded in 1860, thirty-seven years before the rise of Zionism. However, it was the Zionists who converted brotherly aid into a cooperative mass movement involving the whole Jewish people rather than charitable work on their behalf by a handful of rich and influential notables.

For centuries, Jewish philanthropy had been in the hands of "the barons." The Zionists put it into the hands of the people. It was the American Zionists, who, through the People's Relief Committee and the Central Relief Committee, sparked the drive that made Jewish overseas relief a houshold word in the United States, and transformed the Joint Distribution Committee into an authentic Jewish mass movement. And it is the Zionists who have supplied the Joint Distribution Committee with the inspiration, the vision and the leadership that have given the "Joint" its continued hold on the popular imagination. The United Jewish Appeal is another, and even more dramatic, example of the Zionist ability to transform Jewish philanthropy into Jewish brotherly aid on a global scale, exemplifying world Jewish responsibility.

The third idea, the key concept of Zionism, a Jewish national concentration in Eretz Israel—has achieved a phenomenal acceptance among all sections of Jewry. Originally, this idea was met by an almost solid wall of official indifference, skepticism and even outright hostility. Only the enthusiasm and the sacrifices of the masses of the people kept the idea alive. The Balfour Declaration, the first visible sign of practical Zionist success, marked the initial breakthrough of the Chinese Wall of indifference. As it was evidenced by the formation of the Jewish Agency in Palestine, this advance brought many sections of the Jewish community closer to Zionism. But since then, the acceptance of the idea of the Jewish State has been almost complete. In 1943, at the memorable first session of the American Jewish Conference, practically every significant Jewish national organization in the United States, supported the call for the establishment, after World War II, of a Jewish commonwealth in Palestine. When the Zionist leaders spoke before the historic session of the United Nations dealing with the partition of Palestine and the setting up of a Jewish State, they spoke not for the Zionists only, but for all American Jewry.

These three ideas, now almost universally accepted among

Jews in America and elsewhere, have gone far to change the face of the Jewish communities and the nature of Jewish conscious-ness. They have forged world Jewry into a strong, self-conscious ethno-cultural group, intensely aware of its distinct culture and fully alive to its national responsibility. It is true that Jewish self-consciousness and Jewish nationalism are concepts older by several millennia than modern Zionism. But that these ideas have not only survived the Jewish revolution of the past half century and the transplanting from Europe to America, but have also been given new life and added strength, is the crowning achievement of the Zionist movement.

The practical and ideological effects of the historic Zionist achievement are visible in every social institution and every political movement of Jewish life. Today, when practically all of American Jewry is involved in extending economic aid to the State of Israel, we are prone to forget that, for a number of decades, it was the Zionists, almost unaided, who pioneered in that activity. Thus, the Jewish National Fund, the Keren Hayesod and, later the United Palestine Appeal, were originated as the financial instruments of the Zionist Movement, and were supported almost exclusively by Zionists.

Even now, all talk and propaganda to the contrary notwith-standing, the Zionists continue to constitute the backbone of all pro-Israel fund-raising efforts in this country and elsewhere throughout the world. The shock troops of the Jewish Homeland, ever faithful and ever reliable, are the Zionists everywhere, and it is they who have given impetus to the movement of world Jewry, now gathering momentum for the upbuilding of the Jewish State on firm and secure foundations.

The influence of the Zionist revolution has been most pervasive, perhaps, in the field of culture. Herzl proclaimed that the return to Judaism had to precede the return to the Jewish Homeland. In Zionism, a whole Jewish generation found the way back to Judaism and, in that generation, Judaism experienced a recrudes-cence and a flowering that made the period one of the golden ages.

The revival of Hebrew as a living language is almost wholly attributable to the Zionist Movement, which stressed the need for

Hebrew study and the rebirth of Hebrew literature. It was this intoxicating idea that created the cultural ferment that produced such major figures as Lillienblum and Smolenskin, and later Bialik, Tchernikhowsky and Agnon. In a way, modern Hebrew literature, following the Haskalah may be regarded, from the beginning to the end, as a Zionist product.

The renaissance of Yiddish, though not as exclusively attributable to Zionism, undoubtedly owes much to the Zionist stimulus. It has been responsible for the quickening of national and artistic feeling among the great writers of that literature from Frug and Morris Rosenfeld to Yehoash and Leivick and the Yiddish writers of today on both sides of the Atlantic.

Zionism and Yiddish have always lived side by side in a deeply symbiotic and mutually health-giving relationship. Zionism has served Yiddish, and it has also been served by it. The fact is that Yiddish has been the most popular vehicle of Zionist ideas. The Yiddish press has been the greatest Zionist propaganda medium. There was a time, not so long ago, when a Zionist meeting in America had the electric, but heart-warming atmosphere of a Yiddish-speaking society.

The Zionist impact on culture reached into the visual arts with equal vitality and freshness. The Zionist German publication *Ost und West* was, for years, the home of Zionist painters and sculptors as well as Jewish novelists, poets and short story writers. A school of Jewish illustrators and painters was born that found its inspiration in Jewish themes. Lilien, Oppenheim, Gottlieb, Hirschenberg, Glitzenstein, Wachtel, Pilichowski—they all received their first encouragement from the Zionist Movement. And it was these artists who prepared the way for Chagall and Soutine, who represented the entry of the Jewish people into world art, and who had a decisive influence on the twentieth-century school of Paris. For centuries, it had been considered that the Jewish genius was impoverished in this sphere, but the exhilirating touch of Zionism made it shine brilliantly and beautifully.

Originally an intellectual and spiritual movement, Zionism, with its tremendous *élan*, soon spilled over the confining walls of the academy into the midst of daily living, transforming Jewish home life and social life from end to end. It has permeated every modern form of Judaism, acting everywhere as a universal leaven: reforming, recasting, recreating. No organization or institution has withstood its omnipresent force. In fifty-sixty years it has changed everything—the home, the school, the synagogue, the community.

It was Zionism which opened a window to modern life in many a Jewish home. In the Old Country and in many an immigrant home in the New World, Zionism represented the modern outlook on life in general and on Jewish life in particular. Often it brought not peace but a sword, setting brother against brother and father against son, dividing many a family between traditionalists and Zionists, or between Labor Zionists and Mizrachi and Revisionists. But always, in effect, these divisions served to fortify the whole family's sense of Jewishness, its unity in a common heritage.

Zionism did much for the Judaization of the Jewish home on still another level. By reminding Jews of their heritage it brought many of them back to the beliefs and rites of their fathers. Zionism re-introduced to many homes the practice of Jewish ceremony and ritual: the lighting of the candles on the eve of the Sabbath and festivals, the observance of the Seder, the celebration of holidays, and the keeping of fasts. Zionist influence was felt most deeply in the home, and it was the Jewish home that became the dominating force within Zionism, the ultimate moulder of all its agencies and the shaper of all its policies.

Zionism quickly effected a radical change in the Jewish school in Europe. It did not immediately replace the thousand-year-old *heder,* but it set up next to it the *heder mesukon,* the reformed school. In this school, Hebrew was taught as a living tongue: modern teaching methods were employed; and the pupils and teachers shared a passionate interest in the Jewish community in Palestine.

Zionism had an even stronger influence on Jewish education in the United States. In many schools, the very spirit is Zionist, the teachers are Zionists, and the curriculum stresses Zionist ideas and Zionist values. In all types of schools, the celebration of national Jewish holidays, the growing role of Hebrew, and the new approach to the child, bear eloquent testimony to the influence of Zionist ideology upon the Jewish school.

The synagogue, of course, was dedicated to the love of Zion long before modern Zionism: one might go so far as to call it the original Zionist organization. But it is a matter of record that the synagogue, in large part, either opposed Zionism or was indifferent to it. For the synagogue in the Old World, practical Zionist work meant merely *halukah,* supporting aged and indigent scholars in Palestine. But the growth of the Zionist movement has touched the synagogues and brought them new life and new vision. It has had an especially transforming effect on Reform Judaism, where it has combated assimilationism and restored a sense of the central values of traditional religion and custom. It is a far cry from the 1885 Pittsburgh conference of the leaders of the American reform movement and its substitution of Washington for Jerusalem, as the spiritual center of American Jewry, to the Central Conference of American Rabbis with its pro-Zionist declarations. And the Zionist victory in the Orthodox and Conservative synagogues is equally impressive. The Zionization of the synagogue has become so complete that today the synagogue is, as it should be, probably the major center for the dissemination and interpretation of Zionist ideology and for the promotion of Zionist activity.

The influence of Zionism on American Jewish community organization, though less decisive, has been great. Everywhere and at all times, this influence has worked for greater and more efficient democracy. From the very first, Herzl called on the Zionists to go out and conquer the existing Jewish communities, and his method was to democratize them, to take them out of the hands of the assimilationist oligarchs and plutocrats. The rapid penetration of Zionist ideology created a new climate among the Jewish organization of western as well as eastern Europe. Thus, the Kultusgemeinde in Vienna, Berlin and Munich, long the citadels of assimilationism, were gradually compelled to yield to Zionist pressure. Similarly, the Consistoire in France and the Board of British Jews in England slowly but surely turned to Zionism. In east Europe, the 1905 Helsingfors Conference was a signal for a Zionist demand for cultural autonomy in all of eastern Europe and it was the beginning of the so-called *Gegenwarts Arbeit,* which in a difficult time for the Zionist cause, following the death of Herzl, concentrated on the task of modernizing and democratizing Jewish community life in the Diaspora.

In the United States, the drive for democracy in Jewish communal life started with, and was led by, the Zionists. It culminated, at the time of the first World War, in the creation of the American Jewish Congress, which, led by Brandeis, Wise and Lipsky, became a real force in the community. The New York Kehillah, brilliantly led by Dr. Judah L. Magnes, and, for a time, the best hope of Jewish democracy on this continent, was largely a Zionist creation. Finally, the American Jewish Conference, hoping to succeed where the Kehillah and the American Jewish Congress had not fully succeeded, gave buoyancy to the faith in American Jewry's ability to organize its communal life along democratic lines.

No one has yet succeeded in organizing American Jewish communal life into one over-all democratic setup, but the Zionists have labored mightily in the cause, and their efforts have laid the foundation for a richer and more constructive and more cooperative Jewish life. The Zionists have prepared the way for the Jewish Community Councils which have arisen in scores of Jewish communities throughout the length and breadth of the nation, and which seem to constitute that form of Jewish community organization which is most suitable to American conditions.

This, then, is a bare outline of the Jewish revolution which Zionism has accomplished in the Diaspora. That this revolution will grow in size and scope and depth is as certain as anything can be in our uncertain world. The establishment of the State of Israel is not the sort of event that one can note and forget. It is one of those epoch-making phenomena in history that exert a continuing influence on the destiny of mankind. The State of Israel and the Diaspora are linked by an unbreakable bond. Neither time nor space can sever the twain, now that they have met again. Eretz Israel will more than ever shed its radiance on the Diaspora, while the Diaspora, more than ever, will continue to support and reinforce the Jewish Homeland.

The revolution which Zionism has set in motion will set off chain reactions through centuries to come. We have only seen the beginning; the rest is in the hands of the God of Israel.

II

It is hardly necessary to say that Zionism made its tremendous impact on Jewish life through the labors of a host of zealous missionaries, led by inspired and dedicated personalities, who made their dynamic impact upon Zionism. Every country in the world has contributed its share of Zionist fighters as well as generals. Certainly, the United States has given the Zionist Movement some of its most eminent figures. Israel Goldstein, to whom this volume is dedicated, is one of these.

As not only a close observer of, but, also, as an active participant in the Zionist Movement, I have had an unusual opportunity to follow the career of this conscientious, capable and highly articulate thinker and doer. Following the course of his career in Zionism is an excellent way to illustrate the workings of Zionism's impact, because Goldstein gave himself to the Zionist Movement unreservedly, placing at its disposal all his considerable abilities and his high prestige in the American Jewish community.

Goldstein's role in Zionism began in 1921, only three years after the Jewish Theological Seminary awarded him the degree of rabbi and he was elected spiritual head of Congregation B'nai Jeshurun, the second oldest in New York City. In that year, he helped to launch the first national Keren Hayesod campaign. His association with these campaigns lasted for several years, and gave him national prominence that brought him into intimate contact with the leaders of American Zionism, including Wise, Lipsky, Rothenberg and others. As president of Young Judaea, from 1927 to 1931, he helped to prepare a number of the members of the younger generation for their later responsibilities and leadership in the Zionist Movement. For several years, at this time, he served as a member of the Administrative Committee of the Zionist Organization of America. The shaping of the Zionist Movement in those early days owes much to Goldstein's steady and methodical, yet imaginative work.

In 1933, he became president of the Jewish National Fund of America, a position he held for ten years. It is a matter of record that these ten years constituted one of the most successful and progressive periods in JNF history. The financial success of his administration is clearly indicated by the fact that the annual income of the JNF rose from $144,000 the year before Goldstein took office, to $9,000,000 during his last year as president. These figures are singularly eloquent because they speak of matters much more vital than money and are illustrative of the contribution of Zionism to the building of the Jewish Homeland. With this money, and at this time, the JNF bought land in Palestine that subsequently became the territorial foundation of the Jewish State. Without the land there would have been no Jewish State, or, at best, its area would have been tragically insignificant.

Not only did Goldstein raise the intake of the JNF at a crucially important time, he also restored the JNF to its proper place as the prime instrument of Zionist fund-raising activity. For some years, the Zionist leadership had accorded this position to the Keren Hayesod and had tended to underestimate the Jewish National Fund. In order to promote the JNF to parity with the Keren Hayesod, Goldstein carried through an internal structural reorganization of the JNF that revitalized it on all levels. Typical of the new regime, was the appointment of Mendel N. Fisher, a young and dynamic worker, as executive secretary.

Previously, the main source of income of the JNF had been the blue-white boxes. The use of these was, of course, continued, but they were supplemented on a vast scale by new and exciting projects. Most spectacular of these were the *Nachlah* projects in which individual donor and organizations undertook commitments of $25,000 and over, for the acquisition of tracts of land in Palestine, to bear their names. The B'nai B'rith which, it should be remembered, was a non-Zionist organization, subscribed $100,000 for a *Nachlah*. Contributions on a similar scale from individuals also were welcomed; among these was the outstanding subscription of $65,000 by Maurice Levin, the head of a New York City department store.

In 1935, the JNF launched a campaign for gifts and for loans secured by bonds, to finance the draining of the Huleh swamps in northern Palestine. It was the first bond issue of its kind. This campaign was highly successful and contributed in no small measure to the subsequent reclamation of the swamp area, a project that added considerably to the habitable area of the land, thus facilitating the absorption of the later mass influx of returning exiles.

Dr. Goldstein's success as organizer and fund-raiser in chief for Zionist instrumentalities, inaugurated a new era in this activity of the Jewish community of America, with the Jewish Homeland as the chief beneficiary. This practice may be said to have had most far-reaching effects both on the Jewish Homeland and the American Jewish community.

However, he was destined for still larger roles. His achievements had escaped neither notice nor recognition. In 1935, he attended the first World Zionist Congress at Luzerne, Switzerland, as a delegate of the Zionist Organization of America; this honor has been conferred upon him ever since then. He was also elected a vice-president of the Organization in 1936. In 1943, Goldstein was unanimously elected president of the Zionist Organization of America. In the following year, he was elected President of the Synagogue Council of America, a comprehensive organization representing both the clergy and the laity of the Orthodox, Conservative and Reform wings of American Judaism. As president of these two important organizations during the historic war period, Goldstein was in a position to bring the influence of Zionism to bear on the whole Jewish community. The movement for the unity of the Jewish community of America, as a lever for the creation of the Jewish State, dates back to that period.

Inasmuch as America was the leading power among the allies, and as American Jewry was the largest in the world, it was felt that the time had come for bold action to bring about the creation of the Jewish State and that American Jewry was called upon to play a leading role in the fulfillment of the age-old Zionist dream. This idea was officially promulgated at the now-famous Biltmore Conference, under the leadership of Stephen S. Wise, and it was enthusiastically received by almost all sections of Jewish public opinion in America, including non-Zionist and even previously anti-Zionist circles.

Moreover, it was felt that in order to give formal and official expression to this all-Jewish support for the new Zionist program, a new organization, representative of all facets of the community, was needed. This conviction led to the establishment of the American Jewish Conference, composed of organizational representatives and of democratically-elected delegates of local communities. Israel Goldstein was elected from New York with a vote second only to that of the popular idol, Rabbi Stephen S. Wise.

Despite this new organizational development, the major role in mobilizing American Jewish sentiment and support for the Jewish State was played, as before, by the Zionist Organization of America. Largely as the result of this activity, during Goldstein's two-year term as president, the ZOA experienced its largest membership growth up to that time, from 68,000 in 1943 to 138,000 in 1945. And while it was doubling its membership, it was more than doubling its income. The newly-established Zionist-Expansion Fund raised over $300,000 in its first year. At the same time, Israel Goldstein poured his energies and abilities into the all-important political struggle for the realization of Zionist goals. In 1944, he appeared before the House Foreign Affairs Committee of the United States Congress in the course of hearings on a resolution, which was eventually adopted, favoring the establishment of a Jewish State—a new milestone on the road to Jewish statehood.

The rush of history brought with it no little confusion, and clear-headed leadership was more necessary than ever before. At the crucial World Zionist Congress held in Basle in 1946, Goldstein sided with Rabbi Abba Hillel Silver, and other leaders, against the policies of Chaim Weizmann, and insisted on the adoption of a new course aimed at the immediate creation of a Jewish State, and it was this view that carried the day. "In retrospect," says Goldstein, "I have often thought that the policy which brought about the failure of Dr. Weizmann to be reelected president of the World Zionist Organization in 1946, resulted in his becoming president of Medinat Israel in 1948."

Meanwhile, much had to be done to strengthen the Zionist structure. An important step in this direction was taken at the Basle Congress when, acting on instructions from their home organizations, the General Zionist delegates established the World Confederation of General Zionists of which Goldstein was unanimously elected president. This honor was a logical consequence of his long-term labors for the creation of a central agency for General Zionism. As president of the ZOA, he had urged the founding of a General Zionist Party to counterbalance the partisanship and extremism of the parties on both the right and the left. The workers and farmers in Israel were under continual propaganda barrage from both sides, as well as the more persuasive seductions of promises of financial and organizational support, if only they would abandon the moderate center.

The World Confederation of General Zionists gave those at the center—traditionally a large majority of Jews—a spiritual home. It was a loose federation, without a rigid discipline or a fully-elaborated rationale. The Confederation included among its member organizations such important bodies as the ZOA and Hadassah in the United States, and other General Zionist groups all over the world, including Israel.

At the last World Zionist Congress, held in Jerusalem in 1956, the World Confederation of General Zionists was the largest single Zionist party. The organization has invested over four million dollars in Israel, in both agricultural and industrial enterprises, in both the private as well as the cooperative sectors of the economy. At present, one of the major stumbling blocks to its continued growth and influence is the split, in General Zionist ranks in Israel, between the General Zionist Party and the Progressive Party.

It was poetic justice that Goldstein should be privileged to stand at the cradle of the Jewish State. He participated in the meeting of Zionist leaders convened in Paris in 1946 by Ben Gurion, as chairman of the Zionist Executive, on the day when the British arrested the Zionist leadership en masse in Palestine. The question of the partition of Palestine was discussed and the establishment of a Jewish State in a divided Palestine was approved by the Zionist leadership. Nahum Goldmann was charged with the vital mission of sounding out top-level governmental opinion in Washington. He was successful in securing the cooperation of important non-Zionist leaders, notably Judge Joseph

M. Proskauer, the head of the American Jewish Committee. With the virtually unanimous backing of American Jewry, and on the strength of the Congressional resolution in favor of Jewish statehood, Goldmann, aided by David Niles, won the assent of President Truman. With the commitment of the United States government, the stage was set for the United Nations Partition Resolution of November 29, 1947.

These and other signs of concrete progress toward the realization of the Zionist aim so electrified the Jews of America that, during 1947 and 1948, the United Palestine Appeal, of which Goldstein was chairman, and the United Jewish Appeal, of which he was vice-chairman, succeeded in raising together the unprecedented sum of $150,000,000, an amount not equalled since. Every bit of this money, and more, was desperately needed to meet the savage onslaught with which the Arab nations greeted the establishment of Israel.

Goldstein's career as financial wizard continued. When the governmental apparatus of Israel was organized in 1948, Eliezer Kaplan, who had been the treasurer of the Jewish Agency for many years, was pressed into service as the Finance Minister of the new State. Recognizing that the position required a man of rich experience and far-ranging abilities, the World Zionist Actions Committee elected Goldstein to succeed Kaplan. It was an anxious and difficult year. Upwards of 220,000 immigrants flooded into Israel, mostly from east European and Arab countries, almost all of them poor and many of them destitute. They had to be absorbed by the young state. It was just after the Arab war, and the turbulent beginning of the long, uneasy armistice. The obvious solution of halting or limiting immigration was one measure that was never entertained—not even for a moment. The very heart of the new State was the Law of Return.

It was upon the Jewish Agency that a major share of the responsibility of caring for these immigrants evolved. The budget of the Agency, a woefully inadequate $100,000,000 for the year, had to cover not only the absorption of the vast numbers of immigrants, but also the regular expenditures for education, youth work, and the promotion of the agricultural settlements. The treasurer's duties including also the conclusion of purchase contracts, currency exchanges, bank loans and, last but far from least, stimulating fund-raising throughout the Jewish world. In connection with his duties as treasurer, which involved responsibilities for the national housing program, Goldstein also became the first president of Amidar, the Israel national housing company, which constructed and imported many thousands of dwellings for the new arrivals.

All this time, Israel Goldstein maintained an abiding interest in the Diaspora and its problems, as part of his program as a Zionist for the survival of the Jewish people. During war and its aftermath, he was active in various efforts to help the survivors of the Nazi concentration camps and gas chambers. He served with the emergency rescue committee organized by Dr. Wise to see what could be done by way of rescuing some of the Jews within German-occupied Europe, through the bribing of Nazi officers and like measures. Although the results were tragically limited, yet some Jews were saved who otherwise would have been killed.

Two months after the liberation of Germany, Goldstein was the first representative of American Jewry to arrive on the scene with a message of solidarity and help for the surviving remnant of European Jewry. He was well received by the officers of the American Army of Occupation and was instrumental in improving the conditions in the DP camps.

On his return to the United States, after his year as treasurer of the Agency, Goldstein became chairman of the Western Hemisphere Executive of the World Jewish Congress, an office which he continues to occupy. In 1951, he was elected president of the American Jewish Congress. In that capacity, he led the battle for a unified Jewish community in America and to this end helped to transform the National Community Relations Advisory Council from a consultative to a central executive body, of which the American Jewish Congress is still the leading constituent organization.

An essential concomitant of Goldstein's deep concern with the Diaspora was his unceasing effort to strengthen Jewish survivalist forces, particularly in the field of education. It is due to his vision, courage and leadership that American Jewry can now pride itself on the possession of Brandeis University, the first secular university in America under Jewish auspices. After a vigorous ideological drive on behalf of the idea, at a time when American Jewish public opinion was apathetic, if not opposed to it, Goldstein proceeded to follow up the discussion with a succession of bold steps, leading to the implementation of the idea. It was due to his initiative, under his chairmanship, that the campus and buildings of Middlesex University in Waltham, Massachusetts, were acquired for Brandeis University, thus laying, in more than a figurative sense, the cornerstone of a great Jewish university in America. Subsequently, others came to complete the structure, which today occupies so prominent a place in the educational life, not only of the Jewish community, but also the general population of the United States. But the credit for initiating the project and seeing it through its crucial beginnings will always go to Israel Goldstein, who saw in the idea of a Jewish university in America, a significant Jewish contribution to America and to American Judaism.

Thus, on many levels of American Jewish life, the impact of Israel Goldstein's personality, compounded by that of his Zionist ideology, has become manifest through a varied and prolonged activity, which, in half-a-century, has helped to transform the Jewish world and the American Jewish community along with it. Watching him through the years, I have recognized in him the Zionist leader *par excellence*, grounded in Jewish tradition, thoroughly dedicated to the ideal of Zion Restored, and completely committed to the rejuvenation of Jewish group life in all its manifestations throughout the world. It is characteristic of Goldstein, I think, that as a rabbi, he has never confined his interests or activities to his own congregation, large and important as it is, but has, with its cooperation, regarded the rabbinate as an opportunity for full-time service to the whole of the Jewish community and the general community as well. Born in the United States of immigrant parents, Yiddish was his mother tongue, a fact which enabled him to follow and understand the stirrings of the immigrant Jewish masses in America as reflected in the Yiddish press, and the Yiddish literary creativity flourishing on American soil; the spiritual leader of an affluent congregation, he took an active part in general civic affairs such as the movement to promote inter-faith understanding, the fight for equality for negro citizens, and in the Liberal Party in New York, standing for political reform and industrial democracy in America. Eschewing parochialism, he rose to the heights of a national and world Jewish figure to whom nothing Jewish is alien and everything bearing on Israel, Jewish culture and Jewish survival is near and dear. That in him the Zionist revolution has found its most faithful instrument is not only the measure of the man but also the proof of the depth and the intensity of the Zionist Movement.

AMERICAN ZIONISM

IN THE POST-STATE ERA

by Louis E. Levinthal

IT WAS INEVITABLE that the birth of the Third Jewish Commonwealth should have magnified the old difficulties and given rise
to new dilemmas confronting Zionists in the United States.

The relief and rehabilitation of hundreds of thousands of
Jewish refugees, the social and cultural integration of vastly
differing immigrant groups into the more or less homogeneous
people of Israel, the physical security and economic stability of
a small state surrounded by hostile neighbors and blockaded by
implacable enemies—these and similar urgent practical problems
have been the real and articulated concern of all self-respecting
Jews, whether nominally Zionists or not. It is generally known
that the supporters and leaders of the United Jewish Appeal, of
Israel Bonds campaigns, of the American Friends of the Hebrew
University, of Technion, the Weizmann Institute, and many other
philanthropic, economic and cultural agencies, devoted to Israel's
welfare, have included multitudes who have never been enrolled
in any Zionist organization. Because of these facts and the general
misconception of Zionist objectives, the very existence of the
State of Israel has surrounded the term "Zionist" with so much
confusion that, from some quarters, the suggestion has come that
the World Zionist Organization and its constituent bodies have
outlived their usefulness and should be liquidated.

Pre-State Zionism was commonly but mistakenly defined as "a
movement of modern Jews having for its objective the assured

settlement of their people upon a national basis in Palestine."
That definition is erroneous because it is incomplete. Actually,
Zionism aimed not only to rebuild Jewish Palestine, but also to
rebuild Jewish life wherever Jews live. It was Theodor Herzl
himself who taught us that the rebirth of the Jewish State was
not an end in itself, but rather an essential means to a more
glorious fulfillment. He declared: "In Zionism there is not only
the striving for a legally secured land for our people; there is
the striving for moral and spiritual perfection."

Unfortunately, we American Zionists have not been made
sufficiently aware of the truth that the movement of which we are
adherents is simply the dignified attempt to have Judaism play a
vital and continuing role in our personal lives, and in the civilization of the world. We see in the State of Israel an indispensable
means of achieving that supreme ideal. Because we cherish the
Jewish heritage and have faith in Jewish character, we regard
Zion—the Jewish State—as the *Bet Hayyenu,* the fountainhead and
dwelling-place of our spiritual life. Louis D. Brandeis expressed
this idea, with special application to American Jews, in very
clear and simple terms. He put it this way: "Assimilation is
national suicide. Assimilation can be prevented only by preserving national characteristics as other peoples, large and small,
are preserving and developing their national life. Must we not,
like them, have a land where Jewish life may be naturally led,
the Jewish language spoken, and the Jewish spirit prevail? . . .
The glorious past can really live only if it becomes the mirror
of a glorious future, and, to this end, the Jewish Home in Palestine is essential. We Jews of prosperous America, above all, need
its inspiration. . . . Every American Jew who aids in advancing
the Jewish settlement in Palestine, though he feels that neither
he nor his descendants will ever live there, will . . . be a better
man and a better American for doing so."

We American Zionists should, of course, continue to recognize
the World Zionist Organization as the focus and forum of expression of world Jewish interest in the State of Israel and in Jewish
survivalism. We must seek to work within the structure of that
Organization, but with as much autonomy as feasible, toward
the achievement of our aims and the accomplishment of our

tasks. It should be manifest that the Zionist program in America must be formulated in such a way as to guard against needless fragmentation of Jewish life. Our platform should be broad and comprehensive, not narrow and restricted. It should not be characterized by emphasis on secondary or incidental objectives to the extent of losing sight of our paramount objective. Therefore, "party" affiliation by Zionist organizations in America should be discouraged. We must be able to consider all questions affecting the State of Israel, as well as American Jewish life, solely on their merits, and decide all issues independently, free of party interests and ideological prejudices. We must build toward a unified expression of American Jewry's organizational concern in the welfare of the people of Israel as a whole and in the creative survival of the total Jewish community in this country.

The tasks of American Zionism are two-fold in character: (1) as to Israel, the encouragement of continued and increasing Jewish immigration, the absorption and integration of as many newcomers as possible, the stimulation of agricultural settlement and industrial development, the fostering of private capital investment by Americans, the enlightenment of public opinion as to the elementary right of Israel to peace and security; and (2) as to American Jewry, the preservation and enrichment of the values of Judaism, the promotion of Jewish education and Hebrew culture, and the fostering of Jewish consciousness by propagating the Zionist movement.

With regard to the problem of *Aliyah* from this country, we must try to discover why so few Americans have been attracted by the romance and adventure of life in Israel. We should endeavor, through our educational program, to create a favorable climate of understanding and sympathy among our youth. We must also be prepared to employ methods successfully utilized by the Zionists of South Africa, and assist financially those of our young people who may desire to identify themselves personally and completely with the State of Israel. We should make clear that no conflict between American and Jewish loyalties is involved when some of our young people undertake to live in the new State and dedicate themselves there to the ideals of social justice and democracy, shared in common by the United States and Israel.

American Zionists must seek to guide the activities of our existing educational agencies, but in doing so we must realize that American Jewish education must have its own special character—it must be American. *Hakhshara* may be a by-product of our educational program, but it must not be its goal. Except for those who may wish to go to Israel, American Jewish education cannot be preparation for life in the new State. It must rather be preparation for vibrant, self-expressive Jewish life here, in the United States. In a real sense, it is far more difficult to educate our youth for Jewish living in America than in Israel. To be prepared to take one's proper place in the Jewish community here, the Jewish child needs a special kind of education, one in which not only the emotions are stirred by ideals and convictions, but one in which also the intellect is enriched by learning, and conduct is rooted in knowledge. In the face of the competitive diversions and often conflicting interests of our environment, it is not easy to transmit to future generations in this country our religious and cultural heritage as Jews. All the more essential is it for us to concentrate our energies on the problems of education, so that our community may make its specific, its finest Jewish contribution to the civilization of the United States.

Most American Zionists agree that every Jewish child should receive some religious training so that he may have a sympathetic understanding and genuine appreciation of the traditional sanctities of his people. A Jew in Israel may be devoid of religion, and still remain a Jew. A Jew in America, who divorces himself from the Synagogue, from Jewish ceremonials and observances, is in grave danger of ultimately being lost to the Jewish people. Furthermore, as many Jewish children as possible should acquire some knowledge of Hebrew. With the rebirth of the Jewish State, Hebrew has become increasingly essential to the American Jew. In addition to being the sacred tongue, the language of prayer, and the key to the storehouse of our cultural treasures, it is now the living vernacular, the means of communication with the reborn nation of Israel and with educated Jews everywhere. It is obvious that the creative forces in Israel can have little real influence upon our lives here, unless we maintain a spiritual and cultural bond between the people of Israel and ourselves.

In performing these Zionist tasks and in this spirit, we shall attract to our movement, and retain, more and more positive, affirmative Jews, Jews not in name only, but Jews in mind and in heart and in action as well, Jews who are intelligently proud of their Jewish fellowship, devoted to their heritage, and full of faith in the Jewish future. Thus conceived, the Zionist program can be a stirring adventure, a challenging test of the strength of our Jewishness.

It is hardly necessary to stress the obvious need of each generation for the guidance and leadership of strong men dedicated to our ideals. It is indeed fortunate that in our Zionist work in this country we have enjoyed in the past, and may in the future count upon, the ardent support and inspiring direction of many zealous communal servants and not a few gifted rabbis, among whom no one has earned a place of higher distinction than Dr. Israel Goldstein in whose honor this volume is published.

His dynamic personality, his rare gift of eloquence, his limitless capacity for hard work, have made him one of the most successful organizers and efficient administrators in American Jewish public life. He is not only the brilliant rabbi of one of the oldest and largest congregations in this country, but also one of the recognized leaders of American and world Jewry. The versatility and extent of his extra-synagogual activities have been unparalleled. It is, however, manifest that he has at all times given priority, in energy, in zeal and in devotion, to the Zionist cause.

Israel Goldstein's extraordinary record as President of the Jewish National Fund made inevitable his unanimous election as my successor as President of the Zionist Organization of America. He assumed that office at a critical time in the history of the movement. Under his courageous, wise and effective leadership, the ZOA grew mightily in numbers and in influence. In his eloquent inaugural address at the 46th annual convention held in Columbus, Ohio, Dr. Goldstein outlined the program for the American Zionist movement. What he said in 1943 is worthy of repetition, because the articles of faith to which he gave expression then have equal validity today. He said:

Let us join with all our united forces to face and wrestle with the great problems and opportunities which lie before us. Our cause is just. Therefore it must win, if we do our part worthily.

Let me summarize the articles of faith which you and I hold in common as Zionists.

I believe, with the late Justice Brandeis, that Zionists are the best American Jews, best as Americans, and best as Jews.

I believe that Zionism is the leaven of Jewish survival.

I believe that no Jew is a normal Jew who is not a Zionist.

I believe that Judaism as a religion is colorless and without personality unless it is informed by Zionist content.

I believe that a Jewish Palestine will make a major contribution to the peace, democracy, culture and prosperity of the Middle East.

I believe that the treatment which the civilized world will accord the Jewish people will be the touchstone of its national and international morality.

I believe that the just solution of the Jewish problem must be one of the foundation stones of the post-war world.

With prophetic vision he pointed out that one of the essential tasks of the American Zionist movement is the strengthening of every force calculated to aid Jewish creative survival and the resistance of every tendency to weaken the Jewish will to live. The time is not too late for Zionists to heed that admonition.

GENERAL ZIONISM

AS A MOVEMENT

---

by Moshe Kol

[Editorial Note: *The following preface to this article by Mr. Kol sets the broad background of General Zionism before the period beginning with the 1930s which constitutes the special area of Mr. Kol's survey*]

The student of Zionist history will not find it difficult to understand why General Zionism assumed a separate political framework only in comparatively recent years. From the beginning, it represented the broad, middle-of-the-road approach, both in theory and in practice, within the World Zionist movement. It was content to follow the Basle program in the liberal idealistic concept of the classical Zionists. In practical application, General Zionism sought to enlist the cooperation of the masses of the Jews in all countries throughout the Diaspora, in the pursuit of translating the Zionist idea into reality in the building of the *Yishuv*. Its concept was that Jewish national hopes and aspirations could be realized only by the united efforts of all Jews in one broad movement, sufficiently flexible to admit of all shades of thinking and all varieties of approach. To this end, it was deemed essential to strengthen the general national institutions and to stress the over-all unity. The comprehensive political program, Hebrew culture and education, Jewish settlement and the development of the economy of the *Yishuv*—these, rather than individual political parties, the General Zionists felt, were the bases of the movement, its unifying and consolidating forces.

Placing the needs of the building of the nation above separate ideologies, classes or groups, as regards the social and economic foundations of the Palestine community, the General Zionists bade all creative elements to unite in serving the program as a whole. The General Zionists considered that the maintenance of special institutions for education, economic enterprises, social and health needs, by individual parties was not in the best interest of the country as a whole, and insisted that these must be maintained as united general public services.

As issues arose at the Zionist Congresses, producing controversies within the movement, partisan struggles ensued and various factions came into being, each vying with the others on such vital matters as *aliyah,* colonization, etc. The General Zionists, for a time, sought to stem the tide and resolve the differences in the interests of the movement as a whole, but they were soon forced to take a more realistic position. The religious orthodox elements formed the Mizrachi Party in 1902 and began to build its own schools, labor organizations and cultural institutions in the *Yishuv.* In 1907, the socialist element formed the Poale Zion Party and began to build their institutions. As these factions gained in numerical and political strength in the Organization, the danger arose that the basic principles of Zionism would be diminished or eventually overshadowed, with each party seeking to steer the Zionist movement its own way. It remained for the General Zionists to strive to maintain the balance in the movement, to constitute itself as a conciliatory force on a more concrete basis, sufficiently broadminded not to lose sight of the liberal point of view, including the encouragement of middle-class private initiative in the upbuilding of the land.

After the first World War, General Zionism began slowly to crystallize as an organization. About this time, too, the General Zionists, who began arriving in increasing numbers in Palestine, found that in the practical work of state-building, their ideas were not being implemented. The weakness of their position forced them to create an organization which began to exert a growing influence on like-minded groups in various countries of the Diaspora, persuading them of the necessity of becoming organized on a permanent basis. With the cooperation of the labor forces, the more progressive General Zionist elements united in backing the policies of Dr. Chaim Weizmann and the partnership with labor in Eretz Israel. These General Zionists sought a continuation of that partnership while they represented both the middle classes as well as General Zionist pioneering labor settlements. This faction came to be known as Group "A" General Zionists. Opposing them were the middle-class groups, mostly of eastern Europe, called Group "B," which inclined toward the Revisionists led by Jabotinsky. Their chief objective was to strengthen private initiative and to establish an organized force to match the growing power of Zionist labor.

The first attempt to set up a world organization of General Zionists was made at the sixteenth Zionist Congress in Zurich, in 1929, but the vagueness of the proposed platform served only to widen the breach between the "A" and "B" groups. Nevertheless, further efforts to unify General Zionist forces continued. At a conference at Basle, in 1931, the basic principles of a World Union of General Zionists were formulated but they did not include a disciplinary clause. In the course of time, the different views of the two General Zionist groups slowly began to converge, but differences never entirely disappeared. Both groups came increasingly to recognize the importance of private capital and the need of attracting foreign investments to Palestine, as well as the necessity of entrusting to the Zionist Organization and, later, the State, the power of decision in such matters as labor, public health, education, etc.

The developments which led finally to the creation of the World Confederation of General Zionists and its achievements are described in detail in the following article.]

I

WHILE General Zionism has been the cradle of the Modern Zionist movement, it was not until the 1930s that special efforts were made to organize all the General Zionists groups of the world within the framework of one organization which would guide the General Zionist movement and its representatives in its central bodies and in the Jewish Agency for Palestine.

These were the years when mounting political and economic

stress on the Jewish masses in eastern and central Europe and pressure for *aliyah* (immigration into Palestine) rose to maximum proportions. The restriction of Jewish immigration to Palestine by the British Mandatory Government imperilled the existence of the Jews in Europe and resulted in the "illegal" *aliyah* and also in a very bitter fight within the Zionist movement.

The early 1930s were also the years of largest *aliyah*, though its dimensions scarcely satisfied the desire of the Jewish masses to leave the countries of oppression and join in the upbuilding of Jewish Palestine. The political conflict within the Zionist movement, the shortage of immigration certificates, the rivalry of various groups within the Jewish communities and the Zionist movement for positions of influence in matters of immigration and colonization, which were in the hands of the World Zionist Organization, led to a deterioration in internal, social and political relations within the *Yishuv*. During this period, the Zionist Congresses served as an arena for the struggle between the progressive forces in the Zionist movement and in wide circles of the dispossessed Jewish middle class in their respective lands. The former, together with the labor movement, backed the leadership of Dr. Chaim Weizmann, then president of the World Zionist Organization. The latter demanded intensification of the struggle against the Mandatory Government and also opposed the positions of strength and influence of the Histadrut in the *Yishuv*. The latter forces were headed by the Revisionists led by Zev Jabotinsky and were supported by the right-wingers in the General Zionist organizations in eastern Europe, while the great majority of General Zionists the world over, supported Weizmann's political policies and the partnership with labor in Eretz Israel. A special place in this struggle was taken by the small world group of the Radical Zionists, under the leadership of Itzhak Greenbaum, Nahum Goldmann, Robert Shtricker, Menahem Soloveichik and others, who demanded a more energetic fight against the Mandatory Government which had gone back on its promises. The Zionist masses in Poland placed their confidence in Itzhak Greenbaum, who, while leading the struggle for Jewish rights in Poland demanded, at the same time, a change in the political approach *vis-à-vis* the British in order to accel-

erate *aliyah* of the Jewish masses in Poland for whom he saw
no future in their native land. The Radicals, however, were
opposed to the fight against the Histadrut and favored a continuation of the partnership between labor and General Zionism
in order to secure the progressive social character of the *Yishuv*.

When the Passfield White Paper was issued by the British
Labor Government, in 1930, a crisis arose in its relations with Dr.
Weizmann. This led to a rapprochement between the Radicals
and the Progressive General Zionists (Group A), especially
because their approaches to social problems and their support of
halutzic (labor pioneering) colonization were identical. At the
same time, the right-wing General Zionists (Group B) increased
their support of the Revisionists in their fight against Weizmann
and the Histadrut.

The slogan, "Break the Histadrut!" found acceptance among
General Zionist rightist circles in western and eastern Galicia, in
Lithuania and in Austria, but, first and foremost, in the General
Zionist Organization in Eretz Israel. The partnership of the
Group "A" General Zionists and the Radicals with labor in
the Zionist Executive chosen at the Eighteenth World Zionist
Congress in Prague, in 1933, and the intensive struggle waged by
Revisionists and Group "B" General Zionists against this Execu-
tive, headed by David Ben-Gurion, under the presidency of
Nahum Sokolow, added further to the deterioration of relations
between the two camps of General Zionism.

In 1935, a world conference of General Zionists took place in
Cracow. Participants included the General Zionists of Groups "A"
and "B," the Radical Zionists of Poland, and the representatives of
the Progressive Zionists of Eretz Israel, including the delegates
of Hanoar Hazioni (General Zionist youth) and of the General
Zionist group in the Histadrut. This convention represented the
final effort to find a compromise between the various factions of
General Zionists in order to establish one world organization
of General Zionists of varying ideological and political shade. All
those at the conference, shared a will to close the ranks of General Zionism, in the light of the growth of the socialist and the
religious wings of the Zionist movement which were acquiring

influential positions in the upbuilding of the country and in the crystallization of Eretz Israel society, and were also promoting the interests of their members in the Diaspora in respect of *aliyah*. Concurrently, adherents of General Zionism, which had always been the backbone of the World Zionist Organization and which had been concerned with the general interests of the Zionist movement and the totality of the *Yishuv*, were being removed from positions of leadership. This development threatened the unity of the national movement—of the World Zionist Organization. It was urgent that General Zionism be strengthened so that the great instrument for national redemption and for the fulfillment of Zionist aims be not broken, in order that all Jews, irrespective of ideology, class, country of origin, or of party association, feel themselves equal in rights in the State-in-the-Making. But this will to unity was not enough to overcome the divisions in the General Zionist camp and the Cracow convention ended in a split resulting from the failure of the representatives of the rightist General Zionists from Eretz Israel and Galicia to renounce their intention to found a separate workers' organization. The attitude toward the Histadrut and toward the Association of General Zionist workers, either as a faction within Histadrut or as a separate organization outside it, became the dividing line between the Progressive General Zionists and the rightist and class-conscious General Zionists.

Immediately after the split, and at the initiative of Dr. Goldmann, Dr. Kleinbaum and Haoved Hazioni (general Zionist workers), the World Confederation of General Zionists was organized in Cracow, embracing all the Progressive Zionists (Group "A"), the former Radical Zionists and the *halutzic* Hanoar Hazioni, with its workers in Eretz Israel and its *halutzim* in the Diaspora. The group "B" General Zionists remained in the World Union of General Zionists but they were a minority compared with the "Confederation," which comprised most of the General Zionists in the world. Throughout this inner struggle, the great majority of General Zionists remained true to the liberal and progressive traditions of Zionism. Under the influence of the Confederation and its consolidated forces, in cooperation with the labor parties in

Eretz Israel, Dr. Chaim Weizmann was returned to the presidency of the World Zionist Organization, where he served to the end of 1946.

The Zionist Organization of America and Hadassah, in the United States, affiliated themselves with the World Confederation of General Zionists but, in the period before World War II, our American comrades were not yet significantly active or influential in the World Zionist movement. At that time, this was headed by the European Zionists and the representatives of the *Yishuv*.

There is no question that the *halutzic* Hanoar Hazioni played a considerable part in the development of General Zionism. In the early 1930s, the first *halutzim* of the General Zionist youth movements began to arrive in Eretz Israel. Their very appearance in Eretz Israel was a significant event. Theretofore, there had been no workers among the General Zionists in the land, who were of the urban middle classes and of the rural citrus-growing circles. The appearance of *halutzim* and *kibbutz* members of General Zionist persuasion was for them a veritable revolution in realities and terminology alike. Matters came to a head when these *halutzim* declined to organize themselves in a separate trade union. They decided to identify themselves with the General Zionists politically and ideologically, but they insisted upon their right to be an independent group carrying the flag of General Zionist *halutzic* realization within the ranks of the Histadrut— which they saw as the labor organization for all the workers of the land. The appearance of the General Zionist *halutzim* in Petah Tikvah and other colonies heartened the General Zionist progressive and democratic circles, which then constituted a minority in the General Zionist party, and encouraged them to wage ideological and political battle, together with those *halutzim,* against the right-wing class leadership of the General Zionists in Eretz Israel, who were cooperating with the Revisionists, the citrus growers who employed Arab labor, and with all opponents of the democratic organization of the *Yishuv*. This ideological struggle over the form of General Zionism, to give it a progressive face, to keep it true to the *halutzim* and settlers, and to internal democracy in the *Yishuv*, undoubtedly also had an echo in the Diaspora countries, in the resistance to the attempts to identify General Zionism with the middle class and its interests.

II

The creative effort, in the areas of colonization, *halutziut* and education, of Hanoar Hazioni and Haoved Hazioni in Eretz Israel and in the Diaspora took the form of *kibbutzim, moshavim* or *hakhsharot,* under their own name and banner. The *hakshara, kibbutzim* and educational branches of the General Zionist youth movement had the character of a collectivist movement. Activities in the *Yishuv,* in the Histadrut and in the General Zionist camp, were also carried out in the name and with the approval of the movement. The term "creative effort of the movement" was to some extent a novelty in the General Zionist camp. It is not meant to suggest that before Hanoar Hazioni there had been no creative effort in the sectors of colonization, economy or education by General Zionists in Eretz Israel. Indeed, the first settlers during the *Bilu Aliyah* and many of the Second and Third *Aliyot* were "general" Zionists in the classical sense, following no religious, class or party line. Their ideals were: the return to Zion and the realization of Zionism, physical labor on the soil of Eretz Israel, the establishment of Jewish settlements, self-defense, Hebrew education and other Zionist duties. They carried out all these noble tasks in the name of no special party or organization. They came to the land as individual Zionists, and whatever they established or built was their own creation and not the creation of any party or organization. And when the Zionist camp began to fragmentize into ideological groupings and parties, the great majority were General Zionists.

But not only in the vast area of colonization did these Zionists have a large share. They were also among the builders of elementary and secondary Hebrew education in the country. They established industry, based entirely on Jewish labor, and developed the trades. Most of all, they built the first Jewish city in the country, Tel Aviv, and in its wake other cities. These Zionists were also the founders of *Knesset Israel,* the democratic organization of the *Yishuv.*

In the late 1930s, when the pressure for immigration mounted and the Mandatory severely restricted *aliyah,* the "illegal immigration" came into being. The General Zionist *halutzim* refused to be excluded from this sacred task. When, together with the *halutzim* of Hapoel Hamizrachi, they brought the "illegal" ship *Assimi,* general cooperation was established in this field, under the command of Haganah and the Central Zionist institutions. Surely there is no need to emphasize the part of the General Zionists, and just ordinary Zionists from all circles, in the Haganah—in settlement, in town, or wherever they were assigned.

When the struggle against the British intensified before the establishment of the State, Confederation representatives did a great deal to bring about a modicum of coordination between the dissident underground groups—ETZEL and LEHI—and the Haganah. A divided struggle against the British endangered the unity and the very future of the *Yishuv.* The Confederation representatives did their very best to ensure the full cooperation of all segments of the Zionist movement—a true sharing of both responsibility and decision.

III

The catastrophe that befell European Jewry as a result of the Nazi holocaust during World War II utterly destroyed the Zionist movement in every country of Europe invaded by Hitler's hordes. Zionists in the neutral countries, like Switzerland and Sweden, were busy in rescue work and in rendering help to Jewish communities in Nazi-occupied lands. In these countries, the Zionist parties, led by the *halutzic* youth movements, were active even in the sealed ghettos and in the underground. This chapter of Zionist activity during the catastrophe is not known to many, and the important factual material in the Zionist Archives in Jerusalem, in the Yad Vashem Archives and in the Itzhak Katzenelson Museum at Kibbutz Lohamei Hagetaot will enable the researcher who will devote himself to this task to bring before the people and the youth the knowledge of the honor with which General Zionist adult and youth leaders acquitted themselves in sustaining the anti-Nazi underground by continuing the activities of the Zionist movements, the *hakhshara* cells, the youth branches and, above all, in organizing the revolt and resistance in the ghettos and in the partisan movement.

In treating of this period we must mention the help sent by the secretariat of Hanoar Hazioni of Eretz Israel to comrades active in the ghettos of the Nazi-occupied countries. We maintained contact with many of them through Constantinople and Geneva. We assigned people to the aid and contact committees established by the Zionist Executive in Jerusalem (Vaad Hahatzalah) and the Histadrut Executive, and we also independently sent help to comrades in Nazi-occupied Europe and to refugee comrades in Soviet Russia, who were kept alive by the packages sent to them in those trying days. Some of our comrades reached Eretz Israel during the underground immigration period, but some, including many well-known General Zionists and members of Hanoar Hazioni, perished in Soviet labor camps where they had been imprisoned for Zionist activity.

The London headquarters of the World Confederation of General Zionists were virtually paralyzed all during World War II, and the Cracow headquarters were destroyed when the Nazis occupied Poland. Dr. Itzhak Schwarzbart helped maintain contacts with Polish Jews through the Polish Government-in-Exile in London, of whose council he was a member. Itzhak Greenbaum, as head of the Vaad Hahatzalah, accomplished much in the rescue of Jewish leaders and rank and file General Zionists and enabled them to immigrate to, and settle in, Eretz Israel. The contact office of the secretariat of Hanoar Hazioni and of General Zionist *halutz* movement in Tel Aviv, in cooperation with Haoved Hazioni, did not interrupt its work for a day. When the letters received from comrades by the Vaad Hahatzalah and the Histadrut contact offices during the days of the catastrophe and revolt in occupied Europe, see the light, they will tell the story of true comradely solidarity between our movement in Eretz Israel and our adherents in the Diaspora.

The most dramatic chapter in our rescue efforts, towards the end of World War II, is the well-known one of the parachutists who volunteered to rescue our brethren in the occupied countries. Our comrades who participated in this daring enterprise were Abba Berdichev of blessed memory and Hayim

Hermesh. Berdichev was probably killed by the Nazis or their cohorts and the story of his life is set down in a biography published by the Kvutza Alonei Abba on the tenth anniversary of his death. The book "Magen Baseter" which deals with the activities of the Eretz Israel underground in World War II, published in Jerusalem in 1948, also contains testimonials to the heroic roles of Abba Berdichev and Hayim Hermesh.

In summary, we may state unequivocally that there was no field of rescue, help, contact, or any other activity in which we did not fully participate. Many of our comrades were among the volunteers for the various military units recruited by the *Yishuv* institutions and the Zionist movement. Many served in the Jewish Brigade of the British Army and fought in North Africa and on the European fronts. Many were in the Palmah and in other combat and underground units. The Brigade members were the first privileged to meet the surviving remnants of European Jewry, and our liberated comrades in Europe, who later became active in the illegal immigration project and the builders of our movement in post-war Europe.

IV

Following the Allied victory and with the termination of war activities in Europe, we quickly established direct personal contact with the Jewish remnants and with our comrades in Europe. Our emissaries were among the first to leave for the ravaged lands to help the survivors and to rebuild the ruins of our movement. In Poland and Hungary, Italy and Rumania, in western Europe, these emissaries worked under the most trying conditions. They brought the greetings of the *Yishuv* and the movement to the remnants. These were great hours of reawakening to life, to *aliyah* and to Zionist activity. Our comrades in the Jewish Brigade were not satisfied to work only in western Europe and a delegation went to eastern Europe. This was the honeymoon period in the relations between the Allied armies, when the western democracies and Russia were comrades in arms in vanquishing the Nazis. The cold war had not yet begun and travel from west to east was still possible. At that time, too, contact was established between our comrades in the United States and our liberated comrades in Europe.

Dr. Israel Goldstein was then president of the Zionist Organization of America. He came to visit liberated Europe, met the remnants, visited Paris and gave courage to our comrades who had begun to rebuild General Zionism in western Europe. It was a heartening encounter with a happy sequel. Late in August 1945, the first World Zionist Conference since World War II was held in London. Dramatic encounters and a spirit of elation and emotion marked the sessions. A delegation of Polish Jews, headed by Dr. Emil Sommerstein, arrived when the Conference was already underway. This was one of the highest emotional moments of the Conference. Most prominent among the Polish delegation were our comrades who had founded the Zionist Union after the war. At the London Conference we met also comrades who had lived through the Nazi occupation of France, Belgium, Czechoslovakia, and other European lands, or who had lived through the war years in Soviet Russia or in the underground.

During the Conference, the first post-war meeting of the World Confederation of General Zionists took place, with the participation of delegates from Eretz Israel, the United States, Great Britain, Canada, South Africa, Australia, Poland, France, Belgium, the Netherlands, Switzerland, Sweden, Egypt, Italy and Greece. We arrived at the unanimous conviction that the world General Zionist organization had to be revived and reactivated in the field of organization and propaganda; that the activities of our comrades in all countries had to be guided; that emissaries had to be sent to Europe to bolster the movement there; and that the organization had to establish a fund to enable it to extend financial help to the *halutzic* movement in European countries, to the new children's homes and to our colonization efforts in Eretz Israel. The stormy period demanded a new and energetic drive. We had the feeling that we were entering a new phase in our struggle for independence in Eretz Israel, and that our movement had to take its place among the remnants of European Jewry, in organizing them for immigration to Palestine, in the revival of Zionism and in expanding activities in Eretz Israel so as to enable us to absorb all who were preparing to come.

As a result of parleys held in London, it was decided to establish the following regional offices of the revived Confederation: in London, headed by Levi Bakstansky; in Paris, headed by Sam Segal in collaboration with our western European comrades; in the United States, headed by Dr. Israel Goldstein together with an Hadassah representative; in Eretz Israel, headed by Moshe Sneh and Moshe Kol. This was done in order to facilitate the coordination with the Jewish Agency Executive, of our constructive Zionist work on behalf of our *kibbutzim* and our middle-class settlements. A fourth office was to be established in Warsaw for eastern Europe. In this London Conference, representatives of the "Aliyah Hadashah" organization in Eretz Israel participated for the first time, and talks were initiated to unite all General Zionist forces, irrespective of shade of opinion, within the World Confederation. A new executive was chosen for the Confederation, to which it was decided to coopt the members of the Jewish Agency Executive who represented the Confederation.

The first Executive of the World Confederation after World War II, published on August 31, 1945, a manifesto to the General Zionists of the world. This manifesto said, in part:

"General Zionism, which has placed itself in the front-line of the struggle to establish Palestine as a free and democratic Jewish state, calls to the Jewish people, wherever they may be, to rally to the Zionist flag, to increase their effort and to spare no sacrifice until we shall have achieved our aim of bringing to Palestine the remnants of our people and secured for them a life of freedom in Eretz Israel, established as the independent state of the Jewish people. General Zionism considers itself the main factor making for national unity, offering a nation-wide Jewish policy for the Diaspora and for the *Yishuv*. General Zionism stresses the foundation of our existence as one people united by a great historic mission and a common, cruel fate. A strong and influential General Zionism is a guarantee that the differences, which have appeared during our life in the *Galuth*, will be eradicated; it strives to achieve the political, cultural, educational and social unity of those who return to take part in our renewed life in Palestine; it aims at bridging the social differences between the various parts of the *Yishuv* and its classes through common responsibility and mutual understanding. . . ."

We left this Conference aware of the great change that had taken place in Jewish life. European Jewry was destroyed. A remnant was left that turned to Eretz Israel. The centers of Jewish life were destined to be transferred to Eretz Israel and to the United States. In Eretz Israel, there was no prospect of expanding the practical and public activities of our movement, and there was no hope of rebuilding the ruins of the movement in Europe, without the encouragement and help of our comrades in the United States—the Zionist Organization of America and Hadassah. This change in orientation necessitated by reality did not come spontaneously, and certainly not easily, to the Zionist organizations constituting the majority of American Zionism. The leadership of Hadassah and of the Zionist Organization of America had not, in the past, been closely involved in the organized activities of world General Zionism. It is true that Hanoar Hazioni had had ties with the Massada organization even before World War II. But this was a very weak tie and Zionist leadership in the United States had to be convinced that they had to participate actively in the World Confederation to a larger degree and on a new basis. Above all, it was necessary to establish a large constructive fund for the expansion of our economic and *halutzic* activities in Eretz Israel and to help the *hakhsharot,* the children's homes and the comrades who were left destitute in liberated Europe. All parties in Eretz Israel had gone into action but we knew that we could not lift this burden by our own strength alone.

The London Conference afforded us also the opportunity to convince some of the leaders of the Zionist Organization of America of the necessity of an ideological, practical and political compact with their comrades overseas. This was a serious turning point for American Zionism. Dr. Israel Goldstein, then president of the Zionist Organization of America, was one of the first to be convinced, and with all his characteristic zeal and energy he undertook to revivify the Confederation. In November 1945, at the opening of the convention of the Zionist Organization of America, he spoke of the necessity of such a World Confederation of General Zionists equipped with the necessary instruments and possibilities for action. It was the first time that such words had been voiced from a platform of the Z.O.A., words that heralded an ideological and organizational reorientation in American Zionism.

In March, 1946, the founding conference of the European Hanoar Hazioni—Akiva movement was held in Paris. Participating in the conference were several emissaries from Eretz Israel who were already active in liberated Europe, representatives of the newly reorganized movements, and our comrades in the uniform of the Jewish Brigade who had been active in underground immigration. It was a meeting of brethren and comrades that decided to establish our movement anew and to unite all groups and factions within one organizational framework. Great tasks confronted us, and we now also stood before a turning point with regard to our public position and influence in the *Yishuv*.

A month later, the first delegation of the *Yishuv* and of the Zionist Executive left for liberated Poland to meet the remnants of Polish Jewry and our brethren who had been repatriated from Soviet Russia. I had the great honor to be a member of this delegation which visited Poland and the annexed East German territories, and to meet at mass gatherings, scores of thousands of Jews who had not heard about the events in the *Yishuv* during World War II. Let it be noted, to the credit of our comrades, that they energetically reestablished the "Union" as the central Zionist body in Poland and proudly carried the blue and white flag in an atmosphere that was not always friendly. For four years, they worked consecratedly in transferring most of the remnants from Poland to Eretz Israel. Their work was interrupted when the organized Zionist movement was outlawed at the end of 1949.

At the end of 1946, before the Zionist Congress in Basle, the first post-war Congress, the delegates from all General Zionist organizations the world over, including Hanoar Hazioni, the General Zionist Halutz and Haoved Hazioni, met and established the newly united World Confederation of General Zionists.

The Basle Congress was one of the most difficult the Zionist movement had ever experienced. Those were the days of struggle against the Mandatory Government, which had restricted immigration. The Congress had to decide where Zionism was to go from there, and how political independence and the opening of the gates to the remnants were to be achieved. The Congress was divided between the supporters of Dr. Weizmann and the opponents of his political approach, who contended that the crisis in relations with Great Britain, as a result of its anti-Zionist policy, demanded a change in approach and intensification of the struggle. The same division manifested itself in the ranks of the Confederation. Dr. Weizmann was not reelected president at this Congress. Dr. Abba Hillel Silver was appointed to head an American branch of the Zionist Executive, with the participation of Dr. Emanuel Neumann of the Zionist Organization of America and Mrs. Rose Halprin of Hadassah, while David Ben-Gurion was elected chairman of the World Zionist Executive. The leading supporters of Dr. Weizmann were the late Prof. Selig Brodetsky of England, Dr. Nahum Goldmann, the late Dr. Stephen S. Wise and the Hadassah leadership in America. The World Confederation of General Zionists had been founded before the war on the principle that every delegate was free to vote as his conscience dictated and was not bound by any factional discipline in voting at Congresses and in the Zionist Actions Committee. This principle was confirmed at the world convention of the General Zionists in Basle. The Confederation group at the Congress was the largest of all parties, and it made a profound impression upon the whole character of, and the decisions taken at, the convention. At a conference of the delegates of the Confederation present at Basle, it was decided to establish three offices, in Tel Aviv, in Paris and in New York. Dr. Israel Goldstein was elected president of the World Confederation. His election marked the beginning of ten years of a fruitful activity from 1946 to 1956, during which he served as the universally esteemed and accepted leader of the movement, ten stormy years of internal struggle, of great achievement, in the World Zionist Organization, in the *Yishuv* and in the State, after its establishment, and in the lands of the Diaspora.

It was decided in Basle also to establish the Constructive Enterprises Fund (K.M.K.) of the World General Zionist movement, to serve as the financial instrument of the Confederation, and to secure from the Zionist Congress recognition of this fund. Thanks to the agreement of the leaders of the Z.O.A. and Hadassah, the fund was immediately assigned quotas from the United Jewish Appeal in America, such as the Mizrachi Fund and other funds already had. This made possible a fruitful new era of creative endeavor in the fields of colonization, immigrant absorption, economic development of *kibbutzim* and middle-class settlements, establishment of youth villages and educational institutions, bolstering of general education and intensifying of the campaign for unified State education in Israel, and a reinforcement of the General Zionist movement in Israel and in the Diaspora.

V.

The first ten years of existence of the Confederation brought an important change in the status of General Zionism within the World Zionist Organization. The period may be considered as the decade of revival of the General Zionist idea and influence the world over. General Zionism became again the central force in the national renaissance. The General Zionist organizations in all countries of the Diaspora were strengthened and fortified by the recognition that they were an inseparable part of a great world movement which had played, and was continuing to play, an important role in achieving and strengthening Israel's independence. The first two years of existence of the Confederation were devoted chiefly to the struggle of the *Yishuv* and the world Zionist movement for the political independence of Israel. In the United States, the reins of Zionist leadership were in the hands of General Zionists, who organized the campaign in America and at the United Nations for a decision supporting the United Nations Special Committee on Palestine report which recommended the establishment of a Jewish State in part of Palestine. This was a glorious period in Zionist history, which ended with a Zionist victory at the United Nations on November 29, 1947, when more than two-thirds of the member states, including the two greatest world powers, supported Israel's independence. In other countries, too, the General Zionists were in the van of the political effort, mobilizing public opinion and world statesmanship toward a Zionist victory.

In Europe, our comrades were very active also in immigration, both legal and illegal, in the establishment and maintenance of *hakhsharot,* in undertaking constructive and educational enterprises, including children's homes. In France, two children's homes were established under the auspices of the General Zionists and with the support of our comrades in the United States: one at Lyons, with a capacity of 240 children, named after Dr. Israel Goldstein in recognition of his activities in saving European orphans and educating them for a new life in Israel; the other at Brunois supported by the General Zionist Assistance Fund. Our comrades in Europe felt that there was a world center in New York with a branch in Paris, and this cementing of bonds encouraged them greatly. Dr. Goldstein visited them and even reached the Cyprus camps. General Zionist activity was keenly felt in the Diaspora. At the same time, the intensification of constructive activity in Israel, with the help of the Constructive Enterprises Fund, was a turning point in the colonizational, educational and organizational activity of General Zionism in the *Yishuv.* The president of the Confederation and of the World Executive and all its branches remained true to the ideological and organizational tenets formulated in Basle at the founding convention late in 1946.

At this convention it was decided that the world Hanoar Hazioni was the only General Zionist youth organization, and Haoved Hazioni, within the Histadrut, the only General Zionist labor group, recognized by the Confederation. These two decisions had a very basic ideological significance. In the first division the Confederation demonstrated its positive and encouraging attitude toward the General Zionist *halutz* movement. The significance of the second decision was the manifestation of General Zionists positive attitude to the Histadrut as the overall organization of all Israeli workers.

In the resolution to establish the Constructive Enterprises Fund, it was especially emphasized that the object of the fund was to strengthen General Zionist colonization and other constructive enterprises of Haoved Hazioni and to stimulate private initiative among middle-class settlers. In line with these aims, the World Confederation did a great deal to encourage economic pluralism in Israel, a *sine qua non* for the development of the State. Economic pluralism is important also for strengthening democracy, for it insures equilibrium among all economic sectors.

During the first ten years of the World Confederation, General Zionists played a key role in the mobilization of Zionist funds and in the sale and purchase of the Israel independence and development loans. They understood that the young State needed not only a political hinterland but also great help in facilitating the absorption of hundreds of thousands of newcomers and the development of its economy. To strengthen the partnership between the world Zionist movement and the State of Israel, the heads of the Confederation, above all Dr. Nahum Goldmann, then chairman of the American Section of the Jewish Agency, fought for special status for the World Zionist Organization as the representative of Diaspora Jewry in the upbuilding of the State. The "Status Law" approved by the Knesset, Israel's parliament, was the achievement of Dr. Goldmann, who was supported by the entire Confederation, under the leadership of its president, Dr. Goldstein, and by Mrs. Rose Halprin, a member of the Jewish Agency Executive.

At a meeting of the Zionist Actions Committee in 1948, after the establishment of the State, Dr. Goldstein, the president of the Confederation, agreed to serve for a year in Israel as treasurer of the Jewish Agency. This was a year of great financial burdens and of challenging tasks in the economic and fiscal areas. During his term as treasurer of the Jewish Agency, Dr. Goldstein did much to implement the principles of the Confederation firmly to establish all economic sectors, corporate, private, cooperative and public, in order to ensure the full exploitation of every source of initiative and financial aid for immigrant absorption in particular, and the upbuilding of the State, in general.

The country was in need of private investment income parallel to the national income from Zionist funds. There was need to encourage private colonization and professional *aliyah* so as to attract immigrants from western countries. The Confederation declared its support and encouragement of immigration not only from lands of oppression but also from the free world. At that time, the representatives of the Confederation exerted great efforts to keep the apparatus of the World Zionist Organization free from any party bias and demanded that Jewish Agency officials be chosen according to ability and not according to party affiliation.

The support given the General Zionist parties in Israel by the Confederation and its Constructive Enterprises Fund made it possible for the former to strengthen the general education trend and to intensify the struggle for unified State education. These efforts were crowned with success when the Knesset voted to establish State education.

The Confederation and its representatives have always favored, and in word and deed have always emphasized, the importance of the preservation of ethical-religious values in Zionist affairs and in Eretz Israel life. During the past two years, the Confederation leaders have accomplished much in their effort to rally the Jewish people around the World Zionist Organization. The "Presidents' Club," established by seventeen major pro-Zionist organizations, under the leadership of Dr. Nahum Goldmann, president of the World Zionist Organization, is their latest important accomplishment in this area. Now that, since "Operation Sinai," Israel must wage a bitter struggle in the United States and at the United Nations, the importance of such unifying steps becomes manifest.

It was under the presidency of Dr. Goldstein that the Confederation laid the foundations for the organization of General Zionism in Latin America. Before World War II, the Jews of that continent, in general, and the Zionists, in particular, had not especially distinguished themselves for Zionist activity. The Confederation was the first Zionist party to take the initiative in this area. Now Latin American Zionism occupies a place of honor in the movement; the many *kibbutzim* of Latin American *halutzim* are the pride of Israel; its achievements in Zionist fund raising are outstanding; and Hanoar Hazioni is the largest and most active youth movement on that continent.

VI

As we have noted, there have always existed two shades of General Zionism, leading, in 1948, after the establishment of the State of Israel, to the founding in Israel of the Progressive Party.

This new party comprised the liberal intelligentsia and Haoved Hazioni, with its *kibbutz* and labor elements. But this division of General Zionist forces, with the ensuing political and ideological debate in the movement in Israel and throughout the Diaspora, has imposed a strain on the General Zionist movement. At the closing session of the world conference of the Confederation in May 1956, following the twenty-fourth World Zionist Congress, held in Jerusalem, Dr. Goldstein delivered his valedictory after ten years as president of the Confederation. At this session, the representatives of the Zionist Organization of America and Hadassah, General Zionists and Progressives alike, expressed their admiration of Dr. Goldstein and their gratitude for his earnest efforts firmly to establish and advance the organization. In the name of the Progressive Party, I said that Dr. Goldstein symbolized by his personality and deeds all that was positive in all shades of General Zionism. I believe that this was no exaggeration. His ties with the *halutzic* wing of Zionism were always excellent. He had spoken of the need for *halutzic aliyah* not only from Europe and other parts of the old world, but also from America. He had an especially warm feeling for the *kibbutz* (communal settlement) and *moshav* (cooperative settlement) settlers, the laboring and farm folk, whose very lives were a realization of the General Zionist vision.

One of his notable achievements as president of the Confederation was the help extended in the establishment of children's homes in post-war Europe and the support he gave to the expansion of the Youth Aliyah children's villages of Haoved Hazioni in Eretz Israel. The youth farm at Katamon in Jerusalem was named in his honor in appreciation of his labors. He has always maintained a close, active interest in "his" farm, visiting it whenever he happens to be in Israel, listening to its problems, winning it friends, ever alert to means of advancing this youth village of which he is justly proud, as one of the most splendid educational projects on the borders of Jerusalem.

At the same time, Dr. Goldstein has zealously guarded the interests of the private farmers, supporting them in their efforts to found new settlements. The Council for Private Agriculture rightly sees him as patron and great friend. As treasurer of the

Jewish Agency, and since, he has always been their faithful advocate before the councils of the Jewish Agency Executive.

Always interested in immigrants to Israel, he helped found the office for care and help to General Zionist immigrants at the Israel headquarters of the Confederation. The immigrants' hostel on Basle Street in Tel Aviv was named for him in appreciation of his labors on behalf of immigrants and the survivors of the European holocaust.

But no less has his interest been in the development of other areas of Israeli life: industry, the trades, housing. It was during his term as treasurer of the Jewish Agency that he was one of the founders of the national housing company, "Amidar." It is only natural that, as spiritual leader of his Congregation B'nai Jeshurun in New York, the spiritual, cultural and educational problems of the *Yishuv* and then of the State should have become a special object of his interest. The Hebrew University and the other scientific and educational institutions have always been dear to his heart. On his sixtieth birthday, his friends have decided to establish a synagogue in his name at the new university city being built in Jerusalem, and thus to strengthen the religious traditional elements in the student body, the future intelligentsia of the State of Israel.

Behold the man, rich in thought and deed, organizer and toiler for General Zionism throughout the world and in Israel, a role which he saw as a great mission on behalf of the State of Israel and the world Zionist movement. His road as president of the World Confederation of General Zionists was not always an easy one. But today, as he looks back upon this decade, he surely sees it as one of much creative achievement in Israel and in the Diaspora. Above all, he sees the many friends in the General Zionist camp the world over, in every land, class and stratum. He gained this friendship through the admiration for his personality and the principles by which he has guided his life rich in achievement for his people and its historic fatherland.

Part Two

RELIGIOUS
DEVELOPMENTS

JUDAISM AS A MODERN

RELIGIOUS CIVILIZATION

by *Mordecai M. Kaplan*

I

THE RECOGNITION OF Judaism as a civilization would remove once for all a veritable host of false assumptions and distorted notions concerning it. Judaism would then figure in the consciousness of the Jew as the ensemble of all that is generally included in a civilization. It would elicit from him a sense of spiritual rootedness in Eretz Yisrael, a feeling of oneness with the forty-century-old People of Israel, a desire to understand its language and literature, a yearning to cherish its aspirations, and an eagerness to live its way of life, with its mores, laws and arts.

If Jews would try to cope, in this spirit, with their inner and outer problems, they would bring to bear creative intelligence upon whatever task they would undertake, whether it be that of enhancing the State of Israel, of combating anti-Semitism, organizing communal life, promoting Jewish education, establishing congregations, fostering beneficent religion, improving moral standards or encouraging Jewish art. Jews would then no longer content themselves with half-thoughts and compromises which are responsible for the present chaos and demoralization in Jewish life. Their hearts would then be set upon so revitalizing their social heritage, so reconstructing their way of life, and so conditioning their future, that the Jewish People would become a source of spiritual self-realization to the individual Jew, and of marked influence for universal freedom, justice and peace.

If Judaism is to become creative once again, it will have to assimilate the best in contemporary civilization. In the past, this process of assimilating cultural elements from the environment was carried on unawares. Henceforth, that process will have to be carried on in deliberate and planned fashion. In that respect, Judaism will, no doubt, have to depart from its own tradition. That is inevitable, since conscious and purposeful planning is coming to be part of the very life-process of society. No civilization, culture, economy or religion that is content to drift aimlessly has the slightest chance of surviving. It is in the spirit, therefore, of adopting the best in other civilizations and cooperating with them, and not in the spirit of yielding to their superior force or prestige, that Judaism should enter upon what will constitute the next stage in its evolution.

No civilization can afford to become a final and closed system of life. Continuous progress must henceforth be its ruling principle. The realities of the environment and the cultural climate must always be reckoned with. Though this does not preclude the formulation of detailed philosophies and specific lines of conduct, it does preclude their finality, however perfect they may seem at the time of their formulation.

Central to all efforts at Jewish readjustment is the need of clearly defining the status of the Jews in relation to the rest of the world. That status should be based upon the assumption that the dispersion of the Jews must henceforth be accepted as a permanent condition. Jews cannot hope ever again, as a body, to become a nation with a central state to unite them. As citizens of the countries they live in, they cannot aspire to become a trans-national group of a political character, or to function as a political unit. So long as to be a nation means to be a societal unit in which the state is primary and central, Jews throughout the world, including those in Israel, should regard themselves, and be regarded by others, as a "People." A People is not a biological or territorial datum. A People is such by virtue of a cultural pattern which affords it sufficient cohesion to make those who belong to it desire to maintain some kind of unified life (Cf. MacIver, "The Pattern of Social Change in Authority and the Individual," Harvard, p.140).

As a civilization, Judaism requires at least one place in the world, where it may be the primary one for its adherents. Everywhere else, Judaism can function only as a secondary civilization for its members, the primary one necessarily being the civilization of the country they live in. Eretz Yisrael will have to serve as both instrument and symbol of the Jewish renascence and as center of Jewish civilization. Without such a center upon which Jews throughout the world might focus their interest, it is impossible for Jews to retain, for long, the awareness of their unity as a People.

Judaism cannot maintain its character as a civilization, nor can the Jewish People maintain its sense of religio-cultural unity, without a homeland. In Eretz Yisrael, Jewish creativity can express itself in Hebraic form not so easily developed in other lands. There, Jews can attain sufficient autonomy to express their social will in economic and political institutions that might embody their highest ethical aspirations. Albert Einstein once stated the case for Eretz Yisrael succinctly in the following words: "Palestine will become a cultural home for all Jews, a refuge for the worst sufferers from oppression, a field of activity for the best among us, a unifying ideal and a source of spiritual health for the Jews of every country."

What is to be the future of the Jews outside Israel? That is bound up with the following two developments: a) democracy's success in resisting the tendencies that make for a monolithic state, and b) Jewry's success in redefining its own status in conformity with the modern conception of democratic society.

a) The American conception of democracy, which is pertinent to the future of Jews outside Israel, is unmistakably implied in the Federal Constitution. That Constitution, in prohibiting the adoption of any law which would deprive any one of religious freedom, precludes that totalitarian form of State or Church which would declare, for example, Roman Catholics as un-American, because they insist upon identifying themselves with the Vatican and Papacy. Indeed, Jews would never think of asserting their prerogatives to the same extent that the Roman Catholics do. It could never occur to Jews to ask the State to exempt them from school taxes, even if they undertook to provide for the complete education of their children. Since Jews frankly accord primacy to American civilization, there is no basis whatever for charging them with trying to set up a ghetto, or with halting the process of cultural inter-penetration, when they seek to foster their own Jewish heritage.

Religious freedom is meaningless, unless it include the recognition of cultural religious autonomy. Cultural-religious autonomy, on the other hand, does not mean segregation or separation from the life of the rest of the population. Western society is so constituted that, if it is to retain the values of individual personality and freedom, it must do nothing to undermine the two associations which have hitherto been the most potent means of social control, namely, the institution of the family and the religious fellowship. The stability of the former depends upon the stability of the latter. Non-Jews need those two social agencies to counteract the totalitarian tendencies of the modern State. By the same token, Jews need to retain the integrity of their family institution and of Jewish peoplehood.

The fear of being charged either with ghetto-ism or with hyphenated loyalty is largely responsible for the failure of the Jews outside Israel to make the most of their Jewish heritage and individuality. The way to come to terms with that fear is not to try to argue it down, but to create a thought pattern that would remove the very occasion for it. Modern pedagogy teaches that, when a child is afraid of the dark, the best thing to do is to turn on the light. What Jews need at present is such an understanding of their peoplehood as to inspire them with the will to demonstrate the normality of civilizational symbiosis, or living simultaneously in two civilizations, with no less zeal than their ancestors were ready to demonstrate, at all costs, the normality of worshipping only one God. They would manifest such zeal, if they would realize that by fostering their historic civilization simultaneously with their adopted civilization, they have the opportunity of proving, not only in theory, but also in practice, that the diversity of civilizations can become a blessing instead of a curse, and that each civilization should seek not to supplant but to supplement every other, religiously as well as culturally.

b) The present status of world Jewry is so anomalous that its survival outside Israel has been declared an anachronism, which means that Jewish survival does not make sense. The effect of being considered an anomaly cannot but be disruptive and demoralizing. It is impossible to evolve any consistent educational system, any creative cultural pattern, or any inspiring religious beliefs, so long as Jews in the Diaspora are content to remain the enigmatic, anonymous conglomerate they are now. Jews are faced, at present, with a crisis which is succinctly and sharply described in a recent report of the Polish Zionist Federation. "The State of Israel has solved the problem of Jewish homelessness," says the report. "Any Jew may now enter Israel as of right and will receive a very warm welcome. On the other hand, instead of uniting and consolidating the Jewish people all over the world, there is a real danger that the existence of the state may split them into two camps—Israelis and Diaspora Jews—each speaking a different language, thinking along different lines, living in a different atmosphere and absorbing a different culture. Zionism would then have created the Jewish state, but lost the Jewish people" (*N.Y. Times,* Sunday, March 30, 1952).

The only way to remedy this abnormal situation is to have representative Jews from all parts of the world convene in Jerusalem for the purpose of redefining the status of world Jewry as that of a trans-national people. They will have to indicate the historical, cultural and spiritual factors that constitute the unifying elements in Jewish peoplehood. In addition, they will have to formulate the various duties and responsibilities which Jews, wherever they live, will have to accept, and to state how far diversity in modes of life and organization might be carried, without destroying the integral unity of the Jewish People.

All this points to the need of arousing in the Jewish consciousness a demand for the renewal of the covenant by which Jews have lived hitherto as a People. Such renewal will have to prove something more even than the consent of Jews to rededicate themselves to the unity and perpetuation of the Jewish People. It will have to take the form of an impressive demonstration of the fact that Jews still possess a collective will, which can be translated into specific amendments to the Torah, and which would be in line of continuity with the various traditional *takanot,* or Rabbinic provisions, that form part of the Jewish tradition. Those specific amendments would have to define anew the basic rights and duties of Jews throughout the world in their relation to one another.

American Jews have formed all kinds of organizations and federations for specific purposes. These purposes, growing out of the circumstances of Jewish life, are in their very nature inter-dependent. They are treated, however, as though they had nothing to do with one another. The result is that though each purpose may singly be achieved, it does not further Jewish life as a whole. That is true not only of fraternal organization, social service, overseas relief and Zionist activity, but also of the synagogue and the religious school.

The only way to overcome that fragmentation of Jewish life is to have Jews form themselves into organic communities that would function as the instruments of Jewish life as a whole, and that would meet all its needs, in the order of their urgency and importance. Such a community would have to be democratically organized and represent all Jews who wish to be identified with it. Those who at present serve the various organizations and federations would then serve the entire community. Such reorganized communal life would not only coordinate Jewish activities efficiently, it would also integrate the Jew into the living body of the Jewish People, and give him that inner security which comes from belonging and from being wanted and welcomed.

The Reconstructionist movement, therefore, emphasizes the need of finding ways and means of living a maximum Jewish life within the setting of a modern democratic state. Though its program is directed specifically to American Jews, its philosophy applies to Jewish life everywhere. Viewing Judaism as a dynamic religious civilization, it addresses itself to the most urgent Jewish needs of our day, which are the following: 1) to restore the spiritual unity of the Jewish people, 2) to reorganize the communal life of the American Jews, 3) to aid the development of Israel, 4) to revitalize Jewish religion, 5) to encourage Jewish cultural creativity in education, literature and the arts, 6) to intensify participation by Jews in all activities that further the ideals of democracy.

II

So long as religion permeated every phase of human life, and all human needs and interests had to be brought within its orbit, it could afford to be the chief means of self-expression. Now, however, that the esthetic interests have earned, in their own right, a place in the life of the human spirit, to confine Judaism within the limits of what is exclusively religious in character, is to render it irrelevant to most people who are not given to theologizing. For the very sake of religion, it is necessary to foster other interests besides religion. Religion is a quality of life, the substance of which consists of the manifold of human interests, with all their satisfactions and their problems. Community life gives rise to, and depends upon, creative self-expression through poetry, drama, music, sculpture, painting and achitecture, belles lettres, scholarship and philosophy. Only when religion is a quality of such communal living, does it have content, vitality and appeal. Emptied of these concrete manifestations of social and esthetic activity, religion is either a form of theurgy or vacuous mysticism.

It is futile to expect all Jews ever again to profess a uniform type of Jewish religion. That was possible only as long as the world around them was dominated not only by religion, but by one kind of religion. Now, however, with the rest of the world in a state of utter confusion in the matter of religion, diversity of religious belief and practice among Jews is inevitable. But that Jews can be altogether religion-less is paradoxical. Such Jews cannot long remain Jews. Frenchmen and Englishmen, regardless of adherence to the Church will remain loyal to their respective nations. That is because the Church is not an integral part of the life of the Frenchman as Frenchman, or the Englishman as Englishman. The case is otherwise with Jews. Their very peoplehood has always been given a religious significance, and it owes its very survival to that fact. For Jews to try to maintain their peoplehood without their religion is to deprive the former of the principal element by which it can be made into a spiritual asset.

It should not be difficult to render Jewish religion viable in the modern cultural climate. All that is necessary is to accustom the modern-minded Jew to realize that religion is fundamentally a type of human experience which derives from an affirmative and hopeful reaction to life as a whole. So viewed, religion is basically the acceptance of human life as having meaning, that is, as capable of entering into ever-increasing numbers of relations with the rest of reality and of being dominated by purposes of its own choosing. Religion is the ability to discover creative possibilities in the most unpromising aspects of human life. The mystic doctrine that "the sparks of divinity" inhere in all things is what all religion should seek to verify. If we regard human life as deserving that we give it the best that is in us, we necessarily regard it as sacred and divine. If we accept life in that spirit, we are not only religious in the truest and best sense of the term, but also attain the insight which enables us to appreciate what mankind has sought to achieve through religion. We then begin to understand religion as a dynamic and evolving process, and not as a fixed system of beliefs and ordinances to be either wholly accepted or rejected.

In the past, the Jews looked forward to the acceptance of Jewish religion by all the world, as the prerequisite to the coming of the millennium, or to the establishment of the Kingdom of God. Nowadays, however, the very expectation that the religion of any one People or Church can, or should, become the religion of mankind is an anachronism. The main significance of the fact that Judaism is a religious civilization is that Jews cannot expect to function as a People, nor keep their historic civilization alive in the Diaspora, unless they make the beneficient functioning of religion their special concern and interest.

In order that the religious aspect of any civilization function beneficiently, it has to foster the kind of belief in God that is capable of serving as inspiration and sanction for whatever is likely to render man more fully human. That is his destiny and therein lies his salvation. All the world is at present badly in need of such religion. Only such religion can supply a minority people like the Jews with the moral courage to resist being absorbed by the majority populations. The prophet, who first promulgated the mission idea, did not imply that all the people in the world should become Jews. He knew too well that even among his fellow-Jews very few lived by the kind of religion he had in mind. He was fully aware of the spiritual callousness of those he called upon to assume a religious mission. "Who is as blind as my servant, as deaf as my messenger," he cried out. (Is. 42:19).

The Jews were then already dispersed among the nations. Realizing their plight, the anonymous prophet whose words are recorded in the second part of Isaiah, pleaded with them to adopt the cause of beneficent religion as the purpose and meaning of their existence as a People. He stated specifically what he regarded as beneficent religion, in the following words: "I the Lord have called thee in righteousness, and have taken thee by the hand, and kept thee as a covenanted people to be a light of the nations; to open eyes that are blind, to free captives from their dungeon, and them that sit in darkness from out of the prison-house." (Is. 42;6-7). No words could more forcibly convey the truth that the Jews' salvation lay in serving God, by furthering the cause of enlightenment and freedom.

The particularity of Jewish religion derives from the experiences which are peculiar to the Jewish People. That particularity has to be preserved in the process of bringing Jewish religion into live contact with the contemporary universe of values. This can be accomplished by taking into account the entire mass of the traditional ideas and practices which belong to the spiritual heritage of the Jewish People, and reinterpreting them from the standpoint of what are felt to be the most urgent moral and spiritual needs in our day. The reason for this is that those traditional values carry with them the accumulated momentum and emotional drive of our People's past efforts to find and render life meaningful. If those values are shown to be relevant to our day, they can transmit that emotional drive. To render them thus relevant we have to discover what spiritual or ethical urge was latent in the traditional practices, and particularly in the meanings assigned to them.

To illustrate specifically how this approach can revitalize Jewish religion, belief and practice, we shall select from among the traditional Jewish values those of the Sabbath and the Festivals. Those sacred days of the Jewish calendar still have something of a spiritual appeal to all who profess attachment to Jewish life. In the religious tradition, they are assigned meanings which are representative of what that tradition would have us associate with the belief in God.

The following is a tentative attempt to formulate a conception of God in terms that are significant for our day. It is based upon the reinterpretation of the traditional values associated with the Jewish Sabbaths and Festivals.

1. *God as the Power that makes for salvation.* The Sabbath is essentially a symbol of salvation. As such it affirms that all men can achieve salvation, if they avail themselves of the resources that inhere in the world about them and make use of their own abilities. This affirmation is supported by the following teachings expressed, or implied, in the meanings which tradition itself assigns to the Sabbath: a) God is the creative life of the universe; irrevocable fate and absolute evil are deceitful illusions. b) God is manifest in life's holiness which presupposes the working of divinity in the human person. Man's personality is the instrument through which God as the creative life of the world achieves the evolution of the human race. c) God manifests himself in a people's sense of responsibility for contributing creatively to the salvation of mankind. These are the teachings of the Sabbath.

2. *God as the Power that makes for social regeneration.* The modern emphasis upon God's immanence necessitates our reinterpreting the traditional conception of God's sovereignty. As reinterpreted, that conception can function as an aid to the regeneration of society by direct human agency, without reliance on the illusory hope of miraculous intervention. Human initiative and active striving in transforming the conditions under which man lives constitute a manifestation of the divine. These are the teachings of Rosh Hashanah.

3. *God as the Power that makes for the regeneration of human nature.* If we identify God with that aspect of reality which confers meaning and value on life and elicits from us those ideals that determine the course of human progress, then the failure to live up to the best that is in us means that our souls are not in harmony with the divine. That constitutes sin.

The effort of life to achieve and express unity, harmony and integrity, renders life holy. It testifies to the divine possibilities which inhere in human life. Whatever thwarts this effort is sin.

The sins of the individual corrupt the social structure, and the corruption of the social institutions spreads the contagion among individuals. Translated into conduct, the doctrine of the unity of God calls for the integration of all of life's purposes into a consistent pattern of thought and conduct.

Repentance is part of the normal functioning of personality in its effort at progressive self-realization. If human character is to reflect the divine, it must be integrated and self-consistent. This calls for a progressive synthesis of individual self-expression and social cooperation. Such a synthesis is, therefore, evidence of spiritual attainment and the fruit of effective repentance. Whenever we recognize our failure to do justice to the spiritual demands of a new situation, and try to overcome the obstacles that prevent our lives from manifesting the divine, we are practicing repentance, or the return to God. These are the teachings of *Yom Kippur*.

4. *God in nature and in history.* By utilizing the nature festivals to recall historical experiences, the Jews directed the human mind to the consciousness of human history as an ethical and spiritual influence in human life. In contributing to human consciousness the sense of history, the Jews have not only enriched human life but have also created new problems. Both the creative powers in the physical world and the spiritual forces in the human world, that make for personal and social redemption, are treated in Jewish religion as manifestations of the divine. These are the teachings of the Three Pilgrim Festivals.

5. *God as the Power that makes for cooperation.* The tendencies and relationships that augment the unity and value of life, and thus point to the reality of God, are mediated for man chiefly through the organized life of society. Society, therefore, owes it to the individual, in its own interest as well as in his, to give him the opportunity for employing his powers and faculties to the full. Society which deprives men of the opportunity to enjoy and create esthetic values, or which manages its affairs in such a way as to render men godless, bitter and hateful of life, stands self-condemned, as denying men their inalienable right to the pursuit of happiness.

The doctrine of equality does not imply that all men must have identical opportunities for education, employment and esthetic and religious self-expression. It does imply, however, that all have an equal claim to the opportunity to pursue these activities to the limits of their own varying capacities, and in accordance with their own individual interests, insofar as these are not detrimental to the general good. Rights are contentless, unless they are rights to things, or property rights. Only those rights to property, however, which emanate from the concept of personality and are indispensable to its fulfillment are sacred and inviolable.

Cooperation is the chief source of happiness; competition its principal menace. Civilization has become synonymous with the progressive emergence of individuals and groups engaged in internecine struggle for power. The *Sukkot* Festival, with its emphasis on joyous gratitude or happiness, is the protest not against civilization but against its tendency to be a destroyer of happiness. These are the specific teachings of *Sukkot*.

6. *God as the Power that makes for freedom.* The conception of God as the Redeemer of the oppressed has revolutionized the meaning and function of religion, and has placed it as the service of the ethical impulses. Freedom is at the very root of man's spiritual life, and is the primary condition of his self-fulfillment, or salvation. The meaning of religion can be grasped only when social life is based on freedom. The right into which one is born is only potential freedom. Actual freedom is an achievement, with the aid of a civilization, which is based on the high worth of the human person.

When we look to God as the Power that makes for freedom, we expect that He will give mankind no rest until it puts an end to the order of social living in which human beings drudge and slave for aims in which they have no part or parcel. The freedom which means the release of selfhood consists in the right to be honest, different, and creative. These are the specific teachings of *Pesah*.

7. *God as the Power that makes for righteousness—not ourselves.* The moral law must be regarded not as some prudential arrangement or social convention, but as inherent in the very nature of reality. Jewish religion is unique in clearly recognizing that the chief function of the belief in God is to confirm and fortify the moral law. The word "God" has come to be symbolically

expressive of the highest ideals for which men strive. At the same time, it points to the objective fact that nature, both in the world and in man, is so constituted as to make for the realization of those ideals.

Human personality, with its reference to goals of human behavior beyond our capacity, points to a Power that makes for righteousness—not ourselves. What God means to us depends mainly upon our ideal of human life, or life as it ought to be. And the way we conceive that ideal depends upon the level of civilization we have attained. God is thus the Power that endorses what we believe *ought* to be, and that guarantees that it *will* be. Just as the will to live testifies, in an intuitive sense, to the cosmic support of life, so the will to achieve the abundant, or fully human life, testifies to the ultimate attainment of that life. These are specific teachings of the Festival of *Shabuot*.

III

It is incumbent upon American Jews to demonstrate how they expect to solve the problem of living in two civilizations simultaneously. That is a problem which they share with their fellow-Americans who are adherents of historic faiths. Each of those faiths has to be lived in its historic civilizational context, if it is not to be reduced to a series of abstract platitudes. Insofar, however, as their adherents wish to integrate their own lives into the general American civilization, they have the task of enriching it by bringing to it some special contribution from their own historic civilizations. That raises the question: What would Jews have to do to excel in the field of religion in such a way as to enrich American life?

To answer that question we must take into consideration the anomalous condition in which the American people finds itself religiously. To prevent the historical religions, which lay claim to being supernaturally revealed and to being the sole means to salvation, from engaging in mutual conflict for political and cultural domination, the American Constitution has adopted the principle of separation of Church and State. So far as domination is concerned, the Constitution has been effective. But that has not prevented the main religious bodies, like the Roman Catholic

Church, and the outstanding Protestant churches, from seeking to influence legislation and education in favor of their respective ways of life. It has fallen to the lot of the Jews to urge legislation and education in keeping with the principle of separation of Church and State. On the face of it, every such attempt of Jews is made to appear like a move in the direction of secularism and irreligion. In being staunch supporters of the American Constitution, Jews ought to be regarded as good Americans trying to have other Americans live up to their commitment, but life does not work that way.

The fact is that the constitutional amendment pertaining to the separation of Church and State has far-reaching implications, which those who enacted it probably never contemplated. That is where all the trouble comes from. Sooner or later, all Americans will have to face up to those implications. American Jews have to do so now, if they wish to do their share as a group in extricating American civilization from the predicament in which it finds itself in relation to religion.

The separation of State and Church means, in effect, that the Founders of the United States were determined that none of the historical religions, which claimed to have been supernaturally revealed, should form an integral part of the life and culture of the newly-born nation. That does not mean that they expected the civilization of the American people to be devoid of all religious spirit. To ascribe that intention to them is to misread their mind. It is true that there are but few references to God in official documents, but those few bespeak deep religious conviction.

The Founding Fathers, undoubtedly, had in mind some kind of naturalistic religion, like that implied in the well-known phrase, "nature's God." They assumed, no doubt, that such religion would evolve out of the life-experience of the American nation. That is the kind of religion practiced, though seldom professed, by so typical and ideal an American as Lincoln. That is the religion that affects people's lives, without being authoritarian. When the national hymn "America" invokes "Our fathers' God . . . Author of Liberty," it implies a religious interpretation of American experience: A typically contemporary expression of that same religious spirit of America is to be found in the concluding passage of

Adlai E. Stevenson's address in Chicago on Sept. 15, 1953: "We will have to learn to think of the responsibility of leadership . . . as a status in an interdependent world that we Americans . . . must live in, work in, pray for, and pray for on the accents of mercy, justice and faith in a Power greater than ours or any man's."

The framers of the Constitution knew too little about religion as a manifestation of human nature to be able to envisage any practical alternative to the traditional theurgic type of religion. All they could do was to philosophize abstractly about God's being and attributes. Living before the great modern anthropological discoveries, they were sure that institutional religion was either priest-craft or esoteric philosophy. They saw in the growth of modern nationalism the inevitable obsolescence of authoritative religions. But they could not realize that, without free religion to curb and direct modern nationalism, humanity would be rebarbarized. That is why the separation of State and Church has created a religious vacuum, without anything being done to fill it.

The condition of man has undergone a revolution. The range of his knowledge, ability, and resources has been so enlarged that he can obtain most of what he needs in the way of sustenance, security, and health without the aid of theurgic religion. The blood kinship on which he depended, and which was given importance and sanctity by his religion, is now replaced by his economic organizations and his nationalisms. The description of the pre-modern age as "the Age of Faith" is a misnomer, and based on a misunderstanding. Modern man's faith in science, technology, trade unionism, and nationalism is just as intense and as blind as was his faith in the power of prayer and ritual. To be sure, this modern faith is not faith in God. Does that necessarily mean that man can dispense with faith in God? Certainly not, if the God in whom man is to have faith is one whom the present condition of man renders indispensable.

As a result of the widened range of knowledge and resourcefulness, and the substitution of political and economic association for religiously sanctioned kinship, we find ourselves in a state of perpetual tension and foreboding. The threat of global war and universal devastation hangs like a dark cloud over our lives. We have lost faith in man. We have lost our way in life. We are not sure that there is any real difference between good and evil. We seek in vain to drown our fears and boredoms in a welter of action, excitement and self-indulgence. That is certainly not the way to live; it is only a way to make a mess of life.

In the light of this modern condition of man, the primary task of American Jewry is to have the belief in God motivate the following objectives: 1) the utilization of our material progress for purposes of peace and for the enhancement of human life; 2) the pursuit of the human sciences and arts with a view to the elimination of poverty, ignorance, and disease, and to the creation of opportunities for everybody's material, intellectual, emotional and spiritual self-fulfillment; 3) the limitation of the sovereignty of the nations and the translation of their economic interdependence into a workable program for the free exchange of goods and services on a world scale; 4) the inculcation in the individual of a sense of responsibility for doing his personal share toward making the world the better and the happier for his having lived in it.

The second task of American Jewry is to promulgate an indigenous civic religion for the American people that shall act as a unifying influence, uniting all Americans regardless of race, creed, or status, without being authoritative or coercive. That task involves the incorporation into American institutions and practices of those principles in Jewish religion which have a universal import and are therefore transferable to other civilizations.

The universal principles in Jewish religion and their application to American life may be formulated as follows:

1) That God is the God of Israel implies that a People, of which we are a part, should provide the principal experiences on which to base our belief in, or awareness of, God as the Power that makes for salvation. Those experiences constitute the substance which should yield the values that give meaning to human life. As Americans, therefore, we should identify those experiences and strivings in American life and history which would not only give organic character to the American People, but also set it on the road to human progress and perfection. To the extent that American experiences and strivings do that, they reveal God as

the Power that makes for salvation and should be interpreted as such, culturally and educationally.

2) According to the teaching of the Torah and the Prophets, the People of Israel was expected to demonstrate its loyalty to God not merely by worshipping Him, but mainly by practicing justice and righteousness. These are called "the way of the Lord" (Genesis 18:19). In the light of that teaching, failure to walk in that way has brought untold suffering on the People of Israel. Unrighteousness is the offspring of pride which takes the form of rebellion against God, or playing the god. Translated into universal terms, that teaching implies that the religion of a people has to find expression principally in the practice of righteousness in its political, economic, and social affairs. That is the divine law for every people. Violation of that law is bound to lead to failure and disaster.

An illustration of the way those principles should be incorporated in American institutional life is afforded by "The Faith of America." That book contains programs for the religious observance of American holidays, using for this purpose materials drawn from American literature and historical documents. Each holiday is given a specific religious theme. The theme for Lincoln's Birthday, for example, is the ideal of equality and fraternity; for Washington's Birthday, the promise and responsibility of nationhood, and so on with all the other holidays.

Given the wish to survive as a segment of the Jewish People, that wish is bound to seek an outlet in some effort that would give to our persistence as Jews not merely the significance of inertia, but rather the lift that comes from being dedicated to a high purpose. That high purpose should be to contribute to the spiritual life of America the kind of civic religion that will place America in the spiritual forefront of the world, as she is now in the political and economic. That high purpose should be to achieve for ourselves a conception of Jewish religion that is as free and creative as poetry, literature and art, a Jewish religion that is vitally relevant to reality as we know it and live it.

THE SYNAGOGUE IN

AMERICAN JUDAISM

A Study of Congregation B'nai Jeshurun
New York City

---

by Moshe Davis

THE EVOLUTION OF the Synagogue as the basic institution in Jewish group life is central to the history of the Jewish community in America. From the earliest settlements in Colonial days, when there were a handful of congregations all of one pattern, until our own day, when congregations are numbered in the thousands with diversified patterns of belief and practice, the Synagogue has been the cornerstone of the Jewish communal structure. It has at once supported and fashioned the character of Jewish group experience.

The American Synagogue demonstrates clearly the historic process of continuity amid change. Not only has it served as the chief instrumentality to transfer the Jewish tradition from one continent to another, but also, in this very process of transmission, the Synagogue gained new strength. On this continent, for example, the Synagogue had to adapt itself to a continuously developing Jewish community life and to an American environment of freedom of thought and expression. To understand the nature of the American Synagogue is to understand the meaning of American Judaism.

One can often gain insight into a total situation by isolating one of its aspects. The specific, as Rabbi Ishmael teaches in one of his rules of interpretation of the Bible, may hold the kernel of the whole. One of the very few synagogues in American Judaism which affords an opportunity to study Jewish religious history in this light is Congregation B'nai Jeshurun in New York City, whose origin is to be found in the post-Colonial period of nascent American cultural independence and whose history spans the career of American Jewry to the current era.

"Length of days," however, is not the major contribution this congregation offers to our understanding of American Jewish religious history. Rather it is the story of how B'nai Jeshurun squarely met the issues and events of each oncoming age, always seeking to find the balance between the old and the new. Dr. Goldstein reminded his congregation on the occasion of its one hundred and twenty-fifth anniversary: "If we of B'nai Jeshurun are an historic congregation in American Jewry, it is not so much because we have existed for a long time but because we reflect the developments and have played a part in the events of American Jewish history. The rise of American Jewry is reflected in our own congregational constituency. Our congregational families, first, second, third, and fourth generation American stock, as well as immigrant stock with antecedents derived from all the lands of Europe, are a broad cross-section of the flesh and bone of American Jewry." [1]

I

The character of American Jewish congregational life was on the verge of radical transformation in the early part of the nineteenth century, for as American society changed so did its Jewish community, and it was through the Synagogue that the changes in Jewry were expressed. The dominant factor in the changing social and economic scene of early nineteenth-century America is the emergence of the city as the major center of residence and occupation. While, in the American occupational structure, the majority of the population still continued to be occupied in agriculture, yet commercial and industrial pursuits began to involve a new city work force. This was indeed, "The End of Arcadia." [2]

During this period, the country at large was undergoing fundamental economic and social changes. New York State, particularly

New York City, served as the focal point in these changes. In 1825, Governor DeWitt Clinton officiated at a ceremony called the "marriage of the waters," marking the union of the Atlantic Ocean with Lake Erie by means of the Erie Canal. A new epoch began for the City of New York. Already called the "commercial emporium," New York now became the greatest port of immigration in the United States. Within the century, New York City was to become the economic capital of America and the gateway to the New World for millions of immigrant Europeans.[3] Describing New York City as "the new capital," Vernon Parrington found that "the romance of expansion was creating there a new psychology, and this new psychology was preparing the city for leadership in the new age that was rising." [4]

The second decade of the nineteenth century was also a watershed in American Jewish history. The New World, rather than other European countries, became, for the first time in Jewish history, the principal haven for the politically persecuted, the religiously oppressed, and the economically uprooted. The Napoleonic wars, anti-Jewish economic and religious edicts in the southern German States, (e.g., Bavaria, 1813; Württemberg, 1828), and other crises in Poland, forced many Jews to seek refuge on American shores. In literary and social societies, especially in Germany, Jews learned about the liberty-loving people across the seas. Repeated "invitations to America," issued both here and abroad, in American newspaper editorials and in broadsides published and distributed in Europe, interested these people in emigration. America needed human power for its cities and farms; many Europeans needed a refuge and hope.

The Jewish community in America, consisting of some three thousand in 1818, doubled in number by 1826, and rose to fifteen thousand by 1840. In 1825, the general population of New York City consisted of some two hundred thousand residents, while the Jewish population was estimated at between six hundred and a thousand—less than one percent of the total population. But this was the very beginning of a process, which in its unfolding, created in New York City the largest settlement of Jews in the history of the people. At the same time, the American Jewish settlement rapidly assumed the polyglot character of the country as a whole, and consisted of Jews of English, Dutch, German, Polish, Bohemian, Russian, Spanish and Portuguese origin, as well as of native Americans.

Meanwhile, the real drama of growth, tension and change in congregational life was taking place in a series of apparently insignificant acts. The first extra-synagogue philanthropic society in New York, the Hebrah Gemiluth Hesed (later the Hebrew Mutual Benefit Society), was established in 1822 by "18 gentlemen who afterwards became members of Congregation B'nai Jeshurun." Five years later a letter (dated October 6, 1825) was addressed by a group of fifteen Jews in New York City, headed by John I. Hart, to the Parnass and Trustees of the K. K. Shearith Israel, informing them that "we are deputed a committee from a meeting of Israelites held at Washington Hall to announce to you their intention to erect a new Synagogue in this city."

The change wrought in Jewish communal life as a consequence of these two decisions was profound: the monolithic structure of the Colonial Synagogue, organized in accordance with the Sephardic *minhag* and organizational practice, was replaced by a new form of synagogue life—differing not only in ritual practice but also in organizational method and communal outlook. It had been the policy of the Sephardic leadership not to encourage more than one synagogue in a city. For that reason, they demurred in New York, as in Philadelphia and elsewhere, when it was suggested that a second synagogue be established. But they could not deny the need for another synagogue in New York City. As the community grew, Shearith Israel had either to grow—and change—or to admit the right of others to form congregations. Therefore, while we cannot discount entirely the personal factors in the split of the congregation, it was the larger issue which compelled the leaders of Shearith Israel to submit with good grace to the organization of the proposed synagogue. They realized that their own synagogue building was too small to hold all who would come; and if they admitted the Ashkenazim as members, the original Sephardic families would be overwhelmed numerically. Conceivably, then, the ritual practices of the congregation could be changed because of "the increased number of our brethren, and also the probability of many more coming to reside in the city." [5] Men, such as Mordecai M. Noah, himself not an Ashkenazic Jew, supported the new congregation, and the members of Shearith Israel, individually and collectively, participated, on Friday afternoon, June 29, 1827, in the dedication ceremonies of B'nai Jeshurun Elm Street synagogue, the first Ashkenazic congregation in New York City. In a comparatively short period of fifteen years (1825-1840), three additional Ashkenazic synagogues were established in the city.

The chronicle of Congregation B'nai Jeshurun, the story of its relationship with sister congregations, the benevolent and mutual aid organizations which derived from it, its unwavering concern for Jews the world over, the extraordinary contribution to the rebuilding of *Eretz Yisrael* of this congregation—all this is fully described and thoroughly documented in Dr. Goldstein's volume "A Century of Judaism in New York." Here we wish to study the character of the congregation in relation to three themes: the evolution of American rabbinic authority; Jewish education; and the role of the Synagogue in American religious life. Placed against the background of American Jewish life in its formative years, these themes may help us to understand the spiritual motivation of the reoriented Synagogue in America.

II

One of the most difficult problems of American Jewish religious life in the nineteenth century was the relationship between the synagogues in the new country and the mother congregations in Europe, especially the question of rabbinic authority.

In 1825, it could not occur to anyone that American rabbinic leadership would come from native resources. The problem was another one entirely: how to maintain contact with rabbinic authority in the mother country. This question was, of course, not singular to the small Jewish community in America, but rather part of a larger cultural issue. The American people in general had to resolve the question of cultural subordination to Europe.

Though politically independent, the young nation remained under the intellectual and cultural domination of Europe. While it is true that, already in the eighteenth century, a diverse variety of backgrounds existed among the colonists, the cultural pattern which prevailed overwhelmingly was English in origin. Long after it had lost political dominion, England continued to retain its cultural hegemony over the former colony.

But spiritual independence had to follow political independence. In the early decades of the nineteenth century, America entered a period of cultural transformation: it was a nation in search of its own self. A body of opinion began to coalesce which urged the sundering of all cultural ties with Europe. Writers and other cultural leaders argued that America ought to be willing to suffer the inadequacies and immaturities of a "native culture" rather than feed on foreign importations. Let us not imitate, they pleaded; better to create *de novo;* imitation is disingenuous and ultimately suicidal for the young nation; a cultural embargo was urged. Actually these extreme arguments heralded the birth of "American" culture. American ideas of humanitarianism, individualism, and particularism sought and found native expression.

How this process of the particularization of culture affected Jewish life is revealed in the history of Congregation B'nai Jeshurun. The new congregation was patterned after the Great Synagogue in London. The majority of the members being of English origin, they naturally followed the ritual of the service at London. John I. Hart, the *Parnass* of B'nai Jeshurun and the head of the group that left Shearith Israel, was himself the son of the Reader in Portsmouth, England. Readers for the American "branch" were sought in the *London Jewish Chronicle,* and as late as 1837, the half-shekel contributions which were collected on Purim were sent to the Chief Rabbi in England, then Rabbi Solomon Hirschell. It was not a slip of the pen in an entry in the B'nai Jeshurun letter-book which referred to Rabbi Hirschell as the "High Priest of England." Nor was it merely characteristic English phraseology. It indicated the true sentiment of the congregation towards its spiritual leader abroad.[6] "High Priest" or not, Rabbi Hirschell as Chief Rabbi of England, did hold final authority over Congregation B'nai Jeshurun in New York and other Ashkenazic congregations, as the series of specific ritual questions addressed to him amply demonstrates.[7]

On one occasion, the Chief Rabbi did express his wish for "a man to arise in the light of whose learning and virtue the ˈkehilloth' of America could walk in uprightness according to our holy law. But," he added, "until that is the case the intimate connection between your country and England renders it imperative on me to remonstrate against such improper practices [the case of an unauthorized divorce]. You will have the goodness and communicate the contents of this letter to the various 'kehilloth' throughout the union so as to prevent a repetition of these illegal 'Gittin' [bills of divorce]."[8]

Despite their reverence for the Great Synagogue and the Chief Rabbi, it became clear that absentee trans-Atlantic authority could not prevail indefinitely. Slowly the congregation began to grow away from this complete subservience. Even under Rabbi Hirschell's authority, only the more complicated questions had been referred directly to him. When the determination of Jewish law in a given situation was comparatively simple, the congregation consulted Israel B. Kursheedt, in his time the most learned layman in the congregation and a leading public figure. Yet, the vacuum of rabbinic leadership had somehow to be filled. The inadequacy of foreign authority brought about the second, intermediary, phase between complete spiritual dependence and self-sufficiency: the importation of rabbinic authorities from abroad.

Samuel Meyer Isaacs (1839-1849) and Morris Raphall (1849-1868), the first two rabbis of B'nai Jeshurun in this interim period both came from England. These men brought much personal prestige with them, and they conferred that prestige upon the congregation. During their years of leadership, the sermon was incorporated as a regular part of the Sabbath service. Isaacs preached only occasionally, because the sermon during his years was still considered an innovation. But Raphall preached regularly and effectively. The congregation grew in influence and expanded its program under their leadership. Both successfully fought off the advance of Reform, and the congregation maintained its traditional orientation. They achieved their purpose through personal authority and through the strength of enlightened explanation.

Dr. Raphall's ministry was the longer and more effective of the two, particularly in scholarly and religious influence. Recognizing in him the type of rabbi which Congregation B'nai Jeshurun and other traditionally-minded synagogues in America would require, the Board of Trustees formulated its views of model rabbinic leadership in a resolution in 1860, specifying the following qualifications: "No person shall be elected preacher of this congregation unless he be fully competent to deliver religious lectures in the English language; he shall also be sufficiently learned in the Jewish laws to decide ecclesiastical questions that may occur in the congregation; and he shall be competent and it shall be his duty to superintend any educational institute which may be attached to this Congregation." [9]

The indispensability of continuous American rabbinic authority became increasingly apparent during the second half of the nineteenth century, when American Jewry entered into an era of internal ideological and religious struggle. Together with other synagogues of traditional scope, Congregation B'nai Jeshurun was groping for an indigenous expression of the Tradition, an expression which would not only consist of a series of ritual compromises, but would also reflect a constructive approach to the Tradition and to its historic method of adaptation to the needs of a new age. They were groping towards the "positive-historical" approach, as it was called in Europe, or the Conservative approach, as it came to be known later in America. To develop such an awareness, the leaders of B'nai Jeshurun joined forces with several congregations in New York and other cities, to solve the long-postponed problem of local rabbinic education by creating a school for the training of rabbis. Through the preparation of students who themselves would have experienced the nature of American Jewish life, a rabbinate would emerge competent to cope with the contemporary need for change, yet able to conserve the essential character of Judaism. Thus began the third phase in the development of local rabbinic authority, reliance on native training.

The leading proponent in B'nai Jeshurun of an American rabbinical academy was Henry S. Jacobs, rabbi of the congregation during the crucial years from 1876-1893.[10] Henry Jacobs understood the problem of American Judaism. Born and trained in Kingston, Jamaica, in the West Indies, he served at the Ashkenazic synagogue in Kingston, and also held several posts in Sephardic and Ashkenazic communities in the United States before coming for a brief term to Shearith Israel. This wide practical experience taught him to understand the key problem with which American congregations were faced—the lack of a rabbinate properly trained in the sources of Judaism and, therefore, unable to relate the Tradition to life in America.

Jacobs devoted a great deal of effort to the establishment of a school for the training of a native rabbinate. In 1876, he joined the movement to found an American Hebrew College (alternately known as the Hebrew Theological College), as part of the Temple Emanu-El group. He was appointed secretary of a committee which tried to revive plans for this school which had been initiated as early as 1852. Classes were held for several terms, but nothing permanent developed.[11]

Jacobs' religious views made him a natural ally of such "moderate reformers" in the Historical, or Conservative group, as Rabbis Benjamin Szold and Marcus Jastrow. These men had associated themselves with the Isaac M. Wise plan to build an all-embracing Hebrew Union College in Cincinnati. But soon, Jacobs and the others, were disenchanted with Wise and they joined with Sabato Morais and Alexander Kohut to establish the Jewish Theological Seminary. When B'nai Jeshurun formally disassociated itself from the Union of American Hebrew Congregations, the congregation became an active force in the creation of the Seminary. Newman Cowen, a scholarly layman, then treasurer of the congregation, became a trustee of the Seminary, and enlisted support in its behalf. Because of his devotion to the Seminary, Cowen was elected first as treasurer, and later as vice-president of the board of directors. Henry Jacobs also was prominent in the affairs of the Seminary from its inception and was appointed to its Advisory Board of Ministers, assisting as an examiner of students.

For this far-sighted investment in the future of American Jewry, the congregation was amply rewarded. The "seedling" which they had helped plant in 1886 bore fruit, nourishing and sustaining the congregation itself. In 1918, at the invitation of Sol M. Stroock, honorary secretary of the congregation and a director of the Seminary board (later chairman), and at the suggestion of Dr. Cyrus Adler, head of the Seminary, a young graduate, Rabbi Israel Goldstein, was elected spiritual leader of B'nai Jeshurun.

Largely as a result of his continuous service, the congregation has become pre-eminent in American Jewish congregational life.

In the process of struggle with its own problems of rabbinic leadership, B'nai Jeshurun had learned an important lesson: the creation and sustenance of rabbinic authority is a collective enterprise; and it is the concern of the entire American Synagogue. Spiritual leadership requires a people who seek it, as well as rabbis who are trained to exercise it. While the Conservative movement fostered its Seminary, the Reform group strengthened its Hebrew Union College; and before the turn of the century, Orthodox Jewry had established its own Yeshiva. Thus, by a combination of actions, American Jewry had grown into full maturity in its rabbinic leadership, and solved the once seemingly insoluble problem of obtaining adequate native rabbinic authority.

The capital example of this amazing development occurred when Rabbi Joseph H. Hertz, a graduate of the first Seminary class (1894), was invited to become Chief Rabbi of the United Hebrew Congregation of the British Empire (1913). In the years following, other graduates of the three major rabbinical schools were invited to congregations in England and South Africa. One of this group, Rabbi Joel Blau, a former rabbi of Congregation B'nai Jeshurun (1913-1917), was called in 1925 to the position of Senior Minister of the West London Synagog of British Jews. From utter dependence on the rabbinic leaders of British Jewry, the American community had grown to provide rabbis to this same Jewry. The spiritual beneficiary became spiritual benefactor.

III

If, in the area of rabbinic authority, the American Synagogue discovered a direction amid the complexities of the modern world, that measure of achievement has been denied it thus far in an equally vital area of Jewish life, namely, Jewish education. The problem of Jewish education has been one of the permanently unsolved problems on the agenda of American Jewry since the early decades of the past century; and it is an especially acute problem to the congregations of the Conservative movement to which B'nai Jeshurun adheres.

"The Jewish religion," H. G. Wells once observed, "because it is a literature-sustained religion, led to the first efforts to provide elementary instruction for all the children of the community." This very contribution to civilization forced modern Jewry into the throes of a perpetual dilemma, for the system of universal public education has made the problem of intensive Jewish education seem insoluble. As long as the education of their young was the exclusive province of the Jewish community, the Jews were able to educate their children in the discipline of their faith and culture. However, with the advance of universal education, responsibility for the education of the child came to be vested in the State, and religious education became the responsibility of the home and the religious group. As a result, religious education was reduced to a secondary and, at best, supplementary form of learning. The paradox is that the Jewish community conscientiously supported the rise of the public school movement for the enhancement of democracy, and consequently, Jewish life. Yet with the loss of status and time (two crucial factors in any educational framework) how could the Jewish community train a Jewishly learned laity? How could it raise a generation of Jewishly literate Jews? These were the problems posed by the introduction of public education. These problems remain unresolved today.

That an acceptable solution has not yet been found does not suggest that the question has been ignored; tireless efforts and large expenditures of funds have been poured into the quest for the development of a system of Jewish education within the American pattern. If a new approach is now taking hold of leaders in Jewish religious education, it is due to the frustrations and lessons of the past, and to the change of opinion in America generally, with regard to the value and role of religious education in training the youth of the nation. The history of Jewish educational endeavor at Congregation B'nai Jeshurun offers instruction in the perplexities and possibilities of Jewish school training in America.

The Jewish school in Colonial days, as is well known, was an organic part of the congregation. Some of the children went off to Christian private schools, but they were the exception; most Jewish children were educated within the Synagogue. Shearith Israel established the first school of this type in New York, Yeshibat Minhat Areb, as early as 1731. It was, therefore, to be expected that B'nai Jeshurun would also attempt to found an all-day school. A generation was to pass before their plan became a reality. In 1852, under the leadership of Dr. Raphall, an earlier decision of the board of directors was implemented, and the B'nai Jeshurun Educational Institute was established for "males and females, to give them a Hebrew, English and classical education."

The deeper purpose of the Institute, we are told by a reporter in *The Occident,* is "to make our religion familiar to their children, *like household words* . . ." (italics ours).[12] Eighty-eight children were registered in the first school enrollment in 1853. The curriculum was designed to meet the standards of the best schools of the time. Soon the Institute had its own building—"the first school built by Hebrews in these United States." The ambition of the *The Occident* reporter for the educational achievements of the school exceeded even that of the builders of the physical structure: "I trust ere long to be able to speak of Rashi, and Rabbinical classics, Euclid and Latin classics, as integral portions of the instruction . . ."[13]

Altogether, the congregation took great pride in its accomplishment and received praise from other congregations and from leading citizens. Again, the reporter for *The Occident* did not confuse values. Speaking to other generations as well as his own, he mused about the size of the building: "If anything, we thought that everything was too handsome for a school; but it is certainly safer to sin on the side of elegance than on its opposite, the want of it. We could only express the wish that . . . means of instructions will keep at an equal pace with the outward appliances."[14]

Regrettably, the prayers and plans of the founders soon came to nought. The very year of the school dedication (1853), was the year in which the City of New York took over the Public School Society. Formerly the Society had been responsible for the development of public education. This new development, coming after the enactment of a state law (1842) which prohibited the teaching of religion in the public schools administered by the city, eliminated the fear of direct Christian teaching in the classroom and Jewish parents were encouraged to enroll their children in the public schools. Despite the magnificence of the building, the Institute could not withstand the rising popularity of public education. Enrollment fell off drastically, the financial burden became correspondingly heavier and, in 1858, the Institute was discontinued. But, at the very heart of the matter was the mood of the people. "Denominational" education was felt to be a deterrent to the urgent need for social integration of the diverse stocks of immigrants in a cosmopolitan city. It was argued that Jews should be the first to foster the enlargement of American interests; to continue separation in education, it was contended, was to spurn the gift of equality, a gift offered uniquely by America to all of its citizens, Jews among them. The cost—dimunition of religious education, ultimately to affect the very character of the American people—was a consideration unanticipated and, to the extent that it was thought of, the loss was considered less than the gain. Thus ended the brief existence of the synagogue all-day school not only at B'nai Jeshurun but in other synagogues as well. Almost a century was to pass before this type of Jewish school was to be seriously reconsidered.

The educational pendulum at B'nai Jeshurun, as elsewhere, swung in the opposite direction: from a total school situation to the soporific of a Sunday school; from a curriculum of "Rashi and Rabbinical classics" to a smattering of Hebrew reading and catechismic recitations; from a head master who opened his classes with a Hebrew oration to a Jewishly untrained volunteer principal; from full-time daily classes to a brief one-day morning session. This was the B'nai Jeshurun Sunday School which began its classes in 1862. And this was the form of Jewish education which dominated American Jewish congregational pedagogy, virtually unchanged and unchallenged, until the end of the first World War.

It is true that attempts were made now and then to bolster the educational program. For a short while the school schedule was augmented by occasional mid-week sessions; and superior students were encouraged by being given personal instruction. However, these were but feeble attempts which could not possibly produce a literate Jewish community. Who could compete with the social status of French and music classes? And who could create time for religion in addition?

Sensitive to failure and in a spirit of "vicarious atonement," the leaders of the congregation supported a program of philanthropic education. Since their own children repudiated Jewish studies, perhaps the support of other people's children (the children of the poor) who sought a Jewish education might save the losing cause of literacy. The congregation actively supported the Hebrew Free School movement, which emerged in the 1870s, as an intensive supplementary school system, and the children of the Sunday School were encouraged to interest themselves in the Jewish education of their brothers and sisters "downtown." "How explain this contradiction," a contemporary Hebrew writer taunted them and the other Conservative congregations, "that these honorable people fulfill the rabbinical precept 'take heed of the children of the poor, for out of their midst will come forth Torah,' and yet ignore the Biblical law 'and thou shalt teach thy children diligently'?" [15]

B'nai Jeshurun was losing its young, and the future of the synagogue seemed dim. The president reported in 1906: "Where are the children? Have French and music completely ousted religious instruction? These very children who refrain from coming to our religious school will, when they become men and women, be ashamed of their religion or probably of their own ignorance of its tenets. The attendance in our Hebrew School is pitifully small. At the opening day there were but few children present. This portends no good . . ." [16]

The consequences of a truncated Jewish educational system were, strangely, anticipated. As early as 1884, *The American Hebrew* stated editorially that the school is the cradle of the community, and that ultimately a community is bound to take the form in which the school shapes it. "Its [the community's] earnestness and spiritual fervor may be accurately measured and foreshadowed by the efficiency of the religious instruction of the preceding generation." [17] The writers of this and similar editorials were themselves the rabbis and lay leaders of the very synagogues they admonished! Evidently they felt helpless. They faced this dilemma: ardent advocates of the system of public education, they recognized its inherent blessing, deriving from the separation of Church from State, and therefore staunchly defended the system against any incursion; yet, these men could not evolve a Jewish educational program to complement the public school system and to meet their own standards and requirements.

By the end of World War I, several factors brought hope to those who would neither accept the progressive decline of Jewish education nor retreat before the social pressures which militated against its preservation. In the first place, the community itself was fortified in numbers and in quality of Jewish training by the unprecedented flow of east European immigrants. On the world Jewish scene, Zionism had attained a magnificent victory with the announcement of the Balfour Declaration. A new emotional appeal charged students and teachers alike. Zion redeemed was a mission; and the study of Hebrew and Bible was related to the present and the forseeable future, not only to the past. Moreover, the first important results of the native rabbinical and teacher-training schools were now apparent. American-trained rabbis, who spoke the language of the children and shared their interests, assumed the conduct of the schools; young men and women graduates of educational institutes took over the classroom. The old *heder* system was rapidly disappearing. In its place came the communal schools with a Zionist-Hebraist emphasis. In New York City, the now, defunct *Kehillah* organization had bequeathed at least two important legacies: the Bureau of Jewish Education and, even more important, the newly-created calling of American Jewish educators.

Himself the product of an American environment and deeply committed to the new currents of Jewish thought, Rabbi Goldstein directed his attention to the intensification of the synagogue school as soon as he came to the rabbinate of B'nai Jeshurun. Rabbi Goldstein told his congregation: "The real problem of Jewish Education is how to educate the parents to fulfill their responsibility toward the Hebrew training of their children. The child would in most cases readily come to the religious school three times a week if there were more urging, and less coddling in the home. And even if the child occasionally needs to be driven, it is at least as important to drive him to learn Hebrew as to learn French. If the parents would give the Hebrew training of their children the same attention as they devote to those subjects which are only cultural luxuries, the next generation of American Jewry would have more to boast of." [18]

"To make religion familiar like household words"—this was Dr. Goldstein's intention. Coming on the scene seventy-five years after the Educational Institute, Dr. Goldstein found a new kind of Jewish home prevalent among many of his congregants—a home which was greatly "de-Judaized." It devolved on the synagogue to find children who could be inspired to bring up their parents Jewishly. "There are not a few homes in which our pupils will become little missionaries of the Jewish faith to their indifferent parents." [19]

This was the temper of the pulpit at B'nai Jeshurun: how to bring up parents. Dr. Goldstein tirelessly expounded his "surrogate home" thesis. Basing his view on ancient Jewish tradition that "he who teaches his neighbor's child Torah is as if he gave birth to him," Dr. Goldstein spoke out for the responsibility of the entire congregation in the spiritual training of the Jewish child. "No congregation in Israel can afford to adopt the policy of retrenchment and exclusion and discrimination in the matter of Jewish education. If the child's parents are delinquent, the congregation must assume spiritual guardianship of the child . . ." [20]

Under such determined leadership, the school enrollment rose considerably. Very soon, some three hundred students were attending the Religious School; and the three-day-a-week school came into being. The Community Center, which was established to meet the total interests of a Jewish neighborhood, helped to bring the children into Jewish life through social and recreational activities. Children's services on the Sabbath were an added impetus to bring the whole family together in the synagogue. Elementary classes were extended into the high school years. Former students were quickly pressed into service in the religious school and as club leaders, library and office assistants. By 1931, Dr. Goldstein convinced the board of trustees of the importance of approving his policy of concentration on the week-day school, where the number of pupils had by now increased considerably.

Measured against a record of dismal failure in previous decades, these achievements were giant steps forward. However, measured against the objective facts of "de-Judaization" and of widespread ignorance of Judaism, which had sapped the strength of Jewish home life, these achievements were limited; and Dr. Goldstein himself was the first to concede these limitations. Speaking to his congregation in 1928, after a decade of leadership, he asked, in an address remarkable for its candor, "Converting Jews to Judaism": "How many of you would be able to defend your position as Jews in a debate—I mean to defend it intelligently and morally, and present intelligent arguments which, if they could not persuade, might at least impress the challenger? I doubt if the numbers would be very considerable. . . I should like to see Sunday School classes organized not only for children, but for parents, because parents need them just as much as children, and even more, for they are responsible not only to themselves but to their children—to be well-informed about the religion they profess. I should like to see in our own Community Center a parents' group meeting every Sunday morning for Jewish discussions led by a well-versed Jewish layman or by a Rabbinical student." [21]

An offensive was launched to regain the "lost generation." It was part of the adult education movement which began to emerge in the 1930s for the men and women who did not come to receive a Jewish education when they were young and for those who came but did not stay. Perhaps, as adults, these people might start their Jewish lives all over again. Women were the keystone of the educational drive, for as mothers and wives they are the dominant spiritual influence of the home. Classes were arranged in various media: lectures, book review meetings, Hebrew courses, etc. The pulpit itself became an "adult educational institute in Jewish affairs." In addition to his own preaching, Dr. Goldstein brought to his pulpit leading figures in world Jewish life, colleagues in the labor of Judaism.

The response to these efforts encouraged the leadership to assume a more sytematic approach to adult education in the congregation. Rabbi David H. Panitz, who served as Associate Rabbi (1946-1951), and Rabbi William Berkowitz (Associate Rabbi since 1951), were responsible for the development of a new department in the life of the synagogue: The Institute of Adult Jewish Studies. Several hundred men and women were attracted each year to the courses in Jewish history and biography, Jewish classics, Hebrew, etc. The Institute was designed to give the students a sense of regularity in their study. An extraordinary roster of scholars and nationally-known lecturers led the discussions. A review of the courses offered under Rabbi Panitz reveals the earnest effort to make Judaism relevant and comprehensive. Rabbi Berkowitz, building on the work of his predecessor, has attempted to introduce the adult membership of the congregation into the ideas of Jewish religion and thought through the medium of the historic and contemporary cultural experience. Both have sought a way to give the participants in the classes a sense of joy and edification in their adult education.

Nevertheless, despite the variety of activity and intensification of effort, the central goal of Jewish education—the ideal of a literate Jewry—remained far from realization. Neither congregation B'nai Jeshurun nor any other synagogue claims that it has produced a learned Jewish laity in the American environment. In the search for a solution, congregations such as B'nai Jeshurun have been receptive to the new movements toward a better-educated community. The day-school movement, for example, gained new strength largely under the leadership of the Orthodox group. And in the wider American community, the charge of "un-Americanism" has lost its impact before the growing trend toward all-day Jewish schools. Recently, the Conservative movement officially took steps to encourage such schools among its constituents, in the founding of the Solomon Schechter Day Schools.[22]

Dr. Goldstein articulated the new mood in an address to his congregation. Reminding them of the B'nai Jeshurun Educational Institute, in which secular as well as religious subjects were taught, and which provided the equivalent of an elementary and secondary school education, he said: "It is well that today, 100 years later, we should be recalling this chapter, however short-lived, in which our congregation wrote the most splendid single page. For in the past decade or two we have been witnessing an increase of all-day Jewish schools in New York and in other cities in response to the increasing awareness that they offer the most effective opportunity not only for a more extensive Jewish education but also for a better integrated Jewish education, better integrated into the general education of the child. We in B'nai Jeshurun today, like many other congregations, conduct our program of Jewish education as a three session school. It is better than a Sunday School, but not as good as a five session school. For a three session school we are doing as well as any. My view may not be popular with you, but it is nevertheless my view that an all-day school is the most satisfactory answer to the need of Jewish education. Of course, it is costly, and because it is costly it may never become widespread over the American Jewish scene. It is, however, the objection to the all-day school on the ground that it is un-American which I would discount. Some of the best Americans have come out of the Catholic parochial schools and can come out of the Jewish all-day schools. What Congregation B'nai Jeshurun pioneered 100 years ago with the approval of non-Jews as well as Jews, was and is in principle good and proper, and unobjectionable from the American point of view." [23]

Even if the trend for an increased number of day schools continues, private education, it is agreed, will necessarily reach but a fraction of the Jewish school population. And many still feel, that although one may discount the charge of un-Americanism, nevertheless the all-day school is not the most desired form of education in the framework of American life. Consequently, all shades of Jewish religious group life are concentrating on a more intensive complementary school system, beginning with Foundation Schools and including Hebrew Summer Camps. The new challenges are to utilize the leisure time of the child for Jewish learning, and to organize regional and national synagogue programs to help the local congregation meet its problems. Moreover, the proper age of the potential Jewish student is considered to be his entire life. The Jewish adult education movement is now developing its own momentum; its future growth is barely envisioned.

Which of these two approaches will emerge as the dominant form of Jewish education in the future—the all-day school or the intensive complementary program—is as yet quite uncertain. Perhaps a parallel system is the pattern of the future. But this we do know: the Synagogue has finally decided to come to grips with this perennial, unsolved problem. As the history of Congregation B'nai Jeshurun reflects, the Synagogue knows that the problem will remain unsolved unless it breaks through the shackles of Jewish illiteracy.

IV

We have seen the great changes wrought in the character of rabbinic authority and of Jewish education since 1825. A transformation of similar proportions occurred in the role of the Synagogue in American thought and society. Building on its foundations as house of worship, study and assembly for the Jewish community, the Synagogue has recognized its new grant of responsibility in a free society—the duty to help improve the moral tone of the nation. Accepting this obligation, congregations throughout the land have become neighborhood foci to marshal spiritual strength in the struggle for justice and morality, and Jews have joined with citizens of all faiths and creeds to advance the moral and spiritual ideals of the whole American community.

In the meaning of this change lies much of the nobility of the American way of life. Democracy in America has ever been an expanding and changing concept. In a land which the early inhabitants conceived to be "a Christian nation," the Jewish religion has grown to be recognized as one of the major faiths of the country; in a nation whose presidents once referred exclusively to the Christian faith in State proclamations, the Synagogue now stands in its own right in any mention of religious institutions. But one of the greatest forces within American democracy has been the growth of a shared religious experience. Free interchange of religious views among various faith groups, without any fear that such interchange carries with it a concomitant dimunition of individual faith, is a uniquely American experience. In this development, the Jews, who were regarded as exponents of a religious tradition and as the living embodiment of that Tradition, have been given every opportunity to be active participants in the development of the American Idea.

This was not always the case—not even in America. It is true that the Constitution conferred personal liberty and freedom of religious expression upon each citizen, and, with the exception of local battles to be won in some cities and states even to this very day, the issue of religious conscience was settled at the beginning of the nineteenth century. But liberty is one thing, equality another. Liberty could be granted; equality had to be earned.

How this came to be, how respect was earned, is one of the most interesting chapters in American Jewish history. It is the story of the deep love of Jews for this land, of their abiding faith in its future as the moral leader of mankind, as well as their devotion to the principles of the Jewish faith and to the Synagogue. Congregation B'nai Jeshurun participated in the growth of religious and civic cooperation in community relations, and even the achitecture of the synagogues which the congregation built tells the story of the growing and mutually reciprocal confidence of Jewry and America.

During most of the nineteenth century, the masses of Americans knew very little about contemporary Jews. Most of them never saw a Jew, and many of them did not believe that Jews still existed. What they did know about Jews the masses learned from their religious teachers and this information pertained primarliy to Jews in ancient Palestine. On the other hand, many members of the American community did seek out the Jews, and some of them even came to Jewish services. Ezra Stiles, when he was the minister of the Congregational Church in Newport, visited the synagogue, observed Jewish home practice, and recorded his sentiments in a diary. There were many others, too, judging by the various records which have come down to us. By mid-century, with the coming to the United States of some rabbis who could expound Jewish law and history, new possibilities for intellectual exchange developed. For example, Dr. Raphall, whose preaching and lecturing were of the highest order, attracted many Christian listeners. His ministry at B'nai Jeshurun is remembered with such esteem precisely because he brought great understanding of the Jewish tradition to the larger American community. Twice he was invited to the University of Pennsylvania lecture-halls for a series of addresses on the "Post-Biblical History of the Jews." [24] A milestone in his career, and in the career of American Jewish equality was reached when he received an invitation, the first of its kind, to open with a prayer a session of the House of Representatives, thus introducing "the equal rights of Israel's prayers into the halls of Congress." [25] This precedent has since been followed on a number of occasions.

These new responsibilities towards the whole community were reflected in the synagogue program, in worship, in community aid and in wider civic participation. An example of the expansion of the Synagogue's program in observance of a civic quasi-religious holiday is the organization of Thanksgiving services in the 1890s, in cooperation with two other congregations in New York, as a permanent part of the synagogue calendar of B'nai Jeshurun. Of course, during the various national emergencies, including foreign wars, the congregation participated actively in the national cause, both as individuals and as a group. Special services were held, civic rallies were organized, money was raised, sewing-circles functioned. An example of community philanthropy was the creation, during the serious economic crisis in the early 1930s, of an unemployment committee which was formed as a unit of the congregation. This committee distributed large sums of money, bundles of clothing and packages of food, cooperating on a non-sectarian basis with the important social service agencies in the city. The committee also received anyone who came to their doors for help. Out of such community relations, the congregation naturally became an object of interest to people of other faiths. Visiting groups of students and organizations were encouraged to attend religious services. Thus, what had once been a matter of neighborly courtesy evolved into an integral part of the synagogue program.

As a natural consequence of these changes in the synagogue program, B'nai Jeshurun and its affiliated organizations—the Men's Club, the Sisterhood, the youth groups—became an important center for multifarious civic interests and causes. Outstanding leaders of various faith and ethnic groups felt comfortable in its surroundings and were moved to return to the forum of B'nai Jeshurun from time to time. The annual Brotherhood Week observance has become a basic part of the synagogue calendar. And the congregation both encouraged and took pride in the participation of its spiritual leadership in the general community. These efforts were regarded as direct service to the congregation itself. Nor was the hospitality of the synagogue limited to representative personalities. In 1956-57, some fifty-eight organizations conducted their regular meetings and affairs at the Community Center, including various *landsmanschaften*, Zionist groups, general and Jewish philanthropic and aid societies, a Navy Post, and civic youth leagues. Indeed, Congregation B'nai Jeshurun became a home in the community.

The architecture of B'nai Jeshurun reveals this growth of a sense of communal participation and of belonging. In America, where varied religious expression is encouraged, the buildings themselves are manifest symbols of religious freedom and reflect a new attitude. On the other hand, if one scans the pictures of synagogues of eastern Europe, the meaning of personal, economic and political insecurity becomes clear. Even in early America, the trap-door of the Touro Synagogue in Newport and the façade of the Colonial Synagogue expressed the memories of the European past. But the Ashkenazic congregations, rising with the growth of American democracy, were large and beautiful structures. The congregations were not even reluctant to purchase church buildings and convert them into synagogues, and to sell their edifices to church institutions. This seemed to be part of normal American exchange. Towards the end of the nineteenth century, despite the "slavery" to contemporary Gothic, Romanesque or Moorish styles, synagogues were built in every fashion, with distinctive Jewish symbols on the outside as well as within. In recent years, the very buildings themselves are designed to recapture, in the essential design, some authentic aspect of the Jewish past. The large, spacious and dignified synagogue edifice in America today is a result of life in a land of freedom of religions and of expression.[26]

The movement of the B'nai Jeshurun Congregation uptown from Elm Street in 1827, to Greene Street in 1851, to 34th Street in 1865, to Madison Avenue and 64th Street in 1855, to West 89th Street in 1918, indicates much more than the growing need for larger physical settings. It is also a "movement in depth," into a greater security, into the certainty that the congregation as a synagogue has a contribution to make to the intensification of Jewish life and to the American Idea. Each new building bespoke, as it were, greater confidence in America. With each move, the buildings grew taller and taller, and the windows wider and wider. These were windows to the heart of America, to the mind of the world. Men of all creeds and faiths could not help but notice their Jewish neighbors at worship, just as the Jews were free to learn about their neighbors' religions. Consequently, the synagogues built by B'nai Jeshurun, like other fine synagogue buildings, became part of the cause of the civic pride of New York. The dignity of a whole community, expressed in the Jewish religious edifice, symbolized the integration of American Jewry into the larger community. A description of the consecration of the Greene Street Synagogue, in September, 1851, articulated this mood: "Upon the whole it may be assumed that the progress of the Hebrews has fully kept pace with the general progress of the city; and that they need, in no respect, shrink from a comparison with their fellow-citizens of other denominations . . . on the 25th of September last the Synagogue was consecrated with the usual ceremonies; a striking, but most pleasing proof of the influence which free institutions exercise over the fortune, enterprise, and taste of a long oppressed people." [27]

In this land of free institutions, the Synagogue has formed an integral place for itself in American society. As we observe the contemporary scene, we see the rootedness of the Synagogue in the American pattern. While those ethnic groups which are not organized around a religious center seem generally to be disappearing in the American amalgam, there has been continually greater acceptance of Jewish religio-cultural distinctiveness. But we observe also the great need that the people generally have for the message of religion. America is suffering the pangs of the great spiritual turmoil which has gripped the nations of the world. The famine the prophet Amos described has come to us: "Not a famine of bread, nor a thirst for water, but of hearing the words of the Lord." A whole generation is in need of wisdom and spiritual guidance. It becomes the function of the Synagogue in concert with the other religious groups to restore the profound place of religion in the American character, to restore to America its sense of mission to help build a new order for the Ages, the very mission engraved on the Great Seal of the United States: *Novus Ordo Seclorum.*

A spirit of dedication cannot be implanted in the hearts of the people by acts of legislation. Pioneering in the ethical and moral dimensions of life will kindle such a spirit. For this purpose the Synagogue was created and, in the awareness of such responsibility, the American Synagogue has grown. As the history of Congregation B'nai Jeshurun suggests, the Synagogue can best contribute to an understanding of this contemporary challenge if it goes deeper and deeper into its own roots. For if we have learned anything from our experience in this country, this we have learned: In America, Jews speak most eloquently to the conscience of the people through the voice of their own Tradition. A Synagogue that can train its own authoritative leadership, a Synagogue that holds its young and old to Jewish ideals and to learning, a Synagogue that is linked with *Kelal Yisrael* everywhere and that is deeply involved in specific ways in *Eretz Yisrael*—such a Synagogue may speak with the authentic voice of the Jewish tradition to the whole world.

NOTES

[1] *Congregation B'nai Jeshurun Annual Report,* 124 Annual Meeting (January 8, 1950). In my choice of Congregation B'nai Jeshurun as the subject of this examination, I want to express my admiration and regard for the remarkable leadership of Dr. Goldstein and for the Congregation which has enabled him to exercise his initiative and vision to the fullest degree and to serve America and World Jewry with freedom of thought and action.

[2] Arthur M. Schlesinger, Jr., *The Age of Jackson* (Boston, 1945), pp. 8-17. Between 1820 and 1840, the number of people involved in manufacturing increased 127%, while agricultural personnel increased only 79%. These statistics explain the rapid rise of city dwellers and the curtailment of the rural population. In 1820, less than a twentieth of the nation lived in communities of eight thousand or over; in 1840, the proportions had so radically changed that more than a twelfth lived in such communities and more than a ninth in towns larger than two thousand.

[3] For a study treating the social history of New York in this period, with emphasis on the adaptation of the immigrant to American life, see Robert Ernst, *Immigrant Life in New York City 1825-1863* (New York, 1949).

[4] *Main Currents in American Thought* (New York, 1930), vol. II, chapter II, especially pp. 193-202.

[5] David and Tamar de Sola Pool: *An Old Faith in the New World: Portrait of Shearith Israel, 1654-1954* (New York, 1955), p. 275; also pp. 436-439.

[6] Cecil Roth, *History of the Great Synagogue* (London, 1950), pp. 182 ff. For a survey of the relations between the early English and American communities, see J. Jacob Neusner, "Anglo-Jewry and the Development of American Jewish Life" (Typescript, *Yivo* Prize Essay, 1955).

[7] Israel Goldstein, "Ritual Questions Discussed in Correspondence Between Reverend Solomon Hirschell, Chief Rabbi of the Ashkenazim in England and Congregation B'nai Jeshurun of New York," in *Studies in Jewish Bibliography and Related Subjects in Memory of Abraham Solomon Freidus* (New York, 1929), pp. 377-387.

[8] *Ibid.*, p. 386.

[9] Israel Goldstein, *A Century of Judaism*, (New York, 1930), pp. 121-122.

[10] In the period between the ministries of Raphall and Jacobs, the congregation was served by Henry Vidaver (1868-74), Polish-born and trained as a *Maskil*. Rabbi Vidaver's avowed leanings towards innovation, without satisfying the traditionalists, neutralized his effectiveness, and he soon left, in the midst of congregational controversy, to assume a pulpit in San Francisco.

[11] *Jewish Messenger*, vol. XXXIX, no. 18 (May 12, 1876), p. 2; also *Jewish Times*, vol. VIII, no. 14 (June 2, 1876), pp. 213-14; no. 15 (June 9), pp. 232-34; no. 18 (June 30), p. 280. For the background of the New York School, see Allan Tarshish, *Rise of American Judaism* (Hebrew Union College Thesis, 1938), pp. 231-34.

[12] *The Occident*, vol. X, no. 8 (November, 1852), p. 412.

[13] *Ibid.*, vol. XI, no. 4 (July, 1853), p. 232.

[14] *Ibid.*, vol. XII, no. 2 (May, 1854), p. 115.

[15] Moshe Weinberger, *Hayehudim V'Hayahadut B'New York* [Jews and Judaism in New York] (New York, 1887), p. 21.

[16] *A Century of Judaism*, pp. 225-26.

[17] *The American Hebrew*, vol. XX, no. 4 (September 5, 1884), pp. 50-51.

[18] *Report of the Rabbi* (December 17, 1922).

[19] *Ibid.*

[20] *Report of the Rabbi* (December 9, 1923).

[21] *B'nai Jeshurun Topics* (November 21, 1928).

[22] *The Synagogue School*, vol. XV, no. 1 (September, 1956), p. 25.

[23] "New York's Second Oldest Jewish Congregation," in *American Jewry Comes of Age* (New York, 1955), pp. 178-80.

[24] *The Occident*, vol. VIII, no. 9 (December, 1850), pp. 467-73.

[25] The prayer was delivered on February 1, 1860. For the background and events following Dr. Raphall's appearance, see Bertram Korn, "The First Jewish Prayer in Congress" in *Eventful Years and Experiences* (Cincinnati, 1954), pp. 98-124.

[26] See Rachel Wischnitzer's study, *Synagogue Architecture in the United States* (Philadelphia, 5716-1955). For illustrations of B'nai Jeshurun buildings, see pp. 27, 54, 124.

[27] Extract from *The Great Metropolis*, in files of B'nai Jeshurun.

THE RABBINATE—

THE HISTORY OF

JEWISH SPIRITUAL LEADERSHIP

---

by Robert Gordis

THE FULL HISTORY OF the rabbinate as an institution is yet to be written, yet a striking paradox is already clear. On the one hand, the title "rabbi" is the oldest honorific designation in continuous use, far older, indeed, than any honorary degree or academic distinction in vogue today. On the other hand, the functions designated by this ancient title have undergone so far-reaching a transformation in modern times that it may be said to represent virtually a new calling. The term "rabbi," it may be suggested without irreverence, is an old label on a bottle of new wine.

The rabbinate has undergone at least five principal phases, reflecting the kaleidoscopic character of Jewish history. Disregarding fine distinctions of time and space, we may describe these stages in the rabbinate as follows: a) talmudic—(Palestine and Babylonia); b) medieval (western Europe); c) pre-modern (eastern Europe); d) post-emancipation (western Europe); and e) contemporary (predominantly United States and Canada).

The exalted station that is accorded the rabbi in the Jewish tradition is highlighted by the fact that its greatest son, Moses, liberator, lawgiver, creator of the Jewish nation, and architect of the Jewish religion, is not called by any of these titles, but is most affectionately referred to as *Moshe rabbenu*, "Moses, our master, our teacher." It need hardly be added that this title was not applied to him until millenia after the period of the historical Moses. All the extant evidence would indicate that the term did not come into use until after the destruction of the Second Temple in the year 70 C.E.[1]

In the period of the *Tannaim,* the teachers of the Mishnah (70-217 C.E.), two related terms were in use in Palestine, *Rabban,* "our master," which was restricted to the Patriarchs who served as heads of the academy and as official representatives of the Jewish community vis-à-vis the Roman government, and *Rabbi,* "my master," which was applied to every accredited teacher of Torah who was ordained by an older scholar.

In this, the first stage of the rabbinate, the term was used exclusively in a non-professional sense. All the Talmudic sages earned their livelihood by some other occupation. The great Hillel was a wood-chopper, Shammai a builder, Joshua ben Hananiah was a blacksmith, who complained with good reason that the highly-placed patriarch Rabban Gamaliel knew nothing of the tribulations of scholars.[2] Akiba was a shepherd, Johanan was a cobbler, while others were tailors, tanners, laundrymen and even water-carriers. Higher in the economic ladder were the farmers and the merchants among the rabbis. At one period, the rabbis devoted one-third of the day to their livelihood and the remainder to study, but later the situation deteriorated. Rabbi Judah ben Ilai complained that earlier generations spent most of their time in study and less in gainful labor and succeeded in both, while his own contemporaries reversed the emphasis and failed in both.[3] Nonetheless, no salaries or other forms of public support were made available to the rabbis.[4]

With the compilation of the Mishnah by Rabbi Judah the Patriarch (170-217), at the beginning of the third century C. E., the Tannaitic period came to a close and with it ended the hegemony of Palestine as the center of spiritual authority. The Patriarch had striven to prevent the transfer of influence to the more prosperous community of Babylonia by denying full ordination (*semikhah*) even to its most distinguished scholars, Rab and Samuel, who had studied in the Palestinian academies. As a result, the Babylonian *Amoraim,* "expounders of the Mishnah," unlike their Palestinian confreres, did not have the title *rabbi*, "my master," but *rabh*, "master," but that interfered little with their activity as teachers of the Torah (200-500 C.E.). The massive record of their creative labors is the Babylonian Talmud.

It should not be overlooked that their teaching included not only *Halakhah*, which encompassed civil, criminal and religious law, but also *Haggadah*, non-legal material, religious and ethical in character. The *Haggadah* occupies a substantial, if subordinate, part of the Talmud, but it predominates in the vast expanse of the Midrashim. As Zunz showed in his pioneering masterpiece, *Die gottesdienstlichen Vorträge der Juden*, the *Midrash* is often a written record of the homilies delivered in the synagogue and thus bears witness to the antiquity of preaching in Judaism. The interpretation of Scripture had its inception in the days of Ezra and Nehemiah, early in the period of the Second Temple.[5] The process produced both the *Targum*, the Aramaic translation of the Bible, which generally went beyond the literal text, and the *Midrash*.

In Hellenistic circles the influence of the Greek rhetoricians was marked in the structure of the sermons preached in the Alexandrian synagogues and elsewhere.[6] It is likely that the many brief treatises of the philosopher Philo represent transcriptions of sermons he delivered in Alexandria.[7] The great preachers of the early Church, Gregory, John Chrystostom and Ambrose, followed some of these Hellenistic-Jewish models.

In Palestine and Babylonia, preaching was an important activity. Throughout the Talmudic and Gaonic periods, sermons were delivered every Sabbath and festival, as the extant Midrashim demonstrate.[8]

Throughout the Mishnaic and the Amoraic periods (200-500), as well as the succeeding Saboraic (500-540) and Gaonic ages (589-1038 C.E.), the rabbinate remained an avocation in the great centers of Babylonia and Palestine, only the officially-appointed judges being paid for their work, which was primarily a governmental function rather than a spiritual activity. Certain special privileges were accorded scholars by law, such as the remission of taxes, preference in the market-place and other marks of social deference.[9] But the rabbinate did not become a profession until the later Middle Ages. As compact Jewish communities, isolated from the general population, increasingly came into being, there was a growing need of a permanent functionary to supervise the life of the congregation, be available for religious guidance and exercise a judicial role in civil suits among members of the community.

The payment of a salary to a rabbi, however, posed a grave problem from the standpoint of the *Halakhah*. The tradition was clear—the teaching of Torah was a *mitzvah* from which no material gain might be derived. "As I have taught thee freely, so teach thou freely," God said to Moses, according to an old Agada,[10] and the warning against "making the Torah a hatchet to chop with or a crown to glorify one's self with," [11] was taken very seriously. Medieval rabbis in Spain supported themselves by trade, investments, or money-lending, while a very considerable proportion earned their livelihood as physicians.[12]

In a characteristically vigorous statement, Maimonides declared that, though he knew that not all the scholars would agree with him, it is best for practitioners of Torah not to be supported by public funds.[13] He himself was a silent partner in the trading enterprise of his brother David and was free to dedicate himself to study and writing. When his brother was drowned in the Indian Ocean, Maimonides continued to practice what he preached and undertook the arduous profession of physician to the court of Saladin in Egypt. The rigors of his calling Maimonides described in a vivid letter addressed to his beloved disciple, Joseph ibn Aknin, whom he dissuaded from visiting him, because he would have no leisure to spend with him, even the Sabbath being occupied with communal affairs.

Few rabbis, of course, possessed the professional eminence of a Maimonides. The deterioration of the economic position of the Jews that followed in the wake of the Black Death of 1349, and the increasing number of massacres and persecutions from the fourteenth century onward, made it ever harder for rabbis to support themselves by some other livelihood, and so salaries came into vogue. The imperious demands of life met the challenge of the law by defining the salary of the rabbi as *sekhar battalah,* "compensation for being prevented from engaging in a gainful occupation," just as the theory was that teachers were being paid *sekhar shimmur,* "payment for taking care of the children consigned to their care,"—a glorified anticipation of the modern occupation of baby-sitting! Yet, as late as the fifteenth century, Rabbi Simon Duran, who was, incidentally, not "the first Spanish rabbi to take pay," felt constrained to offer a public apology for accepting a salary for his services.[14]

From the fifteenth century onwards, salaries for rabbis were all but universal. The emoluments of the rabbi were, however, minimal, and resourceful spirits sought to make ends meet by auxiliary occupations. The colorful Leo da Modena, who served as rabbi of Venice, kept the wolf from the door by being a printer, a letterwriter, an author, a marriage broker, and, it seems, also a card player, but whether this last occupation proved a financial asset or a liability is not clear.

Most rabbis, who did not possess talents as varied as these, were supported by a small salary, supplemented by communal taxes on wine, meat, or salt, and by fees received for sitting as judges. Their functions included, in addition, the supervision of the *shohetim* or ritual slaughterers, the maintenance of the ritual tradition in the synagogues of the community, and the responsibility for the system of elementary education in the most general terms. The principal function of the rabbi was to be an exemplar of Torah, to spend his days in studying the Talmud, the Codes and the vast expanse of other rabbinic literature, and be available to answer questions of law posed by the congregation. If he possessed the requisite learning, he would be consulted in writing on religious questions by other rabbis and by laymen, and his Responsa (*teshuboth*) to these questions (*sheeloth*) would ultimately be gathered together as a corpus. If his gifts were of a still higher order, he might himself enrich rabbinic literature by writing commentaries on the Talmud and on the Codes, independent halakhic treatises or all-encompassing codes of Jewish law.

The old tradition of regular preaching, however, underwent a decline in the Middle Ages. The addition to the Sabbath and festival services of the *piyyutim,* complicated religious hymns, often quite lengthy, left less and less time for a sermon. Besides, the ever greater preoccupation of the rabbis with *halakhic* details left them little opportunity for, or interest in, developing homiletic skill.[15] Nonetheless, the sermon did not disappear completely from the medieval synagogue. It continued to be cultivated most regularly in Spain, less commonly in France and Italy, and least frequently of all in Germany. The published sermon collections of such gifted preachers as Nahmanides, Shemtob ben Joseph, Isaac Arama and Moses of Coucy,[16] are evidence that preaching remained a significant activity in the synagogue, whether by the permanent rabbinical incumbent or by specially gifted itinerant preachers.

The intellectual attainments of the rabbis in Spain, Italy and the Provence were not limited to the Talmud and its commentaries. Many of them were interested in biblical research and Hebrew philology. Some commanded Arabic, valuable as an adjunct to philosophic studies. Some knew Latin, which they needed for consulting the Vulgate and for participating in the frequently held compulsory public religious disputations. Latin proved useful also in the examination of legal documents in suits coming before them.[17]

It is a tragic paradox of Jewish history that the earlier part of the medieval period, often described as the Dark Ages, was the happier period of the European Jewish experience, while conversely, the later Middle Ages, that saw the breaking of the walls for western Europe through the forces set into motion by the Crusades, the Renaissance, the Protestant Reformation, and the voyages of exploration, brought about a narrowing of the horizons in Jewish life.

In the later Middle Ages, the Ghetto came into being, forcing the Jew, through legal enactments, into limited segregated areas of the cities and towns. The Ghetto established in Germany after the Black Death in 1348-49, was first introduced into Italy in Venice in 1516. It served effectively to isolate the Jew from the general population, eliminating him from the general economic and social life, in which he had previously shared, and depriving him of the challenge and the enrichment of the broadening intellectual horizons that came with the dawn of modernism.

As though the isolation imposed by the Ghetto were not enough, the worsening of Gentile-Jewish relations led to the physical elimination of Jews from western Europe. In 1290, they were expelled from England, not to return until the seventeenth century and then only furtively as nominal Christians. In France, they had been expelled and readmitted time and again as cats-paws in the shifting financial policies of the kings, but in 1394 they were finally and permanently forbidden the rights of domicile. As for the Iberian peninsula, their expulsion from Spain in 1492, and, four years later, from Portugal, was the climax of a long series of persecutions that had converted "the land of delight," as Spanish Jews had loved to call their homeland, into a "vale of tears."

The elimination of the Jews from England, France and Spain meant their concentration in eastern Europe, where there was neither challenge nor inspiration to be derived from the low cultural level of the general environment. As a result, Jewish life retreated into the four ells of the law, the Talmud and its "armor bearers," commentaries, super-commentaries, Codes and Responsa. Such disciplines as philosophy, poetry, history, biblical philology and exegesis, which had shared the interest of western Jewry along with rabbinic studies, now all but disappeared from the orbit of Jewish traditional life. Soon desuetude passed into distaste, so that these studies became suspect as passports to irreligion. The basic intellectual enterprise now became "the battle of the Torah," the legal disputations and casuistic refinements of the German-Polish Talmudists.

The function of the rabbi underwent a corresponding change. There emerged the traditional figure of the Rav, whose presence was the very symbol of the Torah, impressive in appearance, revered for his learning and piety. His communal duties were few: to answer ritual questions, to act as judge in lawsuits between Jews, and to deliver two discourses a year, on *Shabbat Shubah,* when he exhorted the congregation to repent of its sins before the Day of Atonement, and on *Shabbat Hagadol,* the "Great Sabbath" before Passover, when he discussed the laws of *hametz* and *matzah,* which are basic to the traditional Passover. His major occupation was to busy himself with the study of the

Torah. As was the case in the earlier period, a more distinguished rabbi would be consulted on legal questions by laymen and rabbis in other communities and he would write Responsa. A gifted scholar would organize and preside over a Yeshiva or academy that would attract students in proportion to the greatness of its teachers. Essentially, however, his existence was more important than his activity. The average Jew might apostrophize his rabbi in Emerson's words, "I cannot hear what you say, for what you are speaks a thousand times louder."

In the traditional Jewish communities of eastern Europe— Germany, Austria, Hungary, Rumania, Poland and Russia—Jewish life might be narrow in compass, but its roots were deep. The rabbi was not needed to stimulate Jews to Jewish living—no other pattern was conceivable. His basic function was that of the highest religious and legal authority, and the sole patent of his authority was his learning. His scholarship was more significant than his possession of the traditional *semikhah* or ordination which he received from his teachers, which was considerably more limited in scope and power than the *semikhah* of the Palestinian rabbis of the Talmudic period. In fact, at times the *semikhah* took a decidedly unconventional turn, as when it read, "So-and-so is empowered to serve as rabbi in any place where there is no scholar greater than he."

The rabbi's lot was not necessarily an easy one. Frequently, the rabbi had to deal with aggressive lay leaders, and nearly always his meager income posed substantial economic problems for his wife, who generally managed household affairs. But as long as the community itself survived, he was assured of a position of dignity and a modicum of security. For the vast majority of east European Jews, the traditional way of life, with the Rav as its crowning symbol, remained all but unchanged until the beginning of the twentieth century, and in some cases, beyond.

For the Jews of western Europe, however, the Middle Ages came to an end, with the force of an earthquake, in the closing decades of the eighteenth century. The Age of Reason had challenged accepted ideas everywhere, particularly in the fields of religion and morality. As the new ideas of the Enlightenment percolated into the Jewish communities of Germany and France, first in the upper economic strata, and then to the lower levels, the authority of the Jewish tradition was gradually undermined. In the wake of the French Revolution came the emancipation of the Jews which, hesitating and half-hearted though it often was, brought political citizenship, enlarging economic opportunities and new cultural influences into the life of the individual Jew. At the same time, it effectively destroyed the hegemony and cohesiveness of the organized Jewish community. For the first time, defection from Judaism and the Jewish people became not merely a possibility for isolated individuals, but a reality for hundreds and thousands of the most ambitious, gifted and aggressive members of the community. Thousands more, who did not formally replace Judaism by another faith, found their Jewish loyalties and attitudes and, even more, those of their children, being steadily reduced toward the vanishing-point. The ancient commination of Moses became a tragic reality, three millenia after his lifetime: "Thy sons and daughters will be handed over to another people and thine eyes shall behold them and pass out with longing for them all the day and thou wilt be powerless." [18]

But not altogether powerless. The process of defection and decline was powerful and overwhelming, but it was not complete. There were considerable sources of loyalty in the Jewish community which, after the initial shock of the onslaught wore off, reacted against the forces of dissolution. A variety of religious movements came into being, all designed to preserve the Jewish tradition in greater or lesser degree and make it viable in the modern world. And all their schools of thought, conventionally subsumed under varied designations, such as Reform or Liberal, positive-historical or Conservative, and Orthodox or Torah-true, transformed the traditional Rav into the modern rabbi, who was catapulted into a new and challenging environment. In western Europe, where the Jewish community became a religious group, largely parallelling other denominations, the rabbi took on many of the functions and, often even the garb and appearance of his Christian counterparts, particularly the Protestant pastor. But his duties were always more extensive than those of the Christian clergyman, almost never being limited to purely religious functions, such as preaching, conducting services and officiating at marriages and funerals.

This condition was true even in western Europe where the Jewish community retained a quasi-official status, which often included the all-important rights to tax its members and to be maintained by the state. The change in the function of the rabbi was particularly marked in the United States, where no religious group enjoyed any official position and where the Jewish community was completely "voluntary," adherence to, or alienation from it, being a matter of free choice by the individual.[19]

There were three principal reasons for the vast extension of the field of operations of the modern rabbi. First, Judaism faced far greater challenges than Christianity; there were more powerful forces weaning its devotees away, not merely ideological in character, but social and psychological as well. It would, therefore, not suffice for the rabbi to supply the religious demands made upon him; generally he had to labor to create the demand before seeking to fill it. The modern rabbi might believe that he was needed; he rarely had the feeling that he was wanted. His major task now became the stimulation of Jewish life and loyalty on all sectors, in the face of vast, if often impersonal, obstacles.

Second, the expansion of the scope of rabbinical activity found a large measure of warrant in the tradition as well. Judaism had always embraced more than religion. The organic link in Judaism between faith and folk could be loudly denied, but it could never be destroyed, even among those who proclaimed most loudly that they were merely Germans or Frenchmen or Britons of the Mosaic persuasion. The realities of Jewish life, therefore, compelled the rabbi to concern himself with areas like education, culture, community relations, local philanthropy, overseas aid and the ubiquitous problem of anti-Semitism. As Zionism became an increasingly dynamic factor in Jewish consciousness, more and more rabbis of all schools were caught up by its vision and hope.

The third factor which revolutionized the rabbinical calling was the weakening of religious ties among modern Jews, the surrender of the traditional way of life and the decline of Jewish learning among the laity, so that the rabbi's expertness in the law became less and less relevant and less respected. The vacuum thus created had to be filled with new content.

In sum, core and center reversed their roles. Instead of the rabbi being the scholar and the teacher *par excellence,* with a few peripheral functions, his scholarship became secondary, or less than that, and his peripheral functions became central, and these in turn proliferated into a vast complex of activities.

Perhaps the most obvious phase of the rabbi's work lay in his preaching, which now became a regular task, once or even twice each Sabbath and on the festivals. This represented an extreme extension of a function which had existed in earlier phases of the rabbinate. Many of the Talmudic teachers were "masters of the Aggadah," and many medieval rabbis of the west were often distinguished preachers. The east European rabbi had, as we have seen, contracted this activity, almost to the vanishing point. The need for exhortation and inspiration was met not by the rabbis, located in the various communities, but by wandering preachers called *maggidim,* some of whom, like the famous Rabbi Jacob of Dubno, were men of extraordinary spiritual and forensic gifts. The modern rabbi, impelled both by the needs of his community and the example of the Christian minister, was called upon to become a regular preacher.

The older tradition of preaching traced by Zunz, through the medieval period back to the Midrash, had so far disappeared during the latter centuries of the Jewish Middle Ages that its restoration seemed to many to be a "reform" based on Christian models. Thus, as late as 1829, the rabbinical seminary founded in Padua made no provision for the teaching of homiletics in the curriculum. Before the nineteenth century was over, every rabbinical school, whatever its orientation, gave considerable attention to the art of preaching. The ultimate proof of its importance is that the touchstone by which laymen evaluate and choose a rabbi is his sermonic ability, with a greater or lesser secondary interest in his other qualifications. Speaking perhaps *pro domo,* Maybaum, who was professor of homiletics in the *Hochschule* in Berlin, did not hesitate to say, "In small communities as in large, the rabbi is equally obligated to *dedicate the greatest part of his strength and time to the sermon*" (italics his).[20] He goes so far as to caution the rabbi in Germany to be sure not to devote too much time to philological, historical and philosophic studies, but to keep his eye on the sermon as his major goal.[21] The first part of the injunction, at least, is now unnecessary!

Theoretically, the function of the pulpit discourse is the exposition of Judaism, based upon its classical sources in general, and the Scriptural reading of the day in particular. This type of "text-sermon" has survived largely at the Sabbath morning service, when the *Sedrah* of the Torah is read and where the worshippers are largely traditionally inclined. At the late Friday evening service and—during its brief heyday in Reform—at the Sunday morning service, the themes were drawn from the current scene and the treatment was generally that of the lecture or secular address, with relatively little reference to Bible, Talmud or Midrash. Social, political and economic issues that were treated, were illumined only rarely by the light of Jewish teaching. Even books and plays of current interest were utilized as sermon topics. Sermon titles were advertised in the metropolitan press, as well as in the congregational bulletins, in an effort to attract the floating population of "sermon shoppers," who sought the stimulation of sensationalism rather than the spiritual re-creation of religion.

The past decade has seen a distinct diminution in these latter types of rabbinic preachment though they are far from extinct. The new media of mass communication, notably the radio and television, have brought the most eloquent and the most skillful platform orators into every home, so that the appetite for sensationalism has been jaded by surfeit and the individual rabbi can no longer attract a "following" by such devices.

On the more positive side, the new intellectual climate of the age has had a marked effect upon the pulpit. Men and women, who previously could not be attracted to a synagogue or a church on any but the most secular terms, are today manifesting a new interest in religious ideas and values, even if they are unprepared for intellectual acceptance or personal commitment. Increasingly, therefore, the pulpit is concerning itself with religious themes, broadly conceived to include the entire gamut of

Jewish problems, to be sure, but no longer eschewing theological issues.

The second great area of rabbinic activity lies in the field of education. With the rise of the economic level of most congregations, fewer of the rabbis are called upon to teach children in the classroom, professional teachers being the norm, but the rabbi frequently serves as principal of the religious school. He is generally regarded as its titular head, responsible for the broad policies of the institution, such as the content of the curriculum, the number of days and hours of instruction per week, and the general spirit of the school. Special groups of older children, like Confirmation classes and high school groups, will generally be taught, in whole or in part, by the rabbi, on the assumption that his personal influence ought to be brought to bear upon the youth during these formative years.

While important aspects of the educational program thus continue to occupy the rabbi's attention, the tendency is to reduce his work in this area. This trend has been accelerated with the growth of the congregational school at the expense of the communal Hebrew school. A few decades ago, when the more intensive afternoon Hebrew school was conducted under independent auspices, the average congregation contented itself with a Sunday School, often intended for the girls, concerning whom the old prejudice persisted that a minimum program of Jewish education was sufficient. Since the Sunday School met only on Sunday mornings, the rabbi could be expected to devote himself to its supervision. But as the congregational school systems gain in size and complexity, with week-day afternoon Hebrew schools becoming the norm and even day schools on the increase, it becomes clear that most rabbis lack both the experience and the technical knowledge, as well as the time and energy required for school administration. Were the shortage of competent educational personnel less acute, the process of transferring school supervision from the rabbi to the professional educator would have proceeded even more rapidly than it has, but the trend is unmistakable.

It is in the field of adult education that the rabbi has found a challenging area of service. Professionals in the field are few and the conduct of study courses and discussion groups remains a fertile field, in which the rabbi may exercise his functions of teacher.

The uphill struggle to create viable programs of adult education has produced various devices for attracting students, aside from the standard technique of the platform lecture and the classroom. These include Sunday morning lectures, often accompanied by breakfast, and Friday evening study groups, which replace or supplement the sermon at the formal worship period. The social emphasis, which is not always free from the "snob appeal," is utilized in the home study project, where a limited number of families meet at one another's home for study and discussion. Most recently, we have witnessed an extensive growth of Laymen's Week-end Institutes, sponsored by congregations or by a group, as well as the Institutes on Judaism created by national organizations like B'nai B'rith, which recognize that adult education is the basic need of the American Jewish community. In the Laymen's Institute, a group, ranging from 30 to 100 men and women, spend a week-end or a week away from home, generally at a resort-hotel or a summer camp, under the guidance of the rabbi, who generally serves as a member of the faculty. The Institute, under whatever sponsorship, devotes itself to Jewish study, accompanied by a detailed observance of the traditional Jewish way of life, including prayers, grace after meals, Sabbath rest, and *zemirot,* elements that are otherwise remote from the lives of most American Jews. The impact of these institutes on the lives of the participants is undeniable— it still remains to be determined to what extent they will affect the pattern of their year-round living and influence the community at large.

The fourth area of the rabbi's functioning today probably affects the largest segment of the Jewish population, if only at rare intervals—his role as a minister. In Orthodox communities as well as Reform circles, it is a far cry today from the time when a *brith milah* was performed by a *mohel* with no other "clergyman" needed; when a *pidyon haben* required only a first-born male child, the father and a *kohen* in the presence of a *minyan*; when a *bar mitzvah* was called to the Torah immediately after his thirteenth birthday, even on a Monday or Thursday morning, with no attendant pomp or circumstance; when a wedding could be solemnized by any Jew who knew the ritual; and when a funeral was conducted by the family and friends of the departed, who read the order of service themselves. Today all these *rites de passage,* especially the *bar mitzvah,* the wedding and the funeral, as well as the unveiling of the monument approximately a year later, have become rabbinic functions. Undoubtedly, the example of the Protestant minister and the Catholic priest has not been without influence. Even more potent in encouraging the process has been the widespread ignorance among the Jewish laity. On the positive side, it may be conceded that there has been a gain in the dignity and impressiveness with which these significant occasions in life are invested by the participation of the rabbi.

It would be captious in the extreme to oppose a state of affairs merely because it has its analogue in the non-Jewish community. The fact is that, over and above all else, the rabbi has become an ecclesiastic and is regarded by many of his flock as possessing sacramental powers—and this trend represents a transformation of the rabbi's role that is a violent distortion of Jewish tradition.

Closely associated with this clerical function is his role as pastor. In ratio to the reputation that the rabbi enjoys for practical wisdom and human sympathy, men and women turn to him for consultation on their personal and family problems, especially when religious aspects enter into the issue, though by no means only then. This aspect of rabbinic service is growing, as more and more Jews become permanent members of congregations and develop long-standing associations with their rabbis. As against this trend, the increased activity of the personal counsellor and of the psychiatrist has raised important questions with regard to the precise delimitation of function between religion and psychology and the possibility of cooperative endeavor between them.

The modern rabbi's functions have not yet been exhausted. As religious institutions have grown in size, with larger membership rosters and constantly expanding programs, annual budgets have skyrocketed, often reaching six figures. The rabbi has therefore been catapulted into the arduous role of fund-raiser, whether directly in the form of pulpit appeals or personal solicitations from affluent individuals or indirectly by enlarging the membership, "building good-will" and attracting income from other sources. The mechanics of a large institution, with various affiliated groups, has created a new professional, the synagogue executive director, but the rabbi's role in this area is still very pronounced.

Finally, the modern rabbi in America a generation ago won his spurs as the Jewish representative to the larger community. This function as "ambassador to the Gentiles" was particularly important when most American Jews were of foreign birth and of limited general education. Within less than half a century, the bulk of American Jews are native-born, with college-trained men and women plentiful and increasing. Today, Jewish lay leaders in every area of the national life meet their counterparts in the general community. Nonetheless, this function of the rabbi is far from spent. The religious stratification of the American nation along the tripartite division of Catholics, Protestants and Jews, makes the presence of a Jewish religious representative imperative at public functions and in interfaith activities. The efficacy of the "good-will movement" has often been questioned in various quarters, but it continues to be enthusiastically supported by most American Jews. There can be little doubt that even when stripped of the exaggerated claims incidental to publicity and fund-raising efforts, interfaith activity has a vital function to perform in keeping the bridges of communication open among the various elements of the American people.

The capstone in the arch of the rabbi's manifold activities is his role as Jewish spokesman and community leader on the national and the international scenes. The preservation of the Jewish people, the physical succor of the oppressed, the economic rehabilitation of the destitute, the resettlement of the homeless, have created large and complicated agencies that need financial support, administrative direction and statesmanlike leadership. The State of Israel, in spite of its yeoman achievements during its brief history, is not yet a self-sufficient entity, confronted as it is by the herculean task of peaceful reconstruction it has voluntarily undertaken and by the heroic struggle it has had to wage against its hostile neighbors. Great significance, therefore, continues to attach to the various instrumentalities, financial, educational and political, created by the Zionist movement. These institutions, too, require leadership. The Jewish cultural equipment of the rabbi, his forensic gifts, his total absorption in Jewish affairs, his communal experience and his prestige in the general community, make him an ideal public servant of the Jewish community, a statesman, at his best, or alas merely a politician.

To be sure, this type of leadership is by its very nature open to only a few chosen individuals. It is noteworthy how many of the national and international leaders in American Jewry have been drawn from the rabbinate. Dr. Israel Goldstein is a striking example of this type, as he has served on the highest levels of leadership, in the American Jewish community, in philanthropic and cultural endeavor, in Zionist movement, in American liberal politics, in the labor movement and in inter-group relations. In the midst of these public activities he has found the time to produce several volumes of merit. The various chapters of the present volume speak eloquently of this variegated pattern of outstanding activity. Other rabbis of more modest talents and lesser energy have served in fewer areas and on a more restricted scale, but virtually every member of the rabbinate is expected to be a Jewish spokesman and arbiter of policy at least in his own local community.

It will be noted that in this bewildering catalogue of activities, no mention has yet been made of the one function that characterized the traditional rabbi above all others, Jewish scholarship. The truth is that, for many modern practitioners of the rabbinic calling, scholarship has been a prime casualty, crowded out of the program by the imperious demands of an activistic age. With pardonable exaggeration, it might be said that while the old Rav did nothing but study, the modern rabbi does everything but study! The loss of scholarly stature has not passed altogether unwept and unhonored. It is significant that a minority of rabbis, at least, and their number is growing, does sacrifice its hours of leisure and relaxation to maintain the tradition of learning in the rabbinate. Some few do original scholarly research of high quality in Bible, rabbinics, history and theology. Many more interpret and present the results of technical scholarship to the general public in books and through articles in the press. Others seek to give the permanence of print to their more effective pulpit discourses, while still others, like their confreres in Germany before World War II, compile the history of their own congregations and communities and thus supply the sources for the future historian of American Jewry.

As we have noted elsewhere, the decline in scholarly attainment and personal piety of the modern rabbi, as against his traditional predecessor, cannot be compensated for by concrete practical achievements; they belong to different levels of being. Yet the change has not been a total loss. There has been a broadening of cultural outlook and not merely a lowering of the level of Jewish learning in the transformation of the rabbinical calling. Creative scholarship and serious philosophic and theological thought, which had largely been absent from the life of the traditional east European rabbi, have emerged once more in the pattern of activity and thought of some American rabbis.

In surveying the changing role of the rabbi in the modern world, nostalgia for the past is not merely useless; it may prove positively harmful, if it prevents a realistic appraisal of the situation. The metamorphosis of the rabbi's role, from passive contemplation to active leadership in the community, was absolutely called for by the conditions of modern life. Whoever doubts the need for this transformation has only to observe the situation in the State of Israel, where the old rabbinic pattern has been retained in the face of a new and dynamic situation. As a consequence, the rabbi in the State of Israel has sunk to a position of relative insignificance, being little more than a state functionary for registering vital statistics, possessing no vital connection with a congregation of men, women and children. In Israel, the synagogue serves only as a prayer house, playing no dynamic role in the fashioning of Jewish personality or in the solution of the manifold spiritual and ethical problems of a nation in travail.

There are strong grounds for believing that if religion in Israel is to become a vital force and prove an influence for good in the life of the people as a whole, it will come to pass only through the medium of a revitalized synagogue and an active rabbinate. Both can learn more than a little from American synagogues and rabbis at their best.

At the midpoint of the twentieth century, Jewish life is in violent flux. The rabbi, who is the living symbol of the deeply rooted desire of Jews to survive meaningfully through their tradition, is accordingly undergoing a transformation, the end of which is not yet. Prophecy is often as much an effort of the will as it is an enterprise of the mind; the wish is usually father to the thought. But certain trends seem clear with regard to the future of the rabbinate.

All signs point to the growing significance of the rabbi as the central figure in the Jewish community. As Jewish acculturation in America continues to move forward with seven league boots, American Jewry will increasingly take on the form of a religious group. Whether this will mean a narrowing or a deepening of Jewish life, only the future will reveal.

To be sure, the re-structuring of west European Jewry in the post-emancipation period as a *Religionsgemeinde* or a *Consistoire* was accompanied by a progressive decline of vitality. Growing religious indifference, mounting cultural illiteracy and widespread alienation from the community, were everywhere in evidence as elements of an extended process, the end of which was marked by mass inter-marriage and conversion. The fault lay, however, not in conceiving of Judaism as a religious tradition, but in severing the organic relationship of faith, culture and peoplehood, which have always characterized Judaism. There are signs that the modern rabbi, whatever his "denominational" leaning, is increasingly dedicated to such an all-embracing conception of Judaism. His zeal in furthering Jewish life in all its phases will strike a responsive chord among most American Jews. For intuitively, they grasp this organic view of Judaism and the Jewish people, which both the theologians of west European Jewry and the secularist theoreticians of east-European Jewry often failed to comprehend.

At the same time, it is likely that while cherishing this all-embracing view of Jewish life, the rabbi will increasingly be freed from many of the tasks that now harass his days and often give him the frustrated feeling of being a glorified jack-of-all-trades, master of none. The emergence of the educator, the executive director, the social worker and latterly the psychiatrist, will relieve him of certain facets of his local work. The professionalization of fund-raising by Federation, United Jewish Appeal, Israel Bond Drive and countless other institutions, is making his participation in these areas less central and time-consuming than before.

Finally and most important, the much discussed "return to religion" has a vital bearing on the future role of the modern rabbi. While this much touted revival is often exaggerated, it is real; its basic drawback is that genuine as it is for many, it has thus far remained superficial. Nevertheless, the new interest in religion will make it possible for the rabbi to become, in ever greater degree, the teacher and interpreter of Judaism as a world view and a way of life for those men, women and young people who are seeking *hamaor shebayahadut*, "the light that is in Judaism."

This religious revival is not of one piece. It takes the form of a pyramid of three layers. The broad base at the bottom constitutes the new, widespread interest in the message of religion; the middle, narrower segment above it represents an intellectual acceptance, in whole or in part, of the content of religion; the apex, narrowest of all, but the crowning glory of the pyramid, consists of those who have made a personal commitment to the imperatives of religion. Each section of the pyramid poses a challenge and an opportunity for the rabbi, summoning up all his learning and piety, his sympathy and wisdom, his energy and patience.

While other phases of his present activities may pass away, his functions as preacher, as pastor, as counsellor, show no signs of diminution in the future. Quite the contrary, they give every evidence of bulking ever larger. If the modern rabbi succeeds in adding to his life the dimension of "the love of Torah," on however modest a level, he will have established the vital link of continuity with his predecessors in spiritual leadership and thus prove himself not altogether unworthy of being called "master, counsellor and friend."

NOTES

[1] The use of the term "rabbi" in the New Testament which describes actors and events in the decade before the destruction of the Temple is probably an anachronism, reflecting the period of the authors rather than of the figures in the Gospel narratives. Its usage in the New Testament is parallel to its later use in Rabbinic literature as an honorific term employed by a pupil in addressing his teacher (Mat. 26:25, 47; Mark 9:15; 11:21; 14:45 and John 1:38 etc.).

[2] B. Berakot 28a.

[3] B. Berakot 35b.

[4] Cf. B. Berakot 17b; B. Yoma 35b. B. Ketubbot 105a. B. Baba Batra 22a.

[5] Cf. Neh. 8:8, 13.

[6] Cf. J. Freudenthal, Die Flavius Josephus Beigelegte Schrift über die Herrschaft der Vernunft (Breslau 1869).

[7] Cf. op. cit. p. 7, note 3.

[8] Cf. I. Maybaum, Jüdische Homiletik (Berlin 1890) p. 12.

[9] Cf. B. Baba Batra 22a.

[10] Cf. B. Nedarim 37a; Bekhorot 29a.

[11] Cf. Mishnah Abot 2:2; 4:10; 5:23.

[12] Cf. A. A. Neuman, The Jews in Spain (Philadelphia 1942) vol. II, pp. 80, 84f., 90, 99f., who indicates that the authors of fully half his rabbinic sources were physicians. A vast amount of information on the functions of the medieval rabbi is also to be found in S. W. Baron, The Jewish Community (Philadelphia 1942) 3 volumes; see Index vol. 3, pp. 510b-512b.

[13] Cf. his Commentary on the Mishnah, Abot 4:5.

[14] Neuman op. cit. vol. 2, p. 91.

[15] Cf. Maybaum, op. cit. p. 13.

[16] Cf. the excellent study of medieval preachers by Israel Bettan, Studies in Jewish Preaching (Cincinnati 1940).

[17] Neuman, op. cit. vol. 2, pp. 97ff.

[18] Deut. 28:32.

[19] On the categories of natural, compulsory and voluntary community, first proposed by the author, see his The Jew Faces A New World (New York, 1941) pp. 3-31 and Judaism for the Modern Age (New York 1955) pp. 3-29.

[20] Cf. Maybaum op. cit. p. 182.

[21] Cf. Maybaum op. cit. p. 177.

Part Three

IN THE
JEWISH COMMUNITY—
AT HOME AND ABROAD

THE

AMERICAN JEWISH CONGRESS

----

by Justine Wise Polier

THE CREATION OF the American Jewish Congress can be traced to external realities of many kinds during World War I. But, its creation was also, in a real sense, an emancipation proclamation to and for the American Jew. It was a child of the spirit called into being by Jews deeply rooted in American life, deeply loyal to Jewish ideals, and therefore doubly committed to a democratic way of life for Jews as members of the Jewish community as well as for Jews as American citizens.

As one reviews the world of the men of vision who founded the Congress movement one discerns both their understanding of, and distaste for, a continuation of traditions born of oppression in foreign lands that were incompatible with the self-respect of Jews living in a land of freedom. Aware of the need for the *Hof-Jude* or *Sh'tadlan* as intermediary between the Jewish community and its oppressors in European lands, they saw no justification for his counterpart in America. They were as impatient with Jews who, by reason of earlier immigration, wealth or power, assumed the right to become the self-appointed spokesmen of the Jewish people, as they were with the Bourbons in any other area of American life.

During the first World War, many Jews of America became aware of the desperate plight of their brothers in eastern and central Europe and kindled to the hope that, as a result of the war, Palestine would become a homeland for the Jewish people. Soon, however, it became evident that, while, with rare exceptions, the Jewish masses deeply responded, yet Jews of wealth and influence who had long dominated Jewish community life, rejected the hope and stood apart. It was then that the masses of American Jews felt the need to organize more broadly so as to achieve the restoration of Palestine. The founders of the Congress saw the need to articulate the sense of oneness with the Jewish people and the aspirations for a Jewish homeland, and to lay the basis for a Jewish community organization which would reflect their democratic ideals. With increasing clarity they expressed their deep conviction that no persons or groups had a right to speak for American Jews unless they were prepared to work with their fellow-Jews as equals and represent them in democratic fashion.

The idea of an American Jewish Congress, uniting within a democratic framework all Jewish groups for common action on Jewish affairs, was projected by a group of men, including Rabbi Stephen S. Wise, Justice Louis D. Brandeis, Nachman Syrkin, Gedaliah Bublick, and Baruch Zukerman. From the outset, the idea had the support of Judge Julian W. Mack, Dr. Horace M. Kallen, Pinchas Rutenberg, Louis Lipsky, Bernard G. Richards, Nathan Straus, and other distinguished Americans who believed that American Jews should and could be trusted to develop a sound and democratic organization for the working out of Jewish problems.

At a preliminary conference held in Philadelphia on March 26, 1916, Dr. Wise expressed what has remained the spirit and purpose of the Congress movement:

This day is destined to be memorable in the annals of Israel—the more because we are thinking not of ourselves alone, nor for ourselves, but after the Jewish manner, of and for all Israel . . . .

We again solemnly aver that a people is not worthy of respect which does not insist on the right to be heard touching its own affairs, but surrenders the right of judgment and decision to a company of men, however wise and benevolent, who substitute their own opinions and wishes for the convictions and determinations of the whole people. It were little less than a tragedy if the Jewish people, first among the peoples in democratic aim in this land, should succumb to the pressure exerted by those who for one reason or another are distrustful of the capacity of the many to manage their own affairs . . . .

The world cannot be expected to assent to any program touching Israel's future as long as Israel does not unitedly deliberate and speak. Secrecy, always futile as a curative method, has proven disastrous in prolonging and intensifying Jewish woes. We now freely discuss our will where aforetime we furtively listened to the edict of others. A Congress means deliberation not agitation, discussion not division, enlightenment not secrecy . . . .

The only program acceptable to the men in control or our affairs has been a program of palliation, as if nothing more than temporary relief could be hoped for Israel, wounded and oppressed. Relief, alas, is at times sorely needed, was never more needed than today. But relief is not to be exalted as the policy or program of a people unless these be hopeless beggars and that people adopt a program of relief as the only way out. Not relief but redress, not palliation but prevention, not charity but justice . . . is the only program worthy of a great and proud people.

The proposal for the establishment of an American Jewish Congress was opposed by individuals and groups, including a number of national Jewish organizations headed by the American Jewish Committee. There followed negotiations between the representatives of these elements and the Congress organizers, which resulted in the conclusion of an agreement providing, among other things, that a congress should be established "exclusively for the purpose of defining methods whereby, in cooperation with the Jews of the world, Jewish rights may be secured for the Jews of all lands and all laws discriminating against them may be abrogated." It was agreed also that the Congress should adjourn after its representatives had completed their labors in connection with the Peace Conference. Another point of the agreement was that, in addition to the delegates to be elected by local committees, the membership of the Congress should include also representatives of national Jewish organizations participating in the Congress.

Following the conclusion of this agreement, preparations were made for nationwide elections to the new body. On June 10, 1917, for the first time in modern Jewish history, 335,000 Jewish men and women went to the polls to choose their representatives to the first American Jewish Congress.

Owing to the fact that the technical work involved in preparing for the first convention of the Congress occupied more time than was expected, the date of the convention was changed from time to time and, after the entry of the United States in the War, it was decided to hold the convention after the termination of hostilities. It was held at Philadelphia on December 15, 1918.

The resolutions adopted provided that 1) a delegation of not more than nine men be elected to proceed to Europe, where, in conference with representatives of the Jews of other lands, the delegation should do its best to realize the objectives of the Congress; 2) the delegation should be entrusted to cooperate with other Jewish organizations, specifically with the World Zionist Organization, to the end that the Peace Conference might recognize the aspirations and historic claims of the Jewish people with regard to Palestine and might declare that, in accordance with the British government's decree, there should be established such political, administrative and economic conditions in Palestine as should assure, under the trusteeship of Great Britain, acting on behalf of such League of Nations as might be formed, the development of Palestine into a Jewish commonwealth; 3) that the delegation further work to the end that the Peace Conference insert in the treaty of peace, as conditions precedent to the creation of all new or enlarged states which it is proposed to call into being, clauses expressly providing that: (a) all inhabitants of the territories of such states, including war refugees who shall return to them, should for all purposes be citizens thereof; (b) all citizens, without distinction as to race, nationality or creed, should enjoy equal civil, political, religious and national rights, and no laws should be enacted or enforced which should abridge such rights on account of race, nationality or religion, or deny to any person the equal protection of the laws; (c) the principle of minority representation should be provided for by law; (d) the members of the various national as well as religious bodies of the state should be accorded autonomous management of their own communal institutions, religious, educational, charitable, or otherwise; (e) no law should be enacted restricting the use of any language nor should any language test be established; (f) those who observe any other than the first day of the week as their sabbath should not be proscribed from pursuing their secular affairs on any day other than that which they observe nor should they be required to perform any acts on their sabbath or holy days which they should regard as a desecration thereof; 4) that as soon as peace was declared the delegation should take steps, in cooperation with other representative Jewish bodies, for the convening of a World Jewish Congress.

The Congress delegation, consisting of Julian W. Mack, Stephen S. Wise, Louis Marshall, Harry Cutler, Jacob de Haas, B. L. Levinthal, Nachman Syrkin, Joseph Barondess, Morris Winchevsky and Bernard G. Richards, proceeded to Paris in the spring of 1919, where they joined with most of the delegations of European Jewish committees in organizing the Committee of Jewish Delegations at the Peace Conference, in whose name negotiations were conducted with members of the commissions of the United States and other countries for the inclusion of the clauses proposed by the Congress, in the treaties with all new and enlarged states.

The treaties which were finally drafted and signed did include clauses substantially meeting the views of the Committee of Jewish Delegations. These clauses provided for equal rights with the majority population of each country for all "racial, linguistic and religious minorities"—the so-called minority treaties. In the compacts with Poland and Rumania there were provisions concerning specifically the rights of their Jewish populations. Having accomplished their mission, the delegation of the American Jewish Congress returned, and, at a convention in New York City on May 30, 1920, submitted its report, which was unanimously adopted. Then, in conformity with the compromise agreement under which the Congress had been established, it adjourned *sine die*.

However, a large number of the delegates reconvened immediately and appointed a committee to plan the creation of a permanent American Jewish Congress so that the gains achieved in bringing democracy into Jewish life and at the Peace Conference should not be lost. The labors of the committee resulted in a convention in Philadelphia on May 21 and 22, 1922, whose delegates were elected by organizations and by local committees organized by the initiating group. It was at this convention that the present American Jewish Congress was formally established. The following officers were elected: Nathan Straus, president; Aaron J. Levey, Samuel Untermeyer and Stephen S. Wise, vice-presidents; George I. Fox, treasurer; and Bernard G. Richards, executive secretary.

The purposes of the American Jewish Congress were defined by constitution as follows:

1) to safeguard the civil, political, economic and religious rights of the Jewish people wherever these rights may be threatened or violated;

2) to cooperate with other Jewish bodies for the protection of the national minority rights of Jews in countries where such rights have been recognized or incorporated in the law of the land;

3) to fight for equality of Jews everywhere and to give assistance in all cases of injustice, hardship or suffering imposed upon Jews, arising out of the denial of their lawful rights;

4) to fight economic discrimination against Jews, both in America and abroad and to contribute to the economic and cultural development of Jewish life by aiding in the establishment of economic and cultural institutions that may be helpful to this end;

5) to further the development of the Jewish National Homeland in Palestine;

6) to cooperate with Jews of other lands through the World Jewish Congress, to defend Jewish rights and maintain the Jewish status.

Despite the contributions of the Congress movement to safeguarding the security of Jews wherever their security was threatened, and ongoing efforts to organize the American Jewish community on the broadest possible basis in the twenties, its opponents reverted to opposition not only to the Congress movement but also to its frank discussion of public issues affecting

Jewish life, its democratic spirit, and its wholehearted support to the upbuilding of Palestine.

It was the historic understanding of the leaders of the Congress that first began to awaken American Jews and non-Jews to the menace of Hitler and Fascism. Even in the face of this dire danger, the opposition chose to deny its existence or demand silence of Jews lest anti-Semitism in America be increased. They seemed, either through lack of identification, understanding or courage, unable to grasp or face the significance of Hitler's program to destroy the Jewish people. In the first years, they joined the chorus of those who resented "atrocity" stories and demanded silence of the leaders of the Congress movement. Happily its leaders and its members sensed and understood their duty not only to their brothers abroad but also to themselves as free citizens of America. They recognized that, if they were silent or timid because they were Jews, they were not only forsaking their fellow-Jews but also accepting, if not imposing on themselves, a second-class citizenship.

Even after Hitler came to power, the American Jewish Congress not only had to battle to awaken the non-Jewish world to the meaning of Hitlerism, but also had to contend with Jewish leaders who still followed a myopic belief that they could conciliate, that they could "do business' with Hitler. After the American Jewish Congress and the American Federation of Labor had launched the boycott against German goods there were still Jews who wanted to engage in deals to salvage Jewish property. Congress rejected this approach, refusing to ensure the material "security of some Jews through the shame of all Jews. . . . The honor of Israel, the value of civilization, the ideals of mankind are even more precious than life itself."

I shall never forget the early days of March 1933 when Hitler came to power and the Congress leaders decided that the moment had come when they must speak out concerning the menace of Hitler and ask all fellow-Americans to join them in a mass meeting at Madison Square Garden, New York City. Among the great Americans who responded were Senator Robert F. Wagner, who had given up his honorary German citizenship as a protest; Alfred E. Smith, former governor of New York State; William

Green, president of the American Federation of Labor; Bishop William T. Manning of the Protestant Episcopal Church; and that ever-valiant foe against all human injustice, Rev. John Haynes Holmes, pastor of the famous Community Church of New York City. The only unending and terrible pressure for silence came from a small group of powerful and wealthy Jews who, until the last moment, demanded of my father that he call off the meeting and be silent. One distinguished Jew called him and told him that if the protest meeting were held the blood of the Jews of Germany would be on his head. This threat did not shake him because he realized that the group whom this man represented completely failed to understand that, if Jews in America could be silenced in the face of the terror threatening their brethren in Germany, then indeed Hitler would have succeeded in humiliating, if not silencing, the Jews of all lands. Only one message shook my father, and I vividly recall his pacing the floor when he received a cable from the distinguished chief of police of Berlin under the Weimar Republic; the message begged my father to call off the protest meeting. My father knew that this man was a Zionist and a Socialist. The decision to move forward became agonizing. Not until five months later, when he was in Prague, did he learn from this man, who called to apologize and explain, that the cable had been sent by the Gestapo before he could escape from Germany. He told my father how grateful he was that the protest had gone on, and that it had helped at least temporarily. This statement confirmed a message sent from Berlin via Zurich that the foreign protests had prevented "a greater number of kidnappings and bloody beatings and possibly one big general pogrom." The protest had a further meaning to Jews and non-Jews as proof, in the words of the distinguished British member of Parliament Josiah Wedgewood, that "a great people could be trusted to stand on its feet and not crawl on its hands."

While the American Jewish Congress was actively engaged in steps to arouse public opinion in the United States to the dangers of Hitlerism, the Congress was taking steps also to organize a world Jewish congress. The Congress had maintained contact with some of the European Jewish groups which had participated in the Committee of Jewish Delegations at the Peace Conference. This Committee continued to exist for a number of years after the Peace Conference, although some of the delegations which had originally constituted it had withdrawn. In 1921, delegates of the American Jewish Congress participated in an international Jewish conference at Carlsbad and, in 1927, representatives of the American Jewish Congress attended a similar assembly at Zurich, where the Committee of Jewish Delegations was reorganized as the Council for the Rights of Jewish Minorities, with an office at Geneva.

In July, 1931, a conference called by the American Jewish Congress, held at Basle, decided to meet at Geneva the following year to consider the advisability of convening a world Jewish congress. A number of preliminary conferences on this matter were held during the succeeding years, and the calling of a world gathering itself was postponed from year to year because of organizational difficulties. A national electoral conference was finally held at Washington, D. C., on June 13 and 14, 1936, for the purpose of electing seventy American delegates to a world Jewish congress. The Congress was convened in Geneva on August 8 to 15, 1936.

The need for a self-reliant, democratic movement of Jews throughout the world had become increasingly and tragically clear, in the light of what seemed the relentless destruction of Jewish life in Central Europe and the inertia or indifference of the non-Jewish world. There was need for the organization of relief, of securing new homes for refugees from the Hitler terror, and there was great need of finding a way to make clear to America and other democratic lands that their security and peace were also endangered by Hitler. Dr. Wise expressed it in this way:

The world was warned, and we Jews were—as we so often have been throughout history—the object lesson, the shock troops of civilization, first under attack. The challenge of each morning and night was how to make the world, our world, understand.

The American Jewish Congress had been the only responsible American Jewish body to call for, and support, the economic boycott at the beginning of the Hitler regime. The response of great Christian clergymen was the expression of the human conscience. That reaction was heartening in those dark days, when, in addition to its other momentous tasks, the Congress had to defend itself from continuing attacks from Jewish "leaders" who seem to resent the clarity, the fearlessness, and above all the independence of the Congress leaders and the Congress movement. These critics seemed to regard anything they could not control as therefore irresponsible, a reaction repeated throughout history among rulers and those who regard themselves as members of the "ruling class." There was distrust in the capacity of the Jewish people to manage their own affairs through a democratic procedure, and there was fear that Americans would resent Jews who dared to speak courageously as Jews. This latter position reflected not only personal fearfulness but also a lack of confidence in the sense of justice of America and Americans.

Despite this opposition, the American Jewish Congress continued, throughout the tragic decade of Hitler's rise to power, to rally both Jews and non-Jews to an understanding of the meaning of Hitlerism and Fascism, and worked toward the creation of the World Jewish Congress. It also made creative contributions in providing shelter and care for refugees from Hitlerism, both in America and abroad, through its homes here and its projects for children in France. However, even during the grim war years, the leaders of the American and World Jewish Congresses recognized that research and preparatory planning were essential to sound post-war action and they, therefore, created the Institute of Jewish Affairs, under the guidance of distinguished international Jewish scholars. It was here that intensive study was given to problems of relief, reparation, indemnification, restitution, the punishment of war criminals, migration, the resettlement of refugees, international recognition of human rights, and protection of minority groups. These studies have been of incalculable value to governments, the United Nations, and other international agencies. They also provided the basis for the program for the survival of the Jewish people in the post-war world that was developed by the War Emergency Conference of the World

Jewish Congress held in 1944, which was attended by representatives of Jewish communities in forty countries.

While battling against the terrors of Nazism and Fascism, and preparing itself to face the problems of world Jewry in the post-war world, the American Jewish Congress undertook one other momentous task during the war years. On the basis of full commitment to the democratic ideal, the Congress recognized that the combating of specific forms and sporadic manifestations of anti-Semitism, though necessary, was not enough. It recognized that it must assume a more positive program if the Jewish community were to play its total part in the extension of democracy in its full sense to all inhabitants of America. The Congress, therefore, embarked on a two-fold program: First, a fundamental attack on the problem of discrimination based on modern concepts of social science, and rooted in the recognition that the security of no group can be assured until the full rights of all groups are safeguarded. This program required basic research and study, on the one hand, and the implementation of such a positive approach through action, on the other. To meet these needs, the Commission on Community Interrelations was organized in 1944, under the brilliant leadership of Dr. Kurt Lewin, sometimes referred to as the Einstein of social psychology, and a distinguished staff of social scientists. The Commission began studies of group tensions and attitudes which have provided stimulus to much of the work now being done in this field by many other organizations and by universities. Light was thrown on "self-hate" which has so long plagued Jewish life, and understanding was developed of those ways in which men and women can face discrimination with self-respect, and of ways in which attitudes can be changed from fear and hostility to understanding and the will to cooperate. No time was wasted on the preaching of good-will or on the public relations of interfaith activities that had so long produced minimal results. Increasingly, as the evidence warranted it, effort was placed on breaking down walls of segregation, and emphasizing the need for opportunities for people to study, to work, to play, and to live together as equals. Such opportunities were shown to be the most effective basis not only for breaking down discrimination but also for correcting prejudicial attitudes, and so preparing an atmosphere in which democracy and freedom of all men would be truly cherished.

The second aspect of the two-fold program was the responsibility of a Commission on Law and Social Action, under the brilliantly creative approach of Professor Alexander Pekelis. Surveys of such major problem areas as discrimination in employment, in education, and in housing and racial segregation, and the denial of civil liberties, were undertaken. The Congress embarked on programs involving the submission of test cases before courts and administrative government agencies, the drafting of model legislation, and the development of social action campaigns to transform program into reality, so as to provide and protect equal rights for all groups.

As the Congress developed these approaches to the problems that confronted Jews in America, it found a warm response among many young Jews, who saw in its program an opportunity to serve their people and contribute to the progress of their country and the democratic ideal. In these areas also, the Congress faced stiff and angry opposition from some entrenched Jewish organizations.

After some years of lonely leadership among Jewish groups in the struggle for equal civil rights for all Americans, whether Mexican, Japanese, Negro, Protestant, Catholic, or Jewish, the American Jewish Congress became the recipient of the most rewarding flattery, that of imitation. This changing approach was welcome but it, too, led to difficulties. Soon institutional rivalries led to conflict within the National Community Relations Advisory Council, established in 1944, and consisting of representatives of local Community Relations Councils and the national defense organizations. At the request of the N.C.R.A.C., and all its constituent bodies, a study of the work of all the national organizations was undertaken by Dr. Robert M. McIver, professor emeritus of sociology at Columbia University. In his report, Dr. McIver stated that there was considerable duplication and overlapping in the work being done and recommended that the N.C.R.A.C. be given the authority to allocate each task to the organization deemed best fitted to undertake its accomplishment.

The American Jewish Committee and the Anti-Defamation League disapproved of this recommendation, insisting that they have a free hand in deciding which activities they preferred to pursue. In effect, this meant that they claimed the right to duplicate work in this field with funds contributed by the Jewish community. Upon the adoption of Dr. McIver's recommendation by the N.C.R.A.C., the American Jewish Committee and the Anti-Defamation League withdrew from that body. Recognizing the value and welcoming the growth of the Jewish Community Councils in America, the Congress has continued to provide the studies, the analyses, the model legislation, and the technical guidance of court cases in the areas of civil rights and civil liberties to the National Community Relations Advisory Council and its member agencies and communities.

In recent days, since the U. S. Supreme Court decision holding segregation in public schools a violation of the Constitution—a decision which, incidentally, referred to a Congress study in one significant part of its decision—the Congress has found that some of the national Jewish organizations which had imitated it for a while are again timid in the face of community opposition in the South. When asked to be silent by some self-styled Jewish leaders in the South, the Congress has held that it could not have one principle in the North and another in the South, that it could not seek equality and justice for Jews and not be prepared to seek it with equal devotion for non-Jews. And so the Congress alone among the Jewish organizations has, in recent months, been penalized by having its allocations of funds withdrawn or reduced by a few southern Jewish communities. In answer to critics in the South who urge that our forthright position on civil rights is not appropriate for the South, the Congress recalls that when the defenders of slavery excused it on the ground that it was local, Lincoln answered, "Slavery is local, but freedom is national."

The national officers of the American Jewish Congress, and its governing bodies, under the leadership, since 1951, of Dr. Israel Goldstein, have not swerved. They are committed to a program that will expand the frontiers of democracy and bring full equality to all Americans. They are deeply committed to the belief that, as citizens of America, Jews must continue to play their full part in shaping its affairs. This position, they recognize, now as always, involves taking risks in the struggle against inequality, but it alone provides a sound basis for the ongoing effort to create a free society in which justice and peace shall truly prevail for all men.

The acceptance of this responsibility requires not only study, skilled staff and devoted leadership. It calls also for courage in many critical areas of life and thought. Thus, when the "defense against subversion" in the country, under the leadership of Senator Joseph R. McCarthy of Wisconsin, and others, became a disguise for an attack on basic liberties, on political freedom, free association, and the right of dissent, the American Jewish Congress, despite gloomy warnings, opposed all that McCarthyism represented.

Again, when the "defense against subversion" was transformed into a demand for conformity, and then used as a weapon with which to attack or undermine our public schools, the Congress recognized the significance of this threat and mustered its forces, in alliance with other liberal groups, to protect our public schools as one of the most basic democratic institutions of this country.

In the protection of freedom of religion, the Congress has taken leadership in championing the rights of Americans regardless of faith or, indeed, of lack of faith. It has been among the first to recognize the grave danger to religious freedom that would result if the continuing efforts to break down the wall of separation between Church and State should succeed. It has done all in its power to protect religion from interference or control by the State, and the State from interference or control by religious bodies. In these and many other areas, the American Jewish Congress has helped the Jewish community to recognize dangers to the democratic ideal so precious to us as Jews, and as Americans. It has helped to mobilize support for this ideal among Jews and non-Jews and has become recognized as one of those significant forces in America to whom the heritage of freedom is beyond price.

Concerned with creating a democratic structure in Jewish life and with the creative survival of Jews, the Congress has been seeking ways in which fuller understanding of Jewish traditions and Jewish values can become part of the Jewish community. To this end, it publishes *Congress Weekly* (founded in 1933), and supports *Judaism* (founded in 1952), a quarterly edited by an independent board of scholars. It has encouraged adult education and has, through its membership activities, striven to deepen the understanding of, and commitment to, Jewish values on the part of American Jews.

Being neither a religious nor a political organization, the American Jewish Congress has sought so to develop its program that no Jew, who is in fact truly a Jew, should feel excluded from its work, and so that its broad and unifying program would have much to contribute to the life of every Jew.

In the same spirit, while supporting the establishment of the Jewish Homeland, while including projects to strengthen the United Jewish Appeal and the Israel Bond Drive, and providing, through its Women's Division, for the building and the maintenance of the Louise Waterman Wise Youth Center in Israel, the Congress has carefully abstained from participating in Zionist politics. The organization includes in its membership Zionists of all parties, but does not regard itself as having any right, as an American organization, to interfere with the political decisions of the citizens of Israel. The Congress does regard itself, however, as having both the right and the duty to present the truth, as it sees it, to our own government, and to do all in its power to help our government develop a sound and moral international policy with regard to Israel and its people. Through its Commission on Israel and World Affairs, the Congress is collecting significant data and making them available to its membership and the general community. Through this Commission, the Congress hammers out proposed policies and programs in this important area of its activities, and seeks to enlist the cooperation of other Jewish and non-Jewish groups.

To write briefly of the American Jewish Congress or to seek to summarize its contribution to Jewish and American life is indeed difficult. I do, however, feel that I wish to express my appreciation for this opportunity to give a thumb-nail sketch of its philosophy and growing role in Jewish life. This work could not have been achieved without the inspiring leadership of such men as Stephen Wise, Dr. David Petegorsky, the creative and brilliant executive director of Congress until his death in 1956, and the inspiration of such men as Dr. Lewin and Professor Pekelis, or the great and steadfast devotion of the lay leaders, members, and the staff of the Congress who have given of themselves so generously throughout the years. The professional and lay leadership today in the Congress, under the presidency of Dr. Goldstein, who personifies a devotion to the Jewish ideal at its best, a love of Zion and a commitment to the democratic ideal, give promise that the American Jewish Congress will continue to provide light and strength to the Jewish and American community.

THE WORLD JEWISH CONGRESS

AT THE UNITED NATIONS

---

by Maurice L. Perlzweig

THE JEWISH COMMITMENT to the principles and purposes of the
United Nations derives from two sources: the doctrine of man
and his destiny embodied in the Jewish tradition, and the unique
and tragic experiences of the Jewish people as victims of international anarchy and "man's inhumanity to man."

The Jewish doctrine of man is rooted not in an abstraction
called nature, but in a living reality of whom it was written: "In
the image of God created He man; male and female created He
them." The Jewish doctrine of the common origin, the common
right and the common destiny of all mankind is today an integral
element in the faith of all enlightened men, at least in that immense area conquered by the religions derived from Judaism:
Christianity and Islam, to which may fairly be added the world-
wide religion of democracy. The law was promulgated on Mount
Sinai, says an old Jewish tradition, in all the seventy languages of
the nations, so that all might hear and none have the right to
reject it. Its echoes, indeed, may be heard in all the great documents of human liberty, the English Bill of Right, the American
Declaration of Independence, the French Declaration of the
Rights of Man, and the Universal Declaration of Human Rights.
That, no doubt, is why every tyrant who has sought to destroy
these rights has sought first to destroy the Jew.

The Jew who visits the headquarters of the United Nations in
New York may be impressed and even awed by the immense

apparatus of communication through which the delegates speak to each other, though mercifully not in all their "seventy languages." He may be puzzled or fascinated by the modernistic designs which decorate some of the walls. But he will be moved and strangely stirred when he confronts, carved in stone, the celebrated verses from Isaiah and Micah beginning with the words: "They shall beat their swords into plowshares." He may wonder what some of the delegates would think if they realized that these words follow and complete the no less celebrated prophecy on the exaltation of Zion and the establishment of Jerusalem as the spiritual metropolis of mankind. But he will feel at home.

The founders of the World Jewish Congress conceived of the organization not only as a device for the protection of Jewish rights and the furtherance of collective Jewish security, but as an instrumentality through which the Jewish people might bring their heritage to the service of the international community and make their distinctive contribution to the advancement of humanity. Faith and experience united to convince them that liberty, like peace, is indivisible. They realized that Jewish rights could not long survive the denial of human rights, as their successors today realize that a Jewish state remains in peril so long as the world of which it is a part is denied the security of peace. The announcement, therefore, of the proposal to perpetuate and expand the wartime coalition of nations into an international organization dedicated to the ideals of peace and human freedom made an instant appeal to the leaders of the World Jewish Congress. To work in, and give support to, the United Nations has since been one of the principal purposes of the World Jewish Congress.

The representatives of the Congress, who came in 1945 to the Organization Conference of the United Nations at San Francisco, brought with them an experience and a program. The experience had been gained at the League of Nations which, under the minority provisions of various treaties, had sought to protect the rights of minorities in certain regions. The success of the League in this field was limited; but it was real. For a brief period before the expiration of a treaty, even the worst excesses of Hitlerism were held in check in German Silesia. Valuable experience had been gained in a difficult field, and the international community had shown, though in a limited area, what could be done. The program of the World Jewish Congress delegation was to seek, so far as possible, to secure the universalization of the protective activity of the international community so that it might cover human rights everywhere.

It may be that we asked for too much, too soon. If so, we were not untrue to the peculiar tradition of Jewish obduracy which has sustained, unimpaired, the prophetic vision in the teeth of frustration and setback. Our program proved to be in advance of what the great Powers were prepared to concede even in that time of rising hope. Nevertheless, we left San Francisco with the knowledge that a great step forward had been taken.

We were far from being alone. Delegates from church organizations, trade unions, civic and political bodies of all kinds, both national and international, had flocked to San Francisco from many parts of the world, and their pressure was decisive in securing a broadening of the opportunities and obligations which were to be granted to the new international organization in the field of human rights. The Conference had before it a draft of the Charter, known as the Dumbarton Oaks proposals, prepared by representatives of the United States, Britain, France and the USSR, who had met at Dumbarton Oaks, near Washington, in advance of the Conference. This document was, in many respects, timid and defective, not least in the field of human rights. It is the simple truth to say that the major factor which helped to transform it into the present Charter was the determined and unremitting effort of the non-governmental representatives.

There is only one reference to human rights in the Dumbarton Oaks proposals. In the U. N. Charter there are five such references, and the Security Council, the General Assembly, the Economic and Social Council and the Trusteeship Council are each assigned powers and obligations in the sphere of human rights. In addition, the establishment of a new body, the Commission on Human Rights, was made mandatory, and its mere creation ensured that the United Nations would not be allowed to forget or overlook its obligations in this field. In its memoranda submitted to the Conference and in representations to its delegations, the World Jewish Congress had urged that the new organization should be empowered to "protect" or "safeguard" human rights. In spite of the effort of some of the smaller democratic Powers, the Conference was prepared to assign to the new organization the duty only to "promote respect for and observance of" human rights.

Another achievement which has since proved of great practical importance was the authorization given in Article 71 of the U. N. Charter to the Economic and Social Council to confer consultative status on appropriate international non-governmental organizations and to national organizations only subject to the consent of their governments, which meant that consultative status would be conferred, as experience has confirmed, only in the most exceptional cases.

It may here be recorded that the American author of Article 71 told the present writer that one of the organizations mentioned in the discussions as eligible for consultative status was the WJC. The Congress, indeed, was the first Jewish body to be granted such status. One unexpected result was that the United Nations, in all innocence and, as it were by accident, virtually put an end to a controversy which had raged in Jewish communities for many years. Jewish organizations, which had denounced the very idea of an international Jewish organization as dangerous or wicked or both, found themselves in the paradoxical position of being compelled to establish new international bodies as the only means of obtaining official access to the United Nations. The vision of the founders of the WJC had been vindicated by the international community itself.

Very early in its history, the U. N. General Assembly demonstrated that opportunities had indeed been opened up for the international protection of human rights by a decision in favor of the adoption of an International Bill of Human Rights. This Bill was conceived of as consisting of three parts: a Declaration, a Covenant, and Measures of Implementation. Of these, only the

Declaration has so far been adopted, but even standing by itself it has proved to be of historic importance.

At every stage of its formulation, as it passed through the subsidiary bodies on its way to the General Assembly, the representatives of the WJC in London, Geneva, New York and Paris, exerted an unremitting effort to secure the most liberal possible text. The value and importance of this work were publicly acknowledged by members of the Human Rights Commission, and its results are embodied in the texts finally adopted. No instructed student of the Universal Declaration can fail to observe that the draftsmen took into account the lessons learned as a result of the Hitlerite assault on the civilized world. It was the task of the Congress to ensure that these lessons should be fully understood, and its efforts were crowned with a significant measure of success.

In spite of influential opposition, a clause prohibiting incitement to discrimination was included. The draft forbidding retroactivity of legislation was amended, in the spirit of the Nuremberg trials, to make clear that crimes against humanity were punishable under international law even if they were not recognized as such under national law, at the time they were committed. Though in a form weaker than proposed by the Congress, the right to seek and to enjoy in other countries asylum from persecution was affirmed. The right to an education was supplemented, on the proposal of the Congress, by a paragraph defining the aims of education so as to include respect for human rights, the promotion of understanding among all nations, and among racial and religious groups, and the furtherance of the activities of the United Nations for the maintenance of peace. This proposal was made in the light of the misuse of public education by dictatorships in their wars on the ideals and practices of democracy. The Congress regarded its adoption by the Assembly as an achievement of high significance. In its anxiety to ensure that none of the rights enumerated in the Universal Declaration be exploited or perverted by unscrupulous governments, in attacks on the rights of minorities and on democracy itself, the Congress pressed for the inclusion of a safeguarding clause which would avert this possibility. For example, it urged that the highest interests of freedom would be violated if governments were permitted to allow the right to freedom of opinion and expression to become instruments of incitement to hatred and even murder. Accordingly, the Universal Declaration includes the clause (Art. 29[3]): "That the rights and freedoms may in no case be exercised contrary to the purposes and principles of the United Nations." While this clause could well have been formulated in more explicit terms, it nevertheless represents a standard considerably higher than prevails in many countries, where pornography is banned but anti-Semitic agitation of the vilest kind is tolerated as licit in the name of freedom of speech. In its effort to secure the inclusion of this clause, the Congress made sure that the need for solving one of the most difficult problems which confronts democracy should never be overlooked.

The Universal Declaration of Human Rights was proclaimed by the Third Session of the General Assembly in Paris on December 10, 1948, as "a common standard of achievement for all peoples and all nations." It is not a treaty; it defines a goal towards which all nations are summoned to march. But that does not exhaust its significance. While debate continues on its exact juridical status, there can be no doubt that it is no mere academic exercise in definition, but is a document which is having an increasingly important effect on both the ideas and the practices of many peoples. A Belgian representative in the General Assembly expressed a widely-held view when he said: "In this Declaration, voted by the virtual unanimity of all the members of the United Nations, there is a moral value and authority which is without precedent in the history of the world, and it is the beginning of a system of international law."

Subsequent events have fully confirmed this view. Not only have appeals to the Universal Declaration not been seriously challenged, but its provisions have profoundly influenced, or even been incorporated into, new constitutions. In some cases, its authority has been recognized and it has acquired a clear juridical significance by the incorporation of its clauses into international conventions and treaties. A notable example was the

Convention between France and Tunisia, on the status of Tunisia, in which, at the suggestion of the WJC, the binding character of the Declaration was accepted by both governments.

But important though it is, the Universal Declaration does not fulfill the promise implicit in the decision by the United Nations to formulate a complete International Bill of Rights. The next step must be the adoption of a covenant which would take the form of a treaty legally binding on all its signatories. Work on the proposed covenant or covenants has been done in various organs of the United Nations, including the General Assembly itself, and the text has been revised again and again. It must be admitted that, in the present state of international relations, there is little immediate likelihood that these documents will be adopted in a form likely to attract the adhesion of a significant number of signatories. Nevertheless, it is not to be supposed that the present structure of international relations will remain forever unchanged, and the movement of ideas in the camps of the two powerful blocs, which confront each other on the international scene, encourages the hope that there may be fundamental changes and realignments in the coming years. At any rate, the Congress continues to battle unremittingly for an international instrument for the protection of human rights, which will be binding ultimately on all the nations.

In the course of this battle, the WJC has concentrated much of its energy on insisting on the explicit recognition of the right of petition and the opportunity to seek redress. When human rights are invaded or destroyed, the right of petition by responsible and recognized international non-governmental bodies would not only give the victim of persecution a voice, but would also help to take the demand for redress or protection out of the diplomatic struggle and provide an opportunity for a system akin to that of judicial determination. To limit the right of complaint, as is at present proposed, to governments must necessarily mean intervention by one or more states on behalf of citizens of other states, with all the political complications and dangers which such a course must entail. In the present structure of international relations, no other course is available. The results, however, have been so pitifully inadequate and have so often produced nothing but exacerbation of diplomatic conflict, that the time has come for a reappraisal of the whole system. What the Congress has urged, with an increasingly growing response from governments, is that the victim should himself be heard by the international community through his own chosen non-governmental instrument, and that judgment should be passed, if judgment is necessary, by a tribunal which stands above diplomatic conflict and national rivalry.

Though the Universal Declaration represents an important achievement, yet it does not stand alone in the effective work which the United Nations has done in the field of human rights. A whole series of international instruments affecting special areas in this field have been negotiated, ratified by governments, and are now in force. These include the Convention on Genocide, the Convention Relating to the Status of Refugees, and the Convention on the Declaration of Death of Missing Persons. Another, which has not yet come into operation, is the Convention Relating to the Status of Stateless Persons. These documents attempt to deal with highly specialized problems and to give protection or render urgently needed legal assistance to people who have survived the tyranny and persecution in our generation and are now exposed to the pains and penalties which result from a loss of legal status. Though these documents are little known to, or appreciated by, public opinion, including Jewish public opinion, yet their provisions sometimes spell the difference between despair and hope for many thousands of the victims of persecution.

In the formulation of all these instruments the Congress has made a significant contribution. At least one, the Convention on the Declaration of Death of Missing Persons, would hardly have come into existence but for the unremitting efforts of the WJC over a period of years. Its forbidding title covers, and perhaps conceals, an effort on the part of the international community to recognize rights to inheritance, remarriage and adoption which would otherwise be denied to its beneficiaries, and it has thereby opened up new perspectives of hope and opportunity to many survivors of the Hitlerite holocaust who might otherwise have yielded to despair.

Representatives of the Congress have participated, whether by way of formal written or oral submission or informal consultation, in the work of every meeting of the Economic and Social Council (ECOSOC), the Commission on Human Rights, the Sub-Commissions on the Prevention of Discrimination and on the Protection of Minorities, and numerous diplomatic conferences and special conferences and meetings of subsidiary organs under the auspices of ECOSOC. The Congress has made contributions to the work of the International Law Commission, and its memoranda, addressed to the General Assembly, have been brought officially to the notice of the delegations. And during the debates in the General Assembly, on the disposition of the former Italian colonies, its spokesman was invited to address the powerful Political Committee, the only case on record of a hearing granted to a representative of an ethnic or religious minority by that body. The WJC has been equally active in the U. N. Educational, Cultural and Scientific Organization (UNESCO) and its subsidiary bodies, and it has a conspicuous place in the work and leadership of the organizations of consultative non-governmental bodies.

Even a cursory survey of the topics, political, legal, cultural and social, with which the World Jewish Congress has dealt at the United Nations, or of its efforts to develop and expand the possibilities of non-governmental consultation, in both the Jewish and general interest, cannot be attempted within the limits of an essay; it would require a volume. Such a volume was recently published by Dr. Nehemiah Robinson, the distinguished head of the WJC Institute of Jewish Affairs: "The United Nations and the World Jewish Congress" (New York, 1956).

The protection of the Jewish interest in Palestine, before and during the period when that country came under the jurisdiction of the U. N. Trusteeship Council was the task of the Jewish Agency, and, subsequent to the establishment of the State of Israel, the task of the State itself. Nevertheless, support of the State of Israel is one of the objectives written into the constitution of the WJC, and this fact has entailed responsibilities which the

Congress has sought to discharge, at the United Nations as elsewhere, on behalf of the Jewish communities and organizations which it represents in more than sixty lands.

It supported the Jewish Agency at the U. N. Organization Conference at San Francisco in the successful struggle to ensure that Jewish rights in Palestine, under the Mandate of the League of Nations, should be preserved under the Trusteeship system; and it played its part, within the limits of its competence, in securing the support of governments for the historic resolution of 1947, in which the United Nations recognized (though, it must be emphasized, it did not create) the right of the Jewish people to establish a state in its ancient homeland.

Since that event, which marked a turning point in Jewish history, the United Nations has become a battleground on which Israel has been compelled to fight for its sovereign rights and its very existence. A number of Arab states, notably Egypt, have sought to exploit the machinery of an international organization, whose purpose it is to maintain peace, in order to maintain and legalize a permanent state of war. To use the United Nations as a sanctuary from which to wage war, without the risk of retaliation, and to pervert interpretation of the Charter to deny to the victim of a state of permanent aggression the right of self-defence, is to make a mockery of the high purposes of the international organization. Yet, this is what has happened, and great Powers have either stood aside in apparent helplessness or united to compete, in the interests of the politics of power, for the favor of states which have, naked and unashamed, exhibited and proclaimed their predatory policies. Jewish faith in the United Nations has been tried and tested in the crucibles of a bitter experience.

But that faith fundamentally remains unshaken. For to use legalisms as instruments of lawlessness is an old device. Legalisms opened the road to power for Hitler, and today they are being used by Nasser to destroy the Jewish community in Egypt, as tomorrow he will destroy the Christian communities. Even in the most advanced democratic states there are always those who appeal to the Constitution in the very act of undermining it. To say that the United Nations is imperfect is to say that it was built by human hands. But it is no less human, and in the Jewish view more enduringly human, to revolt against injustice. Already voices of protest are being heard in Britain and in France, in the democracies of western Europe and Scandinavia, in Australia, Canada and New Zealand, and in the Congress of the United States, which is to say wherever democracy is deeply rooted and liberalism an authentic way of life. On the other side, are the dictators, the slave owners and states which have not yet recovered from their first draughts of the heady wine of sovereignty.

In this conflict we must believe that Israel and democracy will ultimately triumph or we deny the prophetic faith which made us partisans of the United Nations. The Jew will not abandon the United Nations; he will strive to transform it.

Let the last word on this issue be uttered by the man who, more than any other, has borne the heat and burden of this conflict. Speaking on February 21, 1957, in the Knesset, when Israel confronted the threat of sanctions by the U.N., Prime Minister David Ben-Gurion said:

Undoubtedly the United Nations is still far from perfect and we have grave and bitter complaints against it which are not confined to the last few days. But we will not on that account reject this great world organization. The vision which is personified in the U.N. is the vision of our prophets and the principles on which it is based are the principles of peace, justice and equality among nations. These principles are no less precious to us than to any other people in the world.

Israel Goldstein has been a dedicated partisan of the U.N. from the beginning. Indeed, his support of the U.N. long predated the San Francisco Conference. It is not always remembered that "United Nations" was the name first given to the coalition of Powers which, during the second World War, was resolved to root out the blood-stained tyranny of Nazism and to lay the foundations of a new and free world. That union has suffered many vicissitudes in peace as in war, and it has seemed at times as though its achievement, even as between the western democracies, lay beyond the reach of human frailty. If it has not foundered, it has been because there have been men of high dedication in many lands whose faith has kept the light of hope flickering even through the darkest international storms. In this honored company, Israel Goldstein played his own distinctive part. Throughout the second World War, he stood at the helm of movements of aid to the nations allied to America in a common effort and sacrifice, through which was born a new sense of brotherhood and community of purpose which made the organization of a permanent U.N. possible.

At San Francisco, Israel Goldstein was one of the small company of Jewish leaders who helped to ensure that the new Charter would sustain, instead of undermine, the Jewish rights in Palestine which had been recognized by the League of Nations. At the same time, he lent his powerful advocacy to the non-governmental effort which was chiefly responsible for transforming the narrow and timid human rights provisions of the Dumbarton Oaks proposals into the more generous vision of the Charter.

Since that day he has been tireless in his support, as a preacher and a spokesman for American liberalism, of the ideal which the Charter embodies. He has been among those for whom the U.N. has presented both a special challenge and a special obligation to the United States. In a remarkable address delivered in his capacity as a leader of the American Delegation to the Plenary Assembly of the WJC, held in Geneva in the summer of 1953, he called for a revision of those American policies which had denied endorsement and ratification, by the United States, of a whole series of conventions and other international instruments designed to safeguard the same human rights on the international scene as are guaranteed to American citizens by their own Constitution and Bill of Rights.

Others might have thought it more prudent to remain silent while American policy was under criticism. But he knew himself to be most truly American when he upheld what his convictions taught him were the fundamental values of Americanism. Rather than seem to acquiesce in the creeping isolationism of the moment, or seek refuge in evasion, he spoke out forthrightly though he knew he was challenging, in an international forum, a great and powerful government which was also his own.

This incident is significant not only because it throws some light on the quality of the man, but because it indicates that a great task still lies before him. In a time of crisis when, under the bludgeoning of events, expediency seems often to have displaced principle in the seats of authority, we may draw encouragement from the fact that there are still men among us whose courage and faith forbid surrender to the unworthy fashions of the moment. For Israel Goldstein, his sixtieth birthday marks the beginning of a new era of service and achievement which, under Providence, will be granted him both as an American and as a Jew.

THE ESTABLISHMENT OF

BRANDEIS UNIVERSITY

---

by Julius Silver

THE IDEA OF a Jewish university in the United States had been germinating for almost a hundred years. The desirability of providing secular education on the university level under Jewish sponsorship was initially recognized, in part, in training schools for student teachers and rabbis. Thus, in academies, in which Jewish studies predominated, secular courses were offered in a sort of advanced parochial school atmosphere. No concept of a Jewish institution, ministering exclusively to the secular interests of its student body, developed until the second decade of this century when the idea was discussed in several published articles. However, no practical steps to create such an institution resulted from these intellectual exercises.

A considerable part of such discussion as did take place was evoked by the prevalence, in some institutions of higher learning, especially medical schools, of a quota system limiting the number of Jews in the student body and in the faculty. The establishment of a medical school, under Jewish auspices, that would afford opportunities for study, teaching and research to eligible Jews, who were denied such opportunities because of this *numerus clausus,* was advocated in many quarters. The quota system also prompted proposals for a secular university of first-class rank, under Jewish sponsorship; it was held that such an institution, properly administered, would constitute a living example to the world at large, of an institution rejecting the iniquitous quota system. On the positive side, there were those who advocated such an institution, not only or chiefly as an answer to anti-Jewish discrimination, but as a measure that would place the Jewish community on an equal footing, in the field of higher education, with Christian communities in the United States. The development of higher education in the United States was, in the main, the result of sponsorship by various denominational groups. Thus, Harvard and Yale began as Congregationalist schools, Columbia as Episcopalian, Princeton as Presbyterian, Swarthmore as Quaker, Brown as Baptist, while the Catholics founded Fordham, Notre Dame, Holy Cross and many others.

American Jews as a group had made no significant, identifiable contributions in this field although a number of individual Jews had contributed generously to the funds of various universities. This failure was not generally the result of indifference nor of inadequate appreciation of the importance of institutions of higher learning, but rather was it due to the absence of proper channeling of beneficent impulses.

As always, while those who feel the existence of a social vacuum work tirelessly to fill the need, others hide their inactivity behind a smoke-screen of opposition. In some instances, of course, the motivation underlying the opposition is sincere and honest; in others, the pseudo-intellectual negation is merely rationalized inertia or complacence. Sometimes, the most vociferous opponents of a new movement later embrace it ostentatiously when the idea achieves public acceptance and the risks of failure, incident to immaturity, have been overcome.

So there were pros and cons on the issue of the wisdom of establishing a Jewish university. There were those who urged that such an institution would become an academic ghetto. There were those who contended that such an institution would serve as a pretext for other universities rejecting Jewish students who would be counseled to satisfy their needs among their own people. There were those who succumbed to the notion that identification with a Jewish university would lack the social sanction of the established centers of learning. Still others sincerely hesitated to sponsor an untried institution which could justify its existence only if, and when, it achieved those standards of superior quality which alone would warrant its existence as a Jewish standard-bearer in the academic ranks.

For many years, Dr. Israel Goldstein had given thought to the need for defining the objectives of a Jewish university and for translating those aims into concrete reality. Since 1918, when he was graduated from the Jewish Theological Seminary and was elected rabbi of Congregation B'nai Jeshurun, New York City, he had wholeheartedly dedicated himself to active participation in various communal movements. It was not until the fall of 1945, when his term as president of the Zionist Organization of America was about to expire and when other prior commitments had been satisfied, that he directed his considerable talents and experience to the task of determining whether it was feasible to organize a secular institution of higher learning under Jewish sponsorship.

In defining the objectives of such an institution, he conceived of a prototype university offering undergraduate and graduate courses in academic, as well as professional, fields of study. The institution would be sponsored by a predominantly Jewish group, but without any particular religious sectarianism. Such a school would be open alike to Jewish and non-Jewish students and faculty, who would be admitted or engaged on the basis of merit only.

Neither diverted from his course, nor discouraged by the critics, well-meaning or otherwise, Israel Goldstein proceeded to the task of institutionalizing a concept that was clearly etched in his mind, as a Jewish contribution to the American intellectual scene.

Through a timely coincidence, the physical site for a university became available as the result of negotiations commenced on January 7, 1946. In Waltham, Massachusetts, in an area close to Boston, that great center of American culture and education, near Harvard, Massachusetts Institute of Technology, Wellesley, Boston University, Holy Cross and other ranking colleges and universities, a small school, known as Middlesex University, was struggling to maintain its existence in the face of inadequate facilities and support. It had already been forced to discontinue its medical college; its veterinary school, with an inadequate faculty for even its small student body, was unable to meet even minimum budgetary requirements. Proceedings to abridge the school's charter had been instituted in the Legislature of the Commonwealth of Massachusetts. The professional world looked askance at its standards and its student body.

Nevertheless, Middlesex University was still tenuously maintaining its hold on its charter which granted it power to confer degrees in arts and sciences, medicine and veterinary medicine. The school owned a hundred-acre campus, beautifully situated, and several basic buildings which, in the aggregate, represented an investment of over a million dollars. These physical facilities could not have been duplicated for twice that amount, even if the restrictions of the post-war period had not made materials and labor unavailable for construction.

Dr. Goldstein persuaded the authorities of Middlesex University to transfer control of the institution to a small group of associates recruited by him, in return for a promise to undertake a radical reorganization of the institution and to provide the funds required to meet its budgetary deficits.

What was urgently needed at once was first-class, academic sponsorship, and then a nucleus of supporters who would provide the financial means and community prestige to arrest the unfavorable public reaction to the declining fortunes of Middlesex University.

To achieve these aims, Dr. Goldstein enlisted the cooperation of a number of eminent scholars and scientists, and then, he undertook to secure the endorsement of the greatest academic figure of our age, the world-renowned Albert Einstein. At a conference with the latter, at his home in Princeton, New Jersey, Dr. Goldstein succeeded in obtaining from Dr. Einstein an enthusiastic endorsement of the project expressed in a letter dated January 22, 1946.

Meanwhile, Dr. Goldstein had assembled in New York City, a small initial nucleus of supporters and advisers which included the late Samuel Null, Justice of the Supreme Court of the State of New York; Dr. Israel S. Wechsler, professor of neurology at Columbia University; Dr. Alexander Dushkin, executive vice president of the Jewish Education Committee of New York; Major Abraham F. Wechsler, president of the Madison Settlement

House, Messrs. Milton Bluestein, Albert Rosen and Julius Silver, the writer of this narrative, who served as legal adviser and treasurer of the project.

It was now deemed desirable to add to this group a prominent Jewish leader in Boston who would serve as the local spokesman and who would aid in enlisting the support of the Boston Jewish community. The present writer suggested the name of his friend, Mr. George Alpert, who had attained recognition in various philanthropic activities, and who, as an able lawyer, could be helpful in contacts with the Massachusetts Legislature and the local collegiate approval bodies. On January 24, 1946, two days after Dr. Einstein's letter of approval, Dr. Goldstein and Mr. Silver called on Mr. Alpert in his Boston office and enlisted his cooperation and support. His association with the original group added great strength to the common cause. His notable contributions, during ensuing periods of strain and crisis, marked him as one of the most effective of the stalwarts who helped bring Dr. Goldstein's plans to fruition.

The transfer of control of Middlesex University was accomplished simply by obtaining the resignations of five of the seven members of the Board of Trustees and the election, in their places, of five men nominated by Dr. Goldstein. These were, besides himself, Justice Null, Major Wechsler, George Alpert and Julius Silver.

To broaden the sponsorship, Dr. Goldstein then consulted outstanding educators, prominent figures in public life and leaders of the Jewish communities in New York, Boston and other large cities. He personally interviewed Dr. Karl T. Compton, president of M.I.T.; Dr. Samuel L. Marsh, president of Boston University; Maurice L. Tobin, Governor of Massachusetts; Archbishop Richard J. Cushing of Boston; Dr. Alexander Brin, publisher of the Boston *Jewish Advocate*, who had a large following among the leading Jews of New England; Dr. Alvin S. Johnson, president emeritus of the New School for Social Research; Dr. Morton S. Gottschall, dean of the College of Liberal Arts and Sciences of the College of the City of New York; Dr. Benjamin Fine, education editor of *The New York Times;* Dr. Abram L. Sachar, director of the B'nai B'rith Hillel Foundation, and numerous others.

Meanwhile, with the consent and approval of Dr. Einstein, the Albert Einstein Foundation for Higher Learning (a Delaware corporation) was organized on February 26, 1946 to serve as a fund-raising instrument, dissociated from the unfortunate connotations which the name of Middlesex University had in the public mind. The preamble to the Articles of Incorporation of the Albert Einstein Foundation for Higher Learning was written by Dr. Goldstein, and is quoted in full because of its complete enumeration of the principles which motivated the project:

Believing that the standard of American living which, on its material side, is held up as an example to the rest of the world should also be reflected in a high standard of education which should be made available to all who seek it regardless of race, color and creed, aware of the mounting hunger of American youth for higher learning both as an end in itself and as a means of preparation for the professions, mindful that there are not enough facilities for higher learning and professional training to meet the needs therefor, deeply conscious both of the Hebraic tradition of Torah looking upon culture as a birthright, as well as of the American ideal of an educated democracy and of the "Hebraic mortar which cemented the foundations of American Democracy," and dedicated to the proposition that in the post-war world the American people, entering upon an unprecedented position of world leadership, should lead not only in technical skills and material resources but also in intellectual and spiritual endowments, this Foundation for Higher Learning is established.

The charter of the Foundation provided for a Board of Trustees not to exceed twenty-one members, fourteen of whom were elected at the outset, the remaining places to be filled by new supporters. Dr. Goldstein was elected president; other officers were designated; an office in New York City and an executive staff were provided, and the Foundation thus became an actuality. The board of the Foundation was expected to concern itself not only with the financial aspects of the project but also with policy-making during the interregnum, that is, until the university itself could be named, its program defined, and the key members of its faculty and administrative staff selected.

The creation of an independent fund-raising entity was deemed also to afford greater flexibility in dealing with the

myriad problems incident to the development of the basic prototype university project and of others that might follow later. Its
independent status would, moreover, insulate its activities from
the clouds and storms threatening the newly-acquired assets represented by the charter and physical facilities of Middlesex
University.

Among these clouds were the then pending proceedings before
a committee of the Legislature of Massachusetts concerning the
proposed abridgement of the charter of Middlesex University;
another source of worry was that the Board of Collegiate Authority of the Massachusetts Department of Education would disap-
prove the program of the school of veterinary medicine for the
purposes of Public Law 346 (enabling returned war veterans to
take courses at Government expense). Both of these challenges
were met by Dr. Goldstein and his associates who demonstrated,
to the satisfaction of the public authorities, the ability of the new
sponsors to rehabilitate the ailing institution.

The first public function to introduce the new institution to the
American Jewish community took place in New York City on
June 20, 1946. It was attended by sixty persons who pledged
$350,000, an encouraging initial response preliminary to the
larger public dinner which was scheduled for that fall.

From the outset, it was intended that the name of Middlesex
University would be changed in favor of one more appropriate to
the character of the new institution. There were various suggestions but that of Dr. Goldstein that the institution be named
"Brandeis University," in honor of the late U. S. Supreme Court
Justice Louis D. Brandeis, was unanimously approved. Dr. Goldstein described Judge Brandeis as:

. . . the greatest American Jew of his time, liberal in his Americanism and self-affirming in his Jewishness, who had rendered historic
service to America and to the Jewish people and whose noble life
might well serve as an inspiration to American Jews.

Dr. Goldstein went on to say:

The fact that a large part of his career had been associated with
Massachusetts gave added force to the linking of his name to the

institution at Waltham. His name, moreover, would be a constant reminder of the need to keep the institution modest in size but noteworthy in quality, true to a pattern which Justice Brandeis had often espoused.

Dr. Albert Einstein heartily approved the new name, as did the family of the late Justice Brandeis. The legal formalities for consummation of the change of name were deferred, however, until the program, as a whole, would be further advanced.

A financial plan was now prepared and approved by the Foundation. Its objective was an amount in excess of six million dollars, but it was agreed that the receipt of one million dollars would warrant opening the school. Since 102 returned veterans were involved in the veterinary and pre-veterinary courses, possibilities were explored for obtaining government aid under Federal legislation extending educational privileges to returned veterans.

All the preliminaries were now settled. At this point, the new school had a campus, educational and civic sponsorship, an improved and more tolerant climate of public opinion, the basic elements of the fund-raising machinery and an honored name awaiting a propitious moment for its announcement. Plans were now formulated for the opening of the university. As a step in this direction, an Educational Advisory Committee of eminent educators to cooperate with representatives of the Foundation was appointed. The first duty assigned to this group was "to make a comprehensive study in order to recommend to the Board of the Foundation a man to be selected as acting chancellor of the University to devote himself to the organization of a faculty and the preparation of a curriculum."

During a visit to Dr. Einstein at his home in Princeton, N. J., Dr. Goldstein discussed with him the names of several men who had been suggested for membership on the Educational Advisory Committee. Dr. Einstein agreed to serve and suggested Dr. Otto Nathan, an assistant professor of economics at New York University, as his alternate. Dr. Goldstein suggested that Dr. Abram L. Sachar be considered for the post of chief administrative officer of the University. Dr. Goldstein cited Dr. Sachar's record and, later, sent to Dr. Einstein copies of the books Dr. Sachar had written. Subsequently, in a conversation with Dr. Sachar, Dr. Goldstein asked the latter whether he would be interested in having his name proposed to the Educational Advisory Committee among those to be submitted for its consideration. Dr. Sachar agreed to take the matter under advisement, but no commitment was made by either Dr. Sachar or Dr. Goldstein.

Efforts were now concentrated by Dr. Goldstein toward preparations for the first full-scale public fund-raising dinner which was scheduled to be held in New York City on November 19, 1946.

While the plans for this dinner were going forward, the group enlisted in this great cause, under the leadership of Dr. Goldstein, were appalled by the receipt of a letter from Dr. Einstein severely criticizing Dr. Goldstein for having invited an eminent Catholic clergyman to participate in the program of the forthcoming dinner. It had seemed to the planners of this public function that an endorsement from such a source would strengthen the public acceptance of this fledgling institution, and thus improve the prospect of retaining the charter. Dr. Einstein also criticized Dr. Goldstein for having spoken with Dr. Sachar, despite the tentative and provisional nature of the approach. Dr. Einstein expressed his unwillingness to continue being associated with Dr. Goldstein in the project and, accordingly, proposed to withdraw his support from the institution and the use of his name from the Foundation. Explanations failed to move Dr. Einstein; he remained intransigent in his attitude. With a magnanimity seldom equalled in junctures of this nature, Dr. Goldstein withdrew from his official positions in the University and in the Foundation on September 16, 1946. His associates and supporters protested against this submission to Dr. Einstein's unwarranted criticism, which deprived the project of its guiding spirit. Nevertheless, Dr. Goldstein persuaded these men to recognize the importance of retaining Dr. Einstein's good will, and to continue their interest in the task they had undertaken.

In a resolution which placed on record, and gave recognition to his contributions, his colleagues expressed their deep regret at Dr. Goldstein's withdrawal, in the following language:

WHEREAS, Dr. Israel Goldstein, for many years visualized the urgent need of a Jewish-sponsored university; and

WHEREAS, he grasped the opportunity to realize this need when the closing of the Medical School of Middlesex University and the resultant insecure position of the University in general made it possible; and

WHEREAS, he interested prominent educators, Jewish leaders and business men in the project of aiding Middlesex University; and

WHEREAS, he obtained the support of Dr. Albert Einstein for the project; and

WHEREAS, he caused to be organized the Albert Einstein Foundation for Higher Learning, Inc., as a fund-raising instrument; and

WHEREAS, he succeeded in obtaining control of the physical facilities of the University; and

WHEREAS, he organized an initial group of sponsors prepared to support the project financially and otherwise; and

WHEREAS, he aroused the interest and obtained the approval of the American Jewish community for this project; and

WHEREAS, he organized a fund-raising program and obtained pledges in substantial amounts; and

WHEREAS, he successfully resisted attempts by hostile groups to close Middlesex University; and

WHEREAS, he was active in the application of the Veterinary School of the University for permission to enroll returning veterans under the G. I. Bill of Rights;

Now, THEREFORE, BE IT RESOLVED, that the Board of Directors of the Albert Einstein Foundation for Higher Learning, Inc., recognizing these invaluable contributions made by Dr. Israel Goldstein, and his successful efforts in engineering a most humane project, does hereby express to him, unanimously, its fullest appreciation and gratitude for his services.

Dr. Goldstein's contribution, as instigator and initiator of the new university, was sealed when he withdrew from active leadership. The course he had charted had to be continued by other hands at the helm.

Ironically, despite the sacrifice of Dr. Goldstein's valuable services, Dr. Einstein, shortly thereafter, in June 1947, withdrew his support from the University. His action followed the failure of the Board of Trustees, for many practical reasons, to elect his nominee, the late Dr. Harold Laski of England, as president of the University, which had meanwhile been formally renamed "Brandeis University."

Almost a year later, in April 1948, Dr. Abram L. Sachar was chosen president of Brandeis University. In writing to Dr. Goldstein on June 2, 1948, Dr. Sachar characterized Dr. Goldstein's contribution to the institution, as follows:

> . . . You are really the father of Brandeis University. You put endless energy and devotion into the building of the concept and the corralling of its first support. You expressed confidence in me at the very beginning of the Brandeis history by your discussion with me of possible association with Brandeis . . .

Many new supporters throughout the country now rallied to the cause, and the administrative talents of Dr. Sachar converted this added strength to useful purposes. The student body, the faculty, the physical facilities and the curricula of studies were considerably expanded, while standards of superior quality in all these categories were set and maintained. As anticipated by Dr. Goldstein, Dr. Sachar's leadership has brought Brandeis University to its present high status as an educational institution of which the Jewish community and, indeed, the whole educational world, are justifiably proud. As the institution has grown in stature and significance, it has risen to the challenge which its founder envisioned as its potential. Its prospects for the future are brilliant. But this landmark in the history of American education, with all its glowing promise and achievement, would never have seen the light of day but for the vision and dedication of its founder, Dr. Israel Goldstein.

This fact is attested to by Mr. George Alpert, until recently president of the Board of Trustees of Brandeis University, and now president of the New York, New Haven & Hartford Railroad, in a letter to Dr. Goldstein, dated February 6, 1956:

> . . . It has always been a source of regret to me that difficulties over which neither of us had control resulted in your withdrawal

from active participation. However, your role in the very early days is fixed. Had it not been for your fervor and enthusiasm in those early months, there would now be no Brandeis University. . . .

Dr. Israel Goldstein is the spiritual father and the founder of Brandeis University. This great and growing institution, its name, its physical facilities and its *raison d'etre* are the products of his vision and his energy.

In founding Brandeis University, Dr. Israel Goldstein has added another achievement of vital importance to his career of distinguished public service.

RESTITUTION TO NAZI VICTIMS—

A MILESTONE IN

INTERNATIONAL MORALITY

by Benjamin B. Ferencz

MANY OF THE great movements of history are guided by the inspiration and determination of a few devoted men. The scope and complexity of contemporary life, however, compel a concert of action in which the role of the individual tends to be obscured. It is not the purpose here to place a laurel crown on the brow of any one individual. The work itself must serve to reflect his achievement. The singular endeavor of seeking restitution for wrongs committed against Jews has already carved its place in Jewish history. This program stands as a tribute to the handful of resolute Jewish leaders whose faith and determination made it possible.

When World War II had ended and the fear and anguish had somewhat abated, men could set their hearts and minds to healing some of the profound wounds which remained. During the dozen-year reign of the "Thousand-Year Reich," European Jewry had been decimated. The intellectuals, the artists and the communal leaders had been destroyed. Not even the innocent youth, the stalk of Jewish life, had been spared. Of those who could not flee, only a tattered remnant survived the fanatic Nazi scourge.

With diabolical precision, under the cloak of law, or through mere seizure, duress or terror, Jews had been systematically divested of their possessions. Those who had escaped with their lives were now scattered throughout the world, often living in adversity and need. It was evident that some means would have to be found to restore to the former owners, or their heirs, the property of which they had been so cruelly dispossessed. Nor could the possessions of those who, together with their heirs, had lost their lives in the Nazi infernos, be allowed to remain in the hands of their wrongful possessors. The leading Jewish organizations in the United States, remembering the biblical question "Hast thou killed and also taken possession?", insisted that these heirless assets would have to be retrieved in order to help recontruct the shattered lives of those who had survived. This great humanitarian principle was embodied in the first restitution law passed by the United States Military Government authorities in Germany.

On March 31, 1946, under the provisions of this law, the Jewish Restitution Successor Organization, referred to below as JRSO, was designated as successor to heirless and unclaimed property. In the same year, the Organization was incorporated under the New York State membership corporation law. The incorporators were: The American Jewish Committee; the American Jewish Conference; the American Jewish Joint Distribution Committee; the Board of Deputies of British Jews; the Commission on European Jewish Cultural Reconstruction; Council for the Protection of the Rights and Interests of Jews from Germany; the Jewish Agency for Palestine; and the World Jewish Congress.

Later the following organizations were co-opted: Agudas Israel World Organization; the Anglo-Jewish Association; the Central British Fund; the Conseil Representative Israelite of France; and the Arbeitsgemeinschaft Sueddeutscher Landes-verbaende Juedischer Gemeinden.

In accordance with an agreement reached at the time of the incorporation of the JRSO, the presidency and the chairmanship of the executive committee alternate annually between a representative of the Joint Distribution Committee and a representative of the Jewish Agency for Palestine, in recognition of the special role of these bodies as the operating agents of the JRSO. Since October 1949, Monroe Goldwater of the Joint Distribution Committee and Dr. Israel Goldstein of the Jewish Agency for Palestine have occupied the offices.

Toward the end of 1948, headquarters of the JRSO were established in the Bavarian city of Nuernberg which, ironically, had given its name to the racial laws which divested Jews of their rights in Germany, and to the post-war trials of Nazi war criminals. Jewish lawyers, who had been forced to flee from Germany, were recruited from all parts of the world to help search the records for evidence required to retrieve what had been illegally seized. On the basis of such evidence, each of the many thousands of claims had to be painstakingly negotiated with the current German possessor, or adjudicated by German administrative agencies and courts under the watchful eye of an American Appellate Tribunal. These proceedings, touching the private pocket-nerve of persons long in possession, encountered bitter opposition and hostility. The JRSO was forced to turn to bulk settlements with the State governments as the only feasible means of expediting the recoveries. Upon payment of an agreed sum the German State governments, which had been precluded from obtaining the claims by escheat, obtained them by assignment from the JRSO, and the State assumed responsibility for settling with the current German holder.

These were years of crucial decision for the JRSO. As the wartime alliance between East and West crumbled, United States policy toward Germany underwent drastic revision. Those who were formerly regarded as enemies were now eagerly sought as allies. This reversal brought with it a tendency to forget or minimize the past. German pressure groups demanded the relinquishment of American controls and the abandonment of the restitution policy. Constant vigilance became the Jewish watchword as the attempted assaults were successfully repelled.

In the United States Zone alone, property worth close to $250,000,000 was restored to former owners, now living in sixty different countries throughout the world. In addition, heirless assets worth over $25,000,000 were recovered. These proceeds were used to provide shelter for refugees crowding tent camps in Israel, to aid needy Jews still living in Germany, hard-core medical cases, the aged, the blind and the destitute.

In addition to the rescue of material treasures, the rescue of cultural treasures proved one of the most gratifying aspects of

JRSO work. The Nazis had destroyed the synagogues, libraries and museums of Europe, after looting them, but much of the loot had been transported to Germany. At war's end, the United States army collected these treasures for return to the rightful owners. Acting in collaboration with the Jewish Cultural Reconstruction, an organization of scholars, the JRSO received over a quarter of a million Jewish books which were distributed to *yeshivot* and other centers of Jewish learning throughout the world. Almost a thousand Torah scrolls, and more than 10,000 ritual objects, including Hanukkah lamps, wine goblets, pointers and amulets, were salvaged. A total of 700 works of Jewish art, which had been seized by the Gestapo, were sent to enrich the new museums of Israel. The temples had been destroyed, but these symbols of a great tradition would be seeds of the regeneration of Jewish life.

Besides achieving these satisfying results, the influence of the JRSO overflowed, as it were, into the British and French Zones of Germany. The JRSO served as the pioneer. In the words of Judge Fred J. Cohn, the Chief Justice of the Court of Restitution Appeals, it was "the mainspring of restitution." It was the model for the creation of similar, and related, Jewish successor organizations in the British and French zones, where the pattern was duplicated. In Berlin, the JRSO served as agent for all successor organizations, and everywhere, except in Soviet-dominated areas, Jewish property was returned. In retrospect, it may fairly be said that, of all the declared post-war objectives, restitution was least tarnished with time, and the return of identifiable property as well as the heirless assets was successfully completed.

As JRSO's program was developing, however, it became apparent that the return of identifiable property still provided no compensation to the vast majority of Nazi victims. It was natural that the sharp contrast between Germany's striking economic recovery, and the wretched plight of the thousands of impoverished Jewish refugees, who crowded the barren new settlements of Israel, should arouse a bitter sense of injustice. Those property-less masses who, for years, had suffered the torments of the Nazi concentration camps, the widows and orphans who had lost their providers, those who had been cast out of their professions or businesses, and those who had become permanently disabled remained without redress. A few German Laender (Provinces) in the American zone had enacted indemnification laws providing small payments to select categories of claimants for a number of personal losses, but these decrees were too narrow in scope, too limited in application and too arbitrary in their restrictions to be of help to more than a very small percentage of the victims. There was need for a general law offering personal indemnity to all individuals entitled to redress. Israel appealed to the occupying Powers; the plea was ignored by the Soviets and, though sympathetically received by the West, Israel was reminded that Germany was about to become again a sovereign State.

Before this happened, however, there were indications that the restored State would act favorably on a similar plea. On the eve of the Jewish New Year in 1951, the German Chancellor, Konrad Adenauer, in a solemn statement before the German parliament, publicly acknowledged that "unspeakable crimes were perpetrated in the name of the German people which impose upon them the obligation to make moral and material amends." He announced that "the Federal Republic is prepared, jointly with representatives of Jewry and the State of Israel, which has admitted so many homeless Jewish refugees, to bring about a solution of the material reparations problem in order to facilitate the way to a spiritual purging of unheard-of suffering." For the first time in history, the Jewish people were to see their representatives sitting at a conference table with the representatives of the successor to a government which had systematically sought to exterminate the Jews.

In order to promote the implementation of Adenauer's suggestion, twenty-three leading Jewish organizations established the historic "Conference on Jewish Material Claims Against Germany," on October 25, 1951, in New York City. (This organization will hereafter be referred to as the "Conference.") The chairman was Dr. Nahum Goldmann, head of the Jewish Agency for Palestine, who became the architect of the reparations movement. Jewish public opinion was sharply divided: many, their hearts filled with pain, and distrust of Germany seared into their memory, felt that meeting with the German government could bring only dishonor and disillusion; others, whose sense of pride was not stronger than their sense of justice, were persuaded that the needs and rights of the victims were decisive and that there was no morality in refusing to seek compensation in accordance with normal standards of law. The final decision, reached not without apprehension, was in favor of cautious negotiation. A presidium of five persons, who had faith and who were determined not to reject Germany's offer without trial, was elected to pilot the endeavors. The leaders selected were: Jacob Blaustein, president of the American Jewish Committee; Frank Goldman, president of B'nai B'rith; Israel Goldstein, chairman of the Western Hemisphere Executive of the World Jewish Congress; and Adolph Held, chairman of the Jewish Labor Committee.

On the first day of spring in 1952, in the ancient town of Wassenaar, a suburb of The Hague, the Conference delegation, headed by Moses A. Leavitt, executive vice-chairman of the American Joint Distribution Committee, presented its claims against Germany. It stood side by side with the State of Israel which made independent demands on behalf of its citizens and itself. Jewish extremists threatened and attempted to bomb the meetings which were shrouded in secrecy, and under heavy guard. The negotiations, which were marked by a cold dignity, were difficult and protracted. Disputes arose about the magnitude of the losses, the degree and methods of compensation, as well as Germany's willingness and capacity to pay. Although the presidium remained aloof from the daily sessions, it was in constant contact with all developments and gave directions to the deliberations.

After half a year of difficult negotiations, those who had believed were vindicated, as the final agreements were signed in Luxemburg on September 10, 1952. Israel was to receive close to seven hundred and fifteen million dollars worth of goods within the next ten to twelve years, as collective reimbursement for the funds it had expended in receiving and resettling Nazi victims. Protocol No. 1, concluded with the Claims Conference, contained the outline of new laws to be enacted by Germany, giving individual victims and their heirs the indemnification to which they were entitled for their personal sufferings and losses. Protocol No. 2 provided over one hundred and seven million dollars, to be used by the Conference primarily for the relief and rehabilitation of the most needy victims living outside of Israel.

It was envisaged that The Hague agreements of 1952 would be discharged within ten years. Thus far, the commitments to Israel have been promptly and faithfully met. Vital oil, chemicals, agricultural machinery, railroad equipment, telephone installations and ships from Germany have provided substantial aid in Israel's struggle for economic survival. By a twist of history and faith, Germany, which had witnessed Hitler's mad plan for the annihilation of the Jews, was now helping sustain the new Jewish state.

A uniform Federal indemnification law, providing compensation to large numbers of Nazi victims, was enacted in the fall of 1953. Well over a million claims, about half of them from Jews, were filed under Germany's new law, the administration of which soon bogged down in a maze of bureaucratic red tape and legalistic formalities. Despite the noble sentiments expressed by the German Chancellor and leading parliamentarians, many of the petty officials who administered the law evidenced no enthusiasm for a generous application of its terms. The need for revision, in line with the spirit of The Hague agreements, was apparent to all. The Claims Conference served as spokesman for the Jewish victims of persecution in pressing for improvements. In July 1956, the Federal Republic enacted a revised law designed to accelerate and increase the payments to the claimants.

It has been estimated that the indemnification laws will cost the Federal Republic between one and one-half and two billion dollars, and that they will benefit hundreds of thousands of the Jewish survivors of persecution. Of over 400,000 claims disposed of, only half have been decided favorably, yet over five hundred million dollars have already been paid. On the rolls of beneficiaries of social service agencies throughout the world and in the homes of many thousands of victims, the results of The Hague agreements and Germany's new policy of compensation are beginning to be felt.

Jewish losses were so enormous and the destruction of life so great, that the enactment of complex legislation and the adjudication of countless claims on the merits of provable facts provided only a limited remedy. The funds received by the Claims Conference were designed to help bridge the gap. By the end of 1955, the Conference had received about twenty million dollars as a consequence of The Hague agreements. Needless to say, the demands for these funds far exceeded the amount available.

Established Jewish social service and welfare agencies in all countries, where Nazi victims had taken refuge, became the instrumentalities for the distribution of Conference funds. Current needs were met by grants for cash relief; essential medical aid; care of the aged, the orphaned children, the youth; loan funds, resettlement aid, vocational training and communal rehabilitation. Special funds were provided for rabbis and former community leaders, whose readjustment in new communities was particularly difficult. Close to 50,000 Nazi victims with claims against Germany received legal aid through the United Restitution Organization, which was subsidized by the Conference to help claimants who could not afford private counsel.

One of the most difficult problems confronting the Conference was how to use these funds so that the effect on Jewish life would be of enduring value. The wise counsel of Israel Goldstein, a vice-president of the Claims Conference since its formation, led to the adoption, by the Conference, of the policy that it look beyond the needs of the moment and plan for the distant future. The reconstruction of Jewish life could not begin and end with the dole. A foundation would have to be laid upon which future generations could build.

In line with this policy, the cultural and educational programs of the Conference looked beyond the horizon. Jewish schools were enlarged, teachers and itinerant rabbis were employed, books were published, and *yeshivot* were subsidized in widespread areas where the existing communal facilities could not cope with the demands created by refugee families. Efforts were made to restore the corps of Jewish teachers and intellectuals by providing grants, scholarships and fellowships to students engaged in independent and creative Jewish work, in seminaries, colleges and universities. In an attempt to keep alive the well-springs of Jewish cultural inspiration, research and publications in fields of basic Jewish interest were sponsored. The Conference gave its encouragement and support also to plans for creating a permanent historical record of the Jewish tragedy and for commemorating its victims. The hope was cherished that by striking these sparks the Conference would kindle new flames of Jewish genius which would illuminate the dark shadows which had given them birth.

The Conference has been in existence for only a few years, yet there is hardly a Jewish organization anywhere in the world which has not heard its name or felt its influence. Just as no one can tell where ends the ripple caused by a pebble dropped in a pool, so it is impossible to estimate the limits of the effects of the work of the Conference. It would be premature to venture any judgment now, but indications are that, through Germany's restitution program, a new stimulus has been given to Jewish life.

In contrast with the relatively rapid progress of the negotiations of the Conference with the German authorities, was the slow progress of similar negotiations with the government of Austria. Gay pre-war Vienna had a Jewish population of over 150,000, constituting one of the most flourishing Jewish communities in Europe. When, in 1938, the brown-shirted troops of Nazi Germany invaded Austria, the "Anschluss" was welcomed by jubilant masses of the local population. No time was lost in subjecting the Jews to Nazi brutalities, plunder and murder. The Jews of Austria suffered the fate of their German brethren—mass flight or mass extermination. At war's end, less than 5,000 remained in Austria. The rest were dead or scattered over the face of the earth.

During The Hague negotiations, the Federal Republic of Germany declined to accept responsibility for the plunder of Jewish property in Austria. It was the Austrians who had reaped the benefit, they argued, and it was up to Austria to restore the ill-gotten gains. The Jewish organizations, paralleling the Claims Conference, formed the "Committee for Jewish Claims on Austria." A meeting was arranged between representatives of this committee and the heads of the Austrian state. This historic conference took place on June 17, 1953 in Vienna. The Austrian

Government was represented by Drs. Julius Raab, Chancellor; Adolf Schaerf, Vice-Chancellor; Reinhold Kamitz, Finance Minister; Karl Gruber, Foreign Minister. The joint executive board for Jewish Claims on Austria was represented by Dr. Nahum Goldmann, chairman of the joint executive board; Dr. Emil Maurer, president of the Jewish Community of Vienna and vice-chairman of the joint executive board; Dr. Israel Goldstein, president of the American Jewish Congress; Jacob Blaustein, president of the American Jewish Committee; Adolph Held, chairman of the Jewish Labor Committee; Barnett Janner, vice president of the Board of Deputies of British Jews; Eugene Weill, secretary general of the Alliance Israelite Universelle and Moses W. Beckelman, director general of the American Joint Distribution Committee, who headed up the negotiating team, along with Dr. Nehemiah Robinson, the World Jewish Congress' outstanding expert on restitution problems, who was not able to attend this conference.

The Committee for Jewish Claims on Austria sought legislation to remove existing discrimination against Nazi victims who no longer resided in Austria; measures to benefit the existing Jewish Community by restoring housing, synagogues and cemeteries; and the establishment of a special relief fund to compensate for the heirless property which had been confiscated and was then still in Austrian hands.

The attitude of the Austrian government was most discouraging. It was obvious that Austrian politicians were more interested in providing benefits to former Nazis who could vote, than to Nazi victims who could not. The negotiations were protracted, wearisome and vexatious, but the Committee remained adamant. When agreement was finally reached, late in 1955, it was a far cry from the original expectations and from the concessions obtained from Germany.

Austria agreed to make limited amounts of heirless Jewish assets available to the small local Jewish community, and to establish a fund of about twenty million dollars to aid needy Austrian Jews living abroad. By June 1956, applications to the fund were being received, but no payments had yet been made. Despite this limited success, it is anticipated that substantial numbers of aged and needy Nazi victims from Austria will benefit from the concessions wrung with great travail from the Austrian government.

The history of the Jews is not infrequently a history of persecution. The fearful pattern repeats itself, varying in location, intensity and time. The reaping of the whirlwind has brought in its wake vengeance, hatred and, at times, tribute. The restitution programs here outlined have, however, signalized new directions in man's eternal quest for civilized human conduct. Never before has there been so comprehensive an endeavor to provide individual compensation, varying with the specific circumstances of each particular case, for wrongs such as those heaped upon the Jews of Germany and Austria. The deterrent effort of such a program cannot now be estimated. The ideal of restoring to each, that of which he had been unjustly deprived, has by no means been achieved. Despite shortcomings, however, much has already been gained. There is moreover, a certain movement which is meaningful beyond the compensation paid, and the resuscitation of Jewish life. Long after the restitution funds have all been disbursed and their use has been all but forgotten, the precedent set will still remain. A rule of law has been introduced in an area where, in the past, the tenets of fundamental justice were conspicuously absent. In the words of Israel Goldstein: "It brought into being a new moral standard in international affairs affecting the Jewish people—namely, that no nation can despoil its Jewish population without being held accountable before the bar of justice. The crimes committed by the Nazis, however, were dealt with differently. The Jewish people, united in the face of supreme need and acting in cooperation with Israel, had the dignity to demand restitution and reparation. The amounts total only a meager fraction of the values which had been despoiled. Moreover, there could be no material compensation for the lives which have been destroyed. What has been accomplished marks an historic milestone in international morality."

THE REHABILITATION OF

JEWISH CHILDREN IN FRANCE

---

by Jacob Kaplan

THE SITUATION OF French Jewry in 1944, following the liberation of the country from the Nazis, was catastrophic. The number of Jews who had been deported exceeded 115,000, or one-third of the pre-war Jewish population. One-third of the rabbis had also been deported. Twenty synagogues had been destroyed; all the others had been pillaged and desecrated. The Jews who survived were widely scattered. They had been robbed, their homes and places of business had been confiscated and sold or, had been taken over by the officials of the invaders. Complete reconstruction, moral and material, was necessary.

Efforts in this direction were undertaken without delay. The communities took steps to reorganize. Religious services were resumed in those synagogues which were still in existence, and even in rented halls in places where the synagogues had been destroyed. This spiritual renaissance was facilitated by the fact that, even during the occupation, Jewish life had been maintained insofar as was possible during those terrible years. In some cities, Jewish religious observance continued almost to the day of Liberation. In spite of the risks they ran, the faithful attended divine services even if the synagogue had been the object of a savage attack with numerous victims, as was the case in Lyons, in December 1943. Prayer books had continued to be published, as well as a book of Jewish doctrine and a Hebrew language textbook. Religious courts had continued to function for a long

time. Isolated individuals who asked for Jewish religious instruction were given a correspondence course. Even chanting at
services was not discontinued in some places, notably Lyons, until
as late as April 1944.

In proceeding with the work of reconstruction, begun upon
Liberation, religious revival was not the only task undertaken; social and economic rehabilitation were also promoted. This was developed thanks to the cooperation of the Joint Distribution
Committee, for whose generous aid, both during the emergency
and since, the Jews of France will never be able fully to express
their gratitude.

One of the most grave and agonizing problems was that presented by the situations of many of the Jewish children. In order
to save them from deportation, thousands of them had been
placed in non-Jewish institutions or in private families. It was
of vital importance to withdraw these children from these places
of temporary asylum in order to return them to their parents,
when the latter had not been deported, or, in the case of those
children who had become orphans, to place them in a Jewish
home or institution. The task was the more difficult because a
large number of these boys and girls, even if not baptized, were
being reared as Catholics and Protestants.

Unfortunately, all of these children could not be returned. It was
not always possible to find those who had been placed direct
by their parents or who had been welcomed by neighbors at the
moment of the deportation of their parents, because of the lack
of information regarding the institutions or the individuals to
whose care the children had been confided. Even a government
circular was issued enjoining all who had Jewish children under
their care to declare the fact officially, but there is no way of
knowing to what extent this order was effective. The sad and
shocking case of Robert and Gerald Finaly shows how, in some
quarters, there was no hesitation to baptize such children and to
frustrate all efforts to find these children whose parents had been
deported.

The religious education of these children was our most urgent
task. If it could be hoped that those in Jewish institutions would

receive religious education—a thing that was not always the case because some Jewish institutions refuse, for ideological reasons, to instruct their children in the faith of their fathers—there was the problem of making religious education available to those who were living with their families. In the communities, courses had just been reestablished and were functioning, but lamely. Furthermore, in order to lead these young people back to the Jewish religion, it was not sufficient, as it was before 1939, to have one or two sessions a week, on Thursdays and Sundays; it was necessary to start daily instruction. To achieve this objective, it was necessary to have reception centers for the children after they leave school. In these centers, they would be helped with their school lessons, they would be given lunch, so necessary because of the existing food rationing, and, at the same time, they would follow a course of instruction in Judaism. But, for the community to perform this task, funds were needed and these were, unfortunately, lacking.

Such was the situation when Rabbi Israel Goldstein was in Paris in July 1945. I had come to know Rabbi Goldstein in New York, when I went there, after the Liberation, on a mission on behalf of French Jewry, to which I had been delegated by Isaie Schwartz, the Grand Rabbi of France. I was accompanied by Messrs. Léon Meiss, then president of the Consistoire Central; Baron Guy de Rothschild, now president of the Consistoire; Joseph Fischer, at that time director general of the Keren Kayemeth Le Yisrael and now member of the Consistoire; and M. Joseph Ariel, now minister of Israel to Belgium.

I was very happy to see Dr. Goldstein again in Paris. I was fully aware of the authority he enjoyed not only in his own community but also in American Jewry in general. Nevertheless, the idea of soliciting his aid in behalf of the education of the young did not enter my mind. Madame Kaplan, my wife, deserves the credit. Once, while she and I were discussing, as we had done so often before, ways and means of opening the centers, which appeared to us more necessary than ever, Madame Kaplan was inspired by the thought that, if he were made acquainted with the situation, Dr. Goldstein would surely come to our aid. With this hope in our hearts, we went to see him. I can still recall the close attention with which he listened to my wife's presentation of the urgent need and her moving plea for his assistance. But little time was necessary for Dr. Goldstein to grasp the situation. On the spot, he promised to secure for us the financial assistance we needed to set the center plan in motion. The letter which he addressed to me after this meeting, included the following significant statement:

"During the two weeks that I have been here I have studied the various phases of Jewish life here. It is my opinion that the problem of the Jewish youth here is very urgent. The youth is our future. I am very eager to see a special undertaking here to attract the youth to the Synagogue. I have decided to make available a fund for this special purpose, to be administered by you with such a committee as you may select. You will permit me, I trust, to consider you my representative in carrying out this important activity. The Consistoire, no doubt, will be pleased to see this work undertaken by you. Upon my return to the U.S.A., I shall endeavor to interest some of my colleagues in this activity, though I have no way of knowing now whether they will respond. In any event, the sum now being made available will enable you to make a start in Paris, where I would like to see this sum expended."

This generous donation, coming from the Louis Altschul Foundation and the Sisterhood of Congregation B'nai Jeshurun, was of great importance at this time, because it enabled us to get to work.

By the beginning of October 1945, a center was opened in the Montmartre section of Paris, in a hall of the synagogue of the Rue Ste. Isaure. In a short time, it had seventy pupils, the maximum number the available space could hold. The greater part of the children knew nothing or almost nothing about the Jewish religion. However, the progress they made was such as to make it possible for them to produce a small play in Hebrew the following Purim, March 17, 1946.

A large number of these children had carefully kept, as precious souvenirs, the Christian religious objects which had been given to them by the institutions or families which had sheltered them during the Nazi occupation. It was not long before the children decided to give them up. One little girl, who had hidden her medal to create the impression that she no longer had it, went one day, quite spontaneously, to the headmistress of the center where she had received it, and turned the object over to her, saying, "I have kept it until now because I promised not to part from it. But now I return it because I feel profoundly that I am a Jewess."

In January 1946, two additional centers were opened in the same district, accommodating sixty pupils. Several of them had been living under Catholic auspices of the quarter, to which they had been attracted by the important material advantages offered to them. Great difficulties had to be surmounted before these children could be brought back into the Jewish fold. The nuns in charge of the Catholic institution tried to induce the children to remain by offering to give them a course in Hebrew! As can well be imagined, we had to make incessant efforts to bring our own children back to us. These results, limited but considerable, could not have been obtained without the valuable cooperation of Dr. Goldstein. He made it possible, as he himself said, to set our important project in motion.

Later, I learned that, during his brief stay in Paris, Dr. Goldstein had extended aid also to Maimonides College, a secondary school for Jewish studies, which had, of course, stopped functioning during the Nazi occupation. Its head, Marcus Cohen, who had just returned from Germany, where he had been a prisoner of war, was working hard to resuscitate the institution. The encouragement of Dr. Goldstein and the financial aid extended by him, greatly helped Dr. Cohen to reopen the school. It now has about 1600 pupils and is doing good work under Theodore Dreyfus, who became headmaster when Dr. Cohen was appointed to take charge of a school in Israel maintained by the Alliance Israelite Universelle.

Since then, thanks to God, French Jewry has succeeded in making progress in all communal fields, especially that of religious education. The community has reestablished its courses in religion and has expanded them, it has established schools, both elementary and secondary, and *yeshivot*. It has a young people's aid society and a congregation conducted by youth.

These advances do not mean that everything is running smoothly in this area. A great number of tasks still remain to be done, but it is encouraging to be able to state that the trend is favorable and that progress is continuing. We are sure that Rabbi Goldstein rejoices with us in this fortunate development. To him, who enabled us to get started in our efforts on behalf of our Jewish youth, and to the Louis Altschul Foundation and the Sisterhood of Congregation B'nai Jeshurun, the Jewish community of France tenders the expression of its most grateful appreciation.

THE COURT

WITHOUT A GAVEL

by Louis Richman

TWO FACTORS were chiefly responsible for the establishment of
what has aptly been called "the court without a gavel": the
urgent need on the East side of New York for an agency for the
settlement of such disputes as could not well be submitted to
civil courts, and the traditional Jewish passion for justice.

Jewish courts have played an important part in the lives of
Jews in many countries throughout the centuries. The reputation
of these courts for their sense of justice was so good that not only
did Jews submit complaints to them but also Christians sometimes brought their claims before such courts or before individual rabbis.

Wherever Jewish communities existed, Jewish courts continued, in one form or another, and were often endowed with public
legal authority. One of the most famous examples of a court so
endowed is the Beth-Din of England, of which the late Rev. Dr.
Moses Hyamson was the Chief Dayan until his removal to New
York. Incidentally, he became an officer and an active member of
the Jewish Conciliation Board.

This Board was established in 1919 by a group of rabbis,
judges, lawyers and businessmen of the city of New York. The
original name of the organization, the Jewish Court of Arbitration, was later changed to the present title. The writer of this
chapter was privileged to be one of the founders of this important agency and had served as its executive secretary on a volunteer basis throughout its long career.

The founders of this organization were moved not only by a desire to help the Jews of the community, but also to improve and liberalize the administration of justice in general, and serve as an example for other courts and arbitration societies. Furthermore, protests against the law's delays were just as loud and vigorous then as they are now. By the informal manner of procedure adopted by the Jewish Conciliation Board of America, there was set in motion a simplified method of administering justice quickly, efficiently and inexpensively. To file a "case" with the Jewish Conciliation Board, all that is required, is that the plaintiff come to the office of the Board and state the nature of the complaint. Within a few days, the parties involved are notified to come for a hearing.

While parties are not compelled to appear before the Board, thousands have voluntarily come because of their complete confidence in the integrity of the judges and the high-mindedness of the officers and directors of the Board. This confidence is due, in great measure, to the fact that the Board does not represent any one point of view; it has always sought to represent every segment of Jewish society. Thus, the Board is composed of representatives of Orthodox, Conservative and Reform Judaism. The present composition of officers attests to the representative character of the Board. The president, Dr. Israel Goldstein, is a Conservative rabbi; vice president Dr. Leo Jung is an Orthodox rabbi; while Dr. Julius Mark represents the Reform rabbinate; Judge Jacob Panken, one of the founders of the Board, is a liberal in politics as well as in his religious outlook.

When the parties concerned appear for their hearings, they are first asked to sign an agreement to abide by the decision of the panel of "judges"—a rabbi, a jurist and a business man or woman. The matter is then heard by the panel. The parties may speak either in Yiddish or in English. There being no strict rules of evidence, no involved legal technicalities requiring lengthy argument, the panel is able to discover the truth and justice of the case in a very short time. At the conclusion of the hearing, the judges confer and a decision is rendered. Occasionally in cases involving the disposition of money or property, one of the parties has refused to abide by the decision of the Board. In all such instances in the past, such decisions have been upheld when appealed to the New York State Supreme Court. It is noteworthy that, during the years of the writer's association with the Board, there have been only about a dozen instances in which appeals were taken to a public court. In all other cases, the parties to the disputes cheerfully accepted the decisions of the Board. This remarkable showing is due to the fact that it has always been, and continues to be, the primary object of the presiding judges not merely to make a decision as to who is right and who is wrong, but also to try to find a common ground between the conflicting parties, so that they leave the hearing room not as winners or losers in a legal battle, but as persons who are enlightened, see each other's viewpoints, and are made happier for having had the opportunity of unburdening themselves of their problems before an understanding and sympathetic panel of judges. In other words, the object of the Board is not merely to adjudicate controversies, but, as its name implies, to conciliate the parties involved.

In this informal manner, over 7,500 cases have been disposed of until now by this organization—all without cost to the litigants; no charge whatever is made from the time the claim is filed to the actual hearing at a session or the subsequent follow-up by the social service worker. Thus, the litigants are spared expense besides the strain and anxiety of litigation. However, the Board is not a legal aid society in the usual sense, because it does not deal with claims of an ordinary legal character which can be handled by courts, but only with such cases as arise from problems of internal relations between individuals or between individuals and institutions.

A review and evaluation of the work of the "Jewish Court," as it is commonly called, would be inadequate without some mention of the types of situations that have come to it through the years. The mere mention of the variety of the cases, without going into details, will suffice to show the unique need for this organization. A man claimed that he was unlawfully expelled from his *"landsmanschaft Verein"* after an extended membership of over thirty years; another claimed that he was denied sick benefits to which he was entitled under the by-laws of a mutual benefit organization; another demanded that his society give a financial accounting; and another, that he was denied the privilege of the "floor" by the arbitrary ruling of the president. Other cases involved claims regarding rights of burial; excessive charges for funerals; disputes between husbands and wives; complaints of aged parents that their children failed to support them; misunderstandings between children and their "old-fashioned" parents; difficulties confronting persons in securing admission to homes for the aged; internal disputes arising in congregations; alleged breaches of contract between teachers, rabbis, cantors and other synagogue functionaries, and their congregations; manner of distribution of holy scrolls and other ritual articles upon the dissolution of a congregation; demand by a childless widow that her brother-in-law perform the ancient rite of *"Halitza"* so that she may remarry; demand by a woman that her former husband, from whom she had been divorced, in a civil court, give her a *"Get."* Other cases arise from claims of marriage brokers for compensation for services performed.

In many of these cases, legal redress would have been difficult, if not impossible, and in some instances, such redress, if possible, would be an unbearable financial burden to the persons involved. In many others, the cases would have seemed bizarre, even incomprehensible to a non-Jewish judge. Still others could have been damaging to the good name of the Jewish people. That judges of the courts of the City of New York recognize that the Board is better equipped to handle such matters is evidenced by the fact that they refer them to the Board.

When Dr. Israel Goldstein became president of the Board in 1929, he enlisted the sponsorship of recognized community leadership and he widened the scope of its functions. With characteristic farsightedness, Dr. Goldstein established a social service department, headed first by volunteers from the Sisterhood of the Congregation of B'nai Jeshurun, and later by a full-time professional social service worker. The department helps the parties concerned to adjust themselves to the decisions of the Board, and, if they require aid of other kinds, assists them in approaching appropriate agencies.

The Board has pioneered in another important field. With the improvement of economic conditions with the advent of social security laws, old-age assistance, and labor union welfare benefits, elderly persons are not as dependent upon their children as formerly. Old age holds less terror for them; they approach it with greater confidence and dignity. However, a new type of problem has arisen in the life of the Jews as well as in the community in general. These troubles are caused, it would seem, by the stress and tension of world conditions, and the uncertainties which exist on the national and international scene. In other words, as has so often been said, economic insecurity has been replaced by emotional insecurity.

Long before "pastoral psychology" and the attempt to enlist psychiatry in the service of religion—and vice versa—became the vogue, the Jewish Conciliation Board began quietly providing all-around treatment of family problems, drawing upon the talents of men and women trained in religion, psychology and the law. Dr. Goldstein's advanced ideas in this realm are indeed a credit to his interest in "little people," despite his absorbing occupation with, and interest in, the major Jewish problems here and abroad.

The Jewish Conciliation Board of America takes pride in the fact that it has kept abreast and, in some respects, has been in the vanguard, of the improvement of judicial processes. Fortunately, our organization has remained small; it has not taken on the air of bigness which characterizes the modern trend in many fields. We have tried to give to those who come to us with their problems, a sense of belonging and a sense of relationship which inspire them with comfort and encouragement.

This brief history and evaluation of the work of the Board can be fittingly concluded with the citation of an extract from an address by Supreme Court Justice William O. Douglas on the occasion of the celebration, in January 1954, of the twenty-fifth anniversary of Dr. Goldstein's leadership of the Board. Judge Douglas said:

"The thing that has interested me particularly about the Board is that it has been more interested in justice than in law. Law and justice are not necessarily the same, as you know. Throughout the centuries, law has been trying to catch up with justice. It has not always succeeded. That is one of the great, eternal struggles of man."

"The work of the Conciliation Board, seeking to find what is the truth, trying to apply justice, is a great experiment in a busy community where there are many problems, local and international. It is important to take time out to make adjustments in the little problems of people. That in the end marks the differences between a society which administers to the needs of people, and a society where sores and troubles fester, where the needs and aspirations of the ordinary man are neglected."

Part Four

IN THE
GENERAL COMMUNITY

HUMAN RELATIONS —

THEN AND NOW

---

by Everett R. Clinchy

AS RECENTLY AS the nineteen-twenties, one talked piously in terms of hyphenated Americans. Minority groups were slandered as "mackerel snappers," "kikes," "dagoes," "micks," "Protestant pups" or in sundry other unsavory names that brought fighting results. America was portrayed as a melting pot where its peoples of varied nationality, racial, or religious backgrounds were supposed to become an amalgam, an American type.

The great populations of the East went unnoticed in our schools. The ancient Asian religious cultures that trace back to pre-Bible centuries—civilizations rich in art, industry, and wisdom—were as neglected as though Asian peoples lived on Mars. Africa was the "Dark Continent," actually because Americans were in the dark about it. A stereotyped Africa, as the source of slaves, blocked out any real appreciation of existing African cultures. The West made little effort to understand the morals, values and spiritual meanings of these cultures.

Latin America was generalized as a remote land of revolutionaries. The world at large was divided between the Great Powers and the "backward" peoples who lived in Colonies. The customary prejudice of whites was that, psychologically and biologically, the colored peoples were incapable of becoming quite as human as the Caucasoids. American immigration laws leaned towards the admission of blond, blue-eyed northern and western Europeans. Textbooks were replete with sterotypes. Our big cities were divided into nationality ghettos. Many churches and synagogues were organized on a nationality basis. Our social clubs were highly restricted, as were the choice residential areas and the more desirable vacation resorts.

Catholics, Protestants and Jews lived in tight compartments, each group anxious to prove its Americanism but fearful of losing its identity. American cultural isolationism was a counterpart of its national isolationism.

Yet, the way was prepared for a change in the climate of opinion in the United States. Three developments helped to dramatize the need for a change.

The first was the rise and decline of the Ku Klux Klan. During the nineteen-twenties, it was revealed as a corrupt and un-American organization. The fruit of its work was seen as bad for business, poisonous for politics, and ruinous to religion.

Second, the 1928 political campaign, in which one of the candidates for President, Alfred E. Smith, was the victim of slanders and libels because he was a Catholic, showed the dangerous folly of indulgence of religious animosities in American politics.

Third, internationally, in the early nineteen-thirties, Nazi anti-Semitism showed how wicked and disastrous religious hatred could become as a national policy. Christians began to realize that anti-Semitism is profoundly more devastating and consuming to Christians than to Jews—terrible though the liquidation of six million Jews was.

That the way was prepared for a movement in America which could bring Catholics, Protestants and Jews together to reduce and, where possible, to eliminate racial and religious prejudices, was evidenced by the establishment of several organizations in the early years of the nineteen-twenties. This was a time when religious leaders of all faiths were badly disturbed by the prevalence of flagrant manifestations of anti-Jewish, anti-Negro, anti-Catholic and anti-foreign-born agitation. Besides the Ku Klux Klan, there were other signs of the post-war disillusionment from which a large section of the American people was suffering, and the resulting search for a scapegoat.

In December 1920, the American Committee for the Rights

of Religious Minorities, composed largely of Protestant church leaders, issued an appeal to the American people "to condemn every effort to arouse divisive passions against any of our fellow-countrymen."

Other exponents of interfaith good will during this restless period were the Church Peace Union, the Permanent Commission on Better Understanding Between Christians and Jews in America, and the Committee on Goodwill Between Jews and Christians. The last was instituted by the Federal (now National) Council of the Churches of Christ in America and functioned for four years, from 1924 to 1928.

Although compelled to operate on a very small budget, the work of this Committee, nevertheless, demonstrated the need, and the important possibilties for goodwill of an agency of this kind, given a wider base of membership and generous financial support. The realization of this need by Christian and Jewish leaders led, in 1928, to the establishment of the National Conference of Christians and Jews.

This was an historic step forward in human relations. From 1928, no group had to "go it alone" in its struggle against prejudice. Rabbis, priests and ministers shaped a pattern of cooperation through appearances together on public platforms as trio teams. Today the cooperation of rabbis, priests and ministers is so widespread that every community expects, as a matter of course, that all clergy will cooperate for social and civic ends. This pattern quickly spread to lay cooperation. Catholics, Protestants and Jews working together, retained their unique revelations, but discovered the inherent worth of each other as children of God. As American citizens, Catholics, Protestants and Jews began to live harmoniously to produce a better America.

Outstanding among the founders of the NCCJ and among the members of its original board of directors were: Alfred Williams Anthony, Charles S. Macfarland, Daniel J. Fleming of Union Seminary, Samuel McCrea Cavert, and some of the Federal Council's Committee appointed by S. Parkes Cadman; Louis Wolsey and Abba Hillel Silver of the Central Conference of American Rabbis; Alfred M. Cohen and Boris Bogin of B'nai B'rith; Roger Williams Straus and Arthur Hays Sulzberger of the

Union of American Hebrew Congregations; Cyrus Adler and Israel Goldstein of the Conservative Jewish group; and Herbert Goldstein and David de Sola Pool of the Orthodox congregations. The Catholic representatives included Judge Victor Dowling, Monsignor Michael J. Lavelle, Vicar General of the Archdiocese of New York; Michael Williams of *Commonweal;* and Bernard Rothwell of the Calvert Associates, Boston.

The writer was invited to initiate the program that emerged from that committee. It was then that NCCJ asked social scientists, "How does social change come about?" The answers indicated that people take on the tastes, customs, and traditions of their own basic institutions. People believe in the moral values that their family and their religious agencies inculcate. They observe the taboos, manners, and fashions that their clubs, schools and occupations "fix" or "set." To immunize against anti-Semitism or anti-Christianism, the social scientists advised that it is necessary to persuade the peoples' organizations to bring about the change. To build brotherhood, start with the child.

Drew University, where the late Arlo Brown and James V. Thompson taught, took an interest in our inquiry, "What do religious educators teach the child?" Morris Waldman and Harry Schneiderman, both at that time associated with the American Jewish Committee, read an article we published in the *Christian Century.* It chronicled the repeated emphasis Sunday Schools then placed in their teachings on the Jews as the enemy of the early Church. It disclosed that frequently the Sunday Schools were telling the crucifixion as an example of the evil design of the Jews rather than as the great redemptive story of God's love for Man that it is. As an aftermath of the article's publication, Harry Schneiderman and Morris Waldman persuaded the American Jewish Committee to secure, from the New York Foundation, the funds needed by the NCCJ to set up a three-way study of Protestant, Catholic and Jewish religious textbooks that to this day is bearing good fruit.

The problem of prejudice in public-school textbooks was next attacked. In cooperation with the American Council on Education, NCCJ made a five-year study to guide authors and publishers of teaching materials to the dangers of stereotyping, of generalizations, and statements prejudicial to groups which differed in race, religion or culture. The opportunities for positive teaching of understanding all cultures were accented.

The elimination of prejudicial material in textbooks cleared the way for the injection of creative materials on better human relations. NCCJ worked for five years with a sampling of teacher colleges and school systems. An outgrowth of these studies was a series of publications which affected the American school curriculum, from coast to coast, through an emphasis upon better human relations in the entire curriculum. Thus, *Reading Ladders in Human Relations* stressed the way in which better understanding could be taught through materials in literature. Similar studies showed how better human relations could be taught in the social studies, history and science. The study of the contributions of all groups to world civilization became a focal stress in American education. After World War I, Columbia University pioneered in a course called "The Introduction to Western Civilization," under the guidance of Professor Carlton J. H. Hayes, first Catholic co-chairman of NCCJ. This course was broadened to include Eastern and African civilization, so that the Oneness of the Family of Man might be grasped. Rapidly thereafter, the course was introduced in college curricula throughout the United States. A similar emphasis found its way into elementary and secondary schools of the nation. The result was a new generation trained to think of all men as brothers. "How does it look from where you stand?" was a question we encouraged all to ask.

The enlightened point of view in intergroup relations also entered into private and parochial school curricula. Monsignor George Johnson at Catholic University invited Catholics, Protestants and Jews to help shape a curriculum in the social studies which would enlist the moral and spiritual resources for brotherhood. The result was the Faith and Freedom series now used in most Catholic parochial schools in the United States. The philosophy of human liberties which are derived from God-given rights is an integral part of the series. Social and civic cooperation of Catholics with Protestants and Jews is the keynote of the Civic Clubs which are an outgrowth of the Faith and Freedom series.

The curriculum of the schools could be changed but teachers had to be trained in the techniques of teaching, and the content of better human relations. This was done in major cities first, through NCCJ's Normal School project. At NCCJ's Williamstown Institute of Human Relations, held at Williams College, Massachusetts in 1935, 1937, 1939 and 1941, the idea for a Springfield Schools Plan emerged. School systems from Massachusetts to California then experimented in their own "plans" to teach human relations. The workshop in human relations for teachers became a familiar part of university summer session life. Thousands of teachers, policemen, clergy, and community leaders were trained to do specific jobs in human relations. These leaders in turn helped to train other thousands of students and other teachers in the field.

But training of teachers was only part of the job. Sister Mary de Lourdes of St. Joseph's college wrote that "Every bigot was once a child." *Rearing Children of Goodwill Institutes* brought parents and teachers together to eliminate prejudice in home and school. Direct work with high school and college youth leaders began to produce results in a second generation trained in better intergroup relations. The Parent-Teacher Association was mustered by NCCJ to make one of its goals, "Justice, amity, understanding and cooperation" among Protestants, Catholics and Jews in America.

Here was another historic development. NCCJ and cooperating agencies now began a systematic approach to the five categories of American institutions. Work was done directly in these channels which determine social change:

1. School, college and the home;
2. Churches, synagogues and other agencies of religion;
3. Youth and adult community agencies;
4. Labor unions, industry, business and agriculture;
5. Press, radio-TV, films, theatre and fine arts.

This new approach to the social institutions upon which all human relations advocates relied, was finally formalized in a permanent NCCJ structure which organized five Commissions to conduct programs in the five corresponding areas of social activity.

In the nineteen-thirties, the idea of Brotherhood Week was born. As every religion has its special days to remind people of special values, and as nations celebrate certain dates to mark the memory of national events, so Brotherhood Week was instituted to focus attention of Americans on the need to keep in mind justice in human relations three hundred and sixty-five days a year. It has today become a national institution. In this connection, it is appropriate to mention that Congregation B'nai Jeshurun of New York City, of which Dr. Israel Goldstein is the rabbi, has been outstanding in its observance of Brotherhood Week. In 1944, this congregation established an Annual Brotherhood Award, whose recipients have included Americans who were considered deserving of distinction for their efforts to promote better group relations.

The implementation of truth and justice requires many forms. In 1933, NCCJ organized the Religious News Service to gather and distribute news, features and photos relating to the Protestant, Catholic and Jewish religious groups. Over the years, this agency has acquired world-wide recognition. By promoting better understanding among the three religious groups, it is the journalistic bridge between them.

The scientific study of human relations led to the establishment of Centers for Human Relations at leading universities such as Miami, Boston, Pennsylvania and St. Louis. Today, better human relations training is recognized not only in academic circles but in business and professional training as well. Labor and management have improved relations because they have come to talk to each other as people talk to people. As human relations work takes on the nature of scientific study, it uses knowledge to foster the moral and spiritual resources for brotherhood.

Definitely, the climate of opinion has changed. There are those who become impatient with the educational approach. They wish rapid social change by legislation, even through coercion if necessary. The history of man teaches us, however, that while changes may come about in this way, actually the lasting results are obtained only when men are convinced in their minds and hearts that understanding and love of their brothers are more compelling than hatred and prejudice.

We live today in a world torn by two conflicting philosophies, one based on mutual assistance and love, the other on conflict and hate. Two-thirds of the world's population is undecided as to which way to turn. How we in America settle our own problems of intergroup relations will be a determining factor as to how the peoples of Africa and Asia will decide. We need to give them the encouragement and support which a universally-shared sense of a single Family of Man would make possible. The power of love of God and of fellow-man, which has manifested itself in the United States through a changed climate of opinion, can bring peace to the world.

As this book is published in honor of Dr. Israel Goldstein, the writer believes that it is "only fitting and proper" to mention, in addition to those already cited, a few of the many services rendered by Dr. Goldstein in the cause of the improvement of better intergroup relations. Dr. Goldstein delivered the opening prayer of the founding dinner of the NCCJ; he served, for several years, as the Jewish co-chairman of the Tripartite Commission of Religious Organizations; as chairman of the Synagogue Council, Social Justice Committee and, later, as president of the Synagogue Council, Dr. Goldstein had many occasions for contact and collaboration with the NCCJ.

In his capacity as Jewish co-chairman of the Tripartite Commission of Religious Organizations, Dr. Goldstein was a member of many trio teams, each consisting of a Catholic priest, a Protestant minister and a rabbi, which visited the Army and Navy installations during World War II and carried to the men and women in the armed forces the message of intergroup good will, explaining to them the moral and spiritual significance of the war.

Dr. Goldstein also addressed many meetings in England, and on the Continent, in the formative years of WORLD BROTHERHOOD, an organization that grew out of NCCJ after World War II. The last is a kind of united "mission" in which Christians and Jews may share as partners. To bring about "justice, amity, understanding and co-operation" among all men of good will—Hindu, Buddhist, Moslem, Jew, Christian and all others—is a task that will cement friendship among Christians and Jews in the United States as no lesser goal can.

NATIONAL ASSOCIATION

FOR THE ADVANCEMENT OF

COLORED PEOPLE

by *Channing H. Tobias*

NEVER IN THE HISTORY of the United States of America, has the need for mutual understanding and cooperation among the various elements of the American populace, been more urgent than it is now in these middle years of the twentieth century. The need is not new, for it has been a continuing challenge throughout our national history. What is new is the growing realization that resolution of the internal conflicts stemming from racial differences cannot be safely postponed.

Irrational group discrimination not only penalizes its immediate victims, but also exacts of the total society an alarming toll. Psychologically, it depresses the national morale. Economically, it restricts the national income. Politically, it impairs governmental action at home and engenders distrust abroad. Militarily, it endangers the national defense. An awakening awareness of the debilitating impact of such discrimination has spurred new efforts to assure to all Americans the constitutional rights inherent in American citizenship.

Taking the leadership in efforts to attain this objective, has been the National Association for the Advancement of Colored People which for forty-seven years has carried on an unrelenting struggle to rid our country of all forms of racial discrimination and segregation. The NAACP, a multi-racial and interfaith organization, with 1300 local units in 43 states, seeks its goal of equality for all Americans through constitutional means alone. Through its legal department, it turns to the courts of the land to secure justice and affirmation of constitutional principles. On the legislative front, it works for the enactment of civil rights measures to uphold the constitutional guarantees of freedom and equality. Its educational program seeks the development of enlightened public opinion in support of American democratic ideals.

President Truman, addressing the 1947 national NAACP in Washington, recognized the urgent need for prompt action on the civil rights front when he warned that, "we can no longer afford the luxury of a leisurely attack upon prejudice and discrimination . . . . We cannot, any longer, await the growth of a will to action in the slowest state or the most backward community. Our national government must show the way."

This presidential admonition anticipated the comprehensive report of the Committee on Civil Rights, which Mr. Truman had appointed in 1946, to study the status of civil rights and to make "recommendations with respect to the adoption or establishment by legislation or otherwise of more adequate and effective means and procedures for the protection of the civil rights of the people of the United States."

Unlike the older countries of western Europe, America is a composite of various minorities—racial, national and religious— all with an equal claim to the rights and privileges of citizenship, and all with an equal obligation to assume the common responsibilities and duties of citizenship. Although the American is popularly conceived of as an Anglo-Saxon Protestant, this is a distorted picture, for the present-day citizens of the United States derive from diverse racial origins, from various cultural backgrounds, and profess differing religious faiths. Americanism is the exclusive domain of no single group of whatever race, color, creed or national origin. It is the common heritage of all who have contributed to the development of our nationhood and who adhere to its equalitarian principles.

From the beginning, the nation has been tormented by a deep-rooted moral and political schizophrenia. It has not yet been able to match in day-to-day practice the high idealism of its profession. The author of the immortal declaration "that all men are created equal" and "are endowed by their Creator with certain inalienable rights," was himself a slaveholder, albeit one who was gravely conscious of the anomaly of his dual role as the young nation's foremost spokesman for democracy and as an exploiter of slave labor.

This conflict between practice and profession has continuously beset the nation. No generation of Americans has been able to escape it, although there have been periods during which strenuous efforts were made to stifle the discord by denying the essential humanity of the Negro or by ignoring his very existence. These devices were doomed to failure, for to deny the Negro's humanity was to reject the Hebraic-Christian ethic of universal brotherhood, and to close one's eyes to his presence was to stumble around in foolhardy blindness.

All this was vain, wishful thinking. Like Banquo's ghost, the issue stubbornly refused to vanish, no matter what the incantation. It persistently clamored for attention. It permitted no closing of the eyes or of the mind. Generation after generation, it insisted upon recognition, re-examination and re-evaluation. It harassed and mocked the American people. It granted to the American conscience no enduring peace.

Plainly, the issue is not one merely of Negro rights. Its resolution involves far more than the liberation of the Negro from the shameful shackles of racial discrimination and segregation. It involves also the release of the human spirit, the fulfillment of the American dream, and the vindication of our nation's role as leader of the free world. All these remain in peril as long as basic human rights are denied to any segment of the American people.

Long ago, it became evident that the so-called Negro problem could no longer be considered a sectional issue, the primary, if not exclusive, concern of the South. Today, southerners who formerly asserted a regional proprietorship, point an accusing finger at the rest of the nation and loudly proclaim that the race issue is now a national problem. And beyond our borders, the Europeans as well as the colored peoples of the world have manifested a continuing and critical interest in the persistence of racial discrimination within the United States. At a time when America is engaged in a global contest with a powerful and resourceful foe, race prejudice has become, in the words of President Truman, a "luxury we can no longer afford."

Despite the resurgence of violence and bigotry in the South, as a result of organized resistance to the United States Supreme Court order banning racial segregation in public education, there is mounting evidence that more and more Americans are coming to realize not only the immorality of segregation, but also its economic wastefulness and its impact upon the country's prestige abroad, as well as upon the national security.

This wholesome development is a far cry from the attitudes prevailing in 1909, when the NAACP was conceived. At that time, the new organization stood almost alone in its recognition of the sinister character of compulsory racial segregation and in the demand for its elimination. Although segregation by law was then relatively new, having been imposed by southern legislatures during the latter years of the nineteenth century, it was little challenged except by the heirs to the Abolitionist tradition who organized the NAACP as an instrument to regain the Negro's purloined civil rights. At that time, to espouse full and equal rights for the Negro was to flout the new convention and to defy destiny. The Supreme Court had, in 1896, embraced the shallow doctrine of "separate but equal" and had given legal sanction to compulsory segregation. Upon this judicial sophistry, the whole superstructure of Jim Crow was erected.

This specious doctrine, based upon the false concept of Negro inferiority, remained the law of the land until the Supreme Court ruled, on May 17, 1954, that "in the field of public education the doctrine of 'separate but equal' has no place. Separate educational facilities are inherently unequal." The Court's decision was the culmination of years of NAACP efforts to secure a definitive ruling that segregation *per se* is discrimination and, accordingly, unconstitutional. Until the decision in the public school segregation cases, the Court had shunned every opportunity to hand down such a declaration of public policy.

Even before the Court had ruled, enlightened elements

throughout the nation had come to recognize the unassailable validity of the NAACP contention that equality of human rights is impossible of attainment within the framework of segregation. Religious groups of various faiths, organized labor, youth groups, professional and civic associations, minority group organizations and spokesmen for the Federal government had joined the NAACP in efforts to eradicate the double standard of citizenship. Statesmen, scholars, writers, spiritual and secular leaders had affirmed the need to deal forthrightly with the challenge of the nation's paramount moral and political issue.

From the beginning, the NAACP enjoyed the active support of some of the most eminent leaders of American Jewry. Dr. Henry Moskowitz joined Mary White Ovington and William English Walling in the original planning for the organization. Among the fifty-three signers of the call for a national conference on the Negro which led to the organization of the NAACP were, in addition to Dr. Moskowitz, Rabbi Stephen S. Wise, founder and long-time leader of the American Jewish Congress, and Rabbi Emil G. Hirsch of Chicago.

Many Jewish leaders have served as officers and members of the Association's Board of Directors. Two of the three presidents of the Association were Jews—the late J. E. Spingarn, and his brother, Arthur B. Spingarn, the incumbent. Senator Herbert H. Lehman has long been a member of the NAACP Board and an active supporter of its program. Others of his faith have been actively identified in the work of the Association. There has been a close working relationship between the NAACP and the American Jewish Congress under the leadership of Dr. Stephen S. Wise and subsequently under the leadership of Dr. Israel Goldstein.

The legal work of the Association has been greatly enhanced by the generous and notable contributions of such Jewish jurists as the late Louis Marshall and others now serving on the Association's National Legal Committee. Among these lawyers are Benjamin Kaplan, Cambridge, Massachusetts; Arthur J. Mandell, Houston, Texas; Milton Konvitz, Ithaca, N. Y.; Morris L. Ernst, Osmond K. Fraenkel, James Marshall, Shad Polier, Louis Pollak, Samuel I. Rosenman, Herman Zand and Andrew Weinberger, all of New York City. In the early years of the Association, Arthur B. Spingarn actively directed the legal program.

The fifty national organizations associated with the NAACP in the Leadership Conference on Civil Rights include such Jewish organizations as the American Jewish Committee, American Jewish Congress, Anti-Defamation League of B'nai B'rith, Jewish Labor Committee, Jewish War Veterans, National Community Relations Advisory Council, National Council of Jewish Women and the United Hebrew Trades. Jewish organizations were among those which filed briefs as friends of the court in the historic public school segregation cases.

The continuing devotion of American Jewry to the cause of human rights was reaffirmed in an address by Rabbi Israel Goldstein, successor to Rabbi Wise as president of the American Jewish Congress, in an address delivered at a Madison Square Garden Civil Rights Rally in New York City on May 24, 1956. In that address the Congress leader declared:

"The issue of civil rights is one which affects not any one particular segment or section of the American people but the American people as a whole, since the majority of our people are composed of minority groups—religious minorities or racial minorities. This diversity of its composition is the strength and the richness of America. It is not a melting pot as much as it is an orchestra. Hence the protection of the integrity, equality and security of any group is a protection for all groups.

"Once the abuse of the rights by any American of any other American is tolerated then every American in this multi-racial, multi-religious and multi-cultural nation of ours is threatened. We are all of us members of a mutual insurance company, for we are of one another. Therefore, as we meet tonight under the banner of American civil rights we are not here in the relationship of benefactors and beneficiaries, but in the relationship of fellow-citizens seeking to help one another so that we may together build an American society in every section of the country where American principles shall be matched by daily practices."

Perhaps, because of their long history of religious persecution, many Jews are keenly aware of the injustice of racial oppression. They realize that curtailment of the liberties of any particular racial or religious minority endangers the liberties not only of other minorities but also of the total population. Hitler began by persecuting the Jews and ended in a psychotic attempt to enslave the world. As Rabbi Goldstein pointed out in his Madison Square address, each of us has a vital stake in the preservation of the rights and liberties of every American irrespective of race, color, religion or national origin.

Persons of other races and faiths, too, have joined the NAACP crusade for the abolition of racial injustice. In 1942, Southern-born Pearl Buck, the distinguished novelist and humanitarian, expressed her grave concern about the international implications of racial discrimination in our country. "The importance of facing the situation between white and colored people in our country is twofold," she wrote. "It is upon this rock that our own ship of democracy may go down first, and upon this rock, too, that all peoples may divide into the ultimate enmity. Everywhere in the world the colored peoples are asking each other if they must forever endure the arrogant ruling white race. They feel they have been very long patient, but they cannot be patient forever and they will not."

Upon his return from India where he had served as United States Ambassador, Chester Bowles warned: "Today we must look at the problems of race prejudice in America not only in the light of our own moral convictions, but in the added light of the minimum requirements of world leadership . . . . If we do not soon end the last vestiges of second-class citizenship in America, I have grave doubts about our ability to achieve understanding with the colored peoples of these powerful, rising continents, who represent two-thirds of all mankind and on whom the future peace of the world may depend."

Walter White, the late executive secretary of the National Association for the Advancement of Colored People, repeatedly called upon the country to "awaken to the fact that should the peoples of Asia and Africa follow China in despair into the orbit of the Soviet Union, the Western world would lose much, if not most, of its uranium, cobalt, tungsten, tin, rubber and other essential raw materials."

These and others, who have traveled or sojourned in the Orient and Africa and know the temper of the newly-liberated nations and those on the verge of freedom, agree that the race issue in America is of paramount importance to these uncommitted peoples whose manpower and natural resources could prove decisive in the world struggle for power. Accordingly, they have appealed to their fellow-Americans, with a new sense of urgency, to get rid of the handicap of racial inequality.

Unhappily, the explosive aspects of racial conflict in this country have been much more widely publicized abroad than the news of the steady progress towards elimination of the color bar. The expulsion of Autherine Lucy from the University of Alabama, in response to the harsh demands of an angry mob, is known in every corner of the world. However, the fact that more than 2,000 Negro students have been enrolled in southern universities from which, as recently as 1950, they had been totally excluded is known only to the enlightened few. Likewise, the story of the Negro's economic poverty has been broadcast throughout the world. But it is not generally known that the standard of living of the Negro American, although still well below the national par, is far higher than that of the masses of African and Asian peoples, and surpasses that of most Latin Americans and many Europeans.

Since 1940, *Fortune* Magazine reports in its issue of September 1956, Negro Americans have shared more fully in American prosperity than ever before. "During these years when all Americans have known unmatched prosperity," the *Fortune* article points out, "the income of the Negro has not merely kept pace with the rocketing income of the white population: it has narrowed the prewar percentage gap between white and Negro incomes by more than 20 percent. The Negro population's total cash income after taxes ($15.25 billion) represents today a purchasing power almost matching the value of all merchandise annually exported from the U. S. It denotes a market almost as great as Canada, a market almost twice the size of Australia."

Nevertheless, Negro Americans, as a group, have been kept at the nation's lowest economic level. This has been because of denial of job opportunities and the lack of adequate training for better-paying skilled jobs and administrative positions. Ethnic and religious discrimination in employment, Elmo Roper, the market and public opinion analyst, estimates costs the nation thirty billion dollars a year. Although other minorities are sometimes limited in their job opportunities, Negro Americans are the most frequent victims of such discrimination.

Reporting on his survey of "the high cost of discrimination," Mr. Roper asserts:

If you take into account the amount of purchasing power which is denied minority groups by low wages sometimes on work where machines could do the work even cheaper, if you add the possible contribution to society by workers of minority groups who could move into high-paying vocations where there are manpower shortages— such as medicine, chemistry, engineering and so on, if you add the costs of crime, delinquency, and social maladjustment which can be traced directly to discrimination and prejudice, and if finally you add the costs of segregation which are the direct result of discriminatory practices, you'll find on calculation . . . that this discrimination comes to roughly $10 out of every $75 paycheck, or in total dollar terms, thirty billion dollars lost every year.

But the economic consequences of racial prejudices are measured not alone in lost purchasing power. They are measured also in the high costs of slums in terms of city services, the loss of human resources through the denial of adequate health facilities, and the fantastic extravagance of providing a dual system for education and recreation.

Despite the gains made by Negro Americans in the past fifteen years—and they have been many and spectacular—these citizens are still denied full rights in our American society. The curtailment of the Negro's rights is achieved by outright terror in some communities, by state-imposed restrictions in a vast region of the country, by economic intimidation, by extra-legal and illegal means, as well as by subtle discriminations throughout the country. So pervasive have these efforts been that Roy Wilkins, NAACP executive secretary, characterized them as "a conspiracy to deny equality." The conspirators, he charged, have organized to inflict "refined as well as brutal methods of persecution."

Fortunately, these conspirators do not represent the totality of

American society. They are, at this time, fighting a futile rear-guard action. The trend is against them. They stand challenged by the law as well as by the church and by the public conscience. Even in the Deep South, the color bar, which they so frantically seek to maintain, has begun to crumble. This process, stemming primarily from court decisions, but also extending to areas beyond the courts' jurisdiction, began before the Supreme Court handed down its historic anti-segregation ruling of May 17, 1954. C. Vann Woodward, a southern historian, summarizes this development in his excellent little book "The Strange Career of Jim Crow," in the following words:

"Yet in the face of apparent solidarity of southern resistance to change, a resistance that continues to receive firm and eloquent expression in some quarters, it has become increasingly plain that another era of change is upon the South and that the changes achieved or demanded are in the very area traditionally held most inviolable to alteration. Not since the First Reconstruction has this area been invaded from so many quarters, with such impatience of established practice and such insistent demand for immediate reform. Beginning about two decades ago, but reaching full momentum only in the decade since the Second World War, the New Reconstruction shows no signs of having yet run its course or even having slackened its pace.

"It had not one, but many sources. Perhaps the most conspicuous was the United States Supreme Court and its succession of dramatic decisions down to 1954. But in addition there have been many others, including the pressure and propaganda organizations for civil rights—both Negro and white, northern and southern. There were also executive orders of Presidents, policy decisions of federal agencies, actions by labor unions, professional organizations, churches, corporation executives, and educational leaders. Perhaps the most unusual and at the same time most strikingly effective agencies of radical change were the officers of the Army, Navy and Air Force, acting under orders of both Democratic and Republican administrations. The New Reconstruction, unlike the old, was not the monopoly of one of the great political parties."

Also, unlike the nineteenth century Reconstruction, the present movement has received no positive aid from the Congress of the United States. It has been non-governmental agencies, like the NAACP, the churches, organized labor and others, which have spurred the new movement. It has been the judicial and executive branches of the government which have responded with decrees and orders curbing racial discrimination and segregation.

Not in eighty years has the Congress passed any significant civil rights legislation, despite the obvious need, the quadrennial pledges in the platforms of both major political parties, and the constant needling of the organized liberal forces. To all these, Congress after Congress has turned deaf ears. The road-block in Congress has been the notorious filibuster, the anti-democratic device which enables a tightly-knit minority in the Senate to veto the will of the majority, under the pretext of sustaining the right to "unlimited debate," this minority, maintained in office by a deviously restricted franchise, has for nearly a century succeeded in suppressing every proposal for enlargement of human rights. Until the rules of the Senate are changed to provide an effective means to curb the filibuster, there will be little hope for enactment of any civil rights measure by Congress.

Meanwhile, action to extend the frontiers of human freedom continues through the Federal courts and the national administration, and at state and local governmental levels. Likewise, even in the face of the threats of the newly organized "white supremacy" hate groups, the voluntary associations continue to assert the equality of mankind and, sometimes, proceed to the implementation of their declaration. Contributing to this progress are also the Negro's increasing political awareness and power, his growing importance as a factor in the nation's economy, his steady cultural advances, and the intensification of his drive for recognition and equality as an American citizen.

This goal has not yet been attained. But, for the first time in our history, it looms above the horizon. The youth of the race, and indeed all America, can now confidently look forward to the time when no citizen shall be denied rights and privileges solely because of his race, color, faith or national origin. Then, truly, shall America be the "land of the free."

THE LIBERAL PARTY

OF THE STATE OF NEW YORK

by Ben Davidson

ON TUESDAY EVENING, September 11, 1956, a tall, impressive-looking man arose at the state convention of the Liberal Party and nominated Adlai E. Stevenson as the Liberal Party's standard bearer for president of the United States.

For the more than ten years of its existence, Dr. Goldstein has been exercising important leadership in the ranks of the Liberal Party. At present, he is an honorary vice-chairman of the Party, a member of its committee on international affairs, and a consultant to its policy committee. He has served several times on the Party's platform committee, including the one that drafted the party platform for the 1956 elections.

The Liberal Party of New York State is made up of trade unionists and independent liberals, whose main purpose in politics is the achievement and maintenance of government based on high moral principles, with the public good as its goal. The Liberal Party was founded in 1944 to fight communist and fascist totalitarianism and to oppose reaction of every stripe. The founders of the Party felt that the citizens needed a new and clear-cut political instrument through which they could express their opinions on political questions, work for social progress, a higher political morality and a just and effective solution of problems confronting the people. The founders felt that these necessary and desirable aims could not be achieved through the present political set-up in the country, but that, through independent political action on the part of labor and other liberal forces, more could be accomplished for the attainment of a better community and a better society.

The Liberal Party is composed of county organizations throughout the State of New York, and has approximately one hundred and ten Assembly District clubs in the City of New York. It is the only political party that has a Trade Union Council, composed of scores of trade unions, with an aggregate membership of a half-million workers. The Party also has a Committee at Large composed of liberals in the intellectual, professional and business worlds; a Spanish speaking division with ten clubs; a youth division for high school and college students; and various standing committees especially on the national, state, and municipal legislation levels, which develop programs in all of these important areas.

The Liberal Party has pioneered in the formulation of forward-looking measures such as progressive labor legislation, health insurance, public and cooperative housing, increased aid to education, consumer protection, the needs of our older citizens, planning for prosperity and economic security for the people. Every year, the Party sponsors the introduction, in the New York State Legislature, of bills which set the pace in economic and social legislation and many of whose proposals are later adopted by other political forces, thanks to the educational work of the Liberal Party. On behalf of the interests of the people, it has a permanent legislative representative in Albany and sends spokesmen to public hearings of committees of the United States Congress, of the New York State Legislature, and of the New York City Board of Estimate.

The Liberal Party is especially vigorous and forceful in the fight for civil rights and civil liberties. From its inception, the organization has fought hard to eliminate discrimination and segregation. It has also been in the forefront of the fight for world peace based on the freedom and independence of all peoples. Towards this end, it works for the strengthening of the United Nations and the alliance of the United States with other democracies.

That the announced principles and program of the Liberal Party, and the names of its organizers, aroused the confidence and the support of the public was evidenced in 1944, the very first year of its existence. Political experts were amazed when over 300,000 New York State voters cast their ballots for the candidates of the Liberal Party. Since then, the Party has played a decisive role in bringing about the nomination and election of the candidates of its choice.

The electoral policy of the Liberal Party is both effective and realistic: It throws its strong support behind candidates of the major parties whenever the records and views of such candidates meet with the Party's approval. When neither of the major parties nominates such candidates, the Liberal Party enters its own independent nominees in the electoral contest. This policy helps to set a high standard that advances the public interest, and serves as a source of pressure on the major parties to bring forward the best possible candidates, if they wish to obtain liberal support. The candidates, in turn, value the nomination of the Liberal Party as a badge of honor and as a testimonial to the fact that they have merited the Party's approval in terms of program and standards. The Party's wholesome influence carries over beyond Election Day because elected officials, regardless of party, know that the Liberal Party's significant vote must be taken into account and that the Party will be watchful of the legislative behavior and record of every official.

Although it is a New York State organization, the Liberal Party has influence for good beyond the borders of the state. It has close contacts with the country's trade union forces and is in constant touch with liberal United States Senators and Representatives in different parts of the country.

The officers of the Liberal Party are outstanding leaders in the country's liberal and labor movements. Its state chairman, Dr. George S. Counts, is professor emeritus of education at Columbia University; its first vice-chairman is David Dubinsky, president of the International Ladies Garment Workers Union; its vice-chairmen are Alex Rose, president of the United Hatters, Cap and Millinery Workers Union; professor Reinhold Niebuhr, vice-president of the Union Theological Seminary; professor Roma Gans of Teachers College; Alexander Kahn, manager of the *Jewish Daily Forward;* Benjamin F. McLaurin, international representative of the Brotherhood of Sleeping Car Porters; Charles Abrams, noted housing expert and chairman of the New York State Commission Against Discrimination; Dr. John Bennett, dean of the Union Theological Seminary; Dr. Paul Hays, professor of law at Columbia University Law School; Harry Uviller, impartial chairman of the dress industry and chairman of the New York State Mediation Board; Joseph V. O'Leary, former State Controller under Governor Herbert H. Lehman.

Among its honorary officers, in addition to Dr. Israel Goldstein, are Adolf A. Berle, former Assistant Secretary of State under President Franklin D. Roosevelt; professor William H. Kilpatrick, dean of American educators; Dr. James Shotwell, president emeritus of the Carnegie Foundation for International Peace; Dr. John L. Childs; Dr. Sidney Hook, head of the department of philosophy, New York University; Luigi Antonini, president of the Italian-American Labor Council; Rev. Donald Harrington of the Community Church, and Louis Fischer, well-known author and lecturer. Its membership is of the same high standard, composed of men and women dedicated to social progress and the advancement of the welfare of the people.

It is not surprising that a political party with these principles and policies and such eminent leadership should enlist the support of such a practical idealist as Dr. Israel Goldstein. As already mentioned, Dr. Goldstein has been an active member of the leadership of the Party since its establishment in 1944.

There is not an officer or rank-and-file member of the Liberal Party who does not hold Dr. Goldstein in the highest personal esteem and who does not have profound respect for his political acumen. Even at moments when the pressures on his time are greatest, Dr. Goldstein is always prepared to contribute counsel and energy to the private and public deliberations of our organization.

To Dr. Goldstein, the program of the Liberal Party is at once a political and a human document. He played a leading role in helping to shape that program. He has demonstrated, from time to time, that he is as much at home in the field of domestic affairs as he is in foreign affairs.

Dr. Goldstein shows a keen ability to penetrate to the core of an issue with persuasive logic. This ability to grasp a problem, to help in seeking a proper solution, in creating an atmosphere of justice and not mere compromise, is an attribute that has earned many friends for Dr. Goldstein. Few men have the art of conciliation based on principles, possessed by our honorary vice-chairman. The following extract from an address that he delivered at one of the annual dinners of the Party, will serve as an example of this talent. In speaking of the moral approach to national and international affairs he said:

What must be vigilantly safeguarded, however, is the undisputed right of the people to elect those who shall legislate their will and govern for their well-being. When that right is abridged or abolished or circumvented, and a dictatorship arises which purports to speak in the name of the people, then government, be it ever so benevolent, is bereft of moral sanction, since benevolence can readily change into malevolence, when the consent of the governed is no longer invoked.

Dr. Goldstein has shown concern not only for Israel but for the Middle East as a whole, not only for Jews but for all people who are the victims of injustice and oppression. He speaks out loudly and firmly against injustice wherever it exists, whether in the field of civil rights, civil liberties, immigration, in the economic or social problems of the people. There is never hesitation, once he has reached a decision. We have found him to be independent in opinion, not just a follower, but a leader, not just a spokesman but also molder of opinion. As a molder of opinion, Dr. Goldstein is outspoken and unequivocal in expressing his views. Here is an example of his trenchant style of speech. It is a quotation from the address already referred to:

One of the gravest dangers to which American life is being subjected today is the danger that threatens good old-fashioned American liberalism. In the international tension in which we are living, and in the climate of justified watchfulness against the real peril from hirelings or fanatics in the service of our enemies, reactionaries are finding it easier than it used to be to discredit and pillory patriotic Americans whose only crime is that they are liberal in the best American traditions. Good old-fashioned American liberalism is in danger of being throttled. If Thomas Jefferson were alive today he would probably be labeled by these reactionaries as "subversive," would probably be denied a passport by the State Department on the grounds of "political activity," and would be told by the passport bureau that his travel abroad "is not in the best interests of the United States."

Another example of his powers of analysis of public questions is the following paragraph on the status of Negroes in the United States:

One other moral imperative demands the attention of American politics. It is the status of the Negro citizen. He is not the only victim of group discrimination but he is the most conspicuous victim, the most numerous and the most abused. The inferiority status imposed upon him in a number of states in the Union where he is not permitted to exercise the free right of suffrage, and the widespread denial to him of equal rights in employment, education and housing, is a standing blemish upon the moral credentials of our nation. I am convinced that the effort to suppress equal rights for the Negro is a rearguard battle in a losing cause. A hundred years from now those who are now fighting this rear-guard battle will be looked upon as the twentieth-century vestiges of the eighteenth and nineteenth century slaveholder psychology. But in the meantime it hurts us at home and abroad. A Federal Fair Employment Practice Act with enforcement teeth is overdue. To leave it to the states is to evade the issue. A hundred years ago it was being proposed in many quarters that the issue of slavery be left to the states to decide. But the principle was sealed in blood that the nation had the right to adopt a federal policy against slavery. A federal law to safeguard the equal rights of the Negro in employment opportunities, has in it something of the same moral validity.

Dr. Goldstein is both a thinker and a man of action. He believes in putting programs into effect. He has been active in practically every important election campaign, speaking for the Liberal Party over radio and television channels, and at many public meetings.

In a world in crisis, Dr. Goldstein stands as a beacon of enlightenment and encouragement; he is not only our tower of strength but our good counsellor as well. Together with Dr. John L. Childs, the former state chairman of the Liberal Party, Dr. Goldstein has become "the conscience of the Liberal Party."

It seems appropriate to conclude this statement about the Liberal Party, and our salute to Israel Goldstein at sixty, with another excerpt from the address cited:

"Dr. Chaim Weizmann once said in a critical hour for the Zionist ideal, that he believed in miracles, provided we work for them hard enough. Israel's very existence as an independent State has vindicated his observation. In the light of the war-punctuated history of the human race, the permanent achievement of World Peace, the main purpose of the United Nations, would be indeed a miracle. Let us work hard for it and thus help it come to pass."

SOME ASPECTS OF THE

AMERICAN LABOR MOVEMENT

———————————

by Alex Rose

IT IS INEVITABLE that a man of Dr. Israel Goldstein's liberal inclinations and humane perceptions should support the labor
movement. Dr. Goldstein has given organized labor much more
than lip service. His activities on behalf of trade unionism and
industrial democracy range through governmental, religious and
community functions, emerging as a consistent effort over more
than a quarter century to apply his ethical views and deep understanding of human problems to the strivings of working men and
women.

He is not only deeply committed to a concern with social justice; he is as informed and sophisticated on modern labor issues
as many a labor expert. He has been a member of the National
Labor Relations Board (1935), the Citizens Committee on Unemployment Relief (1933), the Department of Labor Committee
on Immigration and Naturalization (1933), and Public Representative of the Meat, Poultry and Dairy Industry for the Wage and
Hour Division of the Labor Department (1943).

A listing of committees and organizations is hardly sufficient to
provide an idea of the scope of his labors and interests. He has
dealt with the intricacies of labor law; the complex of an industry's operations, pay rates and working conditions; depression
problems and the economic aspects of immigration. Through these
various activities, Dr. Goldstein represents the continuity of an
ancient tradition, the Mosaic and prophetic tradition of social

justice. He frequently cites this guiding source in discussing the most up-to-date issues. It is as much part of his personal background as his work on twentieth-century committees.

His view of trade unionism stems from the integration of Jewish religious philosophy, which, as he has written, "puts human rights above property rights," and his wide experience in the economics and labor fields. Dr. Goldstein credits organized labor in the United States with a high social morality, with active democratic principles, and with the power and the will to advance the welfare of the entire nation. Whether he is addressing a union convention or a congregation, his interpretation of labor issues and events rests on this judgment of labor's ethical value. This interpretation does not prevent him from recognizing the faults and gaps, the occasional betrayals and venalities within labor, but he sees them in perspective, and perspective on unionism is rare.

The labor movement needs such friends, especially today. The forces opposed to organized labor have shifted their attack to a new arena. They are trying to project an image of unions as demagogic, domineering, amoral forces with no responsibility to the nation or even to their own members. Any newspaper reader is familiar with the charges of racketeering and dictatorship, the implication that labor's size and strength alone are threats, the complaints of union "interference" in politics, and so on. It would not be stretching the facts to call this a smear campaign.

The campaign has not yet achieved cohesion, but certainly it has a pattern and a goal. Its aim is to deprive unions and union members of their rights and their strength by creating public acquiescence in measures for "controlling" them. "Control," in the shape of the Taft-Hartley Law and the so-called "right-to-work" laws, is as much a "union busting" method as hired thugs and tear gas bombs once were, but its viciousness cannot be so easily seen.

It is in fighting this sort of attack that labor most needs the support of community and religious leaders. Perhaps they can reach and educate public opinion better than those within labor's ranks.

Dr. Goldstein has tried to educate both the public and the unions. He has used his pulpit to bring a better understanding of unionism to a congregation which is, in general, a fairly well-to-do group. The businessmen and employers he addresses have undoubtedly benefited both ethically and practically from his inclusion of broad social issues and in particular, labor problems, among the topics of his sermons. This process is certainly conducive to a view of ethical life as an every-day matter rather than a Sabbath specialty. Further, it may have helped some employers to avoid the costly effects of misunderstanding in this field. For industrial peace, as for good health, prevention is better and cheaper than cure.

On December 6, 1955, Dr. Goldstein spoke before the historic merger convention of the American Federation of Labor and the Congress of Industrial Organizations. On the day which saw the fulfillment of the hope for re-unification, after twenty years of splits and disputes in the labor movement, and the creation of the greatest free workers' organization in the world, Dr. Goldstein's address contained vital warnings as well as blessings. He asked the delegates to do some "self-analysis, focusing attention upon our inner premises," to examine civil liberties, democracy, racial and religious equality, within unions as well as without, to make sure that labor's "inner credentials are beyond cavil, not only because the instrument must partake of the character of the end which it proposes to serve, but also because democracy, as a way of life, if taken seriously, should be a way of life on all levels of association."

At the same time, he generously called the American labor movement "the most reliable and the most effective force against communism . . . a school in self-government from the trade union local up . . . the most convincing of all arguments for the American system of democracy." The labor movement is all of these things, but has the capacity for being so more fully and effectively. For example, the trade union local school of democracy operates in some locals, but is merely a structural possibility in others. Nevertheless, a lack of internal democracy is more often due to apathy among the rank and file than to dictatorship from the heights. Local union officials work hard to get members to meetings, to arouse their interest in the union and in union affairs. Such efforts as COPE (Committee on Political Education) and the new community service committees are, partially, new forms of practical workers' education, and do as much in activating members to participate in union functions as in spreading labor influence in politics or in the community.

Membership participation, of course, is only one aspect of internal democracy. Admittance, on an equal basis, of all workers, without regard to race, color or creed, is another, and here, too, the actual is something less than the ideal. The ideal is stated in the AFL-CIO Constitution. But in some locals, as Dr. Goldstein pointed out, "there may be resistance to the admission of members 'without regard to race, creed, color or national origin,' resistance reflecting environmental prejudices." These and many other lapses from perfection call for alertness and constant struggle for improvement, but they do not deny the democratic ethos of the labor movement.

We have discussed Dr. Goldstein's views in terms of the labor movement's own principles and problems, in terms of its own morality. Labor is not, and cannot be, involved in the synagogue or church in the same way as religious bodies have involved themselves in labor. Dr. Goldstein recently said that "there has been only one-way traffic between religion and unions." Protestant, Catholic and Jewish religious groups have actively backed trade unionism for decades in America. On the other hand, the labor movement once was antagonistic to religion and is now largely disinterested. While it welcomes and needs the friendship that has been extended, organized labor has not reciprocated in kind. Labor's only claim of a spiritual nature is the inherent morality touched on above, and many labor leaders would even object to a description of union democracy as a "spiritual" quality.

Dr. Goldstein would like labor to be more sympathetic towards religion, "to recognize that religion as interpreted by its modern spokesmen is deeply committed to the ideals of social justice." He has himself been a pioneer in fostering this commitment, in promoting permanent organizations through which it could be expressed, and in developing cooperative links between Jewish, Protestant and Catholic spokesmen on social justice. In 1931, he became the first chairman of the Committee on Social Justice of the Rabbinical Assembly. At that time, he had already reached prominence as a leader of the Jewish community in social action. Two years previously, he had been elected president of the Jewish Conciliation Board of America, an institution he still heads, which seeks peaceful solutions of disputes. In 1935, Rabbi Goldstein headed the Committee on Social Justice of the Synagogue Council of America. These religious groups have been outspoken and specific in their approach. In 1931, they endorsed the five-day week; in 1933, the thirty-hour week, a minimum wage scale, unemployment insurance, Federal relief and public works projects. Twenty years later, they condemned the Taft-Hartley Act as immoral, insufficient and uneconomic.

A recent pronouncement of the Synagogue Council states: "Labor is indispensable to society. The country that has an aggrieved working class is a sick country. America could never have achieved its present status without the toil and industry of its laboring classes, without the vision of labor's leaders who sought for labor its rightful reward." This commendation is typical of those of many religious organizations and individual leaders.

While more knowledgeable on labor issues than many of his colleagues, Dr. Goldstein takes pride in belonging to the liberal, responsible position repeatedly expressed by all three major faiths in this country. In an article on the Taft-Hartley Law, written for a union journal, he returned once again to the religious tradition which underlies his modern philosophy and which has its counterparts in the Catholic and Protestant faiths. "In the Jewish religious tradition," he wrote, "labor and the laborer are invested with dignity and blessedness . . . Just as work is glorified in the Jewish tradition, so a concern for laboring people is also a recurrent theme in Jewish moral law."

In harmony with this tradition, Dr. Goldstein evaluates, and seeks the advance of, trade unionism. "Perhaps most important of all, the trade union has been one of the most effective forces in resisting the dehumanization of the worker which has resulted from the industrialization of our society. It has restored the laborer to his true place—changing him from a mere cog in the industrial setup, a cipher in an accountant's notebook and a mere appendage of a machine to the status of an individual with power within the limits of God's will to control his own destiny."

BRITISH WAR RELIEF SOCIETY

IN THE UNITED STATES

by Frederick W. Gehle

WHEN, IN SEPTEMBER, 1939, without provocation, a Nazi German army invaded Poland and ruthlessly crushed that unprepared country, comparatively few Americans realized that this was the first military step in an endeavor to conquer not only Western Europe but also, as it turned out, Soviet Russia. Very few Americans realized that the crushing of democracy in Western Europe would constitute a threat to democracy in America but, with the invasion of Belgium, again as in 1914, in shameless violation of international morality, and the subsequent fall of France under the Nazi yoke, in May 1940, leaving Great Britain alone as the objective and victim of Nazi bombers and long-range missiles, the peril to democracy became very clear in the United States. An overwhelming volume of articulate public opinion favored the extension of direct aid to Britain to enable that nation to survive. Sensing this to be the attitude of a majority of the American people, President Franklin D. Roosevelt succeeded in persuading Congress to adopt a policy of such aid, short of war with Hitler, as our country could render.

Public endorsement of this policy, however, though overwhelming, was by no means unanimous. In part, the opposition was the expression of pro-German sympathy and even allegiance; the chief exponent of this attitude was the so-called German-American Bund. Some opponents of aid to Britain were motivated by dislike of the British. With Soviet Russia ranged on the side of

Hitler, communists in the United States also condemned help to the British—an attitude the communists were destined to denounce with equal fervor, on the other side, when the Nazis invaded Soviet Russia in the following year.

There were Americans who believed naively, that Nazi Germany was not a peril to democracy in general or to the United States in particular, and that their country, bounded by the protective moats of the Atlantic and Pacific oceans could survive and preserve the democratic tradition, regardless of the outcome of Hitler's war. The leading spokesman of this isolationist sentiment was an organization calling itself "America First," some of whose leaders were highly respected and patriotic citizens. They persistently warned the American people that the "aid-short-of-war" policy was bound sooner or later to plunge the United States into war with Nazi Germany and her allies, Italy and Japan.

Those who fervently favored the aid policy, among whom were many who advocated even immediate intervention in the war, also had their organizations and leaders of great national repute. The most influential of these organizations was the Committee to Defend America By Aiding The Allies, headed by the famous newspaper editor, the late William Allen White. This organization spoke for a cross-section of Americans, yet it was deemed important by some supporters of the policy that the religious forces of the country have their own organ of expression. Prompted by this view, the Reverend Henry A. Atkinson, Rabbi Stephen S. Wise and Rabbi Israel Goldstein, among others, established the Interfaith Committee for Aid to the Democracies.

At the suggestion of the late Dr. Stephen S. Wise, a Jewish section of this Interfaith Committee was established at a conference called by the Americn Jewish Congress. This conference, which was attended by upwards of a thousand delegates from 45 states, enthusiastically accepted Dr. Wise's suggestion and unanimously voted in favor of the affiliation of the Congress with the Interfaith Committee for Aid to the Democracies and the creation of a Jewish section of the British War Relief Society in the United States. Upon the urging of Dr. Wise and other leaders of the Congress, Dr. Goldstein accepted the chairmanship.

The British War Relief Society in the United States, established in 1939, was led by Winthrop W. Aldrich, chairman of the Chase National Bank, later United States ambassador to Great Britain. This Society stimulated the shipment of necessities to the war sufferers in Britain. At the same time, the Society raised funds to finance bulk shipments and similar projects.

The Jewish section of the Society was established at a conference called by Dr. Goldstein. This meeting was attended by representatives of twenty-one national Jewish organizations, including the B'nai B'rith and the American Jewish Congress. This unit set itself the task of raising funds for two main projects, namely, (1) mobile canteens for the feeding of civilians in cities and towns in England that had ben blitzed by the Luftwaffe; and (2) the establishment of nursing homes for children who were removed from blitzed areas to the comparative safety of country districts, with Dr. Goldstein as the chairman.

As the one in charge of the fund-raising activities of the British War Relief Society, the present writer was privileged to have many close contacts with Dr. Goldstein and, on many occasions was moved to express wholehearted admiration of the resourcefulness and zeal of the Jewish section of the Society and of Dr. Goldstein's inspiring leadership. The mobile canteens and the nursing homes made possible by the money gathered by the Jewish section were to aid the needy without distinction of creed. It was agreed that such Kosher facilities as were needed should be provided from the general funds of the Society and not from those received by the Jewish section.

These funds were considerable and made possible the provision of scores of mobile canteens and six nursing homes for children. One of these was named for the late Chaim Weizmann, then president of the World Zionist Organization and destined to become the first President of the State of Israel upon its establishment in 1948. He and Mrs. Weizmann attended a luncheon in his honor at which this presentation was made. Another children's home was named for Dr. Wise. A third was named for Dr. Goldstein, who had occasion to visit it during the war. It was located in Porlock, Wales, and was occupied by children from Plymouth. A very special event was the naming of one of these homes for

Sara Delano Roosevelt, the mother of the President, who had died shortly before. The President was deeply touched by this honor to his mother's memory. He invited Dr. Goldstein to the White House in order personally to express his appreciation. Dr. Goldstein presented the President with an appropriate album which is now in the former President's library at Hyde Park, New York.

Thanks to the earnestness and industry of Dr. Goldstein and his associates, the Jewish section of the British War Relief Society contributed mightily to the general effort. As chairman of its fund-raising arm, I was moved frequently to express recognition of the contribution of American Jews to this cause; Lord Halifax, then British ambassador to the United States, also expressed the thanks of his people to Dr. Goldstein and his associates. I am grateful for the opportunity presented by the publication of a book in Dr. Goldstein's honor to pay tribute to the greatness of his leadership in significant activity in a time which was crucial for civilization.

Part Five

TRIBUTES

נשיא מדינת ישראל

LE PRESIDENT DE L'ETAT D'ISRAEL

ירושלים, יא' שבט תשי"ז

13 בינואר 1957

לכבוד

דר' ישראל גולדשטיין

נ י ו י ו ר ק

ר׳ י. גולדשטיין היקר,

לעונג רב לי לברכך, ידידי היקר,
רבי ישראל גולדשטיין, ליום יובלך, בעברך את מפתן
ששים השנים הראשונות.

ידעתי להעריך את אישיותך האצילה, כסמל
של יהודי שאינו יודע גבולות, בין מזרח למערב, בין
היהדות שבתפוצות ובין זו ששבה־למולדתה וקמה תקומה
ממלכתית.

במסירותך לעברה של האומה ולתקות
עתידה הרימות את קרן הציונות והיהדות בעיני יהודים
וגויים גם יחד, וראה אותך כשותף נאמן לבנינה של
מדינת ישראל.

אחולי לך, ידידי היקר, בשמי ובשם רעיתי,
בריאות ואורך ימים לך, שתזכה לשאת ברמה קרן עמך
בתפקידך הנעלה – בגולה ובישראל – אתה ורעיתך היקרה.

אני מקדם בברכה את יזמת ידידיך וסוקריך
לכבד אותך בהוצאת הספר המוקדש לבעיות ישראל בדורנו,
ויברך פעלכם.

בברכת ידידות נאמנה,

יצחק בן־צבי

בברכות ידידות קלם ?

יצחק בן-צבי

ידיד הן שלקי?

Jerusalem, 11 Shevat 5717
13 January, 1957

Dr. Israel Goldstein
New York, N.Y.

Dear Dr. Goldstein:

It is my great pleasure to send you, my dear friend, greetings on the occasion of your passing the milestone of your first sixty years.

I have learned to appreciate your personality as a symbol of the Jew who knows no boundary between East and West, between Diaspora Jewry and the Jewry that has returned to its homeland and risen again to statehood.

By your devotion to our people's past and to its hope for the future, you have raised the esteem in which Zionism and Judaism is held by Jew and non-Jew alike; and I value you as a true partner in the upbuilding of the State of Israel.

For myself and for my wife I wish you and your beloved wife health and long life to continue your noble efforts in behalf of our people wherever they may be.

I welcome the decision of your friends and admirers to honor you so appropriately by the publication of a book devoted to the problems of contemporary Jewry.

With all good wishes,

Itzhak Ben-Zvi

MY CONGREGATION

AND MY RABBI

---

by Charles H. Silver

AS I SETTLE to the welcome task of appraising the place of our
rabbi in the affairs of our community and in the personal lives
of his congregants, America is prospering and outwardly at peace.
Yet we are living through times infused by a sense of foreboding.
The turbulent state of a world in torment spills over to trouble
even the smallest town and hamlet. It reaches into the home and
disturbs the complacency of every member of the family.

In these times of uncertainty and momentous decision, the
seething unrest of nations leaves its mark on individuals. If such
are the storied "times that try men's souls," our need is greatest
now for those whose responsibility is the ministering to men's
souls. There is evidence of a growing awareness among people
of every faith that secular living is not enough.

Religious precepts have taken on new meaning. The mechanical importance of our civilization and even the advances of
science no longer serve to make us more secure. They may,
indeed, make us a little afraid. We are losing confidence in the
material fortresses we have built on false pride and the empty
quest for profit. We are reaching desperately toward the frontiers
of faith.

The increasingly cosmopolitan character of our modern society,
where few men know their neighbors, has deprived many of us
of a needed sense of belonging. The house of worship, with its
rich and varied communal and social aspects, offers the best and

nearest opportunity to draw together into a warm and rewarding association. In these days, so full of turmoil, so empty of trust, we find ourselves turning toward groups, searching for God.

Upon the minister, the priest and the rabbi, falls the burden of meeting the people's need. He must be more than a spiritual leader in the remote sense of the term. He must be a creative thinker and doer, a teacher, comforter and guide. He must inspire his congregants, fixing their sights steady on eternal truths, lifting their hearts.

I have heard it said that a public office is a public trust. I have come to know of a private trust that is even greater. My rabbi has proved this to me in his precious duty of interpreting the stress and challenge of today through the wisdom of yesterday. That is how his presence and the performance of his day-to-day functions can strengthen his congregation in their hope for tomorrow.

Other pages of this book dwell upon the influence our rabbi exerts beyond the borders of his congregation, indeed beyond the borders of state and nation, race and creed, as a preacher to, and for, the brotherhood of man. They reflect the regard he has earned in high places and beyond the usual province of a minister. But I have known Israel Goldstein for almost thirty-five years, from the days when he was still the young rabbi bearing vital new energies to our city's second oldest seat of Jewish worship . . . and I know the little things, the intimate concern, the small and tender services with such far-reaching effect on the life of every congregant.

Through well over a century and a quarter of its history as America's oldest Conservative congregation, B'nai Jeshurun has constantly widened the concept of its obligation to the community. While sacrificing nothing essentially traditional in its primary function as a place of worship, it has opened new avenues of service as a center of neighborhood activities, instruction and recreation for young and old alike. Above all, it has radiated a spirit of neighborliness that reaches into every corner of our vast sprawling metropolis to touch the lives of all its congregants.

That Dr. Goldstein has been the staunchest advocate and

active worker in these "homey," wholesome, auxiliary functions, clubs, festival and family celebrations, is all the more remarkable because his own horizons have broadened with the years. Although his own community has become the world, yet his heartfelt interest has remained rooted in the local happenings that make up the program of our Community Center. In our many conversations, alert as he is to the international affairs in which he plays so important a role, he has shown that he is equally aware of the progress of our Junior Brotherhood or the needs of our Sisterhood Sewing Group.

Only a few days ago, as I hurried into the elevator, in our Center, at his side, on the way to a meeting of the gravest import at which he was to deliver an address of far-reaching effect on Israeli affairs, I marvelled as he stopped to ask a youngster entering the Center building, "How soon do you need my editorial for our school paper?"

The bigness of a man, I think, is best revealed in such small things. History will gauge the true value of Israel Goldstein's services to Jewry and to all humanity. His congregants need not await that judgment to measure the impact of his warm personality, the inspiration of his eloquence, the depth of his perception. These things are as near and dear to us as a handclasp after sabbath services, a glass of wine together in the sukkah. We know the sincerity of his encouragement, sound advice and practical assistance, because it has become part of our daily lives.

We know, too, that Dr. Goldstein lives what he preaches. We know that his loyalties begin at home, but they do not end there. The influence of a rabbi on the social, ethical and spiritual life of his congregants depends on the rabbi. He must illuminate the timeless values and explain the values that change as times change. As a man of God, he must walk in the flame of divine truth, but never in an inflexible ring of holy or holier-than-thou fire through which his people cannot come to him. And though he may utter words that claim the attention of all mankind, he must yet be ready to whisper consolation to the sorely troubled in his own flock.

There may be some who echo an ancient complaint: "You men of the faith, forsake practical affairs, keep out of politics, don't tell me how to conduct my business and stop trying to tell statesmen how to carry on theirs." These nay-sayers—and there are always a few on hand—ignore the very well-springs of religion.

Is it not the basic purpose of religion to regulate the relations between man and his fellows, to establish a way of life, to mark the borders between right and wrong, good and evil? And is this a set of tenets to be declaimed from a pulpit out of which a minister may not descend to help fashion the better world he has declared to be the will of God? Shall we congratulate each other that we have a rabbi who is tactful and considerate and not be proud that he can also, when necessary, be outspoken, daring, fearless?

The rabbi who best serves his congregation is one, like ours, who does not hesitate to shake the pillars of the temple, to stir the lethargy of men who must be moved, as Isaiah sought to move them, to waken the nations to impending doom—and yet to write his message in the school paper. His ears may be hearing the pulse of momentous events, his eyes may be fixed on distant stars, but his heart abides in the homes of his congregation.

Faithful as he is to the needs of his people, I have still heard Dr. Goldstein confide at times his wish that he had more opportunity to perform, personally, the more intimate pastoral duties of his office. As our neighborhood has changed, and B'nai Jeshurun has drawn its worshipers more and more from areas farther removed from the synagogue, I have heard him remark somewhat sadly that the character of the pastoral side of the ministry changes with the character of a decentralized community. He has spoken, almost enviously, of the advantages of a suburban or small town rabbinate with its daily opportunities for contact with the members.

Though ours is a friendship that would survive disagreement, and we differ on few things, this is a point on which we are not in accord. I am constantly amazed that, while doing so much in larger spheres of influence, he can yet do so much for his congregation. Public life is tyrannical and demanding. Dr. Goldstein is not only a world figure, he is a world traveler. He has made so many trips to Israel that he has achieved the status of a commuter, perhaps its principal commuter.

His work for Israel has been recognized by the establishment of an Immigrants' Hostel in Tel Aviv and a youth village in Jerusalem, both of which bear his name. The recitals of his observations on these journeys, and his reports on the chronic state of emergency existing in that new republic surrounded by hostile neighbors, have made a deep impression on his congregation. As a result, B'nai Jeshurun leads all congregations in America in fund-raising for Israel.

If Dr. Goldstein is devotedly admired by his congregation, he is likewise his congregations's greatest admirer. As he puts it, his congregation understands him; and for a whole congregation to understand their rabbi. . . ! That's not merely admirable, it's almost unbelievable. And even more wonderful, to Dr. Goldstein, is the fact that he's fairly sure there have been times when they didn't understand him, but followed him just the same.

Early in life, our rabbi realized that lack of knowledge of the sources of Judaism, and the elements on which their faith is founded, left many Jews barren of interest and pride in things Jewish. He felt that this was a widening vacuum in which succeeding generations would be lost to the glorious tradition and nourishing faith which their fathers were allowing to falter. He burned with a desire to study, to teach and preach the Torah, and to serve Judaism and Israel, America and humanity.

The years have not dimmed that zeal. He has traversed the oceans and the hemispheres, voicing eternal truths, giving full play to abilities that could never be merely intra-mural. He has spoken in the chambers of man's destiny and his words at times may have altered its pattern. He has spoken not only for today, but his prophetic utterances of yesterday may be recalled during many tomorrows.

With his winning manner and sound counsel, Dr. Goldstein has achieved the almost impossible distinction of meaning so much to so many . . . private chaplain to the distressed at his doorstep, yet ambassador of the world's largest Jewish community to the mighty powers of our time. Author, educator, political leader and champion of the rights of man. . . but also sharer of joys and sorrows, compassionate friend of youth, consecrator of blessed moments, comforter of the bereaved.

This, then, is my rabbi and my friend as I view him from the vantage point of a layman, a member of his congregation. It is a congregation which cherishes the moments we have him to ourselves and proudly shares the glory of those moments he devotes to public affairs.

The young rabbi who sought to touch the lives of others with the warming light of the Torah is still with us, but the light is lifted higher now as its beams seek to kindle understanding among all the races and nations of the earth. B'nai Jeshurun has given some of Israel Goldstein, gladly, to the world, but most of him is here with us, inseparably ours.

He does not depart the temple and the congregation to fulfill his dedicated missions to mankind. In a very real sense, we go with him. And our service to God, through this partnership in the interest of a better future, seems greater the farther it reaches beyond the walls of B'nai Jeshurun into the souls of men.

ISRAEL GOLDSTEIN

AT SIXTY

---

by Pierre van Paassen

MONUMENTAL and uncontradictable as it may appear in the way
it is generally presented to us, the statement that all men are born
free requires, nonetheless, some drastic revision and qualification
at times. Man is not born free. He is born within the bounds and
bondage of society. Outside society he would not even be a man.
He is entirely formed, fashioned and modeled by his environment.
In himself he carries what the ages have poured into his own
tribe's or people's cultural bloodstream but, once born, he has
no other education than the example of his predecessors and contemporaries. He must live as others live. He can neither feel nor
think nor will differently. How can anyone escape these two
constraints: heredity and environment? To think for oneself, to
be really free, is either an illusion, or it is what Tillich calls: the
courage to be, an heroic performance. Which of the two is it?

The truly free man is not he who merely makes a choice between the different courses which society permits him; go to the
left or go to the right, dress in black or dress in gray, vote for
Jack or vote for Harry. "The citizen who is truly loyal will neither
submit nor consent to arbitrary measures." He frees himself from
the laws, the obligations, the judgments, conventions and ideas
by which, it is true, society seeks to protect its members, but by
means of which it also subjects the best of them and their creative
urge to intolerable restrictions.

In the measure that man challenges the conventional, he
liberates not only himself but he prepares and contributes to the

emancipation of others. This process of liberation is, of course, utterly non-violent. It is carried out in full concord with the essential nature and character of an evolving social order. Outside evolution, it would be merely a form of egotism. It is precisely while finding himself in the stream of our evolving civilization that the free man deploys his activity by never leaving well alone, by incessant questioning, and by being constantly at war with the status quo. In doing this, in never ceasing to criticize and to challenge the sacrosanctity of society's constraints, he fulfills the supreme demands of the highest law. He becomes a trail-blazer, a guide to the timid and an architect of the future. Although he may appear an enemy of society to the shortsighted and the chauvinist, in reality he is its best friend. . . .

On the occasion of his sixtieth birthday, I want to honor Israel Goldstein as one of the rare individuals who has shown his contemporaries how one can be a free man in this horribly unfree time of ours. To pay tribute to Dr. Goldstein, I believe, amounts to the same thing as honoring all the high qualities of the human heart and spirit: art, science, liberty and that which is man's noblest possession: the will to dedicate himself, not to a Utopia, but to an accessible, realizable ideal, to what Immanuel Kant called *"das moegliche Reich."* For the sake of that ideal, the free man dares to oppose and defy the thousand and one tyrannies and impediments which the obscurantism and the hatred of the self-righteous place in his path.

Contrary to a superficial allegation, Israel Goldstein, whom I have known and observed for upward of thirty years, has nothing of the "conservative" in him (in the reactionary sense of the word). His apparent serenity, his calm and urbane demeanor are indeed, on first sight, somewhat deceptive, but they veil, I have reason to know, a soul profoundly in love with justice. He is not a neutralist. He always takes sides. He has never, insofar as I know, taken his position on the sidelines in this "time of troubles" for the Jewish people and for mankind as a whole. To the contrary, he was ever in the vanguard with those who kindled the flame of hope anew, who swept away the gathering shadows, and crushed the prejudices of the fearful and the time-servers.

Upon rereading the collections of Dr. Goldstein's published addresses and public statements on important and even critical occasions, I came to the conclusion that we find ourselves in the presence of a man of extraordinary moral courage. Israel Goldstein's statements on burning questions of the day are the more impressive because they are free of histrionics and hysteria and because of their quiet, soberly precise wording. Sensationalism of any kind is alien to the man, a quality which stamps him as a rare exception in our day of brazen self-advertisement and commercialism.

I have heard it said—what doesn't one hear?—that there are two men in Israel Goldstein: the man of imagination and the man of action. I do not think this is true: there are not two superimposed individuals in him. Israel Goldstein is a *Mensch* of one piece: the work and the worker, the rabbi and the orator, the thinker and the agitator for reform and conversion—all form one indivisible unity in him.

Outwardly, Dr. Goldstein certainly does not conform to the mental picture of the somewhat timorous, somewhat naive and absent-minded, old-fashioned rabbinical guide to the perplexed. Israel Goldstein looks like a banker, brisk, efficient, businesslike, or perhaps more like a judge when he, not the judge, is in one of his more solemn moods. Yet, under that exterior of worldly *savoir faire,* such is my experience of him, beats a heart full of compassion for his fellow-men. It is his hatred of iniquity and his aversion to the pettyfogging trivia which, at times, causes his interior to rush into the open and his temper to flare up. I have seen this also happen more than once. This is the streak of prophetic indignation which runs through all his critical observations and actions. It is his detestation of all that is hostile to life and to the free unfoldment of life which is the motive power driving him on, though there is, and this also should be said, nothing of the rigid doctrinaire about Israel Goldstein either in reliigion or politics. He is severe, but his severity is tempered by an all-embracing love of humanity. He knows what man is made of.

In going over the volumes of his sermons in this year of jubilee, it struck me most forcefully that there is one consistent line or pattern to his teaching, an unbroken thread, rather, of emphasis on the community of all flesh. He does not, for instance, see the revival of the Jewish national spirit and the regeneration of mankind as two mutually-exclusive phenomena, but as conditioned, the one upon the other, through the penetration into the world's general thought forms, in whatever shape, of the messianic dream and the messianic longing which are the creation of the Jewish soul.

It follows almost logically that Israel Goldstein has not abandoned, as have some others in his school of Judaism, the Chosen People concept. He is innerly persuaded that the Jewish people still have a mission to perform and that this mission consists of more than mere existence and vegetation.

The rehabilitation of Eretz Israel, to which Dr. Goldstein has contributed enormously through years of devoted and uninterrupted service, is not to him merely the setting up of just one more little Levantine republic, but a mile-post in mankind's advance to the ideal which finds expression in the vision of Zechariah: "When the Lord shall be King over all the earth, and the Lord shall be One and His Name be One." The restoration of the Jewish people in its ancient homeland is to Dr. Goldstein the search for organic unity, the secret binding tie for all mankind. It is the beginning of the brotherhood of man, his emancipation and liberation.

In fact, to Israel Goldstein the restoration of Israel is nothing less, I think, than service of God. He is not out to achieve a delicate consistency of statement on this or any other subject, but to do as much as he can of God's work. He is trying to translate into action the God in his heart and mind. To be sure, God does not need man to build His Kingdom. But man may collaborate, man may place himself at God's disposal. This is what Dr. Goldstein has done and is doing. It may even be said that there pertains a certain obstinacy, a certain dour persistence to his endeavors in this respect. Indeed, when we look somewhat closer, we find that he is seeking to fulfill the Torah's highest demands: for man, with all his soul and all his strength, with his intention and his practice, by the absoluteness of his acts, to purify and to sanctify the world.

If the Jewish people did not have that sense of mission, of which Dr. Goldstein is one of the chief protagonists in our time, or if they should ever lose the consciousness of being charged with a mission, and replace it with a mere desire to be like unto others, they would drop out of sight and disappear from the ken of history.

By his impressive calm, his ability to be a listener (a rare quality indeed amongst *rabbonim*) as well as a speaker, his capacity to see two sides of a question or in a matter under dispute, Dr. Goldstein is indicated as an ideal arbitrator and referee. He is attentive. He lets himself go. He is interested. One feels to be in the presence of a man who is curious about other men. He is simply incapable of withholding his sympathy and, although he does not suffer fools gladly, there is not a trace of condescension about him in his dealings with the most humble. Respect for human dignity is not just a noble-sounding rhetorical phrase to Israel Goldstein.

There is nothing transitory, either, about his sense of humor. The area around his eyes always wrinkled easily, long before he reached his present canonical age. He can even listen to a joke told at his own expense. Whereas, in certain others whom I could name, humor is a protective mechanism or assumed in order to economize mental or emotional effort, in Israel Goldstein it is unfettered, spontaneous and of an almost childlike quality, never sardonic or grim. He has a balanced mind and, *Gott sei Dank,* does not take himself too seriously. Unction and *Wichtigtuerei* are as alien to his spirit as meanness and vindictiveness. You can have a dispute with Israel Goldstein, even a violent dispute, in which passions are unleashed and words fly like angry bolts of lightning, for he is by no means of "the unperturbed and imperturbable" kind; five minutes afterwards, the raging torrent has returned within its banks and the sun shines again. He is as prone to forgive as he is incapable of nourishing a grudge.

I know very well that, in writing of him in the way I am writing, Israel Goldstein does not consider me guilty of flattery. In the first place, men of his kind are immune to flattery and, secondly, it does not lie in my nature to flatter anyone. I have absolutely nothing to gain and nothing to lose. What I want to say yet is this: what in men of lesser caliber is called arrogance —I do not know the equivalent in English of the expression *odium theologicum,* but that is what I mean—is in Israel Goldstein something entirely different. Proud he is: a proud Jew and a proud American, and rightly so, but his is a pride tempered by a gentle and vast native wisdom. It is what the ancient Romans called *superbitas,* by which they meant an awareness of personal superiority, a subconscious assurance of personal value, something which is wholly legitimate, inoffensive and natural. This quality imposes itself not by calculated, highhanded behavior, but subtly insinuates itself and urges itself upon the beholder by means of an indefinable aura and asmosphere surrounding the personality of Dr. Goldstein; it is the aura of sincerity and integrity. He does not regard himself as a possessor, but as a humble seeker, of the truth.

Where Israel Goldstein excels above all is in the art of public speaking. There is nothing flamboyant about his oratory. He does not play for effect or to the gallery. He is not given to dishing out quips and catch-phrases, or to concocting sparkling and startling aphorisms and paradoxes. He doesn't need to have recourse to such tricks; for he has always something to say. He forgets himself and becomes the instrumentality by which the message of the spirit is conveyed. His gestures are few and his physical demeanor does not betray the slightest inner agitation. But the stillness wherein he is heard by vast audiences till this day testifies to the effectiveness and the strength of his discourse. In this respect, he resembles John Henry Newman of whom we are told that he raised his voice scarcely above a whisper, who made not a single motion with his hands, and who but rarely shifted his weight from one foot to the other in the pulpit, and yet held his congregations spellbound while discussing the most abstract propositions. What is the secret here? It is Israel Goldstein's humility, his frankness brought to us wholly without affectation.

But Israel Goldstein is not alone. Behind him and by his side, even when invisible in self-effacing modesty, stands . . . "Bert," the Rabina, a Mother in Israel in spite of her perennial youth, a woman of quiet wisdom and brilliant mind. Mrs. Goldstein is a great and fine person in her own right. It is no exaggeration to say, and not improper, I trust, that without Mrs. Goldstein, Dr. Israel would not be where he stands today, as a defender of the truth, in the very forefront of world Jewry, and in the leadership of the American Liberal Party.

It is an amazing sight to see how these two, "Bert" and Israel, each in her and his own way, alike love and find occasion to expend themselves. If I were permitted to speak on this subject, I would cite Dr. and Mrs. Goldstein as examples of spontaneity in their practice of love of neighbor. With moral rectitude they combine the courage of sensitiveness. It is a marvel to see in them, one by one, a combination of the heart and of the spirit.

Israel Goldstein is the Big Brother in American Judaism. His words and presence always have a reassuring effect. He knows the world, also the world of us *goyim*. In spite of this, he still loves the world and man. This is the quality which stamps him with true greatness.

In order to merit well of him, many walk the road of life with more courage today. For a free spirit alone has the power to engender true faith and confidence in others. Such a free spirit is the rabbi of Congregation B'nai Jeshurun, who enters upon the second stage, and, as we pray, on the most fruitful stage of his career today.

ISRAEL GOLDSTEIN—

A BIOGRAPHICAL APPRECIATION

---

by Levi Eshkol

IN THE LIFE OF every leader, two elements inevitably clash, two
diametrically opposed desires come into conflict, each demanding
considerable sacrifice and deep deliberation. On one hand, the
drive, the need and the will for self-realization and fulfillment
act like a strong magnetic pole on the individual. On the other
hand, the drive, the will and the needs of the group, body, or
people, which the leader heads, pull in the opposite direction.

All the more pronounced is such a conflict when it involves our
people and a son of our people. And yet, from such a conflict can
arise a harmony of action typified by that sage about whom it is
written that "the sword and the book were united." The sword
and the book—*sa'ifa vesafra*—can well summarize the turbulence
of Jewish life in the past few decades and the importance of
balancing problems of existence with problems of the spirit. It
may well sum up the main lines of Dr. Israel Goldstein's character.

Dr. Goldstein first became known as a brilliant member of the
younger generation of American Jewish scholars. Had he been
free to devote to his scholarship those talents and that energy that
were syphoned off into Zionist and Jewish public activity, he
would have made an indelible mark not only on contemporary
American Judaic scholarship, but also on Jewish learning as a
whole.

However, Dr. Goldstein chose to act on the principle that if there is no bread, there is no Torah, and threw himself into the day-by-day struggle to preserve the physical existence of the Jewish people throughout the world, to fortify the structure it was erecting in Palestine, and to develop the State which was proclaimed in Israel. His time, energy and thinking were diverted from scholarship into efforts to raise funds, to mobilize political support, to take part in the strengthening of the Jewish Agency's finances during a most critical year.

Dr. Goldstein is a man with a tremendous capacity for work. This is backed up by a shirt-sleeves approach—"let's see what we are talking about."

For example, we received news that Jewish communities had been discovered in outlying parts of the Morocco, in bandit-infested mountains hundreds of miles from the nearest town, with neither roads nor telephones. When I tried to learn more about them I was told, "Dr. Goldstein can tell you all about them, he was among the first to visit them."

When we worked together in the Jewish Agency, most problems involved places: out-of-the-way work villages in Galilee, new frontier settlements in the Negev, or distant Ma'abaroth. It would emerge, from Israel Goldstein's contributions to the discussion, that he had been there and knew each problem in essence and detail.

In the years that I have worked together with Dr. Goldstein, I found in him that rare modesty of a man who achieves full self-expression in his work and personal life. In the many discussions of theory and principle, which are an inseparable part of a movement, when so few can resist the temptations of rhetoric, Dr. Goldstein is alive, alert and sticks to the point at issue. He listens with an absorbing interest. And when he speaks, Dr. Goldstein says what he has to say, and his words are certainly spoken with *nahat* as befits *"divrei hahamim."*

The fact that he, a General Zionist, has been able to work together, almost without friction, not only with members of all other parties, but *mirabile dictu,* also with members of all factions in his own, bears witness to the strength of his personality. (Perhaps others will even comment on his ability to work together with Levi Eshkol. Who knows?).

A key to his personality is the recognition of responsibility and ability to act on the lines etched out by his understanding of responsibility. Israel Goldstein has, therefore, a great list of achievements and activities: president of the Zionist Organization of America, and of the American Jewish Congress; chairman of the Western Hemisphere branch of the World Jewish Congress; leading member of the Jewish Agency; co-founder of the National Conference of Christians and Jews; founder of Brandeis University; perennial chairman of mass Israel Bond sales events, and these are only *inter alia.*

I do hope that readers will not be tempted to imagine him as some human work-machine, racing through conferences, meetings and stacks of paper-work. Nothing could be further from the truth. It is precisely his rich human personality, his zest for life in all its forms—doing, reading, thinking, and above all, seeing for himself—that have enabled Israel Goldstein to pack so much into so little time, and yet to remain so fresh and sensitive.

Dr. Goldstein assumed the treasurership of the Jewish Agency in 1948, during what was indeed a period of *Sturm und Drang* for the Jewish people. He was treasurer when the tremendous flow of mass immigration swelled the population of Israel, when operation "magic carpet" was beginning to materialize. With characteristic zeal, he took under his wing, Amidar, the immigrants' housing company, and conducted it with absolute dedication. It has since provided roofs over the heads of tens of thousands of Israel's new citizens.

He brought with him into this crucible of Jewish history, the same qualities of *hatmada,* of the *masmid,* which made him a noted scholar. Never departing from the field of Torah, he threw himself wholeheartedly into *avodah*—service to the Jewish people and to humanity in general and *gemilut hassadim*—the dedicated desire and effort to lighten the burden of hundreds of thousands of his fellow-men. For these reasons we honor him, for in his person are united the *sa'ifa vesafra.*

ISRAEL GOLDSTEIN—

THE JEWISH LIBERAL

---

by Abraham Granott

I

AMERICAN JEWRY has a special status within the Jewish people. Its numerical and economic growth has made it a primary factor in the crystallization of the destiny of the Jewish people in the most recent period of our history. In the wake of the large scale immigration to the United States, a powerful Jewish center arose, which radiates its strength to the far corners of the Jewish world.

The changes in the life of our people during the past twenty years, particularly since the great holocaust in Europe, have led to a far-reaching re-evaluation. The leadership of world Jewry passed from the former centers, among them the old European communities of great spiritual stature, into the hands of American Jewry. But for a time, the latter did not have the required experience and the necessary spiritual leadership, which were the hallmarks of the European communities. Spiritual qualities cannot develop at a moment's notice; they grow out of a historical process which, by its very nature, is a long one. The accumulation of forces of leadership was not in proportion to the demographic growth of the American Jewish community and to its economic status, which also improved at a rapid pace. The development of Jewish life and its crystallization were slow and accompanied by many inner struggles, particularly in respect to the manifestation of independent forms of life. The way of life and the original lines of the Jewish mode of living came slowly into relief. In the course of time, distinguished leaders arose, who put their stamp on the setting mold of the American Jewish community. Then the inner Jewishness began to assert itself in this community, until it attained as high a level as that of the Jewish communities of Europe. Only out of an independent Jewish life and within the framework of Jewish experience, can that leadership arise which Jewry needs, the elite which determines the character of life and gives it its unique form.

The Jewish community of America has not yet achieved the desired level and it is too early for it to claim that it has an outstanding, a first-class leadership, in its midst. Actually, American Jewry has not yet had the opportunity to take the place it merits —according to its political and economic strength—the leadership of the Jewish people.

Although the present situation is not satisfactory to all who look to American Jewry to assume even now, in this generation, the leadership of the Jewish people, we cannot shut our eyes to the evident progress American Jewry has made and is making towards the achievement of this goal. On the occasion of the Tercentenary celebration of the American Jewish community, much was said of its growth since the arrival of the first twenty-three Jews in New Amsterdam, to the five and one-half million Jews living in the United States today. A mighty community has developed a multitude of religious, charitable and educational institutions, and social welfare organizations for the Jews of the United States and other lands, besides institutions of great achievement in the rescue and the rehabilitation of large numbers of their persecuted brethren, enabling them to reconstruct their shattered or disintegrating lives.

Also a Zionist organization came into being there, that was always ready to help, support and defend the Jewish undertaking in the land of our fathers. This Zionist Organization of America played an important role in the establishment of the State of Israel, and in the creation of the channels of aid to the *Yishuv*. Another body, the World Jewish Congress, was established for the defense of the rights of the Jews in the Diaspora, to improve the status of the masses suffering in a climate of discrimination. This organization parallels the World Zionist Organization and complements it in several respects. The two organizations have created a wide field for Jewish public activities, and have opened up broad horizons for the realization of the aspirations of our people. They have made possible the establishment of contact between the Jews of the United States and other Jewish communities, large or small. Within these two organizations arose a new Jewish leadership, including men of high quality and great achievement, whose influence has spread throughout the Diaspora. In both organizations the same forces were at work, and the same elite stood at the head of all projects. There is apparently a close relationship between the activities of both organizations, and the very factors that turned the wheels of the Zionist movement awakened the forces that rallied to the defense of our people throughout the Diaspora, and are working in the various avenues of Jewish life to promote a better and more secure future for our people.

II

Israel Goldstein is one of this elite group that arose within American Jewry during recent times and is now in the forefront of leadership, in the United States as well as in world Jewish affairs. Every matter of concern to American Jewry is near to his heart and he is a participant in all communal affairs that are important to them: religion and education, philanthropy and social welfare, the organization of communal autonomy, and Jewish activities in various other areas. Many are the institutions and activities to which he has extended his guiding hand, and given of his strength and energy. Like many Jewish communal leaders in the United States, Goldstein is a rabbi by vocation. Since 1918, he has served as spiritual leader of the oldest Ashkenazic congregation in New York and in the United States, and has molded it into a highly important institution.

The synagogues in the United States have always served as the centers of Jewish communal affairs. This synagogue, too, has never confined itself to religious activities, but has always participated in a variety of Jewish concerns, especially the strengthening of the Jewish national sentiment, which indicates the ideal that American Jews can be loyal citizens of the United States and, at the same time, loyal sons of their people.

Rabbi Goldstein has for many years been among the leadership of the Zionist Organization of America and the American Jewish Congress. If one would define his place in Jewish life, there comes to mind, almost spontaneously, a comparison with that outstanding leader of American Jewry, the late Stephen Wise. In his personality, his qualities and the pattern of his life, Wise served as an example for the younger generation of Jewish leaders in our time. In Wise's activities as the accepted leader of American Jewry, there was an inkling of what American Jewry should and could achieve if it effectively played its part in the people's struggle for a secure future, in the successful outcome of its striving for a well-ordered Jewish life.

Among the leaders of American Jewry, Israel Goldstein comes closest to Stephen Wise, both in sparkling personality and wide range of public activity, and in his colorful and dynamic way of action. Like his esteemed colleague, Goldstein gives all his heart, his unparalleled energy and his great organizational talent to the many problems of his people wherever these may arise. Thanks to his qualities and to the power of his personality, which radiates energy and warmheartedness, he is universally recognized as a communal leader of the first rank. Externally, this general recognition has expressed itself in the fact that he has been called to many of the positions that Stephen Wise, in his time, had occupied: He stands at the helm of the American Jewish Congress, and participates in the leadership of the World Jewish Congress; he is also in the first rank of Zionist leadership. Like his associate before him, Dr. Goldstein has not confined his activities to Jewish affairs alone, but has widened the scope of his interest and activity to include also general problems: the welfare of working men and women; the arbitration of disputes arising in Jewish life; the promotion of honest and liberal government; the fight against racial discrimination; the establishment of better mutual understanding between Jews and Christians—all these and more good works come within the scope of Dr. Goldstein's activities. To those who remember the broad

canvas of Stephen Wise's life, all the problems that were close
to his heart and the activities that filled his days—the similarity
between the fields of endeavor of the two men is apparent.

In addition to the above similarities, largely external, and to
the similar traits of character, mention must also be made of
another common feature. This is apparently a very important
feature and it may well be the one dearest to the heart of our
subject himself: under all circumstances Dr. Goldstein has remained an outspoken liberal. The affinity for a world outlook
that cherishes freedom of the individual and freedom of thought
runs like a scarlet thread through his life and deeds. Anyone
examining his addresses and writings encounters this affinity, and
discovers his liberal ideals, particularly in respect of social problems. Moreover, Dr. Goldstein's liberalism is inextricably intertwined with his Jewish consciousness. Typical is the following
utterance: "Jews feel a sense of responsibility for the betterment
of the social order, as it is written in our prayers. . . ." [1]

In an address on the occasion of the Tercentenary celebration
of Jewish settlement in the United States, he declared:

"The essence of our Jewish existence is but a means to the
realization and a way towards the great objective—a society
built on justice, righteousness and peace." [2]

III

In the long chain of his public activities, Dr. Goldstein's work
for the Jewish National Fund occupies a special place. To be
sure, few are the important Jewish and Zionist affairs in which
his participation was not felt and in which his influence was not
evident. But it seems to me that in his "book of life" there is
no chapter so charged with feeling, so rich in effort, and so dear
to his heart as the ten years (1933-1943) that he dedicated, as
its president, to the work of the Jewish National Fund in the
United States. It is no coincidence that, in this period, Dr. Goldstein reached the acme of organizational and propagandistic

[1] Israel Goldstein, *American Jewry Comes of Age*, New York, 1955,
p. 97.
[2] *Israel and the Jewish People*, in an address delivered before the World
Jewish Congress, August 1953, p. 5.

achievement. This was also a period of exemplary Zionist activity and worthy deeds. This was also an important chapter in the history of the Jewish National Fund, of the institution as such and of its activity in the United States. For Dr. Goldstein this was no ordinary public service but a project to which he dedicated himself, to a greater degree and in a different manner than to other projects, with truly sacred devotion. Perhaps this exceptional interest and drive may have been due to the fact that this activity was especially suited to his talents as an organizer, a talented and resourceful propagandist and a public figure of wide scope. He always found the way to the heart of other people, and his colleagues caught the holy zeal in his heart.

But above all, it was this institution with its popular and traditional character, based on the sublime idea of the national soil, which captured the hearts of the group with whom Dr. Goldstein worked. The national and social significance of this institution was especially close to the heart of Goldstein the liberal, who believes in a social order of justice and righteousness, and who strives for the establishment of society on such a basis. All his life, he has remained true to this institution and to its basic ideals.

Even after giving up his active service for the Jewish National Fund in the United States, in order to carry out other Zionist assignments, he has continued to maintain close ties with J. N. F., zealous for its continued sound development and vigilant for its growth and strength, to fulfill its vital tasks. He has always heeded the call in time of need or when he felt that the precious institution was threatened. This seemed to be the case at the 24th World Zionist Congress (Jerusalem 1956), when it looked as if there was an inclination to introduce drastic changes in the structure of the Jewish National Fund, calculated, Dr. Goldstein and others thought, to reduce its stature and its possibilities. Dr. Goldstein went into action, plunged into the thick of the debate, mustered all his strength, and exerted all his prestige to thwart the attempt to change the character of the J. N. F. In his opinion, based on a decade of service, that would be detrimental to its development and diminish its Zionist and ideological character.

Dr. Goldstein had an important share in the materialization of the principles of the Jewish National Fund, which are one of the pillars of the Zionist world outlook. He sees the J. N. F. as a symbol of the partnership between the State of Israel and the Jewish people, and as an important means in the implementation of this partnership. He was a devoted participant in the implementation of this great social ideal, so dear to the heart of this outstanding liberal, this Jewish liberal.

His liberal approach always comes to the fore in dealing with American problems, with world Jewry and with Zionist activities in general, and the upbuilding of Israel in particular, and also in dealing with the problems confronting Jews in general and Zionists in particular, in the light of developments in the State of Israel. In all these matters, Dr. Goldstein zealously adheres to his liberal Jewish position. We must implement the social and ethical aspirations of Judaism in the life of our people, in the State of Israel and in the lands of the Diaspora—this ideal he proclaims and, for it, he is prepared to work and struggle.

Summing up the task before American Jewry, he says:

"American Jewry faces a twofold challenge. We must do our full share as American citizens toward the preservation and furtherance of the liberal, democratic American tradition especially in times when demagogues and political adventurers, under the cloak of patriotism, attempt to violate that tradition. We must exercise our full measure of responsibility in the program of Jewish survival through strengthening the synagogue, fostering Jewish education, and supporting Israel." [3]

Here we have before our eyes, in all its grandeur, the personality of a Jew who believes with all his heart in the oneness of the Jewish people, who dedicates himself to endless labor for the progress and the betterment of Israel, and for the future of mankind.

[3] *American Jewry Comes of Age*, p. 81

Part Six

BIOGRAPHY

ISRAEL GOLDSTEIN—

A BIOGRAPHICAL SKETCH

---

by Philip Rubin

I. ANCESTRY, YOUTH, SCHOOLING

THE YEARS 1896 and 1897 represented a turning point in modern Jewish history. It was in 1896 that Theodor Herzl issued his revolutionary pamphlet "The Jewish State," calling for the reestablishment of the Jewish nation along modern lines in the ancient homeland, and it was in 1897 that Herzl founded political Zionism by convening, for the first time, an international congress of Jews.

On June 18, of the first of these two years, there was born to David L. and Fannie Goldstein, in the city of Philadelphia, a son, their first-born, whom they named Israel, and who, years later was to leave his imprint on American and world Zionism and on American Jewish communal life generally. He was to be one of the leaders to carry forward the work begun by Herzl in the year of his birth, to help in the creation of that Jewish State of which the immortal founder of modern Zionism could only dream; he was to help nurse the State after its birth.

Israel Goldstein was born in the Jewish quarter of South Philadelphia, in the basement of the Nieziner synagogue, the living quarters of his parents, as his father was sexton of the synagogue. Both his father and his mother came from villages in the province of Vilna, Russia. They came to the United States within a few years of one another, between 1893 and 1895, in the influx from eastern Europe which marked that period. Though neither one of them was of rabbinical stock, the older brothers of both of Israel Goldstein's parents were scholars of repute.

His father, David, had studied in Yeshivoth in the Old Country and for a time came under the tutelage of Rabbi Jacob Reines, one of the great scholars of his time and one of the distinguished pioneers of modern Zionism. Before he was twenty, David Goldstein received *semihah*, i.e., rabbinical ordination. He was also qualified to be a *shohet*, a ritual slaughterer.

Upon arriving in America, David Goldstein, like many others, began to earn a livelihood by peddling small wares in a basket, but after a while accepted the position of sexton of the Nieziner Shul. At the age of twenty-eight he married Fannie Silver, ten years his junior. Both of them worked hard taking care of the synagogue premises, while David was also occupied with religious duties, such as preparing for the daily, Sabbath and festival services, the *Yarzeits*, the funerals.

Thus, from earliest childhood, the synagogue became part of Israel Goldstein's life. He remembers that, at the tender age of four, at every Sabbath service, it was his privilege and duty to go from pew to pew offering a pinch of snuff to each of the male worshippers who desired it. Several years later, during the Sukkoth periods, Israel Goldstein's father assigned him the job of bringing the *ethrog* (citron) and *lulav* (pɔ'm leaves) to the dozen or more homes of those families which had placed orders for them, a job in which the young boy earned some money for the first time.

The boy Israel was given a strict upbringing, because his father, who dominated the household, had stern ideas about child-rearing, thought that discipline was good for the soul. Israel's mother-tongue was Yiddish—both his parents spoke that language at home and it was the medium of conversation in the Shul.

At the age of five, a tremendous new experience came into Israel Goldstein's life. His mother, planning to take a health cure and to visit relatives, took him and his younger brother, Isaac, to Russia, where they were to remain for two-and-a-half years. For an impressionable five-year-old child, this was a new world, indeed. His mother's grandfather and her stepmother lived in Kabilnick, a little village in the Province of Vilna, where his mother's sister's family also lived. It was in Kabilnick where, left by his mother in the care of these relatives while she went to take the cure for rheumatism at the mineral baths near Riga, that young Israel Goldstein began to attend *heder,* learned to read Hebrew and began studying the Bible.

In the *heder,* at nearby Svir, Israel continued the Jewish studies he had commenced in Kabilnick. It was in Svir where his mother's brother's family lived and where he spent a great part of the time during his stay in Russia. Svir was larger than Kabilnick, but was still a small town. His uncle, a lumber merchant, was a learned man. As he had several daughters, the house was frequented by young men of education and was altogether a more cultured and refined environment than his grandfather's house in Kabilnick, where the child had first been placed. In this home, Israel was taught to play the violin by a cousin who had come back from military service where he had learned to be a musician. Because it was unusual for a Jewish child to play the violin, Israel was the object of considerable adulation, besides attracting special attention because he had come from America.

Once his mother took Israel to visit his paternal grandfather in the tiny village of Stayatzchik. This grandfather was a simple, pious peasant type of Jew. Here, Israel had his first opportunity to be on a farm and to ride a horse. Nearby, lived his father's brothers who, unlike their father, were learned Jews.

These years in Russia left an indelible impression upon Israel Goldstein. He recalls the villages he saw as self-sufficient, Yiddish-speaking little worlds in which the surrounding Christians had no part. He has always felt that his experience in Russia had helped to make him more understanding and appreciative of the Old World and its values, that the unusual experience of these childhood years had added a dimension to his Jewish feeling.

Back in Philadelphia, the boy continued his Jewish studies and began his secular schooling. Proud of his violin-playing, his father saw to it that Israel continued to take lessons. Public school, however, was a problem as the boy had to make up for lost time because he had forgotten his English and was going on eight. Simultaneously, Israel was sent to the *heder* conducted by Samuel

Markowitz, the best heder in Philadelphia. This school was regarded as much more modern than, and a great improvement over, the others in town. Among other things, Mr. Markowitz taught *dikduk,* Hebrew grammar, which was an innovation in *heder* instruction.

Young Israel's *heder* career lasted for a little over two years. By the time he was ten, he was conversant with the Bible, the commentaries of Rashi, and a small part of Talmud. On Saturdays, his father would review with him the portion of the week and would occasionally teach him some Talmud. Between public school and Hebrew school and violin practice, little time was left for play. Nor did Israel's father look with favor upon play.

At the age of ten, the boy was transferred to the Yeshiva Mishkan Yisroel, at the suggestion of Mr. Markowitz, who told the father that Israel had nothing more to learn at his *heder.* There, the lad studied Talmud in earnest for the next two years.

In the meantime, his public school education proceeded apace. At the age of twelve, he was graduated from elementary school and entered the Southern Manual Training High School for Boys, which had opened only a year before. Manual training was an innovation in a high school curriculum.

In his father's Nieziner Shul, the boy would hear learned discourses by rabbis, including Philadelphia's renowned Chief Rabbi B. L. Leventhal, and in a nearby synagogue, richer than his father's, he would listen to renowned cantors. His father, ambitious for his first-born, was eager, however, that Israel should also hear good English spoken; so he urged the boy to attend the Sunday lectures at the Ethical Culture Society in Philadelphia, apparently unworried lest his son become "contaminated" by their unreligious doctrine. There, Israel also had his first experience in hearing elevating music. His father's desire to expose him to good speakers even went as far as to suggest that he go to hear the leading Reform rabbi of the city, the Rev. Dr. Joseph Krauskopf.

But, already, at about the age of twelve, Israel Goldstein had begun to venture out on his own in some directions. When the Hebrew Educational Society was established, offering library facilities for Jewish literature and Sunday afternoon lectures by men of eminence in Jewish literature and drama, he became one of its enthusiastic beneficiaries. Thus, the boy formed his first acquaintance with Jewish secular literature in both Yiddish and English. He also became an ardent Yiddish playgoer, and when the stars of the Yiddish stage would come to Philadelphia he rejoiced. A short time later, he was introduced to the English theatre and developed an attachment to it. Also, although his violin lessons had stopped at the age of twelve, young Israel did not neglect hearing good music at the Academy of Music, where the Philadelphia Orchestra played on Friday afternoons.

Zionism came naturally to a child of the ghetto, especially because Israel's father and his cronies did not belong to the extreme Orthodox Jews who rejected the movement. The Jewish National Fund had loyal and active adherents in his family; they were not only patrons but also distributors of the JNF blue boxes and the JNF stamps. Israel helped organize a Zionist club for boys of his age; the club, which was called "Hatikva," consisted of the boys who attended *heder* with him. It offered Israel Goldstein the first of his many presidencies. The office rotated between him and Gershon Agronsky, later, as Gershon Agron, to become mayor of Jerusalem.

Israel's high school career was successful on the academic side, but was wanting in other respects. "I did well in all the subjects except drawing and manual training," he says. "I was never good with my hands, nor had I been encouraged at home to use them. Socially, too, I was backward, partly because I was two years younger than the average, partly because I was not a boy of social inclinations, partly because my *heder* and Yeshiva companionships had not prepared me for a different type of boys at high school, some of whom were Gentiles, while many of the Jewish boys seemed to me to be frivolous. My upbringing at home had looked upon playfulness as an unworthy trait." Yet, despite these difficulties, Israel Goldstein was elected president of his class in his second year.

Simultaneously with his high school entrance, Goldstein also matriculated at Gratz College, a Jewish co-educational secondary school for the training of teachers for Jewish religious schools, to which he was admitted at the age of twelve only because he was already in high school. Sessions at Gratz were held two evenings a week and Sunday afternoons. Jewish history and pedagogy were new subjects to the boy and the study of Hebrew was different in that the Sephardic pronunciation was taught. Among Goldstein's teachers were Dr. Julius Greenstone, a leading biblical scholar, and Dr. Isaac Husik who became renowned in the field of Jewish philosophy. The president of the Board of Trustees was Dr. Cyrus Adler, one of the lay leaders of Philadelphia Jewry.

"While most boys of my age were playing baseball and basketball," Dr. Goldstein recalls, "those recreations were looked upon in my home as fit only for 'loafers'. My physical activity consisted of walking—walking six miles a day to and from high school, and three times a week another six miles to and from Gratz College."

II. HIGHER EDUCATION

At the age of fifteen, Israel was graduated from high school and from Gratz. Being qualified now to teach in a Jewish school, he awaited his opportunity. His family of three sons, Israel, Isaac and Morris, was now increased by the birth of a sister Sarah. In order to realize his ambition of entering the University of Pennsylvania, the boy had to start earning money immediately. And so, during the summer following his graduation, he went to work at Litt Brothers department store as a stock-boy in the stove department at eight dollars a week—his first substantial earnings.

In the fall, he secured a position as teacher in the Hebrew Orphan Asylum at Germantown, in suburban Philadelphia, for five afternoons at fifteen dollars a week, while Sunday mornings he taught Sunday school at nearby Frankfort. This income enabled Goldstein not only to pay his way through college but also to contribute to the family exchequer. This proved to be a Godsend to the family, because just then his father had fallen ill with a lingering circulatory disease which required the amputation of his leg in several stages and long stays in hospitals.

His teaching jobs occupied Goldstein about thirty hours a week, and his college schedule was more crowded than the average, because he was ambitious to complete the four-year course in three years. Though he had little time for extra-curricular activities, he did join the Menorah Society, which had been established shortly before. He did well in his studies, completing the course in three years and being elected to Phi Beta Kappa. One of the men who befriended Goldstein at college was Professor Morris Jastrow, the distinguished Orientalist.

As his graduation was approaching and he was pondering the question of a career, Goldstein thought for a time of entering social service, and he made many inquiries about it. However, both his father and Dr. Cyrus Adler encouraged him to enter the Jewish Theological Seminary in New York. He was then eighteen and his theological views had not yet crystallized. "But I felt that becoming a rabbi was in some respects like being a social service worker—and with full-time Jewish interests—and that appealed to me," says Dr. Goldstein.

World War I had just broken out when Israel Goldstein came to New York to matriculate at the Jewish Theological Seminary, which in 1914 was universally recognized as the greatest institution of Jewish learning in America. Dr. Solomon Schechter, who had become its head in 1901, brought to it from abroad, in addition to his own illustrious Hebrew erudition and mastery of English style, three scholars of renown upon whom, in the main, the Seminary's reputation rested. They were Louis Ginzberg, foremost talmudical scholar; Israel Friedlaender, eminent biblical scholar, and Alexander Marx, outstanding historian and bibliographer. Like his fellow-students, Goldstein was deeply impressed by the privilege of sitting at the feet of such masters. Most of his intellectual stimulation, however, came from Mordecai M. Kaplan, professor of homiletics, who was then beginning to formulate his philosophy of Judaism, which later developed into the Reconstructionist movement.

During his years at the Seminary, a good deal of Goldstein's time was occupied in earning a livelihood. He taught in a week-day Hebrew school and gave private lessons. He lived with a Markowitz family which was related to his *heder* teacher in

Philadelphia. During that year, he became engaged to Bertha, one of the five daughters in the Markowitz family, who was then a senior at Hunter College.

Beginning with the second year at the Seminary, Goldstein began to distinguish himself in his studies. In addition to the Seminary courses, he also began work at Columbia University for his master's degree. At the end of the third year, his student record at the Seminary was at the top of the class. He was the prize-winner in an essay contest on "The History of the Khazars," and he was awarded also the first prize in homiletics for the best sermon.

An unusual circumstance attended that sermon. It was a year of biographical sermons and the subject assigned to Goldstein was "Gamliel of Jabne." This sermon, which was Goldstein's "maiden effort," received the praise not only of Professor Kaplan, the homiletics teacher, the elocution instructor and fellow-students, but was extravagantly commended also by President Schechter. Two days later, Friday, November 17, 1915, Dr. Schechter died suddenly of a heart attack at the age of sixty-nine. The funeral was held the following Sunday. For the ensuing Sabbath services in the Seminary synagogue it was arranged that a eulogy of Dr. Schechter be delivered. The Seminary faculty felt that the life of Rabbi Gamliel of Jabne was so much akin to Dr. Schechter's in its characteristics and significance, that they asked Goldstein to deliver his sermon again as the eulogy of Dr. Schechter. Dr. Schechter's successor as president of the Seminary was Dr. Cyrus Adler of Philadelphia, who had encouraged Goldstein to enter the Seminary.

At the end of his third year, Goldstein was awarded the Steinbach scholarship, the premier award, and a prize for an essay on the Aramaic portions of the liturgy; at the same time he also received his Master's degree from Columbia University. He was elected secretary of the student organization. In his senior year, he was awarded a prize for an essay on "Modern Interpretations of the Book of Job," and, at the graduation exercises in June 1918, he was chosen to deliver the valedictory.

III. RABBI, TEACHER AND PREACHER

Although just graduated as a rabbi, Goldstein already had a considerable amount of rabbinical experience behind him, having held week-end positions with congregations in Rockville Centre, L. I., and Coney Island, New York City, and high holiday and festival preaching positions with congregations in Camden, N. J., Philadelphia, and in the Bronx and Manhattan boroughs in New York. Congregation Beth Elohim in the Bronx, where he had officiated the preceding Passover and Shabuoth, was negotiating with him regarding a permanent position, now that he was about to receive his rabbinical degree.

In the meantime, however, another opportunity, unusual and unexpected, presented itself. Congregation B'nai Jeshurun in Manhattan, the second oldest congregation in New York (the oldest is Congregation Shearith Israel, New York City), was without a rabbi. Among the rabbis who had ministered to B'nai Jeshurun had been such outstanding men as Stephen S. Wise, Joseph Mayer Asher, Judah L. Magnes and Joel Blau. The congregation had moved from its location on Madison Avenue at 65th Street, where it had been steadily declining, to 88th Street west of Broadway, the heart of a growing Jewish neighborhood. Its new building had been completed in May 1918, a month before Goldstein's graduation as a rabbi. At about this time, the officers of the congregation were considering a number of candidates for its pulpit, but had not yet found the one upon whom the Board of Trustees could agree.

It happened that Sol M. Stroock, the honorary secretary of the congregation, who was also secretary of the Seminary Board of Trustees, had heard Goldstein's valedictory at the commencement exercises. He had been so deeply impressed by Goldstein's literary and oratorical talents that he suggested his name to the Board of the Congregation. Goldstein was invited to preach on two successive Sabbaths. He was then elected rabbi for a trial period of six months, at the end of which he was elected for a five-year term.

Before his election, Rabbi Goldstein was hesitant as to whether he should prefer old and wealthy B'nai Jeshurun to young and struggling Beth Elohim of the Bronx. Dr. Adler, however, urged him strongly to accept B'nai Jeshurun's offer, and Goldstein was installed as rabbi there on December 13, 1918. Dr. Adler delivered the installation address in which he said of the new rabbi:

"I knew him as a lad, before he entered the Jewish Theological Seminary, and have watched his career ever since. He has shown fine spirit, great determination, a courage which knew no obstacles that could not be overcome. Under a brave exterior he also has a becoming modesty. When, a few days after the Seminary graduating exercises, you did him the honor to invite him to occupy your pulpit, he was dismayed at the size and importance of the charge, and expressed a preference for a smaller congregation. I advised him to accept the call, feeling sure that he was riper than his years indicated and that he might count upon your full cooperation."

On July 21, 1918, Israel Goldstein was married to Bertha Markowitz in the synagogue of Congregation B'nai Jeshurun. She was to give him two children, Avram and Vivian, and, as "Bert" Goldstein, was to become known as a Zionist leader in her own right, holding among other offices the presidency of the Pioneer Women of America, Labor-Zionist group, co-chairman of the Jewish National Fund of America, and the chairmanship of the New York Women's Division for Israel Bonds. She has accompanied him on many of his visits to Palestine, later Israel, often by virtue of her own position as member of the Governing Council of the World Zionist Organization. In 1932, the entire family went to Palestine to celebrate their son's *Bar Mitzah* in Jerusalem. In 1936, their son and daughter remained for a year's stay in Palestine.

Their son Avram is now professor of pharmacology and head of his department at the Medical School of Stanford University in California; his wife, like him, is a doctor of medicine and does research in bio-chemistry, and they have four children. The Goldsteins' daughter, Vivian, who holds a Ph.D. in psychology, is married to Dr. Paul Olum, professor of mathematics at Cornell University, and they have two children. Dr. Goldstein also has two younger brothers, Issac Goldstein of Philadelphia and Rabbi Morris Goldstein of San Francisco, and a younger sister (Mrs. Herman) Lazarus of Philadelphia.

At the very beginning of his career as Rabbi of B'nai Jeshurun, Goldstein introduced several innovations. For the first time in the history of the Congregation, the late Friday evening service, featured by a lecture, was instituted in the fall of 1918. It was a custom already in vogue in many Conservative and Reform congregations, supplementing or supplanting the sundown service. Another change in the synagogue program was the holding of memorial services on the second day of Shabuoth and on the eighth day of Sukkoth, in addition to the memorial services on the Day of Atonement and on Passover.

A special high holiday service for young people was introduced in 1923. This was held in the vestry rooms and was conducted by students of the Jewish Theological Seminary, who officiated as both preachers and readers. Young people, regardless of whether they belonged to families who were members of the congregation, were free to attend the services. Similarly, there was instituted in 1924, the custom of holding a special service for Jewish collegians on a Friday evening during the mid-winter vacation.

When Goldstein became rabbi of B'nai Jeshurun in 1918, the religious school of the congregation had just commenced its first year on the west side, with a registration of seventy pupils, meeting in the vestry rooms. In 1920, a private dwelling, adjoining the synagogue, was acquired for school purposes. The school population grew steadily, reaching in 1925 the number of three hundred, divided into eleven classes. Even the new building was now inadequate, and a building adjoining it was also purchased.

Although the preponderant majority of the school population attended only the Sunday sessions, several groups met for sessions of one hour each on Tuesday and Thursday. Later, a full weekday school, devoted chiefly to the study of Hebrew, was added to the Sunday sessions. For the confirmation class, consisting of girls as well as boys, attendance at the weekday classes was made compulsory. A high school department was added. The graduates of the high school became eligible to serve as assistants to the religious school staff. All of the regular teachers had to be trained professionals, the volunteer system having been entirely discarded. In 1922, there was organized a Junior Congregation, which held services on Sabbaths, Festivals and High Holy Days.

In order to provide extensive social and recreational facilities for its children and adolescents, and to build up a social and educational program for adults as well, the B'nai Jeshurun Community Center was established in 1921. Seven years later, a six-story community center building adjoining the synagogue in the rear, was dedicated. The center has since become a beehive of activities for Jews of all ages, with a multitude of groups and clubs of a cultural as well as social and recreational character.

The one-hundredth anniversary of the founding of B'nai Jeshurun was celebrated in 1925 and made an impact on the New York community. In this connection, Rabbi Goldstein undertook to write a book containing a permanent record of his congregation's history, against the background of the history of the New York Jewish community generally. After several years of research and writing, the book, "A Century of Judaism in New York," was published in 1930. It was accepted by Professor Alexander Marx as a thesis for the degree of Doctor of Hebrew Literature awarded Goldstein by the Jewish Theological Seminary in 1927. In recognition of his distinguished services to the general community and the Jewish community, he was awarded another doctoral degree, that of Doctor of Divinity, *honoris causa*, by the Jewish Theological Seminary, in June 1945.

IV. COMMUNAL AND CIVIC ACTIVITIES

Even though his was a large metropolitan congregation, Israel Goldstein could never remain a local rabbi. Only a few years after his ordination he started his climb to national Jewish leadership. In 1921, he was elected to his first national office, the presidency of the newly-organized Young People's League of the United Synagogue of America. Since then, Israel Goldstein has been president of more Jewish organizations than probably anyone else in this country.

From the beginning of his rabbinate, Goldstein felt that concern for social justice, in the prophetic tradition, must motivate the rabbi. It was, therefore, a welcome assignment to him to be appointed chairman of the social justice committee of the Rabbinical Assembly of America. A larger opportunity in the same area presented itself later in the Synagogue Council of America, representing national Orthodox, Conservative and Reform rabbinical and Congregational bodies, when he was appointed chairman of its committee on social justice. This brought Goldstein into contact with similar Protestant and Catholic bodies, and with current problems in the realms of industrial relations, inter-race and interfaith problems, Church and State relations, and world peace. It was an opportunity also to educate Jewish public opinion on significant and often controversial questions.

In 1928, Goldstein was one of the founders of the National Conference of Christians and Jews. He became actively interested in its program and served for a number of years on its executive and administrative bodies and as Jewish co-chairman of its commission on religious organizations. He has given the organization aid and support consistently across the years. At times, he was critical of its shying away from important issues, such as that of civil rights, particularly affecting Negroes, and the issue of Zionism, but felt that in general, the Conference was a useful activity in that it did serve to improve Christian-Jewish relations, albeit within a limited range.

Another interfaith effort in which Goldstein became active was the World Fellowship of Faiths established by Kedar Nath Das Gupta. On one occasion when Rosh Ha-Shana was celebrated by this organization by a special program held at the Grace Episcopal Church in New York City, with Buddhists, Moslems and Christians participating, it was Rabbi Goldstein's assignment to respond on behalf of the Jewish community. In 1932, as a delegate from the World Fellowship of Faiths, he attended the Amsterdam Anti-War Congress, on the way back from a visit to Soviet Russia. Upon his return to the United States, he joined the newly-formed League against War and Fascism, but later resigned when he found it to be Communist-dominated.

From 1928 to 1930, he served as president of the New York Board of Jewish Ministers. In his administration, the Board published a volume on "The Problems of the Jewish Ministry." During that period, he headed a committee which raised funds for the Jewish Division of the New York Public Library. In 1938, he served as lecturer in homiletics at the Jewish Theological Seminary. In

1946, on the occasion of his fiftieth birthday, his congregation established the Israel Goldstein Lectureship at the Jewish Theological Seminary of America.

V. ZIONIST LEADER

Dr. Goldstein's first Zionist responsibilities on a national scale began early in the nineteen-twenties. In 1921, he helped, in his congregation and on the West Side of New York City generally, to launch the first Keren Hayesod campaign in the United States, an activity which he continued for years thereafter. Later, he served as a member of the administrative committee of the Zionist Organization of America in the adminstrations of presidents Louis Lipsky and Morris Rothenberg. In 1930, he was elected national president of Young Judaea and served in that office for three years.

Nineteen thirty-three is the year from which Israel Goldstein's long career of top Zionist leadership, a leadership of nearly a quarter-century, dates, for in that year he became president of the Jewish National Fund of America. Having returned from Palestine, a year before, with a special appreciation of the significance of the land redemption program of the JNF, and its idealistic as well as practical values, he was spiritually attuned to the office. Dr. Goldstein regards his ten years activity as president of the JNF, 1933-43, as the greatest single Zionist service he has been privileged to render.

During the year preceding his election, the income of the JNF had been $144,000; when he left the office, ten years later, the income was over $9,000,000. This unprecedented amount represented seventy-five percent of the total world income of the JNF and provided the bulk of the resources which enabled the JNF to play so important a part in the redemption and reclamation of land which became the inalienable property of the Jewish people, on which were established the *kibbutzim, moshavim* and national institutions in Eretz Yisrael.

The Jewish National Fund had been loved but not adequately supported by the Zionists of America. The chief source of income had been the blue-and-white collection boxes. Menachem Ussischkin, world president of the Fund, had come to the United States in 1931 in an effort to stir American Jewry into greater activity in order to provide the funds necessary for carrying out his ambitious plans for redeeming large areas in Palestine. His efforts however, met with virtually no response and he left, embittered and disappointed. This event pointed up the need for a drastic change, both in the internal administration of the JNF and in the methods being employed in educating American Jews to a full appreciation of the vital importance of the JNF in building up a Jewish Palestine.

For a time, Goldstein's efforts brought him into conflict with the Zionist leadership which had come to look upon the Keren Hayesod (Palestine Foundation Fund) as the only important fund-raising instrument of the Zionist movement. The first years of his JNF administration were very difficult ones, but gradually the situation was improved. The internal organization was transformed into a more efficient machine. Mendel N. Fisher, dynamic, young and resourceful, was engaged to replace the retiring executive secretary. In addition to the representatives of the Zionist organizations, new people were brought into the executive board, one of them being Jacob Sincoff who became associate treasurer and rendered valuable service. The Zionist organizations themselves became more intensely activated, and national conferences were held to impress the aims of the JNF upon the consciousness of American Jews.

New fund-raising techniques were developed, including *Nachlah* projects in which organizations and regions were persuaded to undertake commitments of $25,000 and over, for land tracts in Palestine bearing their names. The most conspicuous of these was a $100,000 *Nachlah* undertaken by B'nai B'rith, the leading Jewish fraternal organization in America and in the world. Individual contributions in large amounts were solicited and secured; the foremost of these was a contribution of $65,000 from Maurice Levin, head of a New York department store. In 1935, when the head office of the JNF in Jerusalem announced that it would undertake the drainage and reclamation of the Huleh swamps, the JNF in the United States launched a Huleh gift bond campaign which produced substantial results. Subsequently, a JNF $5,000,000 ten-year bond sale also was successful. His JNF activities took Goldstein into every part of the United States.

American Zionist leaders sat up and took notice. Goldstein's next step was to demand that the United Palestine Appeal accord the JNF parity with the Keren Hayesod in recognition of the importance of the land redemption program. This demand was granted, and, as a result, the JNF income soared. Mr. Ussischkin, in Jerusalem, felt that at last the JNF in America was giving a good account of itself. In his fight for greater support of the Jewish National Fund, Goldstein was enthusiastically backed by Justice Louis D. Brandeis, then the most revered of American Zionists.

In the meantime, Dr. Goldstein's interest and activity in the Zionist Organization of America kept growing. In 1934, he became a vice president. In 1935, as a delegate of the Z.O.A., he attended his first world Zionist Congress; he has been a delegate to every such congress since then. In 1938, he was a candidate for the presidency of the Z.O.A. in a hotly contested election, and was defeated, by a close margin, by Rabbi Solomon Goldman of Cleveland, a Seminary classmate. Five years later, in 1943, Goldstein was unanimously elected president. Thereupon, he retired from the presidency of the Jewish National Fund and became its honorary president.

In 1938, when New York's World's Fair took place at Flushing Meadows, Long Island, and beautiful edifices were put up by the governments of many nations, there was also a Palestine Pavilion showing Jewish achievements in the Holy Land. While not competing in size, the Pavilion did compete in beauty with the other buildings. The project was sponsored by Jewish organizations, with Goldstein as chairman, George Backer as president, and Meyer Weisgal as executive director. The dedication of the Pavilion, in which Mayor Fiorello LaGuardia participated, brought an estimated 100,000 to the World's Fair grounds, the largest attendance attracted by any function in the program of the Fair. It was a striking demonstration of New York Jewry's interest in the Jewish National Home.

The twenty-first World Zionist Congress, which Goldstein attended as member of the Z.O.A. delegation, was held in Geneva, in August 1939, as the world was trembling on the brink of World War II. Only a few months earlier, the British White Paper, restricting Jewish immigration to, and land purchase in, Palestine, was issued. The new policy was a serious setback to Zionist hopes. The Jews in Palestine and throughout the world did all in their power to resist the British policy. Redemption of every available *dunam* of land in Palestine became the chief slogan of the Jewish National Fund during these years of Dr. Goldstein's presidency. The British White Paper policy was the more indefensible in view of the growing menace of Hitlerism and the pressure of fleeing German Jews on the gates of Palestine.

"Aliyah Beth," "illegal" Jewish immigration into Palestine, was one of the principal issues at the twenty-first Zionist Congress. Plans were outlined for the organization of this influx in defiance of the Mandatory Power. After re-electing Dr. Chaim Weizmann as president, the Congress adjourned in a hurry, as war was breaking out. The American delegates barely managed to get back home in time.

Upon the outbreak of World War II, Rabbi Solomon Goldman, president of the Z.O.A., set up a Zionist Emergency Committee. This committee, of which Goldstein was a member, was able to maintain contact with Dr. Weizmann and his colleagues in London, and with the leaders of the Yishuv in Palestine.

In 1943, with the prospects of victory of the Allied Powers beginning to appear brighter, Zionists began to hope that, out of World War II would come at last the fulfillment of the Zionist program, a Jewish State in Palestine, as officially formulated and adopted early in 1943, at a conference in the Biltmore Hotel, New York City.

It was shortly thereafter, that Dr. Goldstein was elected president of the Zionist Organization of America, succeeding Judge Louis E. Levinthal. At the same time, Rabbi Abba Hillel Silver became co-chairman with Rabbi Stephen S. Wise of the American Zionist Emergency Council which was organized on an inter-party basis to serve as a more effective instrument for dealing with crises.

It was becoming increasingly evident to Zionist leadership in America and elsewhere, that vigorous political action was now required and that the mobilization of American public opinion, in support of the Zionist program, was necessary.

As a first step in this direction, the American Zionist leadership wished to achieve, if possible, the support of the entire American Jewish community for the Biltmore program. For this, and other purposes, the American Jewish Conference was organized. It consisted of organizational representatives, as well as democratically elected representatives of communities. In the popular elections held in New York, Dr. Goldstein came out next to Dr. Wise. In its initial stage, the American Jewish Conference included every important national Jewish organization in America. A resolution for the endorsement of the Biltmore program was adopted by an overwhelming majority; this action was followed by the withdrawal of the American Jewish Committee from the Conference. Nevertheless, despite this regrettable event, the Conference continued to function effectively for several years, addressing itself to a number of problems affecting the American Jewish community. It was headed by three co-chairmen, Henry Monsky, president of B'nai B'rith, Louis Lipsky, and Israel Goldstein.

In the mobilization of American public opinion and in the carrying out of the Zionist program, the Zionist Organization of America, the most important of the Zionist groups, had a significant part to play. During Goldstein's two-year term as president, the Z.O.A. experienced its largest membership growth up to that time, from a membership of 68,000 in 1943 to 138,000 in 1945. It enlarged and improved its publication, *The New Palestine*, and brought in as editor Dr. Ludwig Lewisohn, noted author. It established a Committee on Unity to challenge the anti-Zionist American Council for Judaism; it launched the Committee on Hebrew Arts; it organized a series of radio programs in scores of communities; it established the Zionist Expansion Fund, which raised more than $300,000 in its first year, to support the expanded program of the Organization.

In 1944, Dr. Goldstein participated in hearings before the Foreign Affairs Committee of the House of Representatives on resolutions favoring the establishment of a Jewish State in Palestine. The resolution, which was adopted by the U. S. Congress, was an important step in forwarding the political program of Zionism.

In that year, Goldstein also visited London to ascertain the attitude of the members of the British Cabinet toward the Zionist aim and to convey to them the hopes of the American Jewish community for British help in support of Zionist efforts. He was able to see every member of the war coalition Government, except Winston Churchill, who was then not in the country. He saw Anthony Eden, Ernest Bevin, Clement Attlee, Stafford Cripps, Leopold Amery and Herbert Morrison. He found Amery the most friendly and Bevin the most hostile. He reported the results of the interviews to Dr. Weizmann and the other Zionist leaders in London, and to his Zionist colleagues in America.

Toward the end of 1944, when it was becoming increasingly apparent that the war was in its last stages and, in Allied countries, spirits rose high in anticipation of victory, a shattering shock was in store for the Jewish people. Reports were leaking out from Nazi Germany that millions of Jews in Nazi-occupied Europe had been, and were being, exterminated in the greatest mass-murder in history. There were many Jews who felt that many lives could have been saved if the gates of Palestine had been kept open for Jews by the Mandatory. Now it was felt that a stern warning by the Allied Powers to Nazi Germany might stave off further massacre, and that sporadic possibilities existed to save some thousands by arrangements with some of Hitler's lieutenants seeking to store up credits and cash against the day of reckoning which they knew was not far off. Some contacts were brought to the attention of the World Jewish Congress. Dr. Wise, its president, organized an emergency rescue committee consisting of representatives of a number of leading American Jewish organizations to do whatever was possible. Dr. Goldstein was invited to serve on it. With the help of the United States Government, limited rescue actions were accomplished.

In April 1945, when victory over the Nazi-Fascist axis seemed certain and close at hand, the United Nations Organization Conference was held in San Francisco. A number of American organizations were extended the courtesy by the State Department of giving their representatives the status of consultants and associate consultants. Goldstein was named associate consultant to represent the American Jewish Conference.

The representatives of the Jewish organizations attending the San Francisco Conference were particularly concerned with the drafts of the Trusteeship and Human Rights provisions of the U. N. Charter. As between these two, the Trusteeship question seemed to the Zionist and to the American Jewish Conference delegations to be of more immediate concern. They were eager to make sure that Jewish rights with regard to Palestine, existing under the Balfour Declaration, would not be impaired in the phrasing of the Trusteeship section. In connection with its mission in San Francisco, the Jewish delegations saw Messrs. John Foster Dulles and Harold Stassen of the American delegation as well as members of delegations representing other countries. The Jewish delegations' mission in respect of the Trusteeship section of the U. N. Charter was successful. They joined with others in urging the acceptance of the Declaration of Human Rights.

With victory over Hitler and Mussolini finally achieved in May 1945, Zionist hopes ran high. When V-E Day was being celebrated, Dr. Goldstein was in London attending a meeting of the Zionist Actions Committee which was formulating renewed and vigorous demands for the realization of the Zionist program. Because the plight of the surviving remnant of European Jewry was indescribably pathetic, it was hoped that the British White Paper policy would be cancelled and the gates of Palestine reopened.

In July 1945, two months after the liberation of Germany, Dr. Goldstein visited the German camp for displaced persons in the American Zone of Occupation. Coming as the president of both the Zionist Organization of America and of the Synagogue Council of America, he was the first representative of American Jewry to bring a message of fellowship to these survivors of the Hitler holocaust in Germany. He expressed to them the interest of American Jewry in their welfare, held out the hope that the gates of Palestine might be opened wider, and encouraged them to look forward to the renewal of their lives in the Jewish National Home. Having at his disposal a modest amount of money, Dr.

Goldstein was able also to provide a few added material comforts.

In December 1946, at the twenty-fourth World Zionist Congress in Basle, Switzerland, there was a feeling among many of the delegates that time was running out and that it was necessary to serve notice on the Mandatory Power that, bitterly disillusioned with the Mandatory regime, Zionists were resolved to embark on a more militant policy. Many of the delegates felt that Dr. Weizmann's moderate methods of diplomacy, which had achieved so much on previous occasions, were no longer suited to the current emergency. David Ben-Gurion, Abba Hillel Silver and their followers shared this point of view. On the other hand, Stephen S. Wise, Louis Lipsky, Nahum Goldmann and Moshe Sharett sided with Dr. Weizmann. The sympathies of the majority of the Z.O.A. delegation, including Dr. Goldstein, were with Dr. Silver on this issue. Dr. Weizmann was not reelected president of the World Zionist Organization and the office was left unfilled. Ben-Gurion was elected chairman of the Zionist Executive. Goldstein served as chairman of the Political Commission at this Congress. The resolutions adopted by the American Zionists, at the Biltmore Conference in New York, now became the official platform of the World Zionist Organization.

VI. WORLD CONFEDERATION OF GENERAL ZIONISTS

During the Basle Congress, the World Confederation of General Zionists was established. Dr. Goldstein was unanimously chosen its president and has served in that office for a period of ten years. For many years, as far back as 1931, sporadic attempts had been unsuccessfully made to organize the center party in the Zionist movement. During Goldstein's term as president of the Z.O.A., he had urged the advisability of establishing a General Zionist grouping on a world scale, to counteract and temper the partisanship on the right, represented by the Mizrachi, and on the left, represented by the Labor Zionists. In effect, Jewish Palestine was divided politically along party lines similar to those existing among Zionists in the Diaspora. Complaints were being ventilated by many in Palestine that groups affiliated with parties on the right and on the left were receiving financial aid and moral encouragement from their ideological counterparts abroad, and these parties were achieving power positions in the *Yishuv;* the center groups felt orphaned. Similar complaints were heard from the youth in the displaced persons camps and elsewhere who were seeking opportunities to go to Palestine. It was also felt that a General Zionist Confederation would meet some of these complaints and would also enable General Zionists to play a more vital role at Zionist Congresses and intermittent meetings.

The World Confederation embraced the Zionist Organization of America and Hadassah, in the United States, and General Zionist groups in all other parts of the world, including Palestine, and later, Israel. The World Confederation was the largest single party at the last Zionist Congress, held in Jerusalem in April 1956. Under Goldstein's leadership, the Confederation has established a General Zionist Constructive Fund which, during the past decade, has invested over four million dollars in constructive enterprises in Israel, helping agricultural settlements of both the private and cooperative sectors, subsidizing youth villages, and encouraging small industry. The Fund has also built a six-story Immigrants' Hostel in Tel Aviv, named for Dr. Goldstein, and the Jewish National Fund has named a tract of land for him. The Confederation has been subjected to many strains in the course of its existence, chiefly because of the development in Israel of another center party, the Progressive Party.

The year 1947 was a decisive one. The pressure of refugees desiring to come to Israel was mounting and bursting all legal bounds imposed by the British White Paper policy. "Illegal" ships and immigrants, when caught, were being taken to Cyprus where large numbers of "illegals" were being held to await their turn for inclusion in the legal quota. Dr. Goldstein visited the camp in Cyprus and brought a message of encouragement from American Jewry. As president of the World Confederation of General Zionists, he brought a special greeting to the General Zionist youth among the internees. Even in Cyprus, party alignments dominated the scene—the refugees were being prepared for life in Palestine!

Dr. Goldstein was in Palestine when the S. S. *Exodus,* bringing Jewish displaced persons from Germany, was not permitted by the

British to land its passengers in Haifa and several, including a young American, died as a result of injuries inflicted by the British. Mrs. Golda Myerson (now Meir), and Dr. Goldstein were among those who attended the funeral of the victims.

In the meantime, because the Mandatory regime was becoming more and more intolerable, Zionist leadership in the United States, Palestine and England was preparing to submit its case to the United Nations. Zionist leaders in Israel were arrested one Saturday morning and imprisoned in Latrun. As chairman of the Zionist Executive, Ben-Gurion who happened to be abroad at the time, summoned a meeting of Zionist leaders in Paris, and Goldstein was invited to attend this historic gathering. The discussion centered upon the question of submitting to the Great Powers the demand for a Jewish State in a part of Palestine. Dr. Nahum Goldmann proceeded to Washington to sound out the heads of the American Government. He won the support of President Truman for the proposal.

November 29, 1947, when the United Nations adopted the Resolution, authorizing the establishment of a Jewish State in a part of Palestine, was a great day for all Zionists. Dr. Goldstein was part of the group of American Zionist leaders, headed by Dr. Abba Hillel Silver and Dr. Stephen S. Wise, whose labors, added to those of Dr. Weizmann, Mr. Ben-Gurion, Mr. Moshe Sharett, Dr. Nahum Goldmann, Dr. Emanuel Neumann, Mrs. Rose Halprin and their colleagues abroad, culminated in success.

He was then chairman of the United Palestine Appeal and co-chairman of the United Jewish Appeal, which was headed by Henry Morgenthau, Jr. Goldstein's position obliged him to travel the length and breadth of the country for fund-raising. The year 1947-8 proved to be the peak year in total funds raised by the United Palestine Appeal and the United Jewish Appeal. The raising of one hundred and fifty million dollars was stimulated not only by the passage of the U. N. resolution but also, and to a greater degree, by the attacks of the Arab states upon Israel following the passage of that resolution. That income has not been equalled since.

Whether, in spite of this unprovoked aggression, Zionist leaders should proceed with the implementation of the U. N. November 1947 resolution, was the question discussed by the Zionist Actions Committee at a meeting in Tel Aviv held shortly before Passover 1948, which Goldstein attended; Ben-Gurion favored going ahead, though he confided to the Actions Committee that the *Yishuv* had no military planes or tanks and not even enough rifles to go around. Goldstein was designated chairman of the political committee which was to draft a formal resolution. The draft submitted, written and read out by Mr. Zalman Rubashov (Shazar), authorizing the immediate implementation of the U. N. resolution, was accepted almost unanimously. "The die was cast."

The Actions Committee decided to designate an advisory committee, headed by Dr. Goldstein, to sit in New York with the American members of the Zionist Executive. It was an especially crucial time because great pressure was being exerted upon the Zionist leadership by the, then Secretary of State, General George C. Marshall, and by President Truman to agree to a temporary trusteeship arrangement. The majority resisted this pressure and held its ground. On May 14, 1948, Medinat Yisrael, the State of Israel, was proclaimed in Tel Aviv and a Provisional Government, headed by Ben-Gurion, was set up. Eleven minutes thereafter, President Truman proclaimed the recognition of the new State by the government of the United States.

With the establishment of the State of Israel, the Jewish Agency for Palestine and the Zionist movement were inevitably confronted by the necessity of reorientation and reorganization. When Eliezer Kaplan, who had served many years, with great ability, as treasurer of the Jewish Agency, resigned to become the Finance Minister of the State of Israel, the Zionists Actions Committee elected Dr. Goldstein treasurer in Kaplan's place. This new responsibility obliged him to live in Israel. His congregation granted him a leave of absence for a year. He and Mrs. Goldstein established their residence in Jerusalem.

"The year of my treasurership of the Jewish Agency was the most interesting, the most difficult, and in many respects the most important and the most fruitful of my public career," says Dr.

Goldstein. To some it may have seemed strange that a rabbi should be catapulted into such a position. But apparently it was felt by the leadership of the movement that Goldstein's successful experience and service as head of the Jewish National Fund of America, the Zionist Organization of America and the United Palestine Appeal qualified him for the new and difficult responsibility.

The year of Dr. Goldstein's stay was the first year of Israel's statehood and the peak year of immigration, with 220,000 newcomers, adding nearly one-third to the existing Jewish population of the country. The absorption problem was huge. Despite its meager resources and the fact it was still nursing the wounds inflicted during the Arab war, which had ended in an uneasy armistice, Israel was making heroic efforts to solve this problem. The income from the fund-raising campaigns in the Diaspora, approximately one hundred million dollars that year, was woefully inadequate. The entire budget of the Jewish Agency, affecting not only the program of immigration, absorption and colonization, but also education, organization and youth work, came within the purview of Dr. Goldstein as the treasurer of the Agency. He was charged also with the program of purchase contracts at home and abroad, currency exchanges, arrangement of bank loans from the Bank Leumi in Israel and banks in Switzerland and the United States and, not least of all, concern with the fund-raising campaigns in various countries.

One of Goldstein's most important responsibilities as treasurer was the housing program in Israel. He became the first president of Amidar, the Israel National Housing Company, in which the Jewish Agency, the Government of Israel and the Keren Kayemeth L'Yisrael (Jewish National Fund) joined forces. Amidar constructed tens of thousands of housing units and imported many prefabricated wooden houses. One of its most successful projects was the splendid Afridar development in Ashkelon, made possible by an agreement entered into with representatives of South African Jewry.

One of Dr. Goldstein's special concerns was with Jerusalem itself, the beautiful Holy City which had undergone such extraordinary hardship during the Arab siege. As treasurer of the Jewish Agency, he participated in a number of projects aimed at repairing the damaged areas and encouraging new industries.

Before Dr. Goldstein relinquished the post at the end of the year, and returned to his congregation in New York for the High Holiday season of 1949, a youth village in Katamon, a subsection of Jerusalem, was named in his honor. Thereafter, Dr. Goldstein continued as a member of the American section of the Jewish Agency Executive, to which post he was reelected at the sessions of the World Zionist Congress held in Jerusalem, in 1951 and in 1956.

VII. COMMUNAL LEADER

During the nineteen-thirties, when Israel Goldstein became a recognized Zionist leader, much of the time he could spare from his congregational duties was devoted to many causes outside the Zionist sphere. His communal activities gradually grew in number and importance. These communal activities embraced undertakings of a general, humanitarian nature, as well as internal Jewish concern. During the depression years, Dr. Goldstein served on the New York City Citizens Unemployment Relief Committee. In 1933, he was appointed a member of the United States Department of Labor Committee on Immigration and Naturalization. In 1935, he was a member of the National Labor Relations Board. Later, he was a member of a panel to fix minimum wages in the poultry industry.

Among the non-Zionist communal causes which claimed Goldstein's attention for a time was the chairmanship of the American pro-Falasha Committee in 1930. His interest was aroused by Dr. Jacques Faitlovitch, who was giving his life to educating and helping the Falashas of Ethiopia. Dr. Faitlovitch told of 70,000 Falashas (the word means "strangers") who considered themselves descendants of Israelites. These people maintained a way of life based on the Bible, though they had no knowledge of the Hebrew language. Haile Selassie, then newly-crowned Emperor of Ethiopia, supported the effort to establish a school in Addis Abbaba for teaching and training Falasha boys, so that they in turn might become teachers among their people. The Emperor donated a plot of land for the school. The boys were taught Hebrew, Bible, Jewish history and handicrafts. The American Pro-Falasha Committee was asked to provide funds for the building of the school and the maintenance of the program. The undertaking was seen by Dr. Goldstein as a challenge to do missionary work among one of the "lost tribes" who desired to remain Jews.

A communal activity of which Goldstein is particularly fond is the Jewish Conciliation Board of America, a voluntary tribunal for adjudication and conciliation. In 1929, Dr. Goldstein became its president and has continued in that office since.

The "court" deals only with disputes and complaints that would be difficult to submit to the regular courts, such as complaints of aged parents against children for non-support, minor business altercations, synagogue disputes, disputes in lodges and *"landsmanschaften"* concerning sick benefits and death benefits, and a diverse array of social service problems. A panel of three judges, a rabbi, a lawyer and a businessman sit at every hearing. No fees are charged to the litigants. The hearings are conducted in English or Yiddish, as preferred by the persons involved. There are no formalities, no rules of evidence, and no legal technicalities.

When he became president of the Board, Dr. Goldstein instituted a social service department which follows up the cases after the hearings and tries to be helpful to maladjusted homes and individuals and, where necessary, provides financial assistance, psychiatric help and institutional care. The executive secretary of the Jewish Conciliation Board, from its founding, until his death in 1956, was Louis Richman, a volunteer to whose devotion and competent services Dr. Goldstein credits with being a major factor in the success of this uniquely Jewish social service institution.

Dr. Goldstein's work on behalf of the general war effort during World War II represents another fruitful phase in his career as a communal and civic leader. Shortly after the outbreak of the war, and before the United States entered it, there was organized in this country, under the leadership of Dr. Henry A. Atkinson and Dr. Stephen S. Wise, an Interfaith Committee for Aid to the Democracies, for the purpose of winning American public opinion for the British-French alliance in the war. There was a substantial section of American public opinion which advocated isolationism as American policy, being opposed to the policy which President Roosevelt was propounding, to wit, that the Nazi peril was a world peril which must be met by a policy of collective security among the democracies. The Interfaith Committee for Aid to the Democracies supported and urged this approach.

Dr. Goldstein was invited by Dr. Wise to join this Committee. It undertook to cooperate with the British War Relief Society, headed by Winthrop Aldrich, then president of the Chase National Bank, later, Ambassador to Great Britain. A Jewish Section of the British War Relief Society was formed under Dr. Goldstein's chairmanship. The American Jewish Congress, led by Dr. Wise, gave the impetus to this effort, Goldstein succeeded in bringing in a number of other Jewish organizations and individuals. The Jewish Section adopted as its special projects, the provision of mobile canteens for feeding civilians in British cities which had been the victims of the Nazi Blitzkrieg, and the provision of nursing homes for children evacuated from the "blitzed" areas. One such home was established in the name of Sara Delano Roosevelt, the President's mother, who had died shortly before. Other children's homes were named in honor of Dr. Weizmann, Dr. Wise and Dr. Goldstein.

As soon as the United States entered the war in December 1941, Dr. Goldstein became preoccupied with responsibilities connected with America's own war effort. His synagogue, like other synagogues and churches throughout the land, was a beehive of activity, sewing kits for the soldiers, providing cigarettes, holding dances for soldiers, working for Red Cross and raising funds for it and the United Service Organizations. Three hundred of his congregation's boys and girls joined the armed forces, and seventeen gave their lives.

When Soviet Russia entered the war on the side of the democracies in 1941, a Russian War Relief Committee was organized in the United States. Dr. Goldstein became one of its vice-chairmen.

As the Jewish co-chairman of the National Conference of

Christians and Jews' Commission on Religious Organizations, Goldstein joined Dr. Everett R. Clinchy, president of the NCCJ, and other clergymen in the interfaith trio teams sent by the NCCJ to visit army camps, naval stations and other military installations throughout the country, to bring the message of American unity and interfaith comity, and to interpret the moral and spiritual significance of the war against Nazism and Fascism. Along with a Catholic priest and a Protestant minister, Dr. Goldstein addressed thousands of young Americans, many of whom had never seen or heard a rabbi before, and some of whom had distorted ideas of Jews and Judaism.

In 1943, the same year in which he was elected president of the Zionist Organization of America, Dr. Goldstein was chosen president of the Synagogue Council of America, in which are represented the six leading national Orthodox, Conservative and Reform congregational and rabbinical organizations. During the two war years of his presidency, the Synagogue Council worked together with the corresponding Protestant and Catholic bodies, the Federal (now National) Council of the Churches of Christ in America and the National Catholic Welfare Conference, not only in promoting America's war effort but also in formulating the principles on which world peace should be based, stressing the moral and spiritual postulates of American life, the quality of home and family, and the importance of religious worship and religious education. The holding of two of the top posts in American Jewish life, during the war period, gave Goldstein exceptional opportunities for public service at a time when history was being made.

VIII. BRANDEIS UNIVERSITY

Dr. Goldstein's terms as president, both of the Z.O.A. and the Synagogue Council of America, expired at the end of 1945, shortly after World War II had ended. The resulting lightening of the load of organizational responsibilities enabled him to take up a project of which he had been dreaming for a long time, namely, the establishment of a secular university under Jewish sponsorship. Many others had been dreaming, talking and writing about such a university. But it remained for Dr. Goldstein to give the idea a tangible reality, to become the founder of the first Jewish-sponsored secular university in America, Brandeis University. For this achievement, the present writer believes that Dr. Goldstein will be remembered by future generations as much as for any other of his public services.

Dr. Goldstein himself has told the story in his little book, "Brandeis University: Chapter of Its Founding" (Bloch, 1951). Very briefly, it follows.

Early in 1946, Dr. Goldstein learned that Middlesex University, in Waltham, Mass., a Boston suburb, unable to meet the recognized requirements for such an institution, was about to go out of existence. An opportunity presented itself to acquire the school property, comprising a beautiful campus consisting of 100 acres and several substantial buildings.

Dr. Goldstein conferred with the Board of Trustees and persuaded them to turn over the property to a group of friends whom he had organized, including Julius Silver, a New York lawyer, George Alpert, a Boston lawyer, and a number of others. He assured the Board of Middlesex University that his group was prepared to rehabilitate the existing institution, and in time convert it into a university to be sponsored by the American Jewish community. The proposal by Dr. Goldstein, that the Jewish group be given a majority of places on the Board of Trustees of Middlesex was accepted and thus his group acquired control. Goldstein was then chosen president of the University's new Board of Trustees. To serve as fund-raising instrument for the new project, Dr. Goldstein organized a committee which, with Dr. Einstein's consent, he named the Albert Einstein Foundation for Higher Learning. The incorporators were Israel Goldstein, Julius Silver and George Alpert.

Dr. Albert Einstein was interested in the university project and gave it his active support. With his help, a sponsors' committee, composed of the leading figures in American educational, civic, religious and philanthropic life, also was organized. Shortly thereafter, Dr. Goldstein secured the consent of the family of the late U. S. Supreme Court Justice Louis D. Brandeis to naming the new institution "Brandeis University."

At this juncture, an unfortunate rift occurred between Dr. Einstein and Dr. Goldstein over matters of policy. Confronted with the choice between continuing as leader of the project, thereby risking the possible damage to it from Dr. Einstein's public withdrawal, and eliminating himself in order to ensure Dr. Einstein's continued association with the project, Dr. Goldstein chose the latter course, even though a majority of the Board urged him to remain. It was a heartbreaking decision for Israel Goldstein to withdraw from a project in which he believed so profoundly, but just because his heart was so set on the successful creation of Brandeis University, Goldstein felt that his elimination would do less hurt to the project than Dr. Einstein's withdrawal in a hostile mood. It turned out, however, that this self-sacrifice was vain, because not long after this incident, Dr. Einstein withdrew as a result of differences with Dr. Goldstein's successors.

Dr. Goldstein was succeeded, as president of the Board of Trustees of Brandeis University, by George Alpert. But Goldstein's interest in the successful birth of the university continued. His eight months of leadership, beginning with his securing of the campus, the charter, and the name, laid the foundation of the first Jewish-sponsored secular university in America—a highly significant contribution of the Jewish community to the educational resources of this country.

On April 19, 1949, while Dr. Goldstein was in Israel, American Jewry lost its foremost leader in the death of Dr. Stephen S. Wise, president of the World Jewish Congress and of the American Jewish Congress. For the greater part of Goldstein's public life he had worked at Wise's side as a younger colleague in such important organizations as the Z.O.A., the American Zionist Emergency Council, the United Palestine Appeal and the American Jewish Conference. Together they had appeared at the national convention of the Democratic Party in Chicago in 1944, where they had succeeded in having a pro-Zionist plank made part of the platform of the Party. Sometimes, Wise and Goldstein disagreed but, most of the time, they saw eye to eye. Stephen

Wise's last days were illumined by his faith in the emergence of the Jewish State, which he had lived to see.

Shortly after Goldstein's return to the United States, Dr. Nahum Goldmann, acting president of the World Jewish Congress after the death of Dr. Wise, the President, asked Goldstein to become the chairman of its Western Hemisphere Executive. Goldstein has held that office since 1950, participating actively in the program of the World Jewish Congress, which, through its more than sixty affiliated Jewish communities throughout the world and because of the respect in which it is held by governmental agencies, holds a unique position in Jewish life. It played an important part in the work of rescue during the last days of the Nazi regime, and its documentary material and widely respected experts made a noteworthy contribution to the Nuremberg trials of Nazi war criminals. The Congress has intervened with governments, often successfully, in behalf of their Jewish nationals who were threatened with, or subjected to maltreatment or discrimination. It has played an important part in protecting the rights of Jews in Morocco and Tunisia and in tempering their policy on the emigration of Jews to Israel. Similarly, the World Jewish Congress representatives in the Western Hemisphere were able to aid Jews threatened with unjust treatment in several Latin American countries.

In cooperation with other leading organizations in the United States and other countries, the World Jewish Congress performed a historic task, affecting the lives of multitudes of Jews, through its leading part, under the leadership of Dr. Nahum Goldmann, in the establishment of the Conference of Jewish Organizations on Material Claims Against Germany, and a similar organization for pressing claims on Austria.

The Jewish Restitution Successor Organization, composed of eleven leading Jewish organizations, has been successful in negotiations with the German Federal Government and with provincial governments in what was the American Zone of Occupation, for the restitution to their former owners of property unlawfully seized from them. Most of the proceeds from the heirless property has been divided between the Jewish Agency and the Joint Distribution Committee for aid to survivors of Nazi persecution now living in Israel and in other countries. A large number of books, works of art, Torah scrolls and ritual and ceremonial objects that had been seized by the Nazis from Jewish homes and institutions, including synagogues, were turned over to the Jewish Restitution Successor Organization and were distributed to Jewish communities in Israel and other countries. Since 1951, Dr. Goldstein has served in alternate years as president and chairman of the board, respectively.

When the Conference of Jewish Organizations on Material Claims Against Germany was formed in 1951, Dr. Goldstein was a member of its five-man presidium headed by Dr. Nahum Goldmann, which guided the negotiations, on behalf of the leading Jewish organizations, with the Federal German Republic, while Israel was negotiating for the settlement of its claims. These negotiations resulted in the Luxembourg agreements in which the German government agreed to make reparation for the mass murder of Jews by the Nazis; the reparations were to take the form, primarily, of shipments to Israel of machinery and other capital goods to the aggregate amount of close to three quarters of a billion dollars over a period of twelve years. In addition, the agreement provided for an amount of over one-hundred million dollars to be made available to the leading Jewish organizations, to be used for the relief and rehabilitation of the victims of Nazi persecution. It also provided for legislation for indemnification and restitution to individuals. Since then, Goldstein has served as one of the vice presidents of the Conference.

When a similar committee was formed in 1953, to press Jewish claims on Austria, Goldstein was on its executive committee and participated in the opening conference in Vienna with Chancellor Julius Raab and members of his Cabinet. After intermittent difficulties, these negotiations, too, ended successfully.

These negotiations and their results have been, and continue to be, not only of great significance in Jewish history, but also an important contribution to international law. For the first time in the long history of their persecution, the Jewish people, acting through their representative bodies, have succeeded in wringing from the successors to their persecutors a measure of reparations and restitution. International law has been enriched by this precedent which may serve as a deterrent to persecution of minorities in the future.

In 1951, Dr. Goldstein was elected president of the American Jewish Congress. Two years later he was reelected for another term and, in 1956, he was persuaded to accept a third term, which required an amendment to the constitution limiting the tenure of the president to two terms.

The program of the American Jewish Congress was, and is, concerned not only with the welfare of Jews everywhere and with the deepening of the spiritual content of Jewish life, but also with the defense of civil rights and liberties, the maintenance of the separation of Church and State, and the promotion of better community interrelationships here at home. Among the things the American Jewish Congress has fought for, or against, under Goldstein's leadership have been the following:

1. In favor of an organized American Jewish community. It seemed anomalous that Jewish communities in other parts of the world should have been able to achieve a modicum of central organization, while in American Jewry, all attempts in this direction have been abortive. The nearest approximation to a central organization has been the National Community Relations Advisory Council, organized in 1948. In 1952, however, the B'nai B'rith and the American Jewish Committee seceded when the Council decided to allocate functions among the constituent organizations in order to avoid duplication. The American Jewish Congress led the fight for strengthening the NCRAC and has remained its leading constituent organization;

2. In opposition to patrioteering hysteria, symbolized by U. S. Senator Joseph R. McCarthy of Wisconsin, which in the years 1950-54, under the cloak of an anti-communist crusade, endeavored to discredit American liberalism. The American Jewish Congress was in the vanguard of the fight to resist McCarthyism;

3. In opposition to the McCarran-Walter Immigration Act, in which immigration quotas are based upon so-called national origins which, in effect, place the brand of inferiority upon some nationalities, and which include other reactionary and restrictive

features. Representative Francis Walter of Pennsylvania singled out the American Jewish Congress and its president as his initial adversary;

4. In favor of the continuing progress of the retreat of anti-Semitism in America, as manifested in discrimination in employment, education, housing, etc.;

5. In favor of Negro equality in law and in fact. The American Jewish Congress has rendered valuable aid to the National Association for the Advancement of Colored People in its legal battles, including that which led to the historic decision of the U. S. Supreme Court outlawing segregation in public schools;

6. In opposition to attempts to break down the separation between Church and State, such as religion in the public schools, the denial of unemployment insurance benefits to Sabbath observers, etc.;

7. In strengthening the State of Israel, in the face of its hostile neighbors, by mobilizing the economic and moral support of American Jews and non-Jews on Israel's behalf;

8. In opposition to the Arab propaganda campaign in the United States directed against Jews everywhere, taking such forms as the boycott of Jewish business firms, the denial to Jews of travel visas to Arab countries, the exclusion of American Jewish personnel from the American base in Saudia, and the fomenting of propaganda against Jewish citizens in close collaboration with professional anti-Semites;

9. In strengthening Jewish survivalist forces on the American scene by deepening the content of Jewish education and the program of Jewish living.

As president of the American Jewish Congress, and co-chairman of the World Jewish Congress, Dr. Goldstein visited Jewish communities abroad in order to obtain first-hand information about their conditions and their problems.

In 1952, Dr. Goldstein visited Morocco to acquaint himself with the plight of the Jews there. Early in the summer of 1952, on the heels of the Slansky trial in Prague, which set off a wave of anti-Semitism in many of the communist countries, he visited West Germany to acquaint himself with the refugee flight from East Germany. He found that, of the 2,500 Jews in East Germany,

500 had fled to the West, a much larger percentage than the flight of non-Jews, especially in view of the fact that Jews in East Germany are under strict police surveillance and subjected to abusive treatment by the authorities. He found also that only a small percentage of Germans were genuinely contrite over the massacre of six million Jews during the Hitler regime; for the most part, they were uncomfortable at being reminded, disclaimed knowledge of the Hitler program of exterminating Jews, or exculpated themselves by saying they were powerless to do anything.

Upon the formation of the conference of presidents of the leading American Jewish organizations in support of Israel, Dr. Goldstein was invited to join as president of the American Jewish Congress. As the representative of the National Community Relations Advisory Council, Goldstein appeared before the platform committee of the National Democratic Convention in Chicago in August 1956, and helped to secure the inclusion of planks in support of Israel and against anti-Jewish discriminations as a result of Arab policies.

During these recent years of service of the American Jewish Congress, Dr. Goldstein continued his other activities. In 1951, when the Jewish National Fund marked its fiftieth anniversary, he was invited to serve as chairman of the jubilee celebration in the United States. In the fall of the same year, when the drive to sell Israel Bonds was launched in the United States and David Ben-Gurion, Prime Minister of Israel, came to stimulate the effort, Goldstein was entrusted with the chairmanship of the New York executive committee for Israel Bonds and, the following year, when the organization sponsored a celebration of the 3000th anniversary of Jerusalem by holding a huge rally in Madison Square Garden, New York City, Goldstein presided. Similarly, he served as chairman also of the annual Israel Bond Hanukah rallies held in the same place.

When, in 1953, American Jews began preparations for the observance of the 300th anniversary of the settlement of Jews in North America, in 1654, Dr. Goldstein was elected one of the associate chairmen of the American Jewish Tercentenary Committee. In connection with the celebration, he visited Holland, the motherland of the earliest Jewish settlements in America. He brought a message of greeting to and from the Prime Minister of the Netherlands, Dr. Willem Drees. He also visited Recife, Brazil, whence came the original refugee group to New Amsterdam, as well as Dutch Guiana, Curacao, St. Thomas and Jamaica, which are connected with early American Jewish history. Wherever Dr. Goldstein visited, courtesies were extended to him, not only by Jewish leaders but also by government heads. These visits are described in his book, "American Jewry Comes of Age," a collection of tercentenary addresses.

In February 1956, at the historic merger convention of the American Federation of Labor and the Congress of Industrial Organizations, held in New York, Dr. Goldstein, who had been invited to deliver an address, spoke on "Labor, the Cornerstone of the Free World." Believing the objectives of the labor movement to be completely consonant with the humane ideals of prophetic Judaism, Dr. Goldstein has given active support to that movement, both from his pulpit and from other platforms.

For the same reasons, Dr. Goldstein has been active in the leadership of the American Liberal Party in New York, which was formed as a result of the secession of liberal anti-communists from the American Labor Party when this party fell under the control of communists. The Liberal Party, as its name implies, supports those candidates for office who advocate liberal principles. Dr. Goldstein is honorary vice chairman of the American Liberal Party.

In April and May, 1956, the New York Board of Rabbis, observing its 75th anniversary, designated Rabbi Goldstein as chairman of the celebration.

Israel Goldstein's sixtieth birthday was observed by a series of events arranged to help causes near and dear to him. These included:

1. The launching of a birthday fund for the benefit of the American Jewish Congress, at its biennial convention on April 16, 1956;

2. The announcement by the Hebrew University of Jerusalem

that it would erect on its new campus site "The Israel Goldstein University Synagogue." Funds for this purpose have been provided by Dr. Goldstein's friends, headed by Charles H. Silver, president of the New York City Board of Education and now president of Rabbi Goldstein's congregation. The cornerstone-laying exercises for this religious center were held on May 6, 1956, during the twenty-fourth Zionist Congress. Chief Rabbis Isaac Halevi Herzog and Itzhak Nissim, Mayor Gershon Agron of Jerusalem, president Benjamin Mazar of the Hebrew University, and Dr. Nahum Goldmann, president of the World Zionist Organization, were among the many notables who took part in the ceremony;

3. The decision by the agricultural colony Udim in Israel to build a synagogue to bear the name of Goldstein's congregation, "B'nai Jeshurun";

4. The raising of nearly a million dollars for the United Jewish Appeal at a dinner on June 6, 1956, under the joint auspices of the American Jewish Congress and Congregation B'nai Jeshurun, at which Jewish and Christian leaders in American life paid tribute to Dr. Goldstein, and messages poured in from all parts of the world and from the leaders of Israel.

IX. WRITER, SCHOLAR, HUMANITARIAN

As a leader in the Jewish community and in the general community, Israel Goldstein's chief medium of expression has, of course, been oral. His speeches and sermons are those of a man who is gifted with an unusual talent for forceful and eloquent expression. Yet, despite his preoccupation with community problems, he has, thanks to his boundless energy and administrative skill, been able to find time for a considerable amount of writing.

"Though I have published a few books," says Dr. Goldstein, "I have several manuscripts of books still uncompleted, and I have a feeling of guilt at having neglected Jewish study, feel constantly torn between the book and the deed, and cling to the hope that I may be able to extricate myself from my organizational commitments and responsibilities and get to my books."

It is a testimony to Dr. Goldstein's innate modesty that he

should feel guilty on this score, for the record shows that his contributions as an author have not been inconsiderable. He is the author of: "A Century of Judaism in New York," (1930); "Towards a Solution," (1940); "Brandeis University—Chapter of Its Founding," (1951); all of which have been referred to in this chapter, "American Jewry Comes of Age," (1955) and "Shanah b'Yisrael" (A Year in Israel), (1949), containing the addresses he delivered in Israel during the year he lived there as treasurer of the Jewish Agency. He has contributed scholarly articles to the "Encyclopaedia Britannica Yearbooks" of 1947 and 1948, to the "Universal Jewish Encyclopaedia," and the "Encyclopaedia Hebraica," and has written monographs and articles for various periodicals. In the academic year 1954-55, he served as professor of Jewish History at the University of Judaism of the Jewish Theological Seminary, where he gave a course in contemporary Jewish History.

When asked by the present writer which of his numerous activities have given him the greatest satisfaction, Dr. Goldstein replied: "Among the activities which have occupied me in addition to my primary Congregational responsibilities, I have derived the greatest measure of satisfaction from two types of activity. Foremost has been the satisfaction of serving, expounding and propagating the Zionist ideal in the days when it was fraught with controversy, when many abused and others misunderstood it. To have had a share, however humble, in bringing closer the day of Zionist fulfillment, the establishment of Medinat Israel, was itself the richest of all rewards. Next to it, was the satisfaction of having been called to leadership, under the banner of Jewish unity, in such organizations as the New York Board of Rabbis, Jewish Conciliation Board of America, Synagogue Council of America, American Jewish Conference, American Jewish Congress, World Jewish Congress, Jewish Restitution Successor Organization and Conference of Jewish Organizations on Material Claims Against Germany. These organizations and the work they have done, over-arching the internal differences in Jewish life, have demonstrated the possibilities of Jewish unity on programs which embrace the great common denominators of Jewish life."

This writer has known Israel Goldstein since the latter's student days at the Jewish Theological Seminary. During the intervening years he has observed, with absorbing interest, Goldstein's development, his rise to leadership in so many areas of Jewish life and in civic affairs. It is an amazing career, even for one so richly blessed with innate intellectual and spiritual abilities and sheer physical stamina. Dr. Goldstein's accomplishments in less than four decades would have sufficed to fill the lives of half a dozen persons of average stature.

His amazing energy, his spiritual drive, have been dedicated to the advancement of human, particularly Jewish, welfare. In all his organizational activities, Goldstein has not lost the human touch, has not allowed himself to become a mere dynamo generating energy in Jewish communal life in mechanical fashion. Though he berates himself as "an unrabbinical rabbi," he has maintained the rabbi's profound concern in the welfare of individuals as well as of the community as a whole—as witness his deep attachment to the work of the Jewish Conciliation Board, where he meets the plain people and helps them untangle some of their knotty problems.

His innate humanitarianism lies behind Israel Goldstein's understanding approach to people and problems. He not only sympathizes with the sufferings and sorrows of the individual, but also understands and respects his thoughts and ideals even when he disagrees with them.

His many friends in this country, in Israel and elsewhere, love Israel Goldstein for his human sympathies, for his tact, for his special oratorical and organizational abilities, and for his sense of dedication. They all, including this writer, wish him many more years of fruitful activity on behalf of the Jewish people, Israel, America and all mankind.

APPENDIX

Excerpts from the addresses

and writings

of Dr. Goldstein

EXCERPTS FROM THE ADDRESSES AND THE WRITINGS OF

DR. ISRAEL GOLDSTEIN

Selected by the Editor

RELIGION

What Does Religion Say?

What does Religion say? What is its message, divested of its outer habiliments, theological doctrines, organized institutional forms, rituals and ceremonies? X-rayed to its very essence, what is the essential message of Religion?

1. The individual has a worth and dignity of his own. His soul is a part of God. He is more than a cog in a wheel. His pain and his degradation dare not be ignored. Even the ruler of a State is called to account when he trespasses upon the rights of his individual subject witness the Hebrew prophets' reprimand of David and excoriation of Ahab. There are inalienable human rights.

2. Morals and ethics are not timely expedients but timeless imperatives. Standards of right and wrong apply not only to individuals but to nations. The notion that nations, in the eyes of their subjects, can do no wrong is perverted patriotism. Hence the diatribes of the Hebrew prophets against Egypt and Babylonia, Moab and Edom, Israel and Judah, when they transgressed the moral law. Moral standards are universal. No nation dare put itself in the place of God.

3. The unity of mankind is as inevitable in the pattern of man's creation as the flower is inevitably in the seed. To say that God Is One is another way of saying that Man Is One. The Hebrew legend has it that the dust from which Adam was created was gathered from all the ends of the earth. Other religious traditions have legends of similar purport. . . .

4. The human race is improvable. Religion takes a hopeful view of the future. Whether the doctrine is called Messianism or by whatever other name, Religion affirms man's capacity, as a creature endowed with freedom of will, to improve his ways, and to achieve moral progress, however slow the process may be. When one contemplates the disparity between the pace of scientific

advance and the pace of moral advance, one is discouraged; but when one understands why it is so, one is reassured. . . . Considering that civilization is only 6,000 years old, a mere moment compared with the millions of years that the species Man has been upon earth, it is Man's progress, slow but forward, rather than his lack of progress, which is noteworthy. One is justified in looking forward to an evolution of ever higher standards in man's moral concepts and practices. What is important is the long range trend.

5. There is a moral gravitation in human history. Just as there is a physical gravitation which guarantees the integrity and stability of the physical universe, so there is a moral gravitation in human affairs. It is another way of saying that God underwrites the ultimate vindication of the moral verities such as have been embodied in the codes of the great religions.

—"A Free World and Its Spiritual Foundations," *Current Religious Thought,* XII: 1, January-February, 1952

What Religions Have in Common

We are here, thank God, to affirm that Religion need not serve as a barrier but can and should be a bond, that we who profess different religious faiths have more in common that we have in difference.

However much we may differ in the terminology, we have in common an outlook upon life which denies the primacy of material factors. We have in common a conviction of the reality of the spiritual forces in the universe. We have in common a devotion to the establishment of social motivations in human conduct. We hold in common a denunciation and renunciation of war as the goal of a nation's life. We hold in common a hopeful view of humanity's future, a belief in the capacity of the human race for spiritual progress. By these considerations, we are, I believe, bound together.

—"Toward a Solution" (New York: G. P. Putnam's Sons, 1940), p. 71.

On Being A Jew

There is something everyone of us can do to give more content to the Jew within him, intellectual content and emotional content. It can be cultivated by study and by service. Affiliation with Jewish causes

—the Synagogue, Zionism, philanthropy, offer opportunities to act Jewishly and to serve Jewishly. Intellectual content can be acquired by reading and study. Even more imperative than gaining intellectual content ourselves, is the duty of giving it to our children. The most unbearable suffering is to suffer without knowing wherefore. It is doubly tragic that a people should "perish without knowledge." The old Socratic formula, "Know thyself," devolves upon us and upon our children.

What then makes Jews Jews? Is the term "Jew" a racial designation, a religious label or a national epithet? It is none of these alone. Being a Jew, in the broadest definition, means, first, the accident of birth; secondly, the act of choice, choosing to remain a Jew despite the difficulties; thirdly, the act of cognition, learning to know the history and literature of his people so as to understand its soul and appreciate its place in the world; and, finally, the act of transmission, transmitting to the next generation his heritage and the will to carry it on so that the Jewish people may not perish from the earth.

—"Toward a Solution" (New York: G. P. Putnam's Sons, 1940), pp. 84-85.

Nature of Judaism

The program of the Synagogue in its broadest aspect converges on the ennoblement of individual character and the improvement of the social order. The culmination of our daily prayer is the hope "to improve the world under the Kingdom of God."

No religion has defined daily conduct as meticulously as Judaism. In the Old Testament, justice is defined in terms of reparation of damages when a man's cattle grazes in the field of another. Liberty is defined in terms forbidding any men to sell himself into permanent slavery. Tolerance is defined in terms of cautioning against the oppression of the stranger. Charity is defined in terms of the command that the corners of the field and the gleanings of the harvest belong to the poor, the widow and the orphan.

If the Law of Moses is a textbook in practical idealism, the utterances of the Hebrew prophets also project the utlimate goals. They were the first to envisage and proclaim universal Peace, Brotherhood, Justice, the ideals of which have been invoked and repeated since their time by all the protagonists of a better dispensation for humanity.

—"Toward a Solution" (New York: G. P. Putnam's Sons, 1940), pp. 93-94.

THE AMERICAN JEWISH COMMUNITY

Evaluation of American Jewry

I venture the opinion that, while we have fulfilled our American responsibilities well, we have fulfilled our Jewish responsibilities only half well. This evaluation would not be worth much if it did not point up our shortcomings as well as our virtues. Wherein, then, have we fallen short? We have fallen short in the spiritual-cultural quality of Jewish life. Spiritually and culturally as Jews we have been living for the most part on unearned capital, the capital imported from the European homesteads. These transfusions of Jewish vitality from abroad are now virtually at an end, not only because immigration has been reduced to a mere trickle, but especially because the sources have dried up, due to Hitler's holocaust of European Jewry and the fact that the more than two million Jews behind the Iron Curtain are incommunicado and that the vast majority of them have been forcibly alienated from Judaism and Jewish culture. We may as well face up to the fact that, except for such vitalizing influences as may come from Israel, we are on our own. Are we capable of being a self-sustaining Jewry, culturally and spiritually?

The picture has some elements of reassurance but not enough. Our synagogues are numerous and respectable but their influence is superficial. They have broadened their dimensions but they have not deepened their stakes. Religious education has become somewhat more contentful in recent years, but the improvement has started from a very low base. *Yeshivoth* and all-day Jewish schools have sprung up but in relatively small numbers. The majority of Jewish children still belong to the "know-nothing party."

Can such a community be counted on to be the twin pillar to Israel, on which the tabernacle of the Jewish future must rest? Will American Jewry, at least in measure, compensate for the spiritual-cultural casualties we have suffered in Europe, where scores of communities, each an *aym b'Yisroel*—an *alma mater* of Judaism with scholars, poets and saints—nourished the Jewish intellect and spirit everywhere? The answer is in the womb of time. I take no pleasure in jeremiads, but neither can we afford to indulge ourselves in grandiloquent illusions. It behooves us to know wherein we have fallen short. And the awareness of our shortcomings is the indispensable first step toward overcoming them.

—"American Jewry Comes of Age" (New York: Bloch Publishing Co., 1955), pp. 131-132-133.

American Jewry in the Past Forty Years

Not all the New World values in American Jewish life are unmixed blessings. For too many Jews the program of fighting anti-semitism has become a moral equivalent for the Synagogue. We are an over-organized community, yet not organized enough. There is a plethora of overlapping and duplicating organizations. Yet the leading Jewish community, New York, is still without a Kehillah, daunted by the failure of its attempt to organize one forty years ago. On the national level, American Jewry still waits for a framework of democratic unity and, in the meantime, struggles to come together *ad hoc*-wise from emergency to emergency. Only in philanthropy has American Jewry achieved efficient, democratic unity. . . .

American Jewry's shining hour, however, was when it played a notable part, second only to that of the *Yishuv* in Palestine, in providing material support and in winning the political support of the American people and government for the Jewish National Home and then for Medinat Israel. In the final stages non-Zionists joined with Zionists. As it brought strength to Israel, American Jewry strengthened itself as well, for help to Zion nourishes the bond of Jewish brotherhood and feeds the wells of Jewish selfhood. This will be American Jewry's crowning credential in the history of our times.

—"American Jewry Comes of Age" (New York: Bloch Publishing Co., 1955), pp. 118-119.

Jewish Survival in America in Year 2054

Will there be a vital Jewish community on hand in these United States in the year 2054? Jewish survival has been the gauge of our responsibility as Jews from 1654 to the present day. By the same gauge, we of today and our successors of tomorrow and tomorrow will be judged at the time of the American Jewish quatro-centenary. . . .

Barring a world catastrophe or a social upheaval in the United States, there is every reason to look ahead to a *hemshech*, to Jewish continuity. But it will not come of itself. The social forces conducive to the disintegration and the assimilation of the Jewish group culture into that of the general environment will be increasingly pervasive. They will have to be resisted and countered by the forces of survival with the emphasis on maintaining, in consonance with the general culture, the integrity, character and uniqueness of the Jewish culture.

The compactness of Jewish neighborhoods in the cities and the gregarious social trends of Jewish communities in the suburbs will be cohesive factors. Jewish charities at home and abroad will keep Jews mindful of other Jews. I trust that the kind of Jewish self-awareness which reacts only to anti-Semitism will not be part of the picture. Positive stimulation will be available from two sources: one, the Synagogue, the other, Israel.

—"American Jewry Comes of Age" (New York: Bloch Publishing Co., 1955), pp. 133-134.

Higher Education Under Jewish Auspices

If there is still a residue of mental reservation, let it be weighed against the arguments on the other side in favor of the idea, namely the benefits which may result from following the example of other denominational groups, the value of having it known that a Jewish-sponsored university is a non-quota university, so that our fight against the quota system would have a powerful weapon in the very existence of such an institution, and the dignity of the Jewish group which would be enhanced by its contribution to American higher education. . . .

From the point of view of the training of Jewish leadership, it is not to be overlooked that in a Jewish-sponsored university there would be extra-curricular Jewish influences available for the benefit of Jewish students, both secular and religious influences calculated to mold the young people who are to be the leaders of tomorrow in American Jewish life. These influences would not be compulsory but would be so attractive and so accessible as to be compulsive.

—"Brandeis University: Chapter of Its Founding" (New York: Bloch Publishing Company, 1951), p. 131.

ZIONISM

The Concept of a Jewish Peoplehood

Jewish peoplehood is the over-arching term of Jewish identity. It has been, however, characteristic of this people's self-evaluation that it has not regarded its own existence as the absolute end in itself but as a means towards the realization of the larger end—the ideal society of justice, righteousness and peace. "This people have I created that it may declare My glory." It is within that ultimate frame of reference that Jewish peoplehood is the over-arching term of Jewish identity.

There have been periods in Jewish history when the term "Jewish people" was coterminous with the Jewish State. Those periods, however, have been the exception rather than the rule in the 4,000 years of our history. For the greater portion of that span and even during periods when Judaea was a sovereign state, Jewish populations and Jewish communities have lived outside Eretz Israel. Never before, however, was there a situation such as exists today when, during the existence of a Jewish State, four-fifths of the Jewish people lives outside of that State. So the term "Jewish people" has meant and continues to mean more than the term "Jewish State."

The principal concern of the Jewish people, as of every people, is its survival, not only its physical survival, but its cultural and spiritual survival, which, in the case of our people, is the essence of its *raison d'etre*. The primary obligation of every Jew, therefore, is to make his best contribution toward that objective. Whenever and wherever this sense of obligation is lacking, it is a pathological symptom—that there is something fundamentally wrong with him as a Jew.

There have been three main positive factors for safeguarding Jewish survival. One has been the Jewish State, the existing reality, or, when the reality of statehood was suspended, the aspiration for its re-establishment. The other factor has been *Torah u-mitzvot*, the spiritual-cultural-ethical content and the mores of the Jewish heritage. A third factor has been altogether psychological, the sense of Jewish unity, bridging over all the differences of geographical locations and sociological complexions. Whenever and wherever these three factors have been intertwined, the ideal conditions for Jewish survival have existed.

—Address, World Jewish Congress, Third Plenary Assembly, Geneva, Switzerland, August 6, 1953.

What Is a Zionist?

There have been many attempts at defining Zionism. Here is mine. A Zionist is a Jew who desires the survival of the Jewish people physically, culturally and spiritually, recognizing Medinat Israel and working for it as the chief instrument of such survival, who endeavors to invest his own life and the life of his community with Jewish survival content, and who believes that the highest fulfillment of Jewish living can best be achieved in Israel.

According to this definition, a Jew whose help to Israel is motivated by admiration of its pioneering qualities or by the recognition of its value as a haven for the homeless, or as an outpost of democracy, but who is not concerned with the physical-cultural-spiritual survival of the Jewish people or does not endeavor to translate that concern in the pattern of his life and the life of his community, or who feels no limitation upon Jewish self-fulfillment in the Diaspora, such a Jew would be cherished as a valuable friend of Israel but could not be considered a Zionist.

—Presidential address, Conference of World Confederation of General Zionists, Jerusalem, April 22, 1956.

Program for American Zionists

Zionist organizations and individuals should be expected to stress the positive values of Jewish education and the Hebrew language in particular. They should utilize every opportunity to take part in the affairs of the general Jewish community, endeavoring to mold its character more and more Jewishly, and they should play an important role in the effort to safeguard the position of the Jewish Community within the general community, seeking to safeguard its viability and its civic, economic, religious and cultural rights. They should recognize that the ideal Jewish life is life in Israel and even if they themselves might feel constrained to remain where they are, they should encourage others to undertake *Chalutziuth* and *Aliyah*. Non-Jewish public opinion would respect those who would go to Israel because of idealistic considerations just as they understand sympathetically those who go there to escape homelessness, economic misery and political oppression.

—Presidential address, Conference of World Confederation of General Zionists, Jerusalem, April 22, 1956.

Zionism and the State of Israel

A word needs to be said about Israel's relationship to such a Zionist movement. It would have to be a two-way traffic. Not enough has been done by Israel's leadership to make its native youth, the *sabras,* who will be the leaders of tomorrow, feel a deep tie of kinship with the Jewish people the world over. Zionism, in the sense of Jewish collective security, Jewish interdependence and Jewish peoplehood, is needed as much in Israel as anywhere. The *sabra* may resent the necessity of depending upon Jews outside Israel for material help. It is hoped that within a decade Israel will be self-support-ing. Moral, cultural and spiritual interdependence, however, will be a permanent desideratum for the sake of Israel as for the sake of Diaspora Jewry. Otherwise Israel may become spiritually and cul-turally ingrown, sterile and impoverished. The Zionist movement, through its spokesmen and leaders in Israel, has the responsibility to impress this lesson upon the Israeli segment of the Jewish people.

—Presidential address, Conference of World Confederation of General Zionists, Jerusalem, April 22, 1956.

The Jewish National Fund

"What's in a name?" may be a good rhetorical question. The fact is, however, that a name is often the key to the personality of an idea, an institution or a movement. The Jew has intuitively felt great respect for names and has given names with great care. The name of "Keren Kayemeth LeIsrael—Jewish National Fund," with all its impli-cations, sentimental, economic and political, is the key to what it has been in effect, the most popular Jewish institution, the most idealistic, and at the same time the most practically useful Jewish institution, the most characteristic and the most character-building Jewish institu-tion. True to its name, may it prove to be the most enduring institu-tion of the Jewish people.

—"Toward a Solution" (New York: G. P. Putnam's Sons, 1940), pp. 293-94.

The World Jewish Congress and World Zionist Organization

The interaction and the interrelationship between Israel and Dia-spora Jewry is cardinal to the survival of both. Here the World Jewish Congress has an important role to fulfill, complementary to that of the World Zionist Organization. While the Zionist organiza-tion cultivates the Israel-Diaspora tie as a movement which is Israel-tropic and Israel-centered, the World Jewish Congress is Judaea-tropic and Judaea-centered. The suggestion heard occasionally that the Zionist Organization take over the functions of the World Jewish Congress, it seems to me, is not well thought out. It is fraught with danger to the Zionist Organization. The tasks of winning support for Israel and of seeking to protect local Jewish rights require two separate organizations. Situations may arise where the effectiveness of the Zionist Organization in conducting its primary obligation may be weakened or even endangered by its being identified simultaneously with a different function. The two purposes may be complementary but they are not identical. But because the two tasks are complementary, because the World Jewish Congress program lays so much stress on Israel, and because Zionists have been its founders and leaders, Zionists everywhere should see in the World Jewish Congress the natural medium for their participation in the program of protecting Jewish rights on an international scale and in the promotion of the unity of the Jewish people.

—Address, World Jewish Congress, Third Plenary Assembly, Geneva, Switzerland, August 6, 1953.

Promoting the Hebrew Language Among American Jews

The Hebrew language is essential for Jewish cultural and spiritual survival in America. There is no case in Jewish history where a Jewish community survived without an Hebraic culture.

The Zionist movement has a major responsibility to prevent the threat of Jewish cultural bankruptcy in American Jewish life, but it is the responsibility of all Jews and of all Jewish leaders. No American Jew has the right to be called a Jewish leader unless he feels and exercises a sense of concern with Jewish education and Hebraic culture. The Zionist movement has a special responsibility because it places in the very center of its program, Jewish creative living and Jewish cultural survival wherever Jewish communities dwell, and a bond of Hebraic culture between Israel and Jewry outside Israel. Since we lay claim to being the guardians of this sphere of responsibility, we Zionists must be judged more severely in this respect than any other group.

It would be a sin against the *ruah ha-kodesh,* the inspiration of this new day of Medinat Israel, the new springtime of Jewish history, if we neglected to use this springtime for the purpose of stimulating an Hebraic springtide in American Jewish culture. The springtime text of *Shir ha-Shirim* may well be paraphrased. *Et hazamir higiah v'kol halashon od lo nishmah b'artzenu.* The time in which we live, the era of Medinat Israel, is right for the sweet music of the Hebrew word to be sounded, but the Hebrew tones are not yet heard sufficiently in this land.

The Hebrew word must grow and flourish here on the American

Jewish scene. Like the ancient ark in the wilderness, it will carry those who will carry it.

—Address, luncheon of Histadruth Ivrith, April 7, 1957.

ISRAEL

American Policy and the State of Israel

The infant State of Israel is the immediate target for destruction by its hostile neighbors. But also the vital interests of the United States are at stake. I speak not only of considerations of morality and democracy where to be cynical is to be un-American. Of what value are our preachments on international morality and our pretentions to America's place as the leader of the democracies, if Israel, the only genuine democracy in the Middle East, which the United States has helped to bring into existence, is to be thrown to the wolves because it is guilty of the "sin" of being meager in population, in area and in oil?

The Administration in Washington is offering words as a substitute for action, and sometimes the action or lack of action belies the words. We are told that American policy in the Middle East is one of "friendly impartiality" and that "the preservation of Israel is part of American foreign policy." In fact, however, our policy has been pro-Arab, and the preservation of Israel is being jeopardized. Let no one obscure the issue by blaming underlings in the State Department. These policies have been defined and declared at the summit of American responsibility. Our President and our Secretary of State will be accountable to the American people and to the Free World if, God forbid, anything untoward should befall Israel.

We cannot repeat too often that in the strategic Middle East area Israel holds the front line of the Free World's defenses against the Communist threat of penetration. Israel's peril today may be the peril of the Free World tommorrow. The United States cannot be permitted to evade its responsibility.

We believe that the failure of the United States to support the democracy of Israel, in the one area of the world in which there is a clear distinction between democracy and dictatorship, would be unconscionable. We seek for the Arab peoples in the Middle East the same prosperity, the same level of health, the same literacy, the same freedom, the same equality, which we seek for the people of Israel. We want to see the United States extend to them all these forms of aid—but only on condition that they maintain peace with Israel.

—Presidential Address, American Jewish Congress Biennial Convention, New York, April 12, 1956.

What Israel Has the Right to Expect of World Jewry

What has Israel the right to expect of world Jewry?

It has the right to expect a steady sense of attachment to Israel and a steady sense of commitment to its welfare, expressing itself in moral and material support and in contributions of skills and of manpower. *Aliyah* and *Chalutziuth* are important, not only for Israel but also for the Jewish community whence they come, because they are a living bond between both, a ferment of Jewishness in the local community and a nucleus around which Jewish and Hebraic values crystallize. A small state surrounded by Arab neighbors will always require a hinterland of Jewish attachment and support.

Israel has the right to expect of world Jewry an abiding resistance to the forces of assimilation, so that it may have a continuing reservoir of strength on which to draw, and the Jewish people may always have Diaspora Jewry as well as Israel to guarantee Jewish survival.

—Address, World Jewish Congress, Geneva, Switzerland, August 6, 1953.

Diaspora Jewry's Response to Israel's Expectations

Is Diaspora Jewry measuring up to these expectations?

The record of American Jewry in providing manpower for Israel has been meager. Yet the prospects for the future are not to be written off if in Israel greater attention will be given to developing ways and means of attracting non-emergency *Aliyah*. The record of American Jewry in providing material support is impressive, indeed decisive, though still inadequate in proportion to its capacity and to Israel's needs. Its best performance, in my opinion, has been in securing America's moral and political support for Israel. This support has been, next to the heroic efforts of the Jewish community in Palestine, the greatest single factor in the establishment of the Jewish State. It must continue for the sake of Israel's future existence.

If a new test should be in the offing for American Jewry on this front, if there should be inclinations in American political quarters to make some changes in its Middle East policies, will American Jewry stand up to the test of exerting every effort to resist and overcome them even at the risk of unpopularity and abuse in certain circles? I believe American Jewry will not be found wanting, will remember the valiant example of British Jews during the Bevin era, and, best of all, their own splendid record during difficult stages in the Zionist struggle in the United States, where they persisted until the American people and government were persuaded of the righteousness of their cause. American Zionists will again have to provide the initiative and the leadership. It is my conviction that, as happened before, many who are unaffiliated, or who call themselves non-Zionists, will be found worthy in the hour of testing. With the exception of a meager, albeit vociferous eccentric frenetic fringe, the American Jewish community is dominated by a deep and weatherproof love for Israel.

—Address, World Jewish Congress, Geneva, Switzerland, August 6, 1953.

What Diaspora Jewry Expects of Israel

What has Diaspora Jewry the right to expect of Israel?

Perhaps the posing of the question is somewhat premature since Israel has had enough to cope with in the sheer struggle to keep alive. On the other hand, it may not be too early to chart a few desirable directions. Thoughtful Israelis themselves are beginning to project this question upon the consciousness of their people.

Statehood, be the area small or large, is a source of dignity for the people in the state and for their kin outside. . . . The moral and ethical caliber of the Jewish State, the quality of its everyday life, its domestic policies and its stand on world issues constitute its highest justification. Medinat Israel has the opportunity to demonstrate anew the Old Testament synthesis between nationalism and universalism, the State as the instrument of Israel's mission to be "a light unto the nations," a small physical unit become a great spiritual force. Such a state would, of course, redound to the credit of the Jewish people everywhere. Israel must be more than just another statelet on an overcrowded map.

The Jewish people looks to Israel for specifically Jewish nourishment, that it be a cultural-spiritual fountainhead to nourish arid Jewish areas in other lands. Most eagerly the Jews of the world hope that the Jews of Israel may feel a community of interest, understanding and concern with the Jewish people everywhere, an indissoluble bond, and the call of a common destiny. This feeling should stem as much from a sense of Jewish unity and mutuality as from a sense of practical interest in an important source of strength for itself. . . .

—Address, World Jewish Congress, Geneva, Switzerland, August 6, 1953.

INTERGROUP RELATIONS

Brotherhood

Brotherhood is not only a concept but also a responsibility based upon respect for all human beings. It is well that we Americans should test our own sense of brotherhood by the following searching questions:

1. Do we feel the push of conscience to help improve the living conditions of groups in sub-standard environments, or are we satisfied to leave well enough alone?
2. Do we welcome rather than resent the racial and cultural "mores" of our neighbors which happen to be different from our own, recognizing that diversity under unity is an enriching experience for America?
3. Are we ready to admit that other nations may be superior to ours in some respects and that we have something to learn from others?

I think it may be said of America that, both internally and in its relations with other countries, it has made progress in brotherliness. The early American policy of rugged individualism has been in recent years considerably mitigated by a sense of national responsibility to provide increasing safeguards against exploitation of the weak by the strong. In our foreign relations we have expended huge amounts of money, not always wisely albeit well-intentionally, on the premise that our own enlightened self-interest required that we help other nations help themselves economically.

—Address, Brotherhood Award to the Hon. Paul G. Hoffman, at Congregation B'nai Jeshurun, February 16, 1957.

Christian Understanding of the Jew

It is the first principle which needs to be emphasized, though it should seem axiomatic, that the responsibility for harmonious intergroup relations rests chiefly upon the majority group. The achievement of harmonious Christian-Jewish relations in this country is primarily, therefore, a Christian responsibility.

In the fulfillment of his responsibility, the Christian needs first to understand the Jew, and, second, to psychoanalyze his own prejudices against the Jew.

Sometimes the Jew is charged with being clannish. It is averred that even when he has the opportunity of free and easy intercourse with the non-Jew, he fails to make the most of the opportunity, and in many cases even sets up a psychological resistance. As a categorical observation, it is, of course, unfounded. Countless instances can be cited of friendships and comradeships between Christians and Jews which are free from the slightest strain or uneasiness.

Insofar as the observation is true, the Christian who is bent upon understanding the Jew will realize that nineteen centuries of persecution leave a heritage of fear and mistrust which cannot be erased as quickly as desired. He will also come to perceive something of the dilemma which confronts the Jew who, desiring to preserve Judaism and perpetuate it through his children, is troubled as to how far fraternization with the non-Jew can proceed without leading to the breaching of the "fences of the Law," and even to intermarriage.

The Christian who tries to understand the Jew will also understand the feeling of the Jew that, in seeking to preserve and perpetuate Judaism, he is engaged not only in self-preservation, which is a legitimate enough ambition, but also in preserving a culture which by general consent enriches humanity as a whole.

He will understand why the Jew resents Christian proselytizers, and has mistrusted any 'Goodwill" movement which is motivated by an ulterior purpose. Jews concede that Christianity is an adequate religion and way of life for Christians, but insist the Judaism is adequate for Jews and offers them all that is needed both for the here and the hereafter.

He will understand that so-called Jewish manners and mannerisms are not Jewish but traits carried over from former environments. He will understand that the inclination of the Jew to gravitate toward business and the professions is not a racial trait but a sociological aftermath, the result of having been barred from other avenues of livelihood and that, given a chance, as in present-day Palestine, to normalize his life, he can excel in agriculture no less than in business, in handicraft no less than in the professions.

Understanding is the solvent of prejudice. When the Christian understands the Jew he will find it difficult to nurture prejudices against him.

—"Toward a Solution" (New York: G. P. Putnam's Sons, 1940), pp. 56-57.

Anti-Semitism in the United States

I am frequently asked whether anti-Semitism is increasing or decreasing in the United States. Organized defamation by professional anti-Semites continues to decline steadily, with the rabble-rousers unable to gain either popular or financial support and with no indication that they are even attempting to weld their scattered forces into one movement.

The Jewish quota in medical schools will, I hope, soon be a thing of the past. A recent survey in New York State, where the quota was once most severe, showed that almost half of the medical students in ten schools in that state were Jewish. In employment, however, the picture is not so rosy, despite FEPC laws of varying degrees of effectiveness in fifteen states. In Illinois (a state without an FEPC law), a recent survey shows a widespread practice of issuing job orders to employment agencies that contained the legend "No Jews wanted." Generally speaking, seventy-five percent of the Jewish population in the United States are in states where there are fair employment laws, while only twenty percent of the non-white population, principally Negro, are similarly protected. Discrimination in housing continues to be a nuisance, not a menace. There are scattered areas, principally in the suburbs and in swanky resorts, which are *Judenrein*. . . .

One of the most important indications, that of popular attitudes, shows a significant change has taken place in the last ten years, if we can accept the scientific evidence of responsible public opinion polls. They show substantial declines in the amount of Jewish stereotyping, in the amount of latent hostility, and, most significant, in the number of persons willing to act upon their prejudices. . . .

—Address, United Synagogue of America, National Biennial Convention, Kiamesha Lake, New York, November 14, 1955.

Arab Anti-Jewish Agitation

The latest attempt to hurt and degrade American Jews comes from Arab governments and their representatives in the United States. It takes several forms, the boycott of business firms owned wholly or partly by Jews; the Arabs' denial of visas to Americans of the Jewish faith; the prohibition of the right of American Jewish military personnel to serve in the defense forces of their own country on Arab soil; and the well-financed, Arab government-inspired, anti-Jewish propaganda in this country in connivance with fascist anti-Semitic hate groups. American citizens have the right to expect of the American government a modicum of dignity and self-respect in dealing with these offenses. It is nothing less than nauseating to see our State Department cringing and crawling, when the kind of moral issues are involved to which previous administrations, Republican and

Democratic, reacted unequivocally and firmly. . . . We have a right to ask our government why it has yielded to this discrimination against American citizens; why it has denied a group of its citizens equal protection; why it has disowned American tradition; why it has permitted a slavery-ridden Saudi Arabia to determine which Americans may defend America and which Americans may not. We will call upon our government to declare that representatives of foreign lands who, under the cloak of diplomatic immunity, are doing Hitler's work in exporting anti-Semitism to the United States, are *personae non gratae* to the American people.

—Presidential Address, American Jewish Congress Biennial Convention, New York, April 12, 1956.

Reacting to Anti-Semitism

There are two ways in which the Jew can react to anti-Semitism. There is the reaction on the higher level and the reaction on the lower level. Reacting on the lower level, he can cry out against the physical persecution he suffers, and his cry is as right as the instinctive cry of an animal against its attacker. On the higher level, however, the Jew can rededicate himself to his heritage with all the greater zeal, knowing that he stands for eternal values which will prevail long after his opponents' era will have been forgotten.

When we understand that, then we lift our burden from a low plane to a high plane. . . . It makes a great difference in the state of our souls whether we are excoriated for our faults, or we are hounded for our virtues. . . .

There are men, sensitively souled, high-minded men, who, when their cause is just, would rather be the persecuted than the persecutors. We recall on Kol Nidre such a man in Germany, a German professor, Emil Granauer of Hanauer University, who with his wife and children embraced Judaism as a protest against Nazi persecutions. We recall the great French writer, Romain Rolland, who said in an open letter to the Jews of Poland, "I regret I am not a Jew, because I am ashamed of the record of my Christian brothers." Let us be sure that, if the world's wrath we must bear, we bear it for reasons of which we can be proud. Let us become conscious ourselves and make our children conscious of the best motives of our history, and of the highest purposes of our destiny.

—"Toward a Solution" (New York: G. P. Putnam's Sons, 1940), pp, 157-158.

Vision of America

Let our vision for America not fail to encompass the moral aspect. A nation as great as it is strong, whose affluence is matched by its character, a land whose shores contain not so much a melting pot amalgam as an orchestra whose every racial strain and religious heritage lends unique enrichment, a people that still welcomes the stranger at the gate; a nation so confident of its democracy that it is not afraid to expose its mind to the free market of ideas, a land where the color of the skin no longer makes a man less or more than a man, a people seeking to win the world not alone with armaments and dollars but also with ideas and human sympathy; a nation renewing its youth as an eagle, a land reclaiming its title as a new heaven and a new earth, a people under God whose children pronounce a three-fold benediction, once upon its past, once upon its present and once upon its future. To such a vision of America let us be dedicated.

—Address, AFL-CIO Merger Convention, New York, December 6, 1955.

DOMESTIC AMERICAN PROBLEMS

Church-State Relationship

The other problem is that of the Church-State relationship. It holds possibilities of interfaith tensions. There is and probably will continue to be more and more, an insurgent attempt on the part of some of the Christian religious groups to insert breaches, however small, in the traditional American wall of separation between Church and State. The public schools have been selected as the main objective. It is an on-going effort which will persist for many years to come. I shall not repeat the arguments pro and con relating to the proposals for opening prayers, Bible reading, and the teaching of moral and spiritual values based on a belief in God. The fact that the proponents are willing in the final test to accept even the merest and the vaguest of religious affirmations, which cannot possibly have any real influence, leads to the conclusion that they have a long-range, step-by-step strategy in mind. It is not easy for Jewish spokesmen to resist the united Catholic urging and the predominant Protestant agreement. Yet we have no choice but to oppose, for we realize more keenly than the major religious denominations that the American principle of separation of Church and State must be kept inviolate if religious groups are to flourish freely and if the State is not to become the tool of competing Church interests.

—Address, Philadelphia Jewish Community Relations Council, October 3, 1956.

Organized Labor and Civil Liberties

Another important area in which the labor movement can see to it that democracy begins at home is that of civil liberties. The labor movement has not done all that is within its power to do to protect its own members. There are many thousands of employees working for government contractors, or employed as seamen, longshoremen and white-collar workers who are subjected to arbitrary security risks and are often discharged without a hearing on the basis of so-called confidential information—confidential because it cannot stand the light of day. Indeed, there are efforts on foot in Congress to extend the security program to any industrial establishment which may be classified as a defense facility. If this trend continues, every trade unionist will soon have a dossier in the FBI files complete with his fingerprints, photograph and life history of himself and his close relatives. This device can be readily used for union busting. It must be resisted not for that reason alone, but because on all fronts it is high time that the American people recovered its sanity without relaxing its vigilance. It is for labor to insist upon a re-evaluation of our internal Security Program and a close scrutiny of the abuses committed in its name. It would be a healthy development if labor had representation in the U. S. Commission which is looking into the Security Program.

—Address, AFL-CIO Merger Convention, New York, December 6, 1955.

The American Negro Problem

There can be no doubt that the vast majority of the American people have been stirred by the historic decisions of the United States Supreme Court, recognizing them as a long-overdue reaffirmation of the creed of equality that underlies our institutions and shapes our national character.

The fact that inequality and gross discrimination have long existed increases rather than diminishes the need for rapid change. Patience ceases to be a virtue when it requires millions of American citizens to continue to endure injustices that should never have been inflicted upon them. Appeals for moderation cannot morally be made the reason for inaction or for compromise of basic democratic principles. Hence, any program for carrying out the Supreme Court's decisions must have two aspects. In principle, it must be based on acceptance of the constitutional doctrines that were affirmed by the Supreme Court decisions. In practice, it must provide for an immediate beginning of concrete steps toward compliance. We must also demand greater firmness and speed from government agencies dealing with these matters.

The following program is urged:

1. Use of the full powers and influence of the federal government to obtain prompt and full compliance with the decisions of the United States Supreme Court condemning state-imposed racial segregation.

2. Application by all branches of the federal government, Executive, Legislative and Judicial, of the policy that federal funds may not be used to support schools or other institutions that are operated in defiance of the Supreme Court decisions condemning racial segregation.

3. Amendment of the rules of the Senate and House of Representatives to eliminate the filibuster and all other devices that thwart the will of a majority.

4. Vigorous support by the President and adoption by the United States Congress of effective federal laws prohibiting discrimination in employment, giving greater protection to personal security and the right to vote, and strengthening the civil rights activities of the Department of Justice.

5. More vigorous action by the United States Department of Justice to protect security of the person, the right to vote, and the right to resort to the courts for the purpose of enforcing constitutional guarantees.

—Address, Civil Rights Rally, New York, May 24, 1956.

The Immigration Law of the United States

A collateral area which has both domestic and foreign implications is the immigration policy of the United States. The cardinal sin of the present immigration law, the McCarran-Walter Act, is not its restrictive character which may or may not be adequately relieved by a special act for the benefit of refugees, but its determination of quotas on the basis of national origins. This system brands the stamp of inferiority upon some of our best American citizens who originate or whose parents originate from countries which the Immigration Act inferentially condemns as inferior. It makes offensive distinctions between nations and races which are contrary to the spirit of religion. Religious denominations in America, whose basic assumption is human equality, have every reason to throw their strength into the continuing fight to remove from the American statute books this immigration law which is a blemish on America's record before civilization.

—Address, United Synagogue of America, Kiamesha Lake, New York, November 14, 1955.

INTERNATIONAL PROBLEMS

Definition of a Free World

It is advisable to define what we mean by the "Free World" since words sometimes hide rather than express the meaning content. . . . The term "Free World" connotes in our minds not only a group of concepts and practices but also a group of countries, peoples and modes of government. Thus we think of the countries, peoples and governments of the United States, Canada, Great Britain, France, Italy, the Scandinavian countries, the Netherlands, Belgium, Switzerland, West Germany, Austria, Australia, New Zealand and several, not many, Latin-American countries, as constituting the Free World.

What are the characteristic features of the Free World?

We think of a Free World, first of all, as a world free from aggression. . . . A Free World yearns to be free from the fears of aggression, yearns for an orderly peaceful method of settling international disputes, yearns for an international instrument to safeguard world peace.

In its social and economic connotations, we do not mean by the Free World a world in which there is no check upon the individual, we do not mean a world of *laissez faire*, of the individual's unbridled expansionism at the expense of society's well-being. . . . The pattern of a Free World does allow, however, enough freedom and incentive for individual enterprise to be a fillip to energy and resourcefulness.

Among the positive characteristics of a Free World are the following:

1. The free ballot, the right of every citizen to choose government officials and policies by secret ballot.

2. Freedom of speech, press, assembly and worship.
3. The freedom of every child to an education.
4. The freedom of labor to organize and bargain collectively.
5. The freedom of women to equality of political rights.
6. The freedom of minority cultural groups to cultural self-expression.
These add up to the dignity of the individual. To these should be added another freedom which is sometimes overlooked by proponents of a Free World, namely, the right of every man and woman to a job at a living wage, a right to be guaranteed by the State. Without this economic right, other rights often seem to be of only secondary importance. . . .

—"A Free World and Its Spiritual Foundations," *Current Religious Thought*, XII: 1, January-February, 1952.

Religion and a Free World

If the near-range prospect of the Free World is limited to holding its own, the long range prospect, I am convinced, is unreservedly hopeful. The long range is to be measured not in terms of years, but generations. I believe that, in the long range, the Free World is bound to win. You have the right to ask me why I have that faith. My reply will seem naive to some. Yet I make it without hesitation and without apology. I believe the Free World is bound to win because it accords with the precepts of "Religion," and Religion is the tried and tested distillation of the experience of millennia. Under Religion are to be subsumed not only Judaism and Christianity, with which we happen to be most familiar, but other great religious systems whose fundamental teachings are not essentially different from those of the Judaeo-Christian tradition. Herein is the essence of the thesis that the Free World rests primarily upon spiritual foundations and derives its hope for the future from spiritual premises. . . .

The observance of God's Law brings its own ultimate reward in the life of nations and of mankind, reward in terms of well-being and length of days. The transgression of His Law brings its own ultimate penalty in death and disappearance from the world's arena. History has validated this truth again and again.

These propositions, taught, expounded and exhorted by Religion, and distilled from its millennial experience, may be viewed as the safeguards of the ultimate triumph of a Free World.

It is no accident that nazism and fascism regarded Religion as their arch enemy, to be extirpated if possible and curbed whenever extirpation was impossible. Likewise, it is no accident that Communism reviles Religion. Totalitarian systems obviously cannot brook an outlook on life which sanctions and sanctifies the dignity of the individual and espouses the rights of the individual, which applies universal standards of moral judgment, and which seeks to build bonds rather than curtains between man and man. By the same token, the Free World should inculcate these propositions with every resource at its command.

—"A Free World and Its Spiritual Foundations," *Current Religious Thought*, XII: 1, January-February, 1952.

The United Nations

Today, the instrument which best bears that hope for the future is the United Nations organization. It is for the most part still a name, a concept, a seed, and only the beginning of reality; but at least it holds up to view and keeps before our consciousness the ideal of mankind united. Let us not permit its significance to be under-rated. It has not succeeded as yet in ensuring world peace, but neither has it failed as yet. We know of nothing better that can take its place. Its Economic and Social Council and its educational, scientific and cultural organization are engaged in a slow but important work of developing concepts and programs calculated to promote human rights, human progress and world unity. If it fumbles and stumbles, it is fumbling and stumbling in the right direction, forward not backward. Even if it should take one hundred years for the United Nations organization to achieve success, it would be a century well spent. We pray that it may not disintegrate in the meantime. Even as an outlet for verbal battles it is a useful and necessary safety valve. As long as this vessel, the one available international instrument for world peace, holds together, there is hope that the global conflict we fear will not come to pass. The religious forces of the world have no more important mandate than that of winning the respect of public opinion for the United Nations organization, enlisting public support for it, and engaging public interest in its auxiliary bodies.

—"A Free World and Its Spiritual Foundations," *Current Religious Thought*, XII: 1, January-February, 1952.

World Academy for Peace

I have one proposal on the non-political level, which does not depend upon governments and therefore may be more readily implementable than the other proposals.

The moral and spiritual leaders of the world should be harnessed into a permanent collective effort to find a solution for the number one problem of our time—how to abolish war. The goal is of such tremendous importance for humanity's present and future, that even if the chances of success are remote the effort is worthwhile.

It should not be impossible to bring together into a permanent form of association and consultation twenty or twenty-five of the world's pre-eminent moral and spiritual personalities, who would carry authority not by virtue of any official positions but by virtue of their life records and achievements in religious and secular fields. They should be men and women of the caliber of Albert Schweitzer, Thomas Mann, Jacques Maritain, Martin Buber, Bertrand Russell, Bishop Oxnam, Eleanor Roosevelt, Rabbi Leo Baeck, Arnold Toynbee, Toyohika Kagawa, Helen Keller, Edmond Fleg, Nahum Goldmann, and Ralph Bunche (if he will not hold office in the United Nations). Alas, Albert Einstein is no longer alive; he would have been pre-eminently qualified.

These men and women should be politically independent, untrammeled and unbound by commitments to governments. They should be personalities known as citizens of the world whose vision transcends national boundaries. The members of this group should be in communication with one another continuously. They should meet once a year for a period of two weeks in a neutral country such as Sweden, Switzerland or India, in an atmosphere free from political pressure. The group should be small enough to permit of intimate exchanges of views both orally and in writing.

They would constitute a World Academy for Peace. Their findings, published once a year, would inevitably arouse wide repercussions, would stimulate thought and discussion on proposals for ensuring the peace of the world, and would carry considerable moral weight with governments as well as people.

Who would choose the group? One or more of the aforementioned personalities, if approached, may be persuaded to take the initiative in inviting a number of his colleagues to join him. The founding group would then nominate additional members, up to the limited maximum of twenty or twenty-five.

A council of this nature, however devoid of formalities, would nevertheless require a modicum of organization to bring it into being, set it in motion, keep it going, arrange its annual conferences and communicate its findings to the world. It would be a relatively simple organizational procedure requiring a relatively modest organizational budget. It is not unreasonable to hope that one of the great philanthropic foundations, interested in the cause of world peace, would make the necessary funds available.

—Article published as part of Symposium, "Struggle for Peace," in *St. Louis Post-Dispatch*, St. Louis, Missouri, May 31, 1955.

CREDO OF AN AMERICAN JEW

Standing at this juncture between past and future, grateful for the three centuries of American Jewish history and prayerful toward the fourth, may I utter my credo as an American Jew.

I believe that the American in me merges congenially with my Jewish tradition, seeing that the Old Testament was revered by the original colonies as a model and pattern for the individual and the commonweal; and the Jew in me adds an extra dimension to my Americanism, seeing that the difficult but inescapable role of the Jew, by the very nature of his being a persistent minority, has challenged, evoked and defended decency, liberalism and civilization in every society in which he has lived.

I believe that the best hallmark of the Jew and his most valuable credential is his religion; for, as to the rose, which has form and color, fragrance is its quintessence, so to the Jew, whatever else he may be, religion is the quintessence of his historic being. But Judaism is religion in a sense peculiar to itself. The best word for it is Torah. Torah is worship and study, tradition and progress, the letter and the spirit, ethics and ritual, knowledge and character. Torah is as narrow as the fence which must safeguard Jewish self-preservation and as broad as Judaism's outlook on the Fatherhood of God, the brotherhood of man, the triumph of justice and the enthronement of peace. Torah is the mind and the soul of Israel across time and space. And Torah can flourish in America if American Jewry wills it.

I believe that the State of Israel has a special destiny as the natural habitat of Jewish survival, as a light to the nations, as the gifted young sister democracy to the United States, and as the corporate demonstration of Jewish capacity to write a new page worthy of the Old Testament, which will be a vitalizing influence upon Jewish life everywhere.

I believe that America is still a new world, whose newness and freshness, verve and zest, to build here not only a new earth of physical wealth but also a new heaven of human dignity is far from enervated, and that Jewish idealism can help keep America new and fresh.

I believe that the exalted words of Isaiah, Chapter 66, can find fulfillment both here and in Israel, "For as long as the new heavens and the new earth which I make shall endure before me, saith the Lord, so shall your offspring and your name endure."

—Address, American Jewish Tercentenary Closing Assembly, Carnegie Hall, New York, June 1, 1955.

ANNOTATED LIST
OF DR. GOLDSTEIN'S BOOKS

A Century of Judaism in New York: B'nai Jeshurun 1825-1925, New York's Oldest Ashkenazic Congregation. New York, Congregation B'nai Jeshurun, 1930. xxiv, 460 p. Foreword by Cyrus Adler. A detailed and documented history of Congregation B'nai Jeshurun in New York City, against the background of the development of the Jewish Community as a whole. An introduction of 44 pages deals with "The Earliest Jewish Settlements on the American Continent".

Towards a Solution. New York, G. P. Putnam's Sons, 1940. xxii, 345 p. This book traces and analyzes problems, issues, men and events such as the places of religion in society, the role of the synagogue, the relation of Palestine to the solution of the Jewish problem, Christian-Jewish relations, Church and State, and many others. In addition, the book contains several biographical essays.

Mourners' Devotions. New York, Bloch Publishing Co., 1941. (ix), 103 p. The Minhah and Maariv Services and a supplementary section containing selections on death, immortality, the uses of adversity and the origin and meaning of the Kaddish.

Shanah b'Yisrael (A Year in Israel). Tel Aviv, 1950. 70 p., 12 illustrations. Contains Hebrew addresses on problems of Israel, delivered by Dr. Goldstein during his sojourn in Israel (September 1948 to August 1949) as treasurer of the Jewish Agency for Palestine.

Brandeis University: Chapter of its Founding. New York, Bloch Publishing Company, 1951. xi, 133 p. The record of Dr. Goldstein's initiation of the project, resulting in the securing of the campus, the propagation of the idea, the organization of the academic sponsorship, the beginning of the fund-raising, and the obtaining of the consent of the family of the late Justice Louis D. Brandeis for the use of his name.

American Jewry Comes of Age: Tercentenary Addresses, New York, Bloch Publishing Company, 1955. 218 p. In addition to a chapter entitled "The Bonds of Jewish Peoplehood: Report to the World Jewish Congress," this book contains addresses delivered, in many parts of the world, by Dr. Goldstein during the celebration in 1954-55 of the tercentenary of the first Jewish settlement in North America, including addresses on contemporary problems.